# Congress on Measurement, Quality and Data Science (MQDS 2023)



Bordeaux, France
5 - 7 June 2023

ISBN: 978-1-7138-7965-7

**Printed from e-media with permission by:**

Curran Associates, Inc.
57 Morehouse Lane
Red Hook, NY 12571



Printed by Curran Associates, Inc. (2023)



Comite African de Metrologie (CAFMET)
62 av. Notre Dame du Lac
49000 Angers
France

Phone: 33 (0) 6 73 62 32 62
Fax: 33 (0) 2 41 88 84 21

contact@cafmet.com

**Additional copies of this publication are available from:**

Curran Associates, Inc.
57 Morehouse Lane
Red Hook, NY 12571 USA
Phone: 845-758-0400
Fax: 845-758-2633
Email: curran@proceedings.com
Web: www.proceedings.com

# TABLE OF CONTENTS

## PLENARY



## SAFETY, RELIABILITY AND QUALITY



## HEALTH AND ENVIRONMENT



## MANUFACTURING AND ENGINEERING

# Geometrical errors and their uncertainty in goniophotometers: an application to road surface photometry

Johanna Bernasconi[1], Peter Blattner[1], Mikael Lindgren[2], Dominique Renoux[3], and Paola Iacomussi[4]

[1]*METAS, Bern Switzerland*
[2]*RISE, Borås, Sweden*
[3]*LNE Paris, France*
[4]*INRIM, Torino, Italy, p.iacomussi@inrim.it*

**ABSTRACT**: The measurement of luminance spatial distribution of road surfaces provides a full description of the light-material interaction. This quantity is related to road lighting system design and its measurement is performed by goniophotometers. Uncertainty analysis of goniophotometers is usually performed on laboratory instruments with very low beam divergence. Road surface luminance uncertainty budget needs a detailed approach because samples are large and due to the size constraints of on-site measurements, portable instruments tend to have larger beam divergence. In addition, due to the nature of samples, the uncertainty depends on the sample under test. The paper investigates the geometrical errors implicit in luminance measurements made by goniophotometry in the road surface analysis. It presents a theoretical model of a goniophotometer for spatial luminance distribution and provides an evaluation of errors dealing with sensors and source optics characteristics necessary to assess the uncertainty budget of the measurement results.

**Keywords:** Aperture effects, luminance measurements, Uncertainty budget, road surface, luminance coefficient, *r*-tables, BRDF.

**Received** January 1, 2023; **In final form** March 31, 2023; **Published** June 2023



**Corresponding author:** Paola Iacomussi, e-mail: p.iacomussi@inrim.it

## 1. INTRODUCTION

The luminance coefficient of a material is the ratio between the luminance reflected by the material and the illumination from the light source. The knowledge of luminance coefficients of road pavements allows the design of road lighting systems that ensure road safety, while saving energy and complying with the different normative requirements. The luminance coefficient spatial distribution for generic materials is called BRDF (Bidirectional Reflectance Distribution Function) and it is a function of four angles. Two angles identify the lighting direction and two the observation direction. In road surface analysis, the BRDF is simplified and limited to a few lighting directions and only one observation direction, and the values are tabulated (so-called *r*-tables) [1], [2].

Thanks to *r*-table values is it possible to link the intensity emission in a given direction of a road lighting luminaire to the luminance perceived by a driver in a reference position on the road [3]. This approach ensures that the design of road lighting systems (geometries and spacing) is able to fulfil normative requirements, in terms of visibility, to ensure road user's safety.

The entire design approach is based on the knowledge of *r*-tables of the road surfaces: there are reference *r*-tables that can be used, or it is possible to measure on site the *r*-tables of actual asphalt. Due to the geometry of measurement, the luminance coefficient must be known with a high angular resolution. This is true for both the driver's observation direction and all the lighting directions [1], [2]. Specialized goniophotometers have therefore been designed to measure, on site or in laboratory, the luminance coefficient measurements of road pavements. The instruments feature different optical and geometrical characteristics [4], which impact the measurement uncertainty. From this deviation from a perfect measurement geometry, originates an error which we call aperture effect: the paper shows that these geometrical contributions are crucial in the measurement of the luminance coefficient and in its uncertainty determination, especially for on-site measuring devices. The main geometrical factors of influence are the lighting direction and collimation, the illuminated and observed areas, the observation direction and angular field of view. The contribution due to the aperture effect can be determined and corrected, since it is a systematic error. However, some uncertainties are associated with the correction of this effect. In addition, alignment errors of the systems contribute to the total uncertainty.

## 2. METHODS

### 2.1. Luminance coefficient

According to the International Lighting Vocabulary [4], the luminance coefficient, $q$, is defined as the ratio of the luminance $L$ in a given direction at a point on the surface, to the horizontal illuminance $E$, at the same point (definition no. 17-24-079 in [4]). Under specified illumination conditions depending on the targeted normative requirements [3], [5] we obtain:

$$q = q(\alpha, \delta, \beta, \varepsilon) = \frac{L(\alpha,\delta)}{E(\beta,\varepsilon)}, \quad (1)$$

where:

- $\alpha$, $\delta$ are the angles of the observation direction,
- $\beta$, $\varepsilon$ are the angles of the illumination direction,
- $L$ is the measured luminance in the $\alpha$, $\delta$ direction,
- $E$ is the measured illuminance provided from the $\beta$, $\varepsilon$ direction.

The angle $\alpha$ is measured vertically from the horizontal plane of the sample to the observer position and $\delta$ laterally between the observation direction and the reference direction of the sample. $\delta$ is set to zero because road surfaces present isotropic behaviour. The angle $\varepsilon$ is measured from the vertical to the direction of illumination and $\beta$ is the angle between the vertical planes containing the illumination direction and the observation direction. The geometry is described in figure 4 of [6] for the specific case of road surface measurements, as defined in the European road lighting standard series EN 13201. This coefficient is a four-dimensional quantity, measured in $sr^{-1}$. In the application to road surface luminance coefficient evaluation, the reduced luminance coefficients $r(\alpha, \delta, \beta, \varepsilon) = q \cdot \cos^3\varepsilon$ are usually used. The values are determined for specific observation angles ($\alpha = 1°$, isotropy in $\delta$) and specific illumination angles ($0 \leq \tan \varepsilon \leq 12$, $0° \leq \beta \leq 180°$) and the values are usually presented in a so-called $r$-table.

A number of $r$-tables, representative of road surface behaviour, can be found in the technical report CIE 066:1984 [1] for reference.

### 2.2. Measuring instruments for *r*-tables

A deep review of all available instruments for road surface luminance coefficient measurements is available in [5]. These systems can be categorized in two groups of instruments:

- instruments which have collimated or telecentric illumination and detection systems with very low beam divergence,
- instruments without optics or with imaging optics for the illumination and/or the detection.

All instruments suffer from uncertainties in the positioning and the alignment of the system. The most important elements are the position of the light source and its illumination angle, the position and tilt of the sample under consideration, the position and angle of the detection system. The first category of instruments, due to their very low beam divergence, are not subject to aperture effects. The second category is subject to an aperture effect, which depends on the aperture sizes and angles of the illumination and detection system. This effect is investigated in this paper. It yields a systematic error, $k_A$, which can be corrected similarly to other systematic errors due to straylight, temperature variations, nonlinearity of the detector, etc.

### 2.3. Aperture effects

Considering the luminance coefficient definition, the illuminance should be measured at the same point of luminance with the incident light originating from one of the specific directions listed in the $r$-table. In practice, this is not possible since the lighting system and the luminance detector have extended apertures to emit and collect light as shown in Figure 1. As a result, the measured luminance and illuminance are an average over an extended area in a range of angles. Additionally, measured samples like road surfaces, can be highly nonuniform, hence the luminance coefficient will vary at each point and the average across a certain surface is recorded.

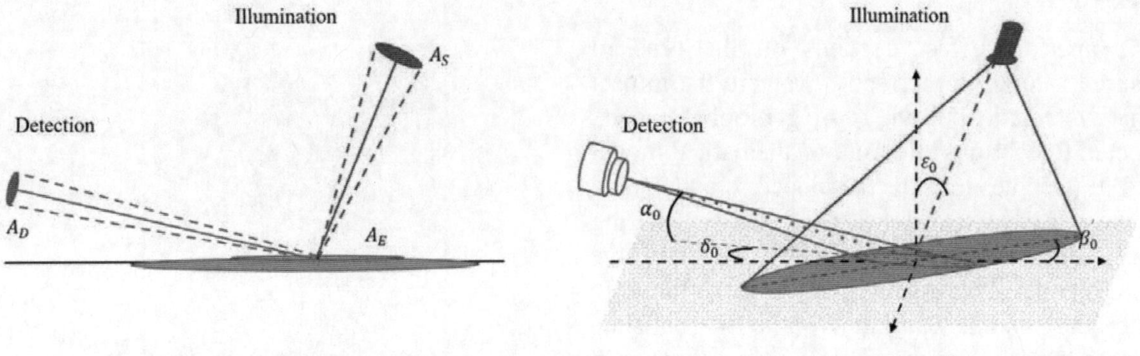


Figure 1. A schematic of the geometrical effects with left) apertures of the illumination $A_S$ with coordinate system ($x_S$, $y_S$), of the detection $A_D$ with coordinate system ($x_D$, $y_D$) and of the effective illuminated area $A_E$ with coordinate system ($x_E$, $y_E$); right) the nominal angles ($\alpha_0$, $\delta_0$) of the detector and ($\beta_0$, $\varepsilon_0$) of the source.

Due to the extended apertures and illumination areas, the measurement system suffers from different systematic effects. Considering the lit area, the actual incident angles ($\beta_E$, $\varepsilon_E$) differ from the nominal values ($\beta_0$, $\varepsilon_0$) (Figure 1) and vary inside the effective illumination field, $A_E$, and depends also on the aperture of the lighting source, $A_S$.

Similar considerations are also valid for the viewing detector: the detection angles ($\alpha_D$, $\delta_D$) differ from the nominal values ($\alpha_0$, $\delta_0$) (Figure 1) and vary across the detection field, $A_D$.

In the ideal case of luminance meters with binary behaviour, only radiation within the field of detection $A_D$ is measured and the detector sensitivity across the field is constant. However, in practice the detector sensitivity may vary slightly across the surface of the detector itself, $k_D(x_D, y_D)$.

In the ideal case, the illuminance field is perfectly homogenous and no light is outside the nominal field, but in practice the illumination field is not homogenous, i.e. $E = E(x_E, y_E)$.

Considering all the aforementioned effects, the collected signal of the luminance detector, $L_D$ differs from the luminance of a perfect instrument $L_0$, because of the aperture effects of both lighting source, detector, and the spatial sensitivity behaviour of the detector into the different fields;

$$L_D = k_A(\alpha_0, \delta_0, \varepsilon_0, \beta_0)\, L_0 = k_A(\alpha_0, \delta_0, \varepsilon_0, \beta_0) q(\alpha_0, \delta_0, \varepsilon_0, \beta_0) E_0 k_{D0}. \quad (2)$$

$L_D$ can also be expressed as a combination of the actual luminance coefficient of the sample $q(\alpha_D, \delta_D, \beta_E, \varepsilon_E)$ and the illuminance on the sample point, $E(x_E, y_E)$, considering the appropriate integration areas (the extended fields in Figure 1)

$$L_D = \frac{1}{A_D \cdot A_E \cdot A_S} \cdot \iint_{A_D} \iint_{A_E} \iint_{A_S} q(\alpha_D, \delta_D, \beta_E, \varepsilon_E) E(x_E, y_E)\, k_D(x_D, y_D), \quad (3)$$

where:

- $A_D$ is the detection field,
- $A_E$ is the illumination field,
- $A_S$ is the aperture of the lighting source,
- ($\alpha_D$, $\delta_D$) are the actual detection angles,
- ($\beta_E$, $\varepsilon_E$) are the actual incident angles,
- ($x_E$,$y_E$) are the coordinates in the illumination field $A_E$,
- $E$ is the illuminance in the illumination field,
- ($x_D$,$y_D$) are the coordinates in the detector field $A_D$,
- $k_D$ is the sensitivity of the detector that varies across $A_D$.

The calculation of $L_D$ of Eq. (3) can be done either by integration of the sixfold integral or by the Monte Carlo method.

To evaluate $k_A$ through simulation, it is essential that the luminance coefficients $q$ are known also at angles around the nominal directions ($\alpha_0, \delta_0, \varepsilon_0, \beta_0$). However, in road lighting, they are known in only very limited directions, given by the $r$-tables.

It is therefore essential to build a general four-dimensional model of the BRDF. Road samples are considered isotropic; hence the values do not change as a function of the $\delta$ angle.

## 3. RESULTS

The aperture effect depends on the type of measured sample: to correctly evaluate the impact of the systematic behaviour of goniophotometers subjected to aperture effects, a mathematical model of BRDF samples must be developed to understand the metrological capabilities of the measuring device. Unfortunately, the BRDF (or q) is the quantity under investigation, so it is difficult to predict the model. Starting from CIE published reference tables to generate BRDF values, two ways are possible: interpolation or modelling. A mathematical model is much faster than the interpolation method and it overcomes the difficulty in interpolating around specular peaks.

### 3.1. BRDF Model

One of the simplest BRDF models is a combination of the perfect diffuse model of a Lambertian sample (with constant luminance), with the scattered specular Phong model [7]. The Phong model is based on the cosine of a given angle, elevated to a given power, which gives the sharpness of the specular reflection. The given angle is the angle between the observation direction and the specular reflection direction. The output of this simple model, well-used in basic physical 3D-rendering engines, can be compared, under the form of solid *r*-tables, in Figure 2 with a reference pavement reflectance (C2) given in CIE 066:1984 [1]. The top pane represents the basic model and the bottom pane the actual behavior of a C2 pavement. It can be observed from this figure, but it happens also for other reference pavements, that the two 3D shapes of BRDF have significant differences.

Additional BRDF models exist but have very limited applications [8], [9], which do not give satisfactory results for road surface pavement. On the contrary, good results have been obtained implementing the aforesaid basic model with supplementary experimental components, as a function with adjustable parameters. Five different road-surface *r*-tables have been modelled: four CIE reference pavements (R1, C2, R3, R4) and a measured sample. The *r*-tables have been chosen with different specular indices $S_1$ to represent the range of realistic road pavements BRDF, with $S_1$ values equal to 0.25, 0.93, 1.11, 1.49 and 0.39. Sharp changes in measured *r*-tables have been observed experimentally for small changes of $\alpha$ with

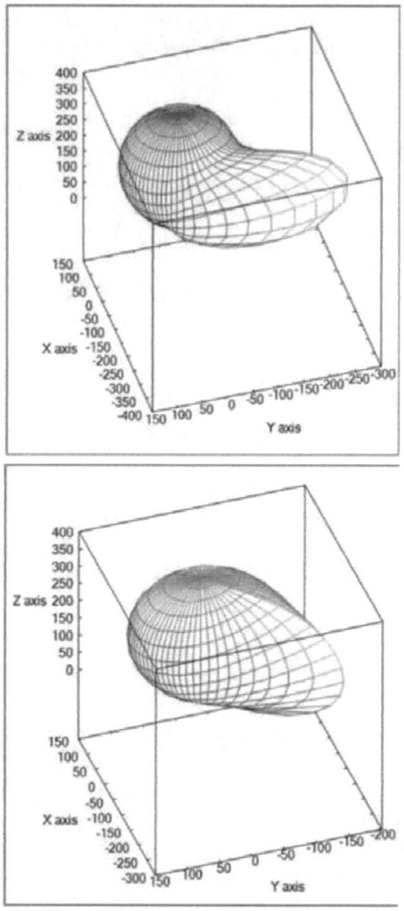


Figure 2. The top pane represents the basic model and the bottom pane the actual behaviour of a C2 pavement.

road pavements measured with laboratory goniometers [10].

This can be partly understood because of masking effects due to the surface roughness. For this reason an additional component, applied as a configurable attenuation factor for grazing angles, has been added to the model to account for this masking effect. In addition, a component representing small scattered retroreflection behaviour was included in a modified Phong model.

Finally, the BRDF behavior of reference road surfaces can be expressed as:

$$BRDF(\theta_i, \varphi_i, \theta_r, \varphi_r) = \Big(k_{\text{diff}} + k_{\text{phong}} \cdot (\cos\Omega)^r + k_{\text{phong-retro}} \cdot (\cos\Omega')^s + k_{\exp} \cdot f(\varepsilon)^p \cdot \left(\frac{\pi-\beta}{\pi}\right) \exp(1 + h \cdot f(\varepsilon)^2)\Big) \cdot g(\theta_i) \cdot g(\theta_r) / g(\theta_r^*), \quad (4)$$

where the nature of components and their corresponding mathematical expressions of terms are presented in Figure 3.

| Model components | Mathematical expression | Parameters |
|---|---|---|
| diffuse (constant) | $k_{diff}$ | |
| scattered specular (Phong model) [8] | $k_{phong} \cdot (\cos\Omega)^r$ | $\cos\Omega = \cos\theta_i \cdot \cos\theta_r - \sin\theta_i \cdot \sin\theta_r \cdot \cos(\varphi_i - \varphi_r)$<br>$\theta_i, \theta_r$ polar incident and reflected angles, equal to 0 at zenith and $\leq \pi/2$<br>$\varphi_i, \varphi_r$ azimuthal incident and reflected angles, $\varphi$ of detector centre is 0 |
| experimental based on an artificial function of incident angles $(\varepsilon, \beta)$ | $k_{exp} \cdot f(\varepsilon)^p \cdot \left(\frac{\pi - \beta}{\pi}\right) \exp(1 + h \cdot f(\varepsilon)^2)$ | $\varepsilon = \theta_i \cdot \theta_r / \theta_r^*$<br>$\theta_r^*$: polar observation angle of fitted *r*-tables (89°)<br>$\beta = \lvert\varphi_i - \varphi_r - \pi\rvert$<br>$f(\varepsilon) = \sin\varepsilon \cdot \frac{\cos\varepsilon}{(\cos\varepsilon)^2 + \mu}$ |
| global attenuation factor for grazing angles of incidence or observation | $g(\theta_i) \cdot g(\theta_r) / g(\theta_r^*)$ | $g(\theta) = \begin{cases} (a \cdot \theta^2 + b \cdot \theta + c)^t, & \text{for } \theta > \theta_l, \\ 1, & \text{for } \theta < \theta_l, \end{cases} \quad \theta_l > 85.3°$ |
| scattered retro-reflected (modified Phong model) | $k_{phong-retro} \cdot (\cos\Omega')^s$ | $\cos\Omega' = \cos\theta_i \cdot \cos\theta_r + \sin\theta_i \cdot \sin\theta_r \cdot \cos(\varphi_i - \varphi_r)$ |

Figure 3. Model components and the corresponding mathematical expressions.

The objective is not to get the same *r*-table values as the considered reference from the BRDF model, but rather to get simulated data representative of realistic BRDF for uncertainty assessment. It is especially important to get similar shape of the specular component, which is the main contributor to the *aperture effect* error. The overall match is very good for the five selected references. The maximal deviation is within ±9 % of the maximal *r*-value. The root mean square deviation is within 2.6 % of the maximal *r*-value. As all the components are not based on physical principles but derived from *r*-tables, the simulated BRDF can only be used for small variations around $\alpha = 1°$ for which the *r*-tables are provided and as commonly done for uncertainty evaluation.

## 4. DISCUSSION

### 4.1. Aperture effect evaluation

The *aperture effect* is considered for any defined geometries and optical systems, by means of a numerical integration of all the possible rays: each ray emitted from the light source, incident on a sample point and reflected toward a point of the detector sensitive field, is weighted by the modelled BRDF at that point. The difference between the integrated modelled BRDF and the modelled BRDF is computed and represents a systematic error. Since this effect strongly depends on the incident angle $(\varepsilon_0, \beta_0)$, the aperture effect is calculated for each incident direction. The systematic error due to the aperture effect can be corrected by means of a relative measurement with a reference close to the targeted sample. The reference is used to determine the correction factor $k_A$ of eq. (2). The whole process is available by a freely available software LUMCORUN developed during the SURFACE project [11] (a Euramet funded project) and downloadable from the project repository [12].

The uncertainties on the angles originate from the positioning uncertainties of the goniometer and the misalignment of the sample. It should be noted that, in principle, there is no correlation between these inputs and the aperture effects.

For the evaluation of the uncertainty budget in luminance coefficient or BRDF measurement, a full measurement model able to include all variables of influences should be developed [13], [14]. When the model is too complex, a Monte Carlo Method (MCM) to quantify the resultant uncertainty on the measurand should be used as suggested in § 7 of [14] using and adaptive procedure.

| tanε/β(°) | 0 | 2 | 5 | 10 | 15 | 20 | 25 | 30 | 35 | 40 | 45 | 60 | 75 | 90 | 105 | 120 | 135 | 150 | 165 | 180 |
|---|---|---|---|---|---|---|---|---|---|---|---|---|---|---|---|---|---|---|---|---|
| 0 | 1.02 | 1.02 | 1.02 | 1.02 | 1.02 | 1.02 | 1.02 | 1.02 | 1.02 | 1.02 | 1.02 | 1.02 | 1.02 | 1.02 | 1.02 | 1.02 | 1.02 | 1.02 | 1.02 | 1.02 |
| 0.25 | 1.03 | 1.03 | 1.03 | 1.02 | 1.02 | 1.01 | 1.01 | 1.01 | 1.01 | 1.01 | 1.01 | 1.02 | 1.02 | 1.02 | 1.02 | 1.02 | 1.02 | 1.02 | 1.02 | 1.02 |
| 0.5 | 1.04 | 1.04 | 1.03 | 1.02 | 1.01 | 1.01 | 1.01 | 1.01 | 1.01 | 1.01 | 1.02 | 1.02 | 1.02 | 1.02 | 1.02 | 1.02 | 1.02 | 1.02 | 1.02 | 1.02 |
| 0.75 | 1.05 | 1.05 | 1.03 | 1.01 | 1.00 | 1.01 | 1.01 | 1.01 | 1.01 | 1.01 | 1.02 | 1.02 | 1.02 | 1.02 | 1.02 | 1.02 | 1.02 | 1.02 | 1.02 | 1.02 |
| 1 | 1.06 | 1.05 | 1.02 | 1.00 | 1.00 | 1.00 | 1.01 | 1.01 | 1.01 | 1.01 | 1.02 | 1.02 | 1.02 | 1.02 | 1.02 | 1.02 | 1.02 | 1.02 | 1.02 | 1.02 |
| 1.25 | 1.06 | 1.05 | 1.01 | 0.99 | 0.99 | 1.00 | 1.01 | 1.01 | 1.01 | 1.02 | 1.02 | 1.02 | 1.02 | 1.02 | 1.02 | 1.02 | 1.02 | 1.02 | 1.02 | 1.02 |
| 1.5 | 1.07 | 1.06 | 1.01 | 0.98 | 0.99 | 1.00 | 1.01 | 1.02 | 1.02 | 1.02 | 1.02 | 1.02 | 1.02 | 1.02 | 1.02 | 1.02 | 1.02 | 1.02 | 1.02 | 1.03 |
| 1.75 | 1.08 | 1.06 | 1.01 | 0.98 | 1.00 | 1.01 | 1.02 | 1.02 | 1.03 | 1.03 | 1.03 | 1.02 | 1.02 | 1.02 | 1.02 | 1.02 | 1.02 | 1.02 | 1.03 | 1.03 |
| 2 | 1.09 | 1.06 | 1.00 | 0.98 | 1.00 | 1.02 | 1.03 | 1.03 | 1.03 | 1.03 | 1.03 | 1.02 | 1.02 | 1.02 | 1.02 | 1.02 | 1.02 | 1.02 | 1.03 | 1.03 |
| 2.5 | 1.12 | 1.08 | 1.00 | 0.98 | 1.02 | 1.04 | 1.04 | 1.04 | 1.03 | 1.02 | 1.02 | 1.01 | 1.02 | 1.02 | 1.02 | 1.02 | 1.02 | 1.02 | 1.03 | 1.03 |
| 3 | 1.17 | 1.12 | 1.01 | 0.99 | 1.04 | 1.04 | 1.03 | 1.01 | 1.00 | 1.00 | 1.00 | 1.01 | 1.02 | 1.02 | 1.02 | 1.02 | 1.02 | 1.02 | 1.03 | 1.04 |
| 3.5 | 1.25 | 1.17 | 1.02 | 0.99 | 1.02 | 1.01 | 0.99 | 0.98 | 0.97 | 0.98 | 0.99 | 1.01 | 1.02 | 1.02 | 1.02 | 1.02 | 1.02 | 1.02 | 1.03 | 1.04 |
| 4 | 1.36 | 1.24 | 1.03 | 0.95 | 0.97 | 0.95 | 0.94 | 0.95 | 0.96 | 0.98 | 0.99 | 1.02 | 1.02 | 1.02 | 1.02 | 1.02 | 1.02 | 1.03 | 1.04 | 1.04 |
| 4.5 | 1.51 | 1.34 | 1.02 | 0.88 | 0.90 | 0.90 | 0.91 | 0.94 | 0.97 | 0.99 | 1.00 | 1.02 | 1.02 | 1.02 | 1.02 | 1.02 | 1.02 | 1.03 | 1.04 | 1.04 |
| 5 | 1.68 | 1.44 | 1.00 | 0.80 | 0.84 | 0.86 | 0.90 | 0.94 | 0.97 | 0.99 | 1.01 | 1.02 | 1.02 | 1.02 | 1.02 | 1.02 | 1.02 | 1.03 | 1.04 | 1.04 |
| 5.5 | 1.86 | 1.55 | 0.96 | 0.71 | 0.78 | 0.84 | 0.91 | 0.96 | 0.99 | 1.00 | | | | | | | | | | |
| 6 | 2.07 | 1.68 | 0.90 | 0.62 | 0.74 | 0.84 | 0.92 | 0.97 | 1.00 | | | | | | | | | | | |
| 6.5 | 2.46 | 1.94 | 0.86 | 0.55 | 0.73 | 0.88 | 0.97 | 1.02 | | | | | | | | | | | | |
| 7 | 2.64 | 2.03 | 0.79 | 0.48 | 0.73 | 0.90 | 0.99 | 1.04 | | | | | | | | | | | | |
| 7.5 | 2.84 | 2.13 | 0.74 | 0.43 | 0.73 | 0.91 | 1.01 | | | | | | | | | | | | | |
| 8 | 3.12 | 2.28 | 0.68 | 0.39 | 0.75 | 0.94 | 1.03 | | | | | | | | | | | | | |
| 8.5 | 3.50 | 2.50 | 0.66 | 0.38 | 0.80 | 1.02 | 1.11 | | | | | | | | | | | | | |
| 9 | 3.66 | 2.55 | 0.59 | 0.36 | 0.82 | 1.04 | | | | | | | | | | | | | | |
| 9.5 | 3.78 | 2.59 | 0.53 | 0.35 | 0.84 | 1.05 | | | | | | | | | | | | | | |
| 10 | 3.92 | 2.63 | 0.47 | 0.34 | 0.86 | 1.07 | | | | | | | | | | | | | | |
| 10.5 | 4.11 | 2.70 | 0.43 | 0.33 | 0.88 | 1.08 | | | | | | | | | | | | | | |
| 11 | 4.30 | 2.81 | 0.40 | 0.33 | 0.90 | 1.10 | | | | | | | | | | | | | | |
| 11.5 | 4.73 | 3.06 | 0.39 | 0.34 | 0.99 | | | | | | | | | | | | | | | |
| 12 | 4.81 | 3.08 | 0.35 | 0.34 | 1.01 | | | | | | | | | | | | | | | |

Figure 4. Ratio $k_A$ ratio among results obtained by a non-ideal instrument and "ideal" instrument. Red cells highlight deviation from "ideal" instruments greater than 100%,

Without aperture effect, a loop over a large number (typically 5000-50000) generates random angles of specified standard deviations and distributions. Those angles are then used to compute the standard deviation of the outcomes, i.e. the values of the BRDF model for comparison with the *r*-tables.

The comparison was done for an actual road surface, measured by an on-site goniophotometer, choosing the reference *r*-table closest to the sample behaviour to calculate the impact of the aperture effect uncertainty. The results displayed in Figure 4 are the calculated systematic errors.

For most of the table, the software result is consistent with the measurement and the software highlights the error for $\beta$ between 0° and 10°. Without any calibration, the error can be very large for specular samples. By calibrating the measurement with the portable instrument with a sample of similar characteristics, the aperture effect can be greatly diminished, the accuracy of the results being determined by how similar the sample under test and the calibration sample are. It is also possible that the straylight from the measurement is higher than what is corrected for, when the light source is illuminating the sample at grazing angles and toward the detector. The results show that the software evaluation also highlights errors which are different from the aperture effect. In particular, the alignment uncertainty adds an uncertainty in some directions, which might compensate some of the errors, or on the contrary, enlarge the errors. The illumination directions with $\beta \leq 20°$ and $\varepsilon \geq 70°$ show the largest values, which corresponds with the peak of the sample BRDF.

## 5. CONCLUSIONS

A model of the geometrical errors in goniophotometric measurement was developed. It was implemented in software (LUMCORUN) that includes the modelling of the geometry of the instrument and the modelling of the behaviour of the sample under test. The model of the BRDF of the sample consists of a diffuse, a specular and an experimental component as well as additional components to fit experimental data, for retro-reflection and grazing angles effect.

A comparison between the results obtained with the software and measurements by a portable goniophotometer was made. Illumination directions corresponding to specular reflection toward the detector provides large systematic errors.

The process highlighted the high dependency of the results on the type of sample used and reference table used to model BRDF. To increase accuracy of the modelling and of the uncertainty evaluation, a good database of up-to-date reference *r*-tables is required.

Thanks to the simulation, it is possible to predict some of the instrument behaviours and therefore, in the future, to correct the systematic effects due to the aperture.

The evaluation by the software can also be used to determine the uncertainty due to the misalignment.

The developed software is a big step towards a better modelling of luminance coefficients and BRDF measurement and is therefore an important tool for the establishment of more accurate uncertainty budgets.

## ACKNOWLEDGEMENT

This research has been conducted in the project 16NRM02 SURFACE and has received funding from the EMPIR programme co-financed by the Participating States and from the European Union's Horizon 2020 research and innovation programme.

## REFERENCES

[1] Road surfaces and lighting (joint technical report CIE/PIARC), CIE 066:1984.

[2] Road surface and road marking reflection characteristics, CIE 144 :2001

[3] Road lighting - Part 3: Calculation of performance, EN 13201-3:2015.

[4] International Lighting Vocabulary CIE S 017/E:2011.

[5] Road lighting - Part 2: Performance requirements, EN 13201-2:2015.

[6] V. Muzet, J. Bernasconi, P. Iacomussi, S. Liandrat, F. Greffier, P. Blattner, J. Reber, and M. Lindgren, "Review of road surface photometry methods and devices – Proposal for new measurement geometries, LRT 1–16 (2020).

[7] E. P. Lafortune and Y. D. Willems, Using the Modified Phong Reflectance Model for Physically Based Rendering" Report CWP197 (Departement Computerwetenschappen, KU Leuven, 1994).

[8] Alexander Basov, Development of a goniophotometer for measuring reflective properties of road surfaces, Master Thesis, (Lappeenranta University of Technology, 2017).

[9] Korobko A.A., Approximation of road surface luminance coefficient, in Proceedings of the CIE Centenary Conference (CIE x038:2013), pp. 1076–1082.

[10] R. B. Gibbons, Influence of Pavement Reflection on Target Visibility, Ph. D dissertation, (University of Waterloo, 1997).

[11] SURFACE consortium, 16NRM02 SURFACE website, https://surface-nrm02.eu, accessed 2023.

[12] D. Renoux, "LUMCORUN", Zenodo (2021), https://doi.org/10.5281/zenodo.5547682.

[13] JCGM 100 :2008, " Evaluation of measurement data. Guide to the expression of uncertainty in measurement", https://www.bipm.org/documents/20126/2071204/JCGM_100_2008_E.pdf/cb0ef43f-baa5-11cf-3f85-4dcd86f77bd6

[14] JCGM101:2008 supplement 1," Evaluation of measurement data — Supplement 1 to the "Guide to the expression of uncertainty in measurement" — Propagation of distributions using a Monte Carlo method, https://www.bipm.org/documents/20126/2071204/JCGM_101_2008_E.pdf/325dcaad-c15a-407c-1105-8b7f322d651c

# How TQM has Impacted the Industry

**Mohammed Alotaibi**

*University of Strathclyde, Department, Faculty, University of Strathclyde, 16 Richmond St, G1 1XQ, Glasgow, United Kingdom, mohammed.alotaibi@strath.ac.uk*

**ABSTRACT**: Total Quality Management (TQM) needs true believers who translate its principles into practices that drive the organization to excellent performance and to be a successful entity in the industry. A model in the paper illustrates TQM in terms of the processes according to the literature review summary of several authors' ideas with an enlargement view. The TQM has parts that are interrelated to build a foundation of QM principles, QM Core, and QM Infrastructure. Putting TQM into practice, a survey was collected from Oil and Gas Drilling Industry field for safety practices which translates the TQM process. In the end, a proposal was discussed in the paper to improve the safety process within TQM and how some factors have impacted the role of risk assessment and root cause analysis methods outcomes under TQM radar.

**Keywords**: Quality Management, TQM, Total Quality Management, Industry Quality, ISO, Performance.

**Received** January 1, 2023; **In final form** March 31, 2023; **Published** June 2023



**Corresponding author:** Mohammed Alotaibi, e-mail: mohammed.alotaibi@strath.ac.uk

## 1. INTRODUCTION

In general, industry performance and monitoring practices have to be understood through Total Quality Management (TQM) concept. This paper reviews literature papers that focus on TQM and analyze the survey that was collected from Oil and Gas (O&G) Drilling Industry experts. The literature review intends to understand TQM measuring performance and develop empirical works on Drilling Industry in O&G for safety practices. The backbone of the discussion is the primary data collection; the survey, which will clarify the weakness and strengths of safety practices under specific indicators used in TQM In addition, connect the literature review to real examples. Many papers have discussed TQM to apply new ideas, approaches, and methods of applications for technical and academic aspects. The interrelationship of TQM processes from authors' reviews and discussions is summarized in the following sections of this paper with a broader picture. The interrelationship elements formed the basis of TQM for QM Principles, QM Core, and QM Infrastructure. The structure of this paper is as follows: Literature Review Search Method, TQM from Literature Review, Survey Analysis, Discussion, and Summary and Conclusion.

## 2. LITERATURE REVIEW SEARCH METHOD

A mapping tool was used to filter related papers and tap on, precisely, the industrial impact from QM and ISO to narrow the search. Among several search and mapping tools available for scholars, Connectedpapers website (Papers, 2023) has been selected, a tool that can map key papers by clustering the prior and derivative works. The keywords "quality management models and methods" was used to show suggested papers, as in Figure 1.

Figure 1. Connectpapers.com search suggestions.

The selected paper is "Clustering quality management models and methods: systematic literature review and text-mining analysis approach." It is the core paper to build a graph for related papers, as in Figure 2.

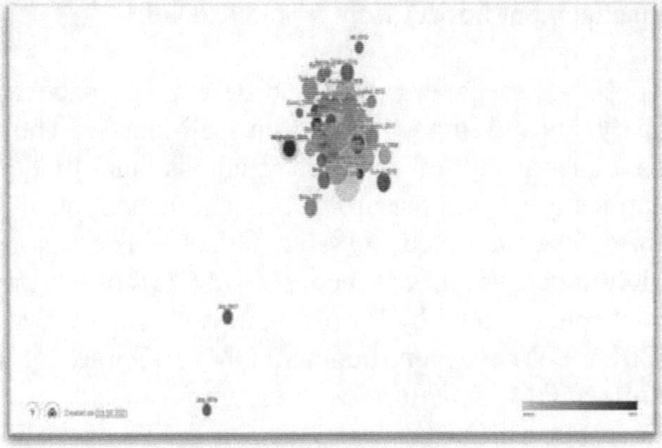

Figure 2. Connectedpapers.com clustering graph.

Below are the criteria used to refine the generated list from the core paper which mapped papers that connected to QM:

- Most fitting abstract that has QM focus
- Most appropriate paper with higher citations and references

As a result, 41 papers emerged from the core paper, as shown in Figure 3.

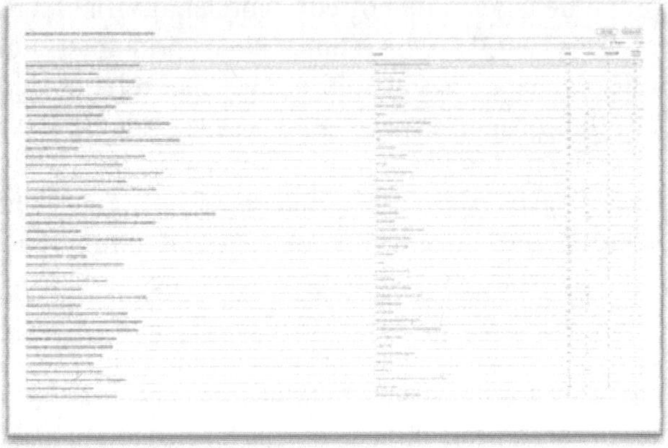

Figure 3. Connectedpapers.com papers connected to the core paper.

Nine papers, including a key paper, were selected for analysis with an 8+ "similarity ranking score," which connectedpapers.com uses in its ranking option, as in Figure 4

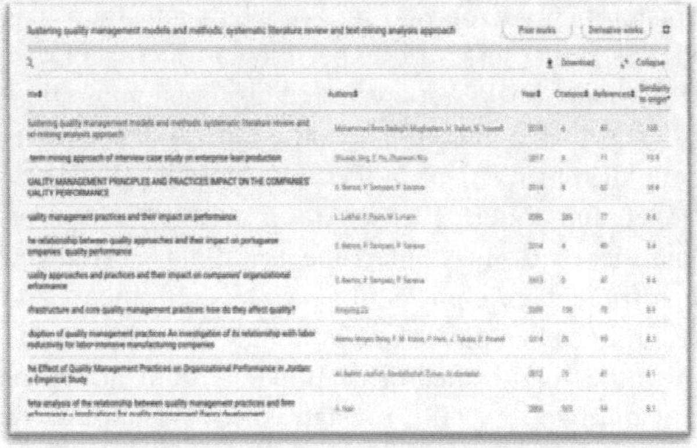

Figure 4. Connectedpapers.com ranking papers.

Those selected papers have a year range in as Table 1, with a mix of method approaches as in Table 2.

Table 1. Papers Ranged by Year

| **Range** | **Year** |
|---|---|
| Oldest | 2006 |
| Newest | 2019 |
| Average | 2013 |

Table 2. Papers Method Approaches

| **Methodology** | **Number** | **Percentage** |
|---|---|---|
| Qualitative | 3 | 33% |
| Quantitative | 1 | 11% |
| Mixed | 5 | 56% |

Two of those nine ranked papers were excluded because they have a low relationship to the topic and need more citations. An additional paper has been added for QM's historical review purpose, "Theory of Quality Management: Its Origins and History."

## 3. TQM FROM LITERATURE REVIEW

According to Síria Alves Barros, Sampaio and Saraiva (2014a) TQM definition is "Total quality management (TQM) described as a collective, interlinked system of quality management practices (QMPs) that is associated with organizational performance. An understanding of quality management principles is the foundation of any improvement activity." which draws a meaning of literature review in terms of TQM industrial impact. Historically, in Japan, the quality movement evolved from just inspection techniques to total quality control. The idea in Japan followed the epistemology proposed by Shewhart and then was given to the scientific experimentation for PDCA (Plan-Do-Check-Act cycle). This epistemological of TQM is a mixed phenomenon, and scientists sought improvement in the PDCA cycle, (Koskela, Tezel and Patel, 2019). Along with other broad historical discussions, the authors criticized insufficient references for established ideas and techniques that play a fundamental role in TQM. On the other hand, the International Organization for Standardization (ISO) established principles of TQM as the foundation of ISO standards; for example: "Customer focus, Leadership, Engagement of people, Process approach, Improvement, Evidence-based decision-making, Relationship Management (International Organization for Standardization, 2015)". The definition and history of TQM draw brief lines for the next section, the selected papers that focus on TQM's industrial impact.

### 3.1. TQM's Industrial Impact

The authors from the selected papers discussed new ideas, approaches, and analysis results that reach out to the concept and definition of the TQM and its impact scale on industrial. In relation to the aforementioned TQM definition, its core meaning is relaying on practices performed by the organizations which impact organizations' performance ends. This concept unlatches ideas and interrogates for academic and industrial practitioners to examine TQM, measuring its actual impact.

In the beginning, the objective of the key paper "Clustering quality management models and methods: systematic literature review and text-mining analysis approach" was to examine the models used in QM through a historical perspective, (Sadeghi Moghadam, Safari and Yousefi, 2019). This key paper's literature review search method was about extracting and reviewing the quality management techniques from collected documents (text mining). Because of their study limitations, they introduced only three QM tools (FTA, FMEA & RCA). According to their review, emerging trends for QM are primarily focused on corporate social responsibility, supply chain, knowledge management, and sustainable development. Still, from several other studies, additional works have been discussed, such as leadership, customer focus, employee involvement, HR management, continuous improvement and innovation, and other QM practitioner tools, such as PDCA and the fishbone diagram. This knocks the door for the subsequent seven papers regarding quality management impact from a practical side.

These seven papers have a different approach to analyzing the impact of QM on the industry. They have a variety of research methods and theory applications to measure the performance results from the adopted QM practices. The most highlighted argument about QM's origin is the conceptual model by Barros, Sampaio, and Saraiva, (2014b). They identified ten QM principles and thirteen QM indicators, as in Figure 5.

Figure 5. A Model for the Relationship of QMPPs and Quality Performance (SÌria Alves Barros, Sampaio and Saraiva (2014b)).

In their study, the ground-breaking comprehensively identified a model that includes practices for QM, which translate the principles into performance. They could prove the relationship between principles and indicators through their research method (survey). However, the study would have been more interesting if they had included the results from implementing QM practices from the company performance indicators end.

Further exploring the relationship between QM practices and the impact on performance, Lakhal, Pasin and Limam (2006) have proposed a model that explains the direct effects of management practice (to the left-hand side) and three performances indicators; financial performance, operational performance, and product quality (to the right-hand side), where both are linked to around infrastructure practices and core practices (in the middle), Figure 6. They claimed that the path analysis approach in the conceptual model showed an association between management practice, infrastructure and core practices, and performance. Their findings showed interesting positive effects of QM practices on organizational performance if companies' manager implements TQM. However, their argument relies heavily on qualitative analysis only for implementing the model with associated aspects of QM, with no quantitative analysis.

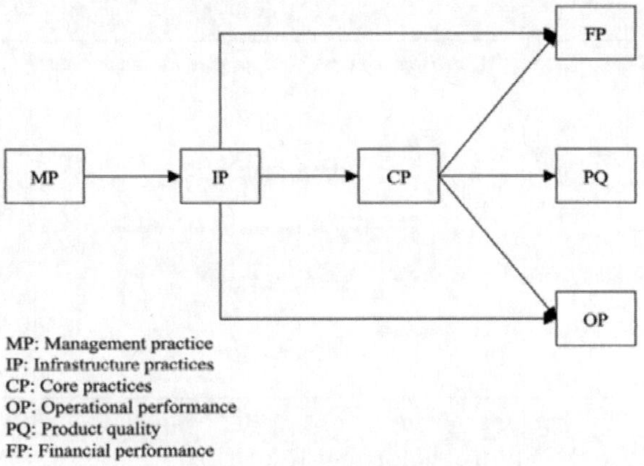


Figure 6. A Model for the Relationship of four Dimensions "Management Practice, Infrastructure Practices, Core Practices, and Performance" (Lakhal, Pasin and Limam, 2006).

Also, a conceptual model developed by Síria Alves Barros, Sampaio and Saraiva (2014a) (in their second paper), Figure 7, identified approaches to QMPs that have a significant impact on QM performance in Portuguese companies, but this may not apply to other organizations because of local regulation or business cultural. Their literature reviews generated nine generic QM performances "Leadership, customer focus, employee involvement, and commitment, HR management (incentive and recognition), strategic planning management, process management, supply chain management, continuous improvement innovation, and Quality tools and Business Excellence Models." They identified indicators for measuring organizational performance, proofing consistency outcomes and results. In their comprehensive qualitative analysis research, an investigation is needed to explain the efficiency of QM when implementing the proposed model.

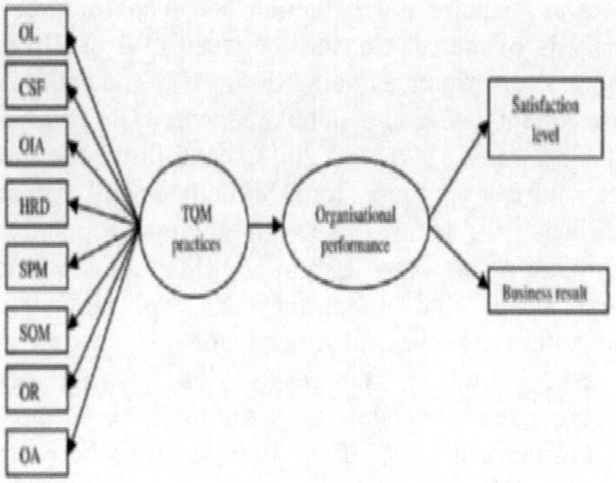


Figure 7. A conceptual proposal model of TQM practices Síria Alves Barros, Sampaio and Saraiva (2014a).

Moges Belay *et al.* (2014) made tremendous attempts to study the relationship between TQM practices and labor productivity. The measuring method is the revenue per employee and asset per employee to determine the QM adaptation level. The findings from this study, statistically, the correlation coefficient of TQM practice level and total asset per employee is 0.639 with a significance level of 0.05. The r-value is not less than 0.05, which shows a positive relationship between revenues per employee and TQM practice and adoption level. Since they focused this study on labor-intensive manufacturing companies, findings can't be extrapolated to other sectors, i.e., oil and gas, where technology has a significant portion of their operational activities. Though, observation suggested a strong influence from TQM on the organization's performance.

On the same momentum, Jaafreh (2012) had a similar approach; his six hypotheses were statistically tested, with QM practices as independent variables and organizational performances as dependent variables. Leadership, strategic planning, customer focus, and employee relation have a significant direct impact, while supplier quality and process management have no significant. It reveals that quantitative and qualitative analysis prove a relation between TQM and its effect on performance.

The last paper has heightened the need for meta-analysis of the relationship between QM practices and the performance (Nair, 2006). After the author's assessment using the published empirical studies data between 1995 and 2004, he followed seven determined hypotheses for QM methods and overall performance. He revealed an aggregate positive correlation between several QM practices and performance, but low on the plant level. However, the author believes an investigation is needed to assess the indirect link between management/leadership and operational performance and the direct/indirect links between supplier QM and financial performance, customer service, and product quality.

## 4. SURVEY ANALYSIS

The concept behind the survey is to analyze current practices in the drilling industry and learn from the real practice in the field which would lead to exploring TQM pitfalls in safety monitoring and performance. The method is survey-based through Qualtrics.com online software application. It is about collecting primary data from field subject matter experts who hold positions in health, safety, environmental, QA, Operation, and Maintenance. It is targeting specific drilling contractors who are working in the O&G drilling industry in Saudi Arabia. The questions were designed to evaluate the QM system in assisting safety management systems by applying risk assessment (RA) and root cause analysis (RCA) methods. A safety control can be systematically actionable by measuring control and corrective action, which are important in Quality Management System (Tashi, Mbuya and Gangadharappa, 2016).

Although, in the survey, assessing the experts' opinion is often difficul but a subjective judgment is often practiced, for instance, using the weight technique to clear the blurry opinions (Jiskani *et al.*, 2022). These methods (RA and RCA) are widely used applications for problem correction and uncovering symptoms or signs, which will help to develop prevention practices to stop incidents from reoccurrence. Figures 8 and 9 represent the RA and RCA feedback from the field experts with the following rating scale type:

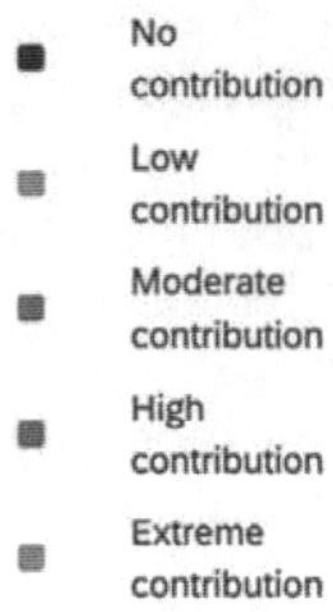


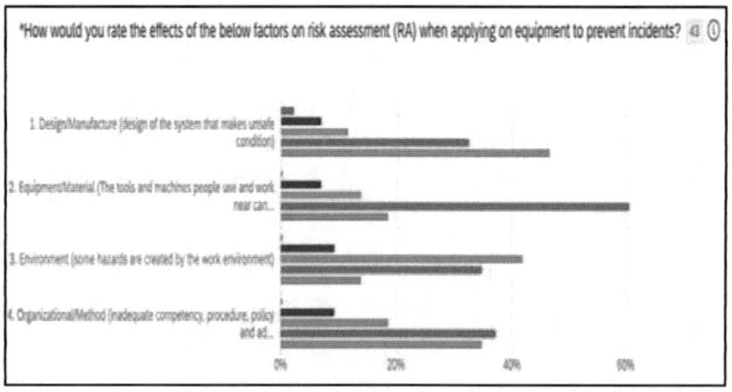


Figure 8. Factors that affect RA.

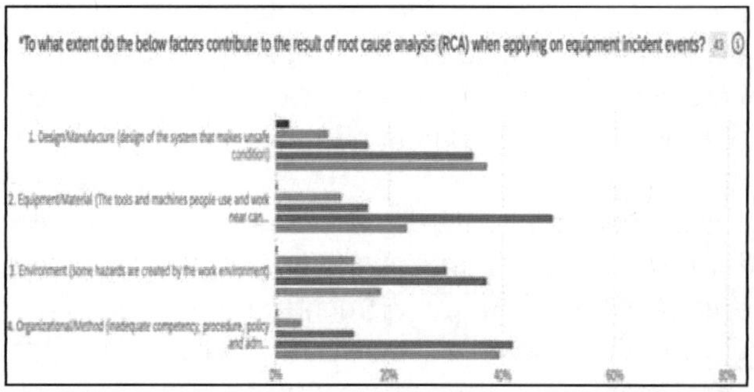


Figure 9. Factors that affect RCA.

Both questions show that a majority of responses identify Design/Manufacturer and Organizational/Method factors as having an extreme level of contribution for RA and RCA. The other two factors, Equipment/Material and Environment, have a second level of contribution. The highlight from the field survey shows an extreme impact on the quality of conducting RA and RCA on drilling incident events from those factors. This led to revisiting TQM processes and applications to manage indicators and practices, which will be discussed in the next section.

## 5. DISCUSSIONS

First, the model in Figure 10 shows TQM in terms of the procedures in accordance with the literature review summary of the ideas of various authors with the enclosing cycle. Leaders who adhere to TQM view it as a crucial philosophy and benefit from a higher output from their staff in terms of efficiency and profitability because it inspires them to find solutions to issues. TQM components are linked to form the QM principles, QM Core, and QM Infrastructure, which form the basis of TQM. All of these are consistent with the central idea or value used by the majority of authors to define high-level principles, which are: 1) Leadership, 3) Strategic Planning, 3) Supplier Quality, 4) People Management, 5 Organizational) 6) Process Management 7) Customer Focus 8) Product 9) Information and Analysis.

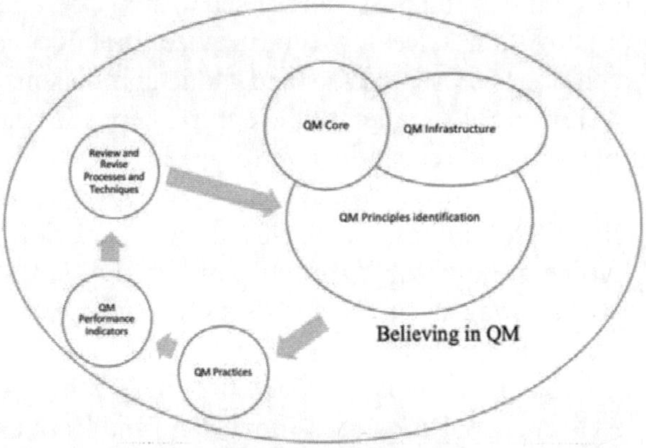


Figure 10. literature review summary of authors' ideas for QM.

QM practices are the third step in the cycle. It is the implementation stage of the QM and tests the return from it. Authors have identified several practices (top management support, customer relationship, supplier relationship, workforce management, quality information, Product/service design, and process management), and they prove of relationship to performance as statistically presented in many papers. Those practices connected the central concept to performance indicators. A summary in Table 3 from Síria Alves Barros, Sampaio and Saraiva (2014a) mentioned the most important indicators that QM could be measured.

Table 3. Performance measures proposed by different authors (Síria Alves Barros, Sampaio and Saraiva (2014a)

| Author(s) | Measure | Indicators |
|---|---|---|
| Prajogo and Sohal (2004) | Organization performance | • Quality performance<br>• Innovation performance |
| Lakhal *et al.* (2006) | Organization performance | • Financial performance<br>• Operational performance<br>• Product Quality |
| Lin *et al.* (2005) | Organization performance | • Satisfaction level<br>• Business results |
| Fuentes *et al.* (2006) | Organization performance | • Operational performance<br>• Market and financial performance<br>• Employee performance |
| Sila *et al.* (2007) | Performance measure | • Organizational effectiveness<br>• Financial results<br>• Market results |
| Sit *et al.* (2009) | Organization performance | • Customer satisfaction |
| Shieh and Wu (2002) | Organization performance | • Project performance |
| Feng *et al.* (2006) | Organization performance | • Quality performance<br>• Innovation performance |
| Ooi *et al.* (2008) | Organization performance | • Job satisfaction |
| Zakuan *et al.* (2010) | Organization performance | • Employee performance<br>• Customer satisfaction<br>• Business results |

The last step is to review and revise processes and techniques for implementing QM in the organizations. Although "review and revise processes and techniques" is sometimes included in principles. However, the control cycle PDCA model was added as a standalone element to revisit the central concept (QM principles, QM Core and QM Infrastructure) to identify gaps and follow the control cycle again.

The industry has a significant portion of this paper. It is a steppingstone to identifying the impact of the TQM on the industry. In conjunction with survey results, field feedback has implied that the most affected factors from the survey are big concerns about safety practices that the drilling industry demonstrates in their QM processes for safety practices, in terms of RA and RCA methods.

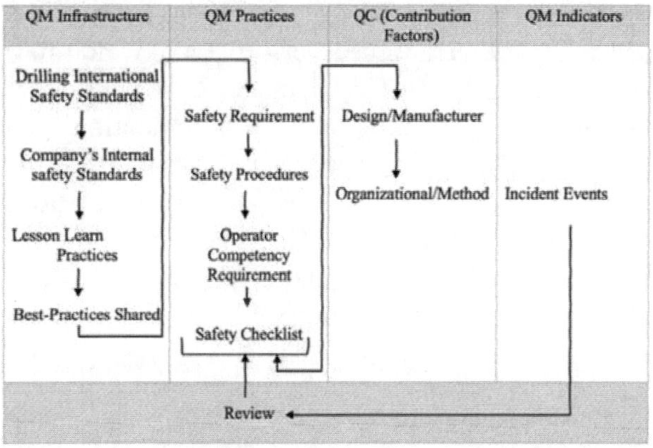


Figure 11. Drilling Industry TQM with Survey Outcomes

Within the approach that was discussed previously, TQM should have the Infrastructure, Practices, Indicators and Review processes to improve the drilling safety process. The survey feedback incorporates this approach with specific QM performance and monitoring indicators. Figure 11 demonstrates the approach: The first column is the several standards to build the QM Infrastructure, which has already been adopted by drilling companies. In the following column QM Practices, which is putting QM Infrastructure into motion mode, consists of safety procedures to run drilling operations and machines, that must be in compliance with safety requirements. These QM Practices also have already been adopted by drilling companies. The next move of the TQM process is the Quality Check (QC) for the factors that have an extreme contribution to safety control methods (RA and RCA). The two factors (Design/Manufacturer and Organizational/Method) have to meet the requirements and criteria from the previous columns. In design/manufacturer factors, QC will review and verify if suppliers provide equipment specification that meets safety standards for drilling operations. Also, for organizational/method, if the supplier provides enough manuals and procedures to run equipment and associated activities in a safe manner. The last column is the QM Indicators, which has an incident event indicator. This indicator shows the quality of previous processes. When incidents indicate causality related to contribution factors, then a review process will go back to improve procedures to avoid such pitfalls in the quality process.

Most authors have proof of the relationship of the QM to the organizations' performance, which to a certain degree, they show evidence either by higher returns or by gaining a higher reputation and customer loyalty. This paper is a foundation for the next TQM dilemma in the industry operations performance gauging. TQM is one of the methodologies that improve performance and monitoring systems for safety.

## 6. CONCLUSIONS

If a business is to succeed and assume the lead in its sector, it needs a true believer to put QM's principles into action. First of all, executives who believe in quality management see it as a basic sense that will increase worker productivity and profitability. The cornerstone of TQM under the "Believe in QM" umbrella is a mix of the three components: QM Infrastructure, QM Core, and QM Principles. Which all adhere to the definitions of basic concepts and tenets that are consistent with the ways in which the majority of authors have described them.

The QM is implemented through QM practices, which evaluate its effectiveness. Numerous papers have statistically demonstrated the connection between various practices and performance. These practices include top management support, customer and supplier relationships, workforce management, quality information, product and service design, and process management. These procedures linked the main idea to success metrics. However, when necessary, this has to be reviewed; the methods and procedures used to apply QM in the organizations. Review and revise practices and techniques presented as stand-alone components for cycle control to reiterate the central concept, search for gaps, and repeat the control cycle.

The literature review serves as a foundation for knowing how the QM will affect the industry. Drilling Industry in Oil and Gas serve as an example in this paper. Data was collected through a survey to evaluate factors that impact the quality of safety performance. Risk Assessment (RA) and Root Cuse Analysis (RCA) methods which indicate the quality of safety outcomes to prevent incidents. In the survey, experts show an extreme contribution of two factors that impact RA and RCA quality, Design/Manufacturer and Organizational/Method.

A proposal process for TQM was demonstrated in this paper under columns for each component of TQM, with the survey results. The process gives a mean to review the impacts of the factors on the safety practices and enhances performance and monitoring systems for safety management systems.

## ACKNOWLEDGEMENT

I am grateful to Prof. Matthew Revie and Dr. Steve Paton, who provided extensive personal and professional guidance during my doctoral career. And nobody has been more important to me in pursuing this paper and learning journey than my parents, wife, sons, and daughters, whose love and guidance are with me in whatever I pursue.

**REFERENCES**

[1] Barros, S.A., Sampaio, P. and Saraiva, P. (2014a) 'The relationship between quality approaches and their impact on portuguese companies quality performance'.

[2] Barros, S.A., Sampaio, P. and Saraiva, P.M. (2014b) Published. 'QUALITY MANAGEMENT PRINCIPLES AND PRACTICES IMPACT ON THE COMPANIES' QUALITY PERFORMANCE'. 2014b.

[3] Jaafreh, A. (2012) 'The Effect of Quality Management Practices on Organizational Performance in Jordan: An Empirical Study'. Journal of Financial Research, 4.

[4] Jiskani, I.M. et al. (2022) 'Improved Z-number based fuzzy fault tree approach to analyze health and safety risks in surface mines'. Resources Policy, 76 102591.

[5] Koskela, L., Tezel, A. and Patel, V. (2019) Theory of Quality Management: Its Origins and History.

[6] Lakhal, L., Pasin, F. and Limam, M. (2006) 'Quality management practices and their impact on performance'. International Journal of Quality & Reliability Management.

[7] Moges Belay, A. et al. (2014) 'Adoption of quality management practices'. Benchmarking: An International Journal, 21 (1), pp. 77-100.

[8] Nair, A. (2006) 'Meta-analysis of the relationship between quality management practices and firm performance—implications for quality management theory development'. Journal of Operations Management, 24 (6), pp. 948-975.

[9] Papers, C. (2023) Connected Papers | Find and explore academic papers. Available at: https://www.connectedpapers.com/.

[10] Tashi, T., Mbuya, V.B. and Gangadharappa, H. (2016) 'Corrective action and preventive actions and its importance in quality management system: A review'. International Journal of Pharmaceutical Quality Assurance, 7 (1), pp. 1-6.

[11] Sadeghi Moghadam, M.R., Safari, H. and Yousefi, N. (2019) 'Clustering quality management models and methods: systematic literature review and text-mining analysis approach'. Total Quality Management & Business Excellence, 32 (3-4), pp. 241-264.

# Human factors and interfaces between operators, processes, and plants in the technical standards: the Italian experience

Romualdo Marrazzo[1], Domenico Barone[2]

[1]*VAL-RTEC, ISPRA. Via V. Brancati n.48 - 00144 Roma, Italia, romualdo.marrazzo@isprambiente.it*
[2]*Tecnologie Sicurezza Industriale Srl. Via Lomazzo n. 51 - 20154 Milano, Italia*

**ABSTRACT**: The Seveso III Directive 2012/18/EU imposes an obligation to take into due consideration the human factors and the interfaces between operators, processes, and plants, as part of the implementation of the Safety Management System for Prevention of Major Accident. In the national technical standard that provides guidelines for implementing a safety management system, specific attention is paid to the human-machine interface in close connection with the prevention and assessment of human error. A good designed man-machine interface, in the control room of a process plant, allows you to minimize the possibility of operator error on the panel. The assessment of the possibility of human error must be used in the reliability analysis to verify if the procedures and operational controls adopted to improve the behaviour of the operator or the instrumental controls give the best contribution to the safety of the system. In addition, a fundamental role is represented by training activities and emergency drills. The consideration of the human factors and the interfaces between operators, processes, and plants, must be based on: detecting any problems at the interfaces, monitoring the status of systems, using proper labelling of equipment, improving the reliability of operators' performance; implementing an effective system of operational controls.

**Keywords**: HMI, Seveso, Inspection, Standards, Human factors, Safety Management System.

**Received** January 1, 2023; **In final form** March 31, 2023; **Published** June 2023



**Corresponding author:** Romualdo Marrazzo, e-mail: romualdo.marrazzo@isprambiente.it

## 1. INTRODUCTION

The Seveso III Directive 2012/18/EU [1], implemented in Italy by a legislative decree issued in 2015 - D.Lgs. 105/2015 [2], is aimed at the prevention of major accidents involving dangerous substances. The D.Lgs. 105/2015 covers establishments where dangerous substances may be present (e.g. during processing or storage) in quantities exceeding certain thresholds. Operators of the establishments are obliged to take all necessary measures to prevent major accidents and to limit their consequences for human health and the environment.

Depending on the amount of dangerous substances present, establishments are categorised in lower and upper tier, with different obligations. The requirements include, among others: notification of all concerned establishments; deploying a Major Accident Prevention Policy (MAPP) through the implementation of a Safety Management System for Prevention of Major Accident (SMS-PMA); producing a Safety Report (SR) for upper-tier establishments; producing an Internal Emergency Plan (IEP) for upper tier establishments; providing information in case of accidents.

As part of the implementation of the Safety Management System, the D.Lgs. 105/2015 imposes an obligation to take into due consideration the human factors and the interfaces between operators, processes, and plants.

During the control activities it is in fact necessary to verify that training programs and emergency drills are implemented to improve operator behaviour. It is therefore fundamental that in the risk analysis the human factor and the conditions in which significant activities for the safety of the establishment must be carried out, giving a particular attention to the interfaces between operators and processes in the phase of operational control of the plants.

## 2. METHODS

### 2.1. Human factors in the control activities

In Italy, the SMS inspection are conducted to verify the suitability of the operator MAPP carrying out a planned and systematic examination of the systems being employed at the establishment, whether of a technical, organisational or managerial nature.

The human factors and the interfaces between operators, processes, and plants are specific items of interest during the SMS control activity [3]. In fact, the commission must:

- Verify that training and drill programs exist and are implemented to improve the behaviour of the operator.
- Verify that the work shifts, and the distribution of tasks have been established taking into account the psycho-physical stress to which the workers are subjected and that mechanisms are put in place to verify that the appropriate psycho-physical conditions are maintained.

Among the tools available to the inspection commission during the documentary verification, it is possible to verify directly, also by consulting the documentation relating to the health and safety at work analysis, the compliance with the indications relating to the maintenance suitable psycho-physical conditions of the workers.

During the "on-site" visit, the possible insights concern interviews with the employees both on the management methods of ordinary and extraordinary management, maintenance, emergency interventions, and on their involvement in the drafting and/or revision of the operating instructions.

### 2.2. The consideration of the HMI and the human error

The national technical standard UNI 10616:2022 (Establishments with major-accident hazard-Safety management systems-Guidelines on implementation of UNI 10617) [4] provides guidelines for implementing a safety management system, describing the procedures and technical tools useful for achieving specific objectives for the prevention of major accidents in industrial establishments (national technical standard UNI 10617:2019) [5].

It deals with most of the hazards and major accident risks present both in simple installations and in more complex installations where the process risks can be preponderant compared to those connected to the simple loss of containment. The application of the contents of the standard must be commensurate with the specificities of the major accident hazards present in the establishment.

In the standard, specific attention is paid to the human-machine interface (HMI), meaning the system that separates the operator, who is using a machine (i.e. the control panel located in the control room in the case of the process industry), from the machine itself, while ensuring a constant connection.

Among the objectives for the continuous improvement of the SMS-PMA, which arise from the results of the identification of the hazards and the assessment of the risks of a major accident, the improvement of the quality of the interface between the operator and the plant/process can also be included (i.e. promptness, accuracy and punctuality in reporting anomalies).

In close connection with the HMI, it is considered the prevention and assessment of human error, a fundamental aspect of process safety management.

To strengthen and disseminate the culture of safety, the site manager should also operate through the implementation of a company policy which clearly and transparently identifies the criteria for distinguishing acceptable behaviour from that which cannot be considered as such, distinguishing situations involving intentional misconduct from human errors attributable to organizational causes.

The awareness of the people who carry out a work activity in the plant, involved in activities relevant to safety, can in fact be verified through knowledge of the potential negative consequences deriving from a failure to comply with the specified procedures, with consequent human error, and the possibility of even a major accident. The need to verify the system procedures, on the other hand, may derive from the possible analysis of the accidents and/or near misses connected to the ascertained human error.

## 3. RESULTS

### 3.1. Design of the man-machine interface

The functionality of the interfaces between operators, process and systems, consisting of the instrumentation located in the control room with related switchboards/monitors/buttons/optical and acoustic signalling panels, including wireless devices, must be ensured through the periodic check program of the active safety systems, consisting of toxic and/or flammable gas detectors, fire detectors, alarms and blocks for critical operating parameters. The displays must report process variables, alarms, automatic blocks, recordings, as well as actuators for control actions on the process, such as starting/stopping pumps and compressors, opening/closing valves, changing the regulation and operating parameters set.

The main functions of an interface are:

- Presentation of process information.
- Immediate implementation of control actions.
- Support for diagnosis, decision making or planning.

Important elements of an interface are usability, to make the HMI easy to use (reducing the possibility of errors), and accessibility by the panel operator. A correct design of the control, alarm and automatic blocking systems must take into account the analysis of the operator's tasks at the switchboard and the optimal ergonomic and specific environmental factors for correct operation of the systems and plants.

A good designed man-machine interface, in the control room of a process plant, allows you to minimize the possibility of operator error on the panel, both during normal operating conditions and during emergency situations, throughout the process life cycle and in case of plant or process changes. These interfaces must be considered throughout the life cycle of the process and during plant or process changes.

Particular control provisions must in fact be adopted to manage any modifications/changes made, in conditions of necessity and under specific responsibility, to the switchboards or control equipment. Obviously, these changes must not reduce the ergonomic design characteristics as well as they must take into account other project requirements, such as accessibility for maintenance or periodic checks.

### 3.2. Practical schemes of control rooms

In order to represent some practical examples of control room [6], with the relative representation of process parameters and data on the screen of a DCS (Distributed Control System), the case of a typical process industry was investigated.

In the following, schemes of correct design and distribution of spaces in a control room, with the relative minimum requirements are presented [7]:

- Figure 1: Illustrations of definitions associated with workstation visual display
- Figure 2: Visibility of large screens and the widths of corridors
- Figure 3: Travel routes and collaborative operation among units

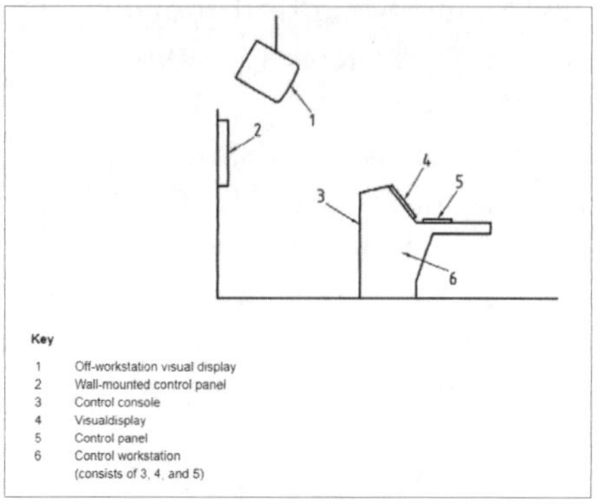


Figure 1. Illustrations of definitions associated with workstation visual display.

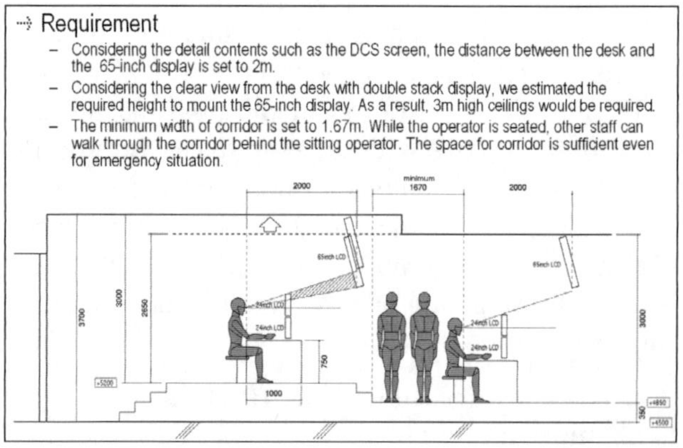


Figure 2. Visibility of large screens and the widths of corridors.

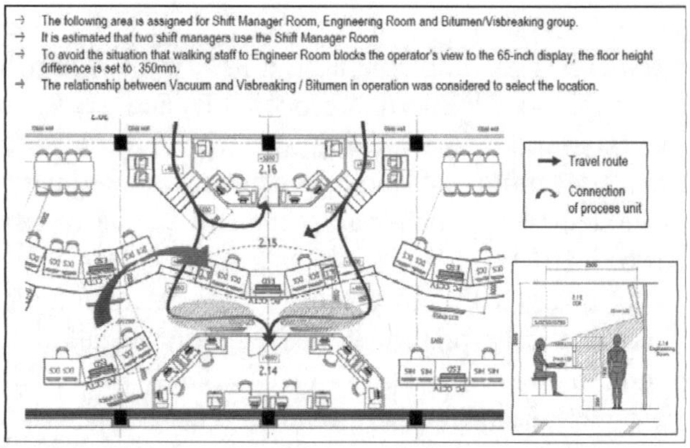


Figure 3. Travel routes and collaborative operation among units.

The key points for the adequate representation of data and information on a screen, in order to improve the man-machine graphic interfaces [8], are:

- Color graphic representation (Figure 4)
- Device status display (Figure 5)
- Representation of data values (Figure 6)

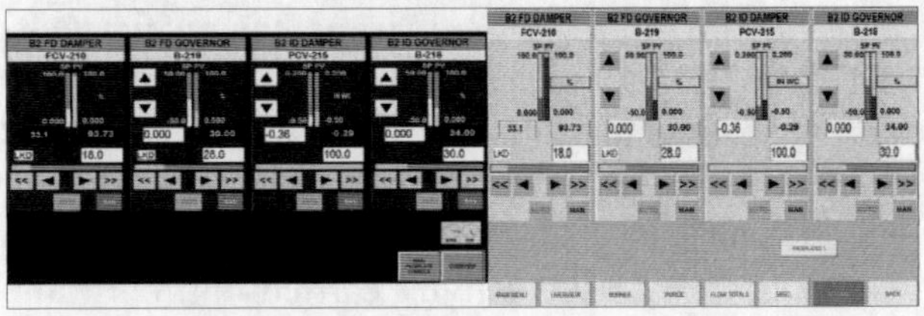

Figure 4. Color graphic representation.

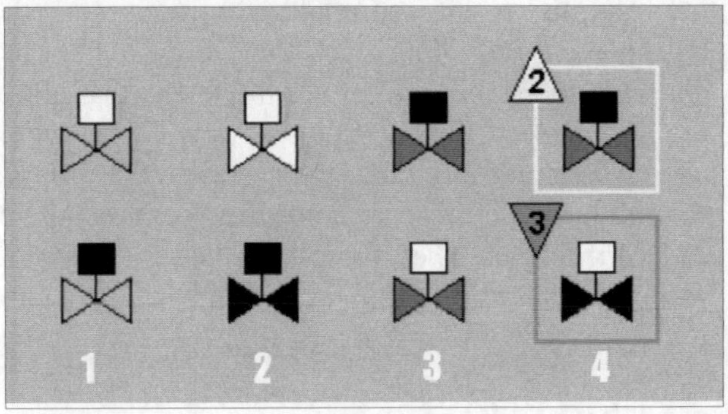


Figure 5. Device status display.

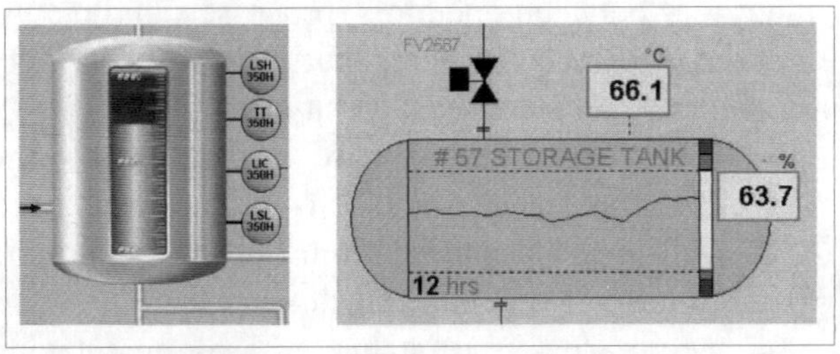


Figure 6. Representation of data values.

Typical examples of control panels are finally given in the following, as taken from the DCS (Distributed Control System) in the control room [9]:

- Figure 7: Plant overview
- Figure 8: Process Air Unit Process

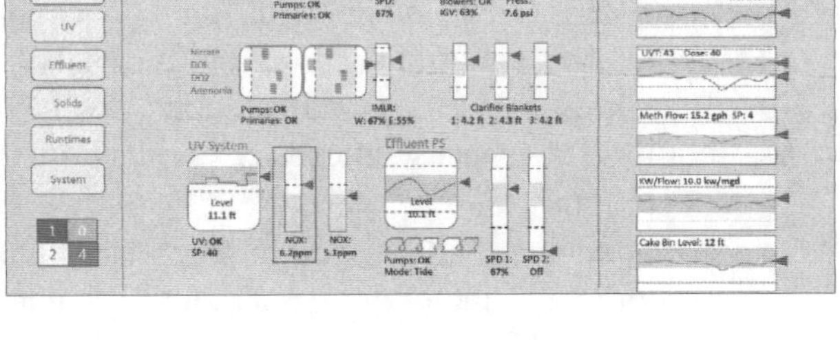


Figure 7. Plant overview.

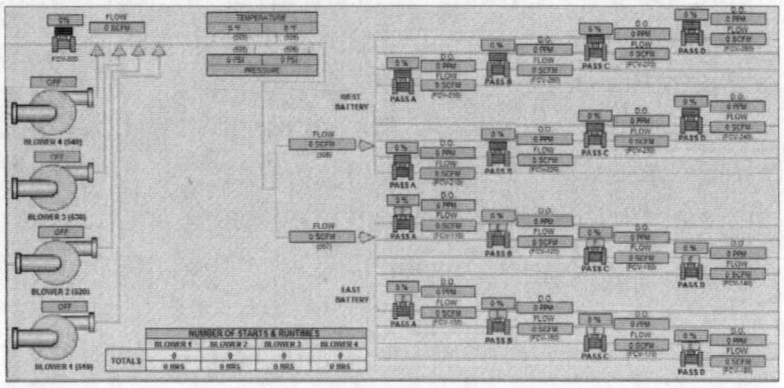

Figure 8. Process Air Unit Process.

### 3.3. The prevention of the human error in a process plant

The prevention of human error cannot ignore the knowledge of the potential negative consequences deriving from non-compliance with system procedures, with the possibility of a major accident. The assessment of the possibility of human error must be used in the reliability analysis to verify if the procedures and operational controls adopted to improve the behaviour of the operator or the instrumental controls give the best contribution to the safety of the system.

The management by the workers of operating anomalies and/or emergency situations must be verified both in the actual conditions of occurrence of the events and in the simulations, in order to highlight any deficiencies connected to the human factor. The analysis of non-conformities relating to procedures, regulations, operating instructions, detected as a result of inspections and/or accidents/near-accidents, generally linked to human error, can highlight deficiencies related to the behaviour of people, the organization and the work environment. Such deficiencies must be subject to appropriate corrective actions.

Emergency drills are an important element of evaluation. They must be carried out according to a specific path that goes from planning to the critical analysis of the results, in order to prepare any corrective actions, also in terms of response times and emergency management of the operators in order to reduce the possibility of accidents related to human error.

## 4. DISCUSSIONS

Based on the experience coming from the control activities conducted on some Seveso Italian establishments, in the following the discussion about examples and indications of particular or recurring situations are given about the consideration of the human factor in the SMS.

The inspections must mainly be aimed at evaluating how much the company policy, and therefore the management system, require that human factors are actually taken into consideration in the conduct of the plant's activities, identifying any deficiencies. The aspects that must be taken into consideration are the organizational elements, the policy and standards followed in the design and modification phases of the plants, the operating conditions, including problems related to process management, and the working environments.

As regards the design phases of new processes or operating systems, it must be evident that the company policy or the standards adopted foresee the consideration of human factors. Indicative of the fact that human factors have been considered is, for example, the evidence of the analysis of the aspects related to the spaces available to the operators, the accessibility of the equipment, the correct construction and location of the control panels and the use of prototypes and pilot plants also for the analysis and revision of the operator-plant interface.

At an operational level, information on work shifts must be acquired, for example by verifying that the available resources are distributed in a homogeneous manner, or in any case congruent with the workload, that the responsibilities have been clearly identified and are commensurate with the experience and ability of the employee to identify the cause of an error which may also cause a major accident. In fact, it must be considered that stress and fatigue can be the result of incorrect personnel management. To identify a possible deficiency in this sense, one could, for example, analyse the criteria for allocating resources within the various operational areas, verifying whether both the physical and aptitude characteristics and the degree of experience, which must be possessed by the person responsible for the critical tasks of the plant, have been specified.

With regard to the operating procedures available to operators, the main aspects to consider are that these are clear and complete, written in a language that operators can understand, that their involvement in drafting and revision has been envisaged and, most importantly, that these procedures provide employees with all the elements that enable them to identify and manage unforeseen situations.

It should be remembered that the conditions of the working environment (lighting, temperature, exposure to noise, vibrations or chemical agents, etc.) also play a fundamental role in the employee's ability to interact with the systems and equipment. In this regard, it will be important to verify not so much that the values of these parameters are compatible with the activity carried out, but rather that national and international standards have been considered in the organization of the activity for the definition of optimal conditions in the workplace, providing, in the procedures, the analyses to establish what are the levels that allow to guarantee efficiency and safety. Finally, it should be considered that the system must provide for the periodic measurement of these parameters, to verify that the pre-established limits are respected, adopting compensatory measures in case it is not possible to respect the limit.

## 5. CONCLUSIONS

The consideration of the human factors and the interfaces between operators, processes, and plants, in the correct implementation of a safety management system must be based on:

- The detection of any problems at the interfaces, thanks to the feedback information coming from both the operators and the maintenance technicians.
- Monitoring the status of equipment and systems. It is important that equipment is visually inspected throughout the work shift. Reading the instruments placed on the equipment makes it possible to verify the reliability of the parameters reported by the remote-control systems in the control room. Furthermore, only through visual inspections anomalous situations can be promptly identified. The information found must be recorded on special checklists which must be reviewed on a periodic basis by the supervisors so that what is reported is consistent with other data and that any anomalous situations are promptly resolved. In addition, it is good practice to have equipment checks integrated with normal operations.
- An adequate maintenance of work tools and equipment, including maintaining good

conditions of cleanliness and order in the workplace (s.c. house-keeping).

- The use of correct labeling and signaling of containers, pipes, equipment, etc., also through appropriate color codes, to allow immediate knowledge of the risks and the identification of systems and components. Of specific importance, for example, are the methods for signaling automatic blocks to the switchboard, especially in the event of a bypass due to contingent plant requirements, with the relative operating management procedure.
- The maintenance of good lighting conditions, essential for identifying the equipment, reading the instruments and identifying possible problems.
- The improvement of the reliability of the operators' performances. Particular attention should bc paid to the procedures for handing over deliveries between shift managers and/or switchboard operators during shift changes in the plant and in the control room, keeping adequate traces in the system documentation.
- The implementation of an effective system of operational controls based on procedures, permits, inspections, etc., that allows to prevent or promptly identify any human errors before they cause accidents.
- The functionality of the operator/process and operator/equipment interfaces to make it easier for the operator to monitor the process, identify any anomalies or emergency situations and implement the foreseen intervention methods. Consider, for example, the problem of managing a maximum number of alarms on screen in the event of a generalized emergency, or the problem of assessing reliability/redundancy for critical alarms (in the event of a power failure).

## REFERENCES

[1] Directive 2012/18/EU of the European Parliament and of the Council of 4 July 2012 on the control of major-accident hazards involving dangerous substances, amending and subsequently repealing Council Directive 96/82/EC Official Journal of the European Union 55 L197. (2012).

[2] DECRETO LEGISLATIVO 26 giugno 2015, n. 105 "Attuazione della direttiva 2012/18/UE relativa al controllo del pericolo di incidenti rilevanti connessi con sostanze pericolose". (Gazz. Uff. 14 luglio 2015, n. 161, S.O.). (2015)

[3] APAT. Linee guida per lo svolgimento delle verifiche ispettive sui sistemi di gestione della sicurezza in impianti a rischio di incidente rilevante. Manuali e linee guida 23/2003. ISBN 88-448-0095-0. (2003).

[4] UNI 10616:2022. Stabilimenti con pericolo di incidente rilevante - Sistemi di gestione della sicurezza - Linee guida per l'applicazione della UNI 10617. (2022).

[5] UNI 10617:2019. Stabilimenti con pericolo di incidente rilevante - Sistemi di gestione della sicurezza - Requisiti essenziali. (2019).

[6] ISO 11064-3:1999. Ergonomic design of control centres — Part 3: Control room layout. (1999).

[7] T. Naito et al. Control Room Design for Efficient Plant Operation. Yokogawa Technical Report English Edition Vol.54 No.1. (2011).

[8] https://boomtsps.medium.com/%E0%B9%81%E0%B8%99%E0%B8%A7%E0%B8%84%E0%B8%B4%E0%B8%94%E0%B8%81%E0%B8%B2%E0%B8%A3%E0%B8%AD%E0%B8%AD%E0%B8%81%E0%B9%81%E0%B8%9A%E0%B8%9A-human-machine-interfaces-for-process-automation-systems-isa101-concepts-868590d7dd5a. (20/03/2023).

[9] R. Kowalski et al. NEXT-GENERATION SCADA HIGH PERFORMANCE HUMAN MACHINE INTERFACES - Configuring HMIs to Display "Operator-centric" Information. Arcadis 2016. (2017)

# Method for the control of blockchain exploitation

Mor DIOP[1], Saïd TAZI[2], Yves DUCQ[1]

[1]Univ. Bordeaux, CNRS, IMS, UMR 5218, 33405 Talence – France
[2]Univ. Pau & Pays Adour, E2S UPPA, LIUPPA, Anglet, 64600, France
mor.diop@u-bordeaux.fr

**ABSTRACT**: These Blockchain is considered a digital, decentralized and distributed registry of relevant data, assets and transactions that is shared among members of a network. This technology attracts many sectors and his choice depends on several factors. For this, the ideal would be to consider all stakeholders from start to finish to allow everyone to be at the same level of information on "why" blockchain would add value to the processes in place both on functional and organizational levels. Several researchers and industries have studied the issue to come up with a solid management method as there is no single rule to succeed in this need. Research has shown that the notions of costs, and lead time are difficult to respect because of a lack of governance during the blockchain project and after its implementation. So, it is clearly established that the management of a Blockchain project is important to achieve all the phases, but it is also important to manage its exploitation. Our contribution is focused in this direction by proposing the different axes of management for a good exploitation of this technology keeping in mind that a previous contribution was published to managed the design and implementation phases. The results obtained are satisfying and allow us to take an important step in the governance of the blockchain.

**Keywords**: Blockchain (BC), operational management, performance indicators.

## 1. INTRODUCTION

During the management of a blockchain (BC) project, several factors come into play, both on functional and organizational levels. Although research is important and efforts are considerable, management challenges are still present and require a solid method. The main causes of failure of blockchain projects are related to costs, governance and delays. However, taking an inclusive approach is still an effective way to engage multiple stakeholders and prioritize efforts based on needs. In addition to that, the distribution of decisions would allow to define an appropriate management structure for the project by integrating all the operating hypotheses and the correction of detected inconsistencies and dysfunctions. The GRAI method, with its ability to model the company's decision-making systems based on the theoretical basis of references and structured approaches would be an effective way to represent these levels of decisions. Our contribution is based on the decisions to be taken at the strategic, tactical and operational levels in order to ensure a good exploitation of the blockchain. The coupling of this method with cost and time indicators is a good strategy to measure the effectiveness of decision taken at each level of decision, hence the need to combine them to obtain a more effective approach. In this paper, we will focus in the second part on the state of the art of the different works in this direction and the third part will focus on the distribution of decisions at these three levels of decisions (strategic, tactical and operational) accompanied by performance indicators to support this distribution.

## 2. STATE OF ART

Blockchain is a technology composed of a network that shares a single distributed database. It allows two or more parties to interact in transactions without any intermediary thanks to the cryptographic proof used to control the exchanges. At the beginning, this technology was typically reserved for the financial domain but since a few years it has become a subject to be exploited in other domains like supply chain, etc. Blockchain is one of the innovative technologies that are disrupting all sectors of the enterprise. The proper conduct of a blockchain project remains a major concern for all stakeholders interested in this technology. In [1], Ghassan Al-Mazrouai et al argued that the agile method can be a good approach to manage a blockchain project. Similarly, Duch Jonama et al used SCRUM after arguing that it will provide better adaptability and flexibility [2]. However, most of the researches focus on the contributions of blockchain in different domains, but little attention is paid to the costs of implementing blockchain, and even less to their reduction [3,4,5,6,7]. However, it is clearly proven that the management of a BC project is important to achieve all the phases, but it is also important to manage its operation. The exploitation of the BC requires a lot of subtleties and good governance to escape from the overheads and to take advantage of the latter. In [8], the notion of energy consumption has been much debated in the use of blockchain. It was concluded that this notion was one of the causes of high costs. In [9], the authors argued that a lack of control can be a bottleneck that would prevent the goals from being reached in the long run. Indeed, with its quality of a "trustless network" the control rules remain a trust factor that will link the different users and eventually the providers of blockchain services. These good steering rules are directly translated into the technical approaches and design to ensure in addition to performance, security, reliability, etc. [10]. Adopting a common approach and following a guideline to ensure the exploitation of blockchain remains a necessity if the difficulties related to its governance have been well integrated. This lack of coordination remains the most delicate point and is most often neglected. According to [11], "This lack of overall consensus - except maybe a consensus on blockchain's potential and hype - has been a critical blockchain adoption barrier". This situation is unfortunately noticed late. Indeed, because of these bottlenecks several projects could not see the light of day. In the survey by Mehrdokht Pournader et al, only 8% of 26,000 blockchain projects were successful in 2016[12]. In [13], causes that would be at the origin of these failures have been reported (see table 1).

**Table 1: Blockchain project discontinuation survey 1 (N = 600).**

| Cause of project discontinuation | Response percentage |
|---|---|
| Cost | 51% |
| Unsure how to start | 45% |
| Lack of governance | 45% |
| Users did not realize benefits | 10% |
| No executive buy-in | 9% |
| Compliance/Audit demands | 7% |
| Regular discomforts | 6% |

In addition to what is noted above, barriers between organizations and external barriers related to cultural differences, collaboration, ethics, competitiveness were raised in [14].

Despite this craze, it is noted that the profitability of blockchain so far requires substantial work. The number of transactions and the large amounts of data that define the supply chain force in the current context to think about the effective exploitation of blockchain (if used in this sector) to reveal the challenges in this area. This paper is proposed in this context to contribute with:

- The proposal of decision making at different levels.
- The proposal of performance indicators.
- The proposal of risk reduction.

## 3. CONTRIBUTION

### 3.1. GRAI Grid for BC control

The "GRAI Grid" aims to represent a mapping presenting the distribution of decisions:

- Strategic: the decisions at this level aim to impact the long-term objectives. The dashboards of this level offer a strategic vision of the company and allow the actors to pilot properly. In general, the indicators of these dashboards focus on internal processes, financial results and customer satisfaction.
- Tactical: the decisions at this level aim to define and implement at medium term the means to reach the strategy. This dashboard offers the possibility to locate the possible problems of these gaps and to bring solutions. Depending on the company, this type of dashboard is established by term or by month.
- Operational: This part represents a short-term steering tool and allows to measure the evolution of the detailed performance. In other words, it is the actions taken using the means defined in the tactical part. The operational level is synonymous with rapid decision making.

In table 2, are represented these different control levels. This repartition refers to the ability to conduct well the phases of a blockchain project and provides precise answers for the decision needs.

### 3.2. Costs and delay indicators

1. Choice of indicators

The use of performance indicators remains an efficient way to evaluate the relevance of decisions taken during the management of a project. In addition to this, these indicators offer a precise and synthetic vision that would allow decision-makers to have a clear indication of either success or failure. After the decisions taken in the previous GRAI grid, the objective of this section is to propose a list of performance indicators for each phase of the proposed methodology (from initialization to exploitation) to allow the relevance of the decisions taken to be assessed. With the evolution of the market and the multiple risks linked to competition and customer requirements, performance is no longer based solely on the financial aspect. More and more there are models of performance measurement that consider other internal and external non-financial aspects as described in [15] where the actors are based on the linkage of the objectives and strategies of the company to calculate the performance indicators. In this paper, the notions of costs and delay have been put forward to propose a series of performance indicators that would allow the project decisions to be properly measured (refer to table 3). The control of cost and time is a sine qua non condition for the success of a blockchain project because it has been revealed in several surveys that the latter is a real bottleneck [16].

2. ABCD method

This part explores the possibilities of reducing the risks associated with the costs and delays of the method. Based on the ABC method, which allows the analysis of costs by activity, our contribution consists in adding the notion of delays, hence the ABCD method. For each phase, the risk drivers are reported (costs and delays) and their management plans are proposed. As a reminder, the costs and delays associated with blockchain projects were a real bottleneck. These problems are caused by, among other things, a lack of control, a poor management method, an unmanaged budget, unclear use cases, etc. The ABCD method focuses on these potential risks at each phase of the method and the opportunities to reduce them, which allows to anticipate these problems and manage the associated costs and delays (refer to table 4). In sum, to evaluate the effectiveness of the GRAI chart, it is essential to have the measurement indicators. These indicators are a sufficient starting point for measuring performance and proposing areas for improvement, because these indicators basically play a verification role, this verification being only an entry point for steering.

## 4. DISCUSSIONS

This paper aims to show the need to adopt a control method to exploit blockchain technology. Several efforts are noted in the application of this technology in the supply chain. After these valuable contributions noted it was decided to propose a way of management using the GRAI method to define different levels of decision. Cost and time indicators were selected to test the effectiveness of these decisions. Finally, was selected a set of cost and time risk inductors and methods to reduce theme which, for the most part, represent bottlenecks.

## 5. CONCLUSIONS

As since its emergence the technology blockchain has conquered many sectors by its ability to meet many challenges. Alongside this enthusiasm, reality has shown that there is still a long way to go to make the most of the potential of this technology. However, although he has successful projects with great satisfaction, many other projects fall through as mentioned in [12,13, …] by being optimistic and based on successful projects, we can defend the idea that this technology could, like any new technology, contribute to the current challenges with the improvement of its maturity. Our future perspective will be to propose implementation of some GRAI grid items to help better make decisions.

**Table 2: GRAI grid**

| Functions / Decisions | External information | To Manage Initialization & Feasibility | To Manage Strategic Definition | To Manage Design | To Manage Development | To Manage Evaluation & Exploitation | Internal information |
|---|---|---|---|---|---|---|---|
| **Strategic**<br>**H=5 years**<br>**P=6 months** | • Competition<br>• Ecological challenges | • Decide on GO / NOGO<br>• Define the macro planning<br>• Define the type of application(public/private)<br>• Identify the most interesting partners<br>• Define first partner list<br>• Establish a sourcing plan (list of criteria) for BC professionals<br>• Anticipate the behavior of future users (Combalberd 2018)<br>• Define a crisis prevention plan (CCIM 2020)<br>• Define the economic risk | • Decide on GO / NOGO<br>• Define the rules<br>• Choose the BC professional who gives the best guarantees in relation to the needs<br>• Identify investments (ASLOG.Ch 1.10)<br>• Define contract with partners<br>• Integrate technical and human constraints | • Define the requirements<br>• Establish a test plan<br>• Define the development strategy<br>• Define a quality plan for deliverables<br>• Break down the project (deliverables)<br>• Prioritize the processes | • Invest in material and human resources<br>• Create internal skills for future developments<br>• Manage the response time<br>• Define an alternative solution in case of failure(store transactions somewhere if BC down) | • Define a plan for collecting feedback from future users<br>• Define measurement indicators<br>• Define Operations Strategy<br>• Define Evaluation Strategy | • Build customer loyalty<br>• Traditional tool: evolution problem/need for innovation<br>• Migration to NTIC<br>• Need for process optimization<br>• Need to ensure interoperability with the exterior<br>• Anticipation<br>• Quality approaches |
| **Tactic**<br>**H=1 year**<br>**P=3 months** | • Customer requirements<br>• Market evolution<br>• Technological evolutions | • Define/ analyze the nature and sources of crises<br>• Select close or distant partners<br>• Establish a crisis management plan<br>• Planning of outsourced activities<br>• Balance resources to be provided with customer/market requirements<br>• Define a project plan (provisional)<br>• Choose the BC professional giving the best guarantees<br>• Clearly define your needs | • Manage data sources<br>• Adopt team management practices (ASLOG.Ch.1.4.9)<br>• Set up a crisis cell (VAN2015/Hafyane2012)<br>• Define a strategic change plan<br>• Share the project needs with the different parties | • Define the project life cycle<br>• Break down the project<br>• Define a Functional Change Plan<br>• Adopt a development method<br>• Choose the tools to use<br>• Identify priorities | • Establish technical training<br>• Define a project development framework (a room, computers, servers, etc.)<br>• Define a secondary storage plan for transactions in case of unavailability of the CB<br>• Establish a transaction plan for the same user<br>• Define a technical change plan | • Define a training plan for users<br>• Run simulations<br>• Manage user feedback (opinions, suggestions)<br>• Define a plan for the evolution of the technology | • Customer feedback/suggestions |
| **Operational**<br>**H=2 weeks**<br>**P= 1 day** | | • Organize workshops<br>• Define POC<br>• Study the economic relevance | • Establishing an action plan<br>• Managing reluctance<br>• Convincing through practice (simulation, etc.) | • To make the documentation<br>• Establish the balance of the constraints | • QRQC<br>• Documentation | • Controls (ISO 9001)<br>• Non-conformity management (ISO9001.10.2)<br>• User training | |

| | | | | | | | |
|---|---|---|---|---|---|---|---|
| | | | | • Make the tests reliable | | • Quality audit (ISO9001.9.2) | |

**Table 3: Cost and delay indicators**

| Function | Performance indicators | |
|---|---|---|
| | Cost | Delay |
| **Initialization & Feasibility** | • Environmental cost<br>• Energy cost<br>• Crisis prevention budget<br>• Budget invested in R&D | • Negotiation time<br>• Average response time/solicited partner<br>• Time to manage a crisis |
| **Strategic Definition** | • Strategic communication costs<br>• Recovery budget in case of failure<br>• Delivery cost | • Estimated project time |
| **Design** | • Prototyping cost<br>• HR cost<br>• Material cost<br>• Subcontracting cost | • Time to process a request<br>• Average response time/query |
| **Development** | • Material purchase cost<br>• Technical training cost | • Sprint delivery time<br>• Number of technical training hours |
| **Evaluation & exploitation** | • Training cost<br>• Cost of use<br>• Rate of return on investment<br>• Maintenance cost | • Evaluation time<br>• Feedback processing time (opinions, suggestions, etc.)<br>• Training time (getting started)<br>• Operating time<br>• Maintainability time<br>• Daily use time |

**Table 4: ABCD Method**

| Function | Risk's inductors | | Opportunities to reduce risks | |
|---|---|---|---|---|
| | Costs | Delay | Costs | Delay |
| **Initialization & Feasibility** | • Provider Cost<br>• Partner Cost<br>• Unrequested Services Cost | • Total delivery time | • Provider competition<br>• Legal contract definition<br>• Only consider the necessary needs | • Choose your service provider well<br>• Propose to manage the control points |
| **Strategic Definition** | • Overall project cost<br>• Uncertainty Cost | • Overall project duration<br>• Overtime<br>• Lead time between design and development | • Define a detailed budget<br>• Monitor additional costs closely<br>• Provide a management plan if the budget is exceeded<br>• Minimize overload | • Define a master project plan<br>• Identify potential risks<br>• Define a risk management plan<br>• Refer to existing solutions<br>• Regularly measure progress rate |
| **Design** | • Design Cost | • Design time | • Refer to specifications<br>• Perform accurate modeling | • Require clear and precise specifications<br>• Report regularly<br>• Focus on agility |
| **Development** | • Development Cost<br>• Other Software Cost | • Technical training time<br>• Development time<br>• Uncontrolled Lost Time | • Negotiate technology transfer<br>• Assess training needs<br>• Internally manage the project's-controlled parts | • Select dates by deliverables<br>• Regularly monitor progress of sprints (minutes, meetings, etc.)<br>• Provide value for service providers<br>• Measure skills required in each phase |
| **Evaluation & exploitation** | • Profitability Cost<br>• Maintenance cost | • master's time | • Own and manage the control points internally | • Offer training<br>• Allow time for adaptation |

## REFERENCES


[1] V. Vijayakumar, V. Neelanarayanan, P. Rao, et J. Light, Éd., *Proceedings of 6th International Conference on Big Data and Cloud Computing Challenges: ICBCC 2019, UMKC, Kansas City, USA*, vol. 164. Singapore: Springer Singapore, 2020. doi: 10.1007/978-981-32-9889-7.

[2] D. Jonama, « Trains energy meter system using Blockchain », p. 78.

[3] PricewaterhouseCoopers, « Blockchain: A new tool to cut costs », *PwC*. https://www.pwc.com/m1/en/media-centre/articles/blockchain-new-tool-to-cut-costs.html (consulté le 2 septembre 2022).

[4] « The 70% value of Blockchain lies in the reduction of costs », *Softtek*, 10 juillet 2018. https://www.softtek.eu/en/tech-magazine-en/cybersecurity-en/70-of-the-value-of-the-blockchain-lies-in-the-reduction-of-costs/ (consulté le 2 septembre 2022).

[5] PricewaterhouseCoopers, « Time For Trust: How blockchain will transform business and the economy », *PwC*. https://www.pwc.com/gx/en/industries/technology/publications/blockchain-report-transform-business-economy.html (consulté le 2 septembre 2022).

[6] B. Kfoury, « The Role of Blockchain in Reducing the Cost of Financial Transactions in the Retail Industry », p. 13.

[7] S. Valeria, D. Vitaliia, T. Kateryna, H. Rostyslav, et Y. Oleg, « The Impact of Blockchain Technology on International Trade and Financial Business », *Universal Journal of Accounting and Finance*, vol. 10, n° 1, p. 102-112, janv. 2022, doi: 10.13189/ujaf.2022.100111.

[8] R. S. Kaplan et D. P. Norton, « Transforming the Balanced Scorecard from Performance Measurement to Strategic Management: Part I », *Accounting Horizons*, vol. 15, n° 1, p. 87-104, mars 2001, doi: 10.2308/acch.2001.15.1.87.

[9] A. I. Sanka, M. Irfan, I. Huang, et R. C. C. Cheung, « A survey of breakthrough in blockchain technology: Adoptions, applications, challenges and future research », *Computer Communications*, vol. 169, p. 179-201, mars 2021, doi: 10.1016/j.comcom.2020.12.028.

[10] J. Golosova et A. Romanovs, « The Advantages and Disadvantages of the Blockchain Technology », in *2018 IEEE 6th Workshop on Advances in Information, Electronic and Electrical Engineering (AIEEE)*, Vilnius, nov. 2018, p. 1-6. doi: 10.1109/AIEEE.2018.8592253.

[11] L. Koh, A. Dolgui, et J. Sarkis, « Blockchain in transport and logistics – paradigms and transitions », *International Journal of Production Research*, vol. 58, n° 7, p. 2054-2062, avr. 2020, doi: 10.1080/00207543.2020.1736428.

[12] M. Pournader, Y. Shi, S. Seuring, et S. C. L. Koh, « Blockchain applications in supply chains, transport and logistics: a systematic review of the literature », *International Journal of Production Research*, vol. 58, n° 7, p. 2063-2081, avr. 2020, doi: 10.1080/00207543.2019.1650976.

[13] A. I. Sanka, M. Irfan, I. Huang, et R. C. C. Cheung, « A survey of breakthrough in blockchain technology: Adoptions, applications, challenges and future research », *Computer Communications*, vol. 169, p. 179-201, mars 2021, doi: 10.1016/j.comcom.2020.12.028.

[14] S. Saberi, M. Kouhizadeh, J. Sarkis, et L. Shen, « Blockchain technology and its relationships to sustainable supply chain management », *International Journal of Production Research*, vol. 57, n° 7, p. 2117-2135, avr. 2019, doi: 10.1080/00207543.2018.1533261.

[15] S.Dalmas,P.Duvaut,G.Gonthier,et G.Jacovetti, « Les verrous technologiques des blockchain», *Massive Online Open Course*, avr.2021, ISBN : 978-2-11-162212-8.

[16] Raritan Inc,«Comment concevoir une infrastructure blockchain performante», *2019.*

# Reliability test monitoring: detection of time-to-failure with specific instrumentation

Arnaud Maire[1], Marco Bonato[2]

[1] *Valeo Thermal Systems France, 8 rue Louis Lormand, La Verrière; 78322 Le Mesnil Saint-Denis, France. arnaud.maire@valeo.com*

[2] *Valeo Thermal Systems France, 8 rue Louis Lormand, La Verrière; 78322 Le Mesnil Saint-Denis, France. marco.bonato@valeo.com*

**ABSTRACT**: The final design validation of automotive components is carried out on benches that verify the mechanical resistance under various types of environmental and in-service stress loads. The components must endure for a period of time specified by customers, expressed in hours or number of cycles, and which represents an equivalent lifetime of the vehicle. If the product shows a functional failure before the end of the test, its design needs modification. It is therefore essential to identify the failure zone and to provide an accurate estimation of the time-to-failure. Some of these tests can be long, and potential failures might occur at night or weekends, i.e. during a period of time when no lab technician is present to detect the failure. Therefore, in these cases, the exact time of the failure is not known with precision. Moreover, when several failures are observed afterwards, it is difficult to conclude which failure occurred first.

This paper will provide some practical examples of instrumentation that has been applied to the validation of Valeo products (mainly heat exchangers) during accelerated validation tests, with the goal of measuring with accuracy the time of the first failure.

**Keywords**: Failure detection, automotive, Heat Exchangers, Reliability, Physical Measurements.

**Received** January 1, 2023; **In final form** March 31, 2023; **Published** June 2023



**Corresponding author:** marco.bonato@valeo.com

## 1. INTRODUCTION

Modern automotive industry is experiencing a fast pace revolution. This concerns not only the mobility (electrified, autonomous and connected vehicles) but also the way both suppliers and carmakers deal with the reliability of the components and systems. Indeed, modern reliability engineering has to take into account the on-going numerical transformation that is shaping the mobility industry[1].

Road load data collections from the final users, on a dedicated fleet of cars, and during vehicle measurements, (the so-called "big road load data" [2]), allows to collect and post-treat an ever-increasing amount of measurements. The definition of usage mission profiling nowadays rely on big data analytics, and deep learning and data visualisation tools are useful tools to better exploit the results of all possible data recorded during product validation tests [3].

Nevertheless, there is still a small niche of expertise that requires a fundamental background of engineering judgement, knowledge of physical phenomena, and the ability to perform measurements that allows to determine the exact time to failure during accelerated bench tests (design validation durability tests) [4],[5].

This paper illustrates practical case studies where expertise of sensor mounting and measurement is applied to the monitoring of design validation tests on both mechanical and electric parts. The objective is to be able to determine the time to failure with a high level of accuracy and be able to stop the test at the appearance of the first failure. We will highlight the consequence of such an approach on the prediction of the reliability of the component under validation, and the implication on the overall goal of ameliorating the design and the performance of thermal system components.

## 2. METHODS

This paper presents several case studies of reliability test monitoring techniques applied to the recording of the exact time of the first failure during the design validation phase of automotive components. Each case study starts with a short introduction of the product and the importance of recording the time of the first failure, during the accelerated bench test. The second session describes in detail the test set-set up and the measurement methodology. The third session illustrates how the accelerated reliability test is carried out and the results of the measurements.

The final session resumes the conclusions and the implication of the methodology for improving the reliability of the components under investigation.

## 3. WCAC BRACKETS

The design of the water cooled intercooler (WCAC) has to take into account the high level of vibration stress that the part will undergo. The product is mounted on the cylinder head of the car combustion engine, where the stress loads are intense from both a mechanical and thermal point of view. To validate the design, the WCAC is tested on the shaker via an accelerated vibration signal.

In the example here considered, the component is compliant with the validation specification proposed by the carmaker, i.e. no leakage, deformation or cracks appears at the end of the vibration tests. The test is performed on the product rigidly mounted on its fixture (stand alone) (Figure 1). The brackets, designed by the carmaker, were not available at the time of the design validation. Only during the final customer's validation test on the engine block (the so-called "dyno test"), the steel brackets holding the WCAC to the cylinder head are integrated and the accelerated vibration test performed.

Several failures were registered at the end of this dyno-test test.

The system, composed by the WCAC with the steel brackets, was analysed in depth. The failure was detected by the appearance of cracks and the breakage on both the WCAC and the brackets. The carmaker claimed that the first failure was to be ascribed to the failure of the WCAC and the consequence "loose" movement would provoke the failure on the bracket. On the other hand, it could be that the initial failure of one brackets was behind the further failure of the WCAC.

### 3.1. Measurements Set up

A new technique to control the test in a more precise manner (in particular, the behaviours of WCAC) was needed during the vibration test. This was achieved by sticking several accelerometers on the product and near the brackets. The real time frequency response of each sensor would be measured, and time series data recorded. The reasoning was that any failure would modify the dynamic response of the system resulting in a shift of the first mode.

### 3.2. Endurance Vibration Tests

The vibration tests were then relaunched, and stopped when the drift of the modes to lower frequency of the WCAC were detected. This set up proved that the first failure of the system was ascribed to the steel brackets and not to the WCAC. Therefore the part that needed a design change to endure the vibration test was one of the OEM brackets.

### 3.3. Conclusions

This project was very useful to point out:

1) The importance of testing the part in its real environment at design validation phase
2) The importance of measuring the dynamic response of the component under investigation

Figure 1. Water cooled intercooled rigidly fixed (without brackets) on vibration shaker.

The same method found a useful usage during a research project dealing with fatigue of short fiber polymer specimens [5]. The time to failure were recorded thanks to real time measurements, moreover the shift in the 1$^{st}$ natural frequency could be used as an indicator of the incoming failure (crack propagation until rupture of the specimen) together with an increase of the damping ratio (decrease of the stiffness) and used to predict the time to failure for specimens with different fibers orientations.

## 4. STRAIN MEASUREMENTS ON A ROTATING MACHINE.

On combustion engine cars, a system of heat exchangers are placed on the front of the car, so that the air coming in through the apertures contributes as much as possible to the cooling of the elements (the engine cooling radiator, the condenser, the intercoolers etc.). In case of additional cooling need, a fan system provides a complementary air flow. The ensemble of heat exchangers and the fan system is known as the engine –cooling module.

A new engine-cooling module is to be mounted on a new platform of combustion engine cars, with a particular structure of the front air intake. In order to guarantee better aerodynamic performances, the front end module (FEM) of the car has an asymmetric air intake geometry, with higher air mass on the bottom than the top. This configuration rises some questions about the effect of such asymmetric airflow on the fan system. It is believed that the asymmetric air intake flow could generate a wind milling effect on the helix, provoke additional stress on the bearing of the electric motor holding the rotating shaft which is carrying the fan helix. The asymmetrical air flow through the front air grill could induce perpendicular moment and effort on the ball bearing, resulting in a premature failure. This would be detrimental for the durability of the fan system (both in terms of thermal and acoustic performance).

To confirm the hypothesis, a specific test was set up to measure the moment and effort on the plastic fan. Then, a tailored endurance test was carried out to reproduce the failure due to the over-sized stress load.

A slip ring assembly is screwed on the shaft (Figure 2). This assembly is connected with one static strain gages is glued on the center of the helix, near its mounting point with the electric motor (intersection with the shaft). The strain gages were from Kyowa (KFGS-1N-120-C1-23, K = 2.1 with thermal compensation factor alpha = 23 µm/m/K for aluminum).

Note that thermal compensation factor for aluminum used for the plastic fan is expected to introduce an offset deviation of signal with temperature (plastic thermal coefficient is between 30 to 65 µm/m/K). Nevertheless, in our case the temperature variations were limited during the measurement, (few °C), and the thermal compensation would affect mainly on the offset, not on the strain difference induced by the air flow or the rotating fan.

Figure 2. The fan electric motor is equipped with the slip ring assembly.

The calibration of the stress value is obtained by recording the force induced to the bottom of the helix that provokes a given measure strain deformation. This is not an absolute Force value, it is therefore called "Newton equivalent" (Neq). A mechanical force of 10N is applied at the bottom of the helix. The corresponding strain is measured on the fan at the shaft mounting point. From this calibration value, the strain obtained during measurements at various air flow configurations was converted to the corresponding Neq.

### 4.1. Testing Methodology

Since previous aeraulic tests had confirmed the hypothesis that an asymmetrical airflow induced high stress on fan, the goal of the testing procedure was to reproduce the stress by mechanical force on fan external ring which corresponded to various configuration of coverage of the air shield top model, then measure the stress as Neq at various fan speed.

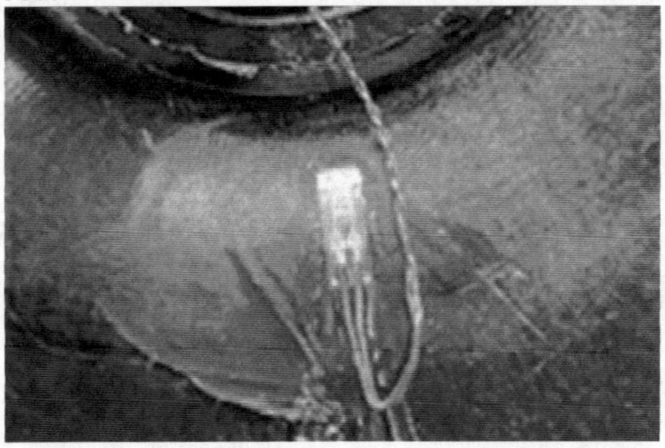

Figure 3. Strain gages on the front of the fan helix, near the shaft of the motor

During dedicated tests, the complete cooling module was placed in the aeraulic chamber, and exposed to critical conditions of in-service air flow (representing the possible range of vehicle speeds). Various configurations of the airflow were tested: by considering a symmetric air flow, and with increasing degrees of surface air shield on the top of the module (25% to 50% of coverage) and for different speeds fan rotation. For each configuration, the maximum strain amplitude associated, was extrapolated from the strain measurement, and the strain value converted to the stress exerted on the shaft bearing. The conversion from strain to Neq is possible thanks to the previously explained calibration. The critical combination of the testing parameters would give an equivalent stress of 18.3 Neaq

### 4.2. Endurance testing

Once the strain measurements have permitted to associate a Neq to the most critical air intake configuration, a new test set up was built to perform durability endurance test on the fan system under the external asymmetrical force.

A special ball bearing rolling pulled over the fan ring with adjustable force, so that the stress on the fan shaft would reach 21,6 Neq (in this case more than the maximum Neq recorded during the areolic tests) and the fan put under rotation until failure.

The duration of this accelerated stress test was correlated to the fan system field usage.

No failure of the bearing was detected after hundred hours of testing.

### 4.3. Conclusions

No failure occurred during the mechanical endurance Test. The duration of this accelerated test exceeded the expected hours of fan usage profile in the vehicle (representing 15 years and 300 000 km).

The conclusion is that the asymmetrical stress of wind milling on the vehicle will not induce fan failure, therefore there is no need to robustify the original design of the product.

## 5. BALL BEARING STRESS ON E-MOTORS.

During the development of a brushless electric motor, several endurance tests are run to validate its design. These accelerated life tests validate endurance of the product facing environmental stress.

The HVAC blower controls the airflow for both cabin heating and cooling. The rotation power is delivered to the fan by the magnetic attraction between the rotor and the stator that induces the rotation of the shaft. As for the engine-cooling fan system, the shaft is sitting and surrounded by ball bearings, they have the role of both supporting and facilitating the rotation of the shaft. To avid fast degradation between contacts of the metal, the capsule containing the bearing is lubricated by mineral oil. One specific endurance test (high temperature test) verifies that there is no oil degradation that would result in loss of lubricant function and early wear out of the bearings.

One of the key aspects of bearing assembly is the ability of leaving enough clearance to allow a smooth rotation, without forcing too much the capsule heatsink and leaving an excess of residual stress. During the rotation, stress is induced in the vertical (Z) and transversal axes (Y). At the manufacturing phase, during motor assembly, misalignment of ball bearing or tightening of rear ball bearing introduces extra axial force (X axis) inside the motor.

In order to define the tolerance limit for a specific electric motor design, a tailored test set up was defined with the goal of induced a controlled stress in X direction, and measure the endurance of the part before early bearing degradation.

### 5.1. Measurements and Test Setup

The goal of the test was to verify the motor endurance while applying an axial force that corresponds to the maximum force predicted during the assembly process. This stress load had to be directly applied on the rear side of the shaft. To monitor the response of the electric motor, three physical parameters were constantly measured: the input voltage, the temperature of the shaft near the bearing mounting points, and the voltage of the safety fuse.

### 5.2. Endurance testing

To perform the endurance test, the rear cover was removed to access the shaft. The motor was put under pressure via a pressure tool that pressed the shaft in the X direction, on its rear side. The electrical motor was supplied with 11V to activate the rotation of the helix. The results showed that the induced axial force on the rear side of the shaft increased the motor current consumption by

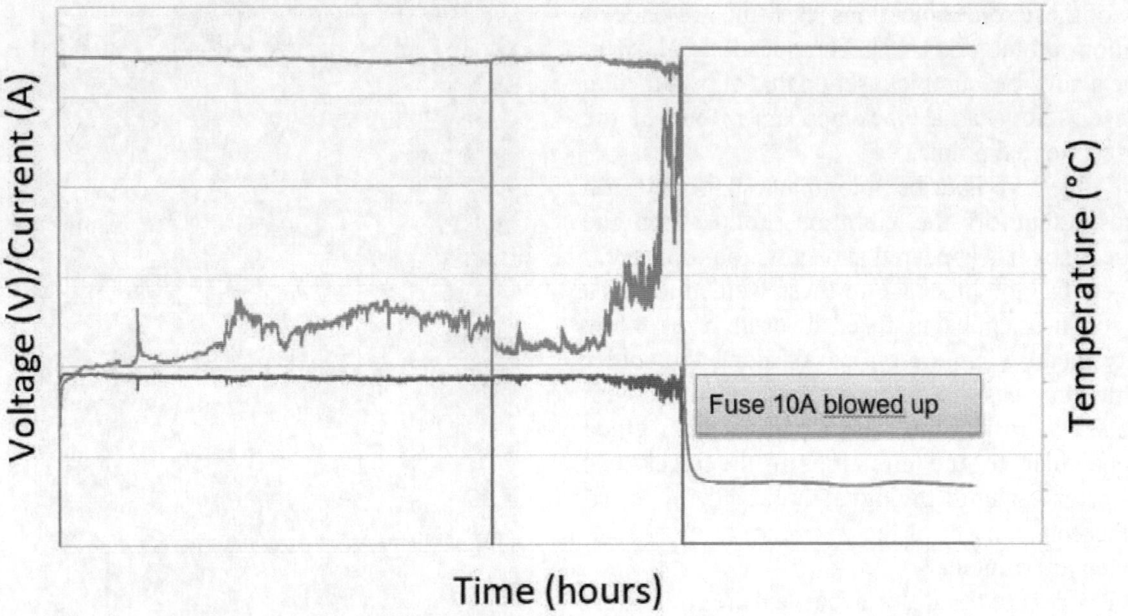


Figure 4. Bearing endurance test monitoring until failure. Orange line: motor voltage; light blue: shaft temperature; dark blue: current intensity.

increasing losses in ball bearing. The consequent ball bearings wear out would increase rotation torque, resulting in a rapid increase of the shat temperature until blowing of the fuse.

The failure was declared at the moment when the fuse blew, therefore the measure current intensity suddenly drop to zero (Figure 4). Thanks to the recording of the endurance test, the exact time to failure was known.

### 5.3. Conclusions

The accurate analysis of the front ball bearing is necessary to determine the failure to cause (bearing degradation by friction, or fatigue). In conclusion, this test set up and the measurements output allows to define the time to failure of the electric motor bearings for given assembly conditions, and to optimize the assembly process so that it is within the tolerance limit for the specified product durability.

## 6. BATTERY COOLER SOLDER JOINTS

Given the importance of the battery thermal management for increasing the battery life and the autonomy of the car, it comes as no surprise that an ever-increasing number of carmakers are demanding an extension of the warranty period of the battery thermal management module (BTM).

The core of BTM of the hybrid and electric vehicles is the battery cooler: a heat exchanger made of aluminium plates and connectors whose role is to keep the battery at the optimum working temperature (during driving, charging and pre-conditioning).

From a supplier perspective, the acceptance of extended warranty conditions (5 to 8 years) really depends on the knowledge of the product design margin.

This is very important in order to provide realistic reliability predictions, and also a robust starting point to derive design rules. It is therefore of fundamental importance to be able to measure where the location of the first failure, both in terms of location and time to failure.

In this example we investigate the durability of the BTM facing vibration fatigue loadings, by illustrating a methodology that allows it to stop the vibration test when the first failure is detected.

### 6.1. Measurements

During preliminary design validation obtained by finite element simulations, the battery cooler here investigated had shown several zones of vibration stress concentration, in particular located on welding joints. After the optimization of the design the initial prototype parts are undergoing vibration tests. For reliability predictions, the test needs to continue until failure, and be stopped when one of the failures is recorded by modification of the resonance of the part (see section 3.1). After an initial killer test, a close inspection reveals that many of these solder junctions show the presence of vibration fatigue cracks[7]. The question is how to define a new measurement set up that allows to stop the test as soon as a crack appears in one of the exposed welded points.

The objective is to be able to automatically stop the test (shut off the vibration table) when the fatigue crack has appeared and starts to propagate.

To control the breakage of these welded joints, a series of "mechanic wire fuse" are used. A set of low dustily metal wires are pulled all along the cooler and glued across the expected zone of failure with polyester insulation. The wires are glued perpendicular to the direction of the cracks. A multimeter transmits the signal through the wire, so that the connectivity of the wire circuit is verified, but once interrupted.

The wires are fixed along the weld area of critical joints, mounted in series, and connected to the test bench by a closed loop emergency stop device.

The principle being that the breakage of the stud, entails the cut-off of the power supply of the closed loop and the stop of the test.

In case of crack initiation, the force induced on the wire would provoke a brittle failure of the glued wire, and the opening of the circuit (Figure 5). The cut off would affect the loop of the circuit connected to the shaker table, the result is that the test is stopped and the exact time to failure known from the shaker control unit (the recorded logs).

### 6.2. Endurance testing

The vibration signal here used is a random power spectrum density from the ISO 12405-1 (2011) standard, with a frequency range of 5 to 200 Hz. The battery cooler shows no failure after the scheduled testing time (21 hours), and the test is continued until the first failure is detected.

Thanks to this optimized test setup, it has been possible to launch accelerated vibration test to failure, stop the test at the moment of the first failure and be able to record the time and the location of the failure (corresponding to the broken wire of the loop).

### 6.3. Conclusions

The recording of the exact time to failure and the location of the first failure has permitted us to clearly identify the design margin of the battery cooler. This information is fundamental to be able to perform reliability prediction in case of extension of the warranty period.

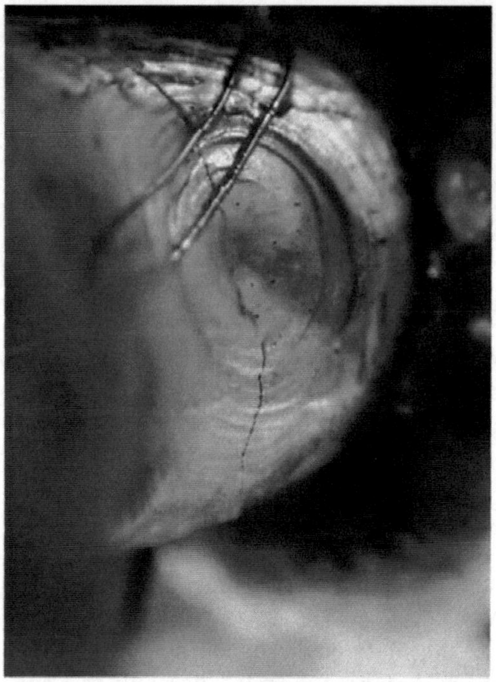

Figure 5. Close-up of the welding joint with wires after detection of the failure (crack).

## 7. CAPACITOR ROBUSTNESS DURING VIBRATION TESTS

The cooling capability of electric vehicles rely on a cooling loop which is alimented by an electrically driven compressor (eDC). The eDC offers numerous advantages compared to the mechanical compressor: higher energy efficiency for the vehicle thermal management (cabin and battery), lower power consumption, better acoustic performances and size reduction.

In contrast to the swash plate principle, which is primarily used in the belt driven compressor field, the high voltage compressors use the scroll principle to compress the refrigerant. The benefits are that the weight is reduced by approximately 20 and there is a reduction in the cylinder capacity of the same amount whilst the output remains identical

In order to generate the right amount of torque for the drive of the electric compressor, a DC voltage of over 200 Volt is used.

The electric control unit of the eDC is the inverter driver PCB circuit control board. This assemblies several electronic subcomponents. The design of the inverter and the sizing of the components is optimized to endure the in-service stress loads, especially the vibration stress.

The initial design validation is generally carried over by FEA simulation, and the time to failure predicted. The sub-components that shows the major reliability risk is the capacitor (Figure 6). Its relatively heavy weight makes it more sensitive to vibration displacement and fatigue failure.

To correlate the preliminary FEA simulation showing the failure of the capacitor, a dedicated test set up a unit to record the failure of the capacitor wire running highly accelerated vibration tests on the whole component.

Figure 6. Example of electrolytic capacitors mounted on a PCB (source: Wikipedia).

### 7.1. Measurements and Testing

The vibration test was carried out by placing the eDC with the brackets on a fixture in the shaker test. A tri-axial power spectrum density signal (a vibration validation developed internally and taken as standard reference of design validations) was used. The capacitance of the compressor integrated inverter was continuously monitored by a sensor connected via an open-source electronics platform (Arduino). The acquisition system was connected to the vibration table control unit, so that when the value of the measured capacitance went below a threshold (considered as a limit to declare the failure of the capacitor), the vibration table would stop. This new methodology replaces previous less accurate test control methods and time to failure recordings, such as having the test stopped at regular intervals to control the capacitance, or setting the capacitance monitored but with the laboratory technicians manually monitoring every 15 minutes.

### 7.2. Conclusions

Facing the need to know the exact time of the first failure of the PBC of a newly designed electric compressor, we have developed a methodology that permits to stop the vibration test at the exact time of the failure.

The knowledge of the exact time of the first failure is important because it gives the elements to correlate the simulation results, to determine the design margin of the product, and if needed to further improve the design.

## 8. GENERAL CONCLUSIONS

The reliability predictions for both mechanical and electronic automotive components strongly rely on the accuracy of both the exact time of the first failure mode. Failing to determine whose component or zone failures first makes it difficult to improve the product design facing in-service and environmental stress loads. The inaccurate determination of the time to failure makes the reliability predictions unrealistic. It is therefore essential to have developed within the organization the know-how to be able to monitor the component under test and be able to stop the test at the appearance of the first failure. In this paper we have shown several applicative case studies, and emphasize the importance of the multi-discipline approach. Each test monitoring requires particular expertise on sensor mounting, measurements and data post processing. The difference in the failure modes detection should rely on a creative approach based on the knowledge of the physics of the failure under investigation.

## ACKNOWLEDGEMENT

The authors would like to acknowledge Ewelina Czerlunczakiewicz and Marco Bencivenga for the support of the vibration case studies (section 3 and section 7).

## REFERENCES

[1] https://www.valeo.com/fr/challenge-la-revolution-de-la-mobilite-numerique/

[2] Frédéric Kihm, Tudor Miu, Marco Bonato, Fatigue Damage estimation in vehicle from minimal instrumentation thanks to a mixed Engineering / Data Science approach, Procedia Structural Integrity, Volume 38, 2022, Pages 12-29

[3] Marco Bonato, Murali Krishnamoorthy and Philippe Goge, Data Mining and Machine Learning Methods for Robust Reliability Predictions on Automotive Components 2022 Annual Reliability and Maintainability

Symposium (RAMS) Year: 2022 | Conference Paper | Publisher: IEEE

[4] Bracke et al. Reliability engineering based on operating data and monitoring systems within technical products: *Challenges, requirements and approaches, Safety and Reliability – Safe Societies in a Changing World,* 1st Edition, 2018, CRC Press.

[5] L. Pierrat and M. Bonato, Outliers detection at the lower tail of a small statistical sample originated from test results of strength, Proceedings of the 31st European Safety and Reliability Conference ESREL2023, Anger, France.

[6] P. Hayes et al., Vibration Fatigue Analysis of Composite Materials, Proceedings of the 5th Symposium on Structural Durability in Darmstadt May 17-18, 2017.

[7] S.S. Manson and G.R. Halford, Fatigue and Durability of Structural Materials, ASM International, 2006.

# A Smart Solution to Plant Growth Monitoring and Control in Greenhouses: Methodology and Instrumentation

Radhwen Ben Kahla[1], Feiza Ghezail[2], Imen Harbaoui[3]

[1]*Université de Tunis El Manar, École Nationale d'Ingénieurs de Tunis, LR11ES20 Laboratoire Analyse, Conception et Commande des Systèmes, École supérieure privée d'ingénierie et de technologie, Tunis, Tunisie, radhwen.benkahla@esprit.tn*

[2]*Université de Carthage, Institut National des Sciences Appliquées et de Technologie, LR11ES26 Laboratoire d'Informatique pour les Systèmes Industriels, Tunis, Tunisia, feiza.ghezail@insat.ucar.tn*

[3]*Université de Tunis El Manar, École Nationale d'Ingénieurs de Tunis, LR11ES20 Laboratoire Analyse, Conception et Commande des Systèmes, Université de Carthage, Institut National des Sciences Appliquées et de Technologie, Tunis, Tunisie, imen.harbaoui@insat.ucar.tn*

**ABSTRACT**: The application of artificial intelligence in urban agriculture provides the farmer with the ability to predict soil properties, weather conditions, and crop production rates, as well as to manage irrigation, production, breeding and harvesting, thus producing higher quality crops at a lower cost. Among the techniques of industry 4.0 applied to agriculture, such as the Internet of Things, cloud computing, big data, and augmented reality, we will focus on artificial intelligence and more specifically on machine learning and computer vision to manage weather conditions of green houses. In this field, our project consists in building an autonomous system to control an intelligent greenhouse. This paper describes the infrastructure of the project, defines the set of sensors and actuators required for the application, and explains the methodology that will be applied in the next step of the project.

**Keywords**: Precision agriculture, agriculture 4.0, smart green houses, data mining, decision making, machine learning.

**Received** January 19, 2023; **In final form** March 31, 2023; **Published** June 2023



**Corresponding author:** Radhwen Ben Kahla, e-mail: radhwen.benkahla@esprit.tn

## 1. INTRODUCTION

The new technologies and innovations of industry 4.0 has impacted the agricultural industry by providing an automatic and connected aspect, which improves control and supervision of the different production phases, and optimizes the different actions that the farmer performs throughout the plant cycle. It thereby improves quality, increases production capacity and decreases production cost.

The deployment of connected sensors, control equipment and automated actuators managed by computerized systems, based on data analysis and statistics, will reduce errors in the decision-making process compared with the conventional method, in which the farmer is the sole decision-maker on the action to be taken [1].

In this context, several management and decision support systems have been developed and applied in urban agriculture, such as vertical farming, hydroponics, and aquaponics. These systems are used to predict greenhouse climatic conditions, reduce energy costs, detect diseases and weed growth, predict the required treatments to avoid weed growth, and predict production yields according to climatic parameters.

Yuwen Liu et al. [2] have developed a greenhouse climate prediction model, using a long short-term memory-based model to predict the climate and artificially control its evolution.

In turn, Pradyumna K. Tripathy et al. [3] have developed a decision support system that controls temperature and humidity, provides accurate monitoring of soil and its moisture, detects and prevents plant pathologies, periodically collects data, and provides an interface for communication and interaction with human actors.

Otherwise, a predictive controller has been applied by Gabriela Cáceres et al. [4] in a case study of a strawberry field to predict and control where and how much to irrigate, in order to minimise the amount of water and energy consumption, without compromising crop yield.

To build such efficient systems, several artificial intelligence techniques have been used, such as machine learning, deep learning, fuzzy logic, swarm intelligence and computer vision.

For instance, to boost agricultural production with less energy consumption, Faisal Jamil et al. [5] applied an optimal smart contract integrated with the prediction, optimisation, and control of the autonomous greenhouse environment, and proposed a blockchain-based secured and reliable platform for the integrity of the autonomous greenhouse.

In addition, convolutional neural network "CNN" are widely used for phenotype detection of four grain crops. Different CNN models including VGG, YOLO, Fast R-CNN, and Mask R-CNN have been used for image classification, object detection, semantic and instance segmentation [6].

This work presents an experimental framework designed to monitor the growth of plants (lettuce) according to climatic and nutrient solution parameters, fully controlled by means of a set of sensors, actuators, and computer vision algorithms. In another way, the proposed approach allows updating the target variables by updating the control setpoints according to the variation of the growth rate of the plants to obtain the best growth result.

## 2. RELATED WORK

The method described in the current paper, which provides greenhouse management and regulation setpoints adjustment by controlling the plant growth rate, is one of many applications of artificial intelligence in agriculture. These applications enable controlling and managing many factors affecting plant growth, and contributing thereby to successful outcome of agriculture industry in urban environment.

Navarro-Hellin et al. [7] developed a decision support smart irrigation system based on climate and soil variables using PLSR and ANFIS technics of machine learning.

A non-linear control model has been designed by Jalal Javadi Moghaddam et al. [8] to be used in greenhouse climate control systems, based on the concepts of equilibrium points and zero dynamics of system theories. The model uses information provided by sensors installed inside and outside the greenhouse.

Usharani Bhimavarapu et al. [9], proposed an improved optimizer function (IOF) to generate accurate prediction, then implemented the proposed IOF with the long short-term memory (LSTM) model, the function was applied on paddy, red gram, sugarcane, cereals, pulses, groundnut, and chilli.

An SVM with radial basis function was applied by Rumpf et al. [10] as a kernel-based model to early detect and identify sugar beet disease. In turn, Sethy et al. [11] used deep features ResNet50 besides SVM model with a dataset of 5932 diseased rice leaf images to identify rice leaf disease.

Kamir et al. [12] proposed a fuzzy hybrid ensemble classification and estimation method using remote sensory data to assess yield for wheat crop.

An MPC method, proposed by Chiara Bersani et al. [13], was applied in a smart innovative greenhouse located in Italy. This method showed that the greenhouse saved about 30% of electric power compared with a relay control method guaranteeing a consistent and reliable indoor temperature profile.

According to Manas Wakchaure et al. [14] who have reviewed the potential impact of the various artificial intelligence techniques, including fuzzy logic (FL), artificial neural network (ANN), genetic algorithm (GA), particle swarm optimization (PSO), artificial potential field (APF), simulated annealing (SA), ant colony optimization (ACO), artificial bee colony algorithm (ABC), harmony search algorithm (HS), bat algorithm (BA), cell decomposition (CD) and firefly algorithm (FA), etc., in the field of agriculture. The authors analysed 155 paper and interpreted that AI is implemented in:

1) Cultivation phase: by planning crop to be planted, land preparation, water irrigation, and seed sowing.
2) Monitoring phase: by continues monitoring, data collection, disease identification, weed control, fertilization use, and pesticide spraying.
3) Harvesting phase: by segmentation, cutting, picking crop and fruit, storing, and selling.

Otherwise, Abia Katimbo et al. [15] have studied the potential of ten machine learning models (Artificial Neural Network (ANN), Long Short-Term Memory (LSTM) Support vector machine (SVM), K-Nearest neighbour (KNN), Categorical boosting (CatBoost), Multiple linear regression (MLR), Random Forest (RF), Stacked Regression (Stacked-Regr), Stacked Random Forest (Stacked-RF), and Weighted average Ensemble (Weighted-Ensemble)) in predicting crop evapotranspiration and crop water stress index for irrigation water management. They found that stacked regression performed best in estimating evapotranspiration and CatBoost was the best in predicting crop water stress index.

Divyanshu Varshney et al. [16] have investigated 4 kinds of machine learning classifiers for plant identifying diseases and found that more diseases are detected with high accuracy by the CNN classifier. They reported that, in the future, the Navie Bayes classification supervised approach should only be used to classify diseases in crops and to help people automatically diagnose all types of diseases in crops using machine learning approaches from other classifiers, such as the decision tree.

Along with Pallipati Vasavi et al [17], who reviewed crop leaf disease detection methods using machine learning and deep learning algorithms by visual symptoms, the system allowing to identify the crop leaf diseases can be developed in 5 steps: (i) image acquisition, (ii) image pre-processing, (iii) image segmentation, (iv) feature extraction, and (v) classification. The techniques used in classification and in other previous steps, such as Machine Learning, Deep Learning, Transfer Learning, Deep Siamese Neural Networks, LSTM, Optimized CNN, SqueezeNet, Ensemble Models and many other classification techniques, differ according to the image acquisition method. For instance, capturing the images from drones, smart mobile phones, digital cameras, and UAVs requires image processing by image augmentation. Then, image segmentation techniques are applied using K-means, Principal component analysis Clustering. Afterward, features are extracted based on texture, shape and colour, and finally, classification is performed using a machine learning algorithm.

Another method based on IoT has been used by Khaled Obaideen et al. [18]. The conducted study revealed the several benefits in irrigation system IoT offered, mainly a better crop management by monitoring product conditions in real time, a reduction in the overall water consumption, and a prevention of diseases. The used method also presents a number of limitations, including a high-power consumption of devices, a short battery life for equipment, weak communication signals, and unavailable internet connection in all locations.

## 3. CASE OF STUDY

The proposed method consists of adjusting climatic control setpoints, according to the growth rate of a greenhouse hydroponic culture. For this purpose, we have built a laboratory in the form of two greenhouses and a separate control room, in order to set-up a sensor management system and actuator management system that allows us to control and monitor the crops with a minimum of disturbance.

The greenhouse management system is comprised of three subsystems (detailed in figure 6): (i) a growth rate monitoring system to control and calculate the plant's growth rate variation, (ii) a nutrient solution management system to control the nutrient solution of the plants, (iii) and a climate management system to control the climate parameters. In the next sections, the hardware and software environment to be deployed in the future works will be described.

### 3.1. Buildings and infrastructure

The laboratory shown in figure 1 covers a total area of 90 m² and a minimum height of 2.3 m in the form of two separate and isolated greenhouses.

Figure 1. Greenhouses building

The roof is made of sandwich panels and the walls of glazed aluminium, 3 windows on the roof of each greenhouse and 3 fans on the walls are used for air evacuation.

An external control room is built to gather the necessary equipment for the supervision, control, and data processing of both greenhouses.

Figure 2. Photovoltaic array

A photovoltaic array of 9 kWp shown in figure 2 is available to supply equipment and ensure greenhouses autonomy. Moreover, a wind turbine and a solar concentrator will be installed to evaluate the different forms of renewable energy for the benefit of an intelligent and autonomous greenhouse.

### 3.2. Data acquisition system (DAS)

Meriem Soussi et al. [19], who reviewed climate control and cooling systems in greenhouses under hot and arid conditions, indicated that the main control parameters are temperature, humidity, Carbone dioxide concentration and solar radiation. And as reported by Abhinav Sharma et al. [20], the most used sensors in precision agriculture are the accelerometer (ADXL345), Air humidity (HTU21D), Air temperature (SHT11), Camera (PixyCam, Raspberry Pi), Capacitive Touch (MPR121), Depth (Microsoft Kinect 1 & 2), Force (Flexiforce A20-25), Indoor Localization (iBeacon), Light (GL5528), RGB Colour (TCS34725), Soil Moisture (SEN0114), Sound (SEN-12642), Distance (HC-SR04), Pulse Oximeter (SP02), Temperature (Max30205) and Piezoelectric (PZT).

In the current work, the data acquisition system (DAS) shown in figure 3 is comprised of the data acquisition card and all sensors used to measure ambient temperature, air humidity, $CO_2$ level, sunlight intensity, nutrient solution level, nutrient solution temperature, and nutrient concentration. Furthermore, cameras will also be installed to be used as visual sensors.

The sensors communicate with the data acquisition card via Wi-Fi and the collected data is processed by the climate monitoring system and the nutrient monitoring system. Simultaneously, data is saved in the data repository. Three visual sensors are installed on 3 sides of the plant and at a fixed distance to allow size plant recognition. On each side, the machine learning algorithm measures plant length and width, and records the values in the data repository. These values are used to calculate the variation of growth rates.

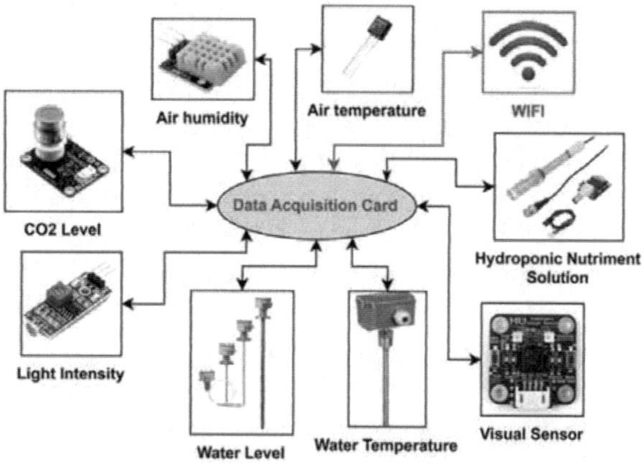


Figure 3. Data Acquisition System (DAS)

### 3.3. Actuator management system (AMS)

The actuator management system (AMS) shown in figure 4 is comprised of a control board that communicates instructions to the organs, allowing to adjust the plant growth variables, and the extractors and windows allow the evacuation of air, which can be used to regulate the temperature and the internal humidity. Moreover, a $CO_2$ dispenser and a fogger act on the $CO_2$ content and on the humidity levels, heaters and air coolers provide temperature adjustment, insecticides and pesticides spraying system prevent plant diseases, a pumping system allows the supply and circulation of the nutrient solution, fans installed inside the greenhouses homogenize the climate and provide more accurate data values. In addition, an artificial illumination system (LED) and automated curtains are used to vary the photoperiod of the culture.

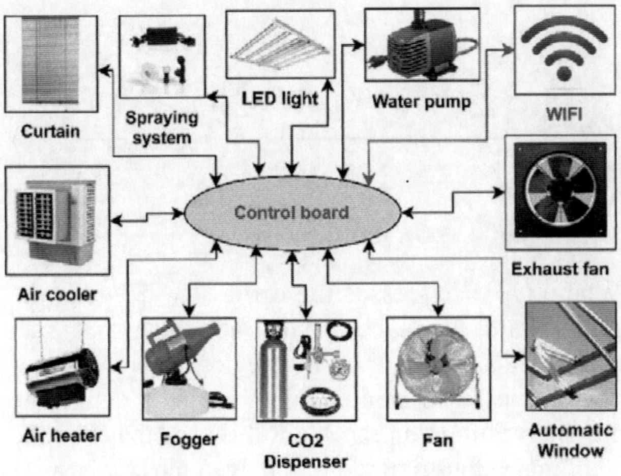


Figure 4. Actuators Management System (AMS)

## 4. PROPOSED APPROACH

The experimentation consists of developing a machine learning algorithm, allowing to recognize the length and width of 3 sides of the plant, the dimensions are saved in the data repository with all data collected from sensors. A dynamic database provides the regulation setpoints to the climate monitoring system, to the nutrient monitoring system, and to the growth monitoring system.

The climate monitoring system processes the data from the data acquisition system in real-time, controls the climate parameters according to the set points defined in the dynamic database, and acts on the actuators through the control board, while the nutrient monitoring system processes the nutrient solution parameters.

The growth monitoring system treats the images and recognizes the dimensions of each side of the plant, then calculates and saves the growth rates in the data repository, before comparing the calculated values to determine if growth rate is improving, remaining constant or decreasing. This allows to decide if the variation of the air temperature, the humidity and the $CO_2$ content are favourable or not. The changes in the growth rate can also be used to determine the harvesting time with high precision. In the dynamic database, the input set-point values are firstly adopted based on the ranges recommended in the literature.

According to measurements and statistics conducted by Kyungdeok Noh et al. [21] on a home cultivation system, the most influencing variables on lettuce germination are temperature and photoperiod. Indeed, the maximum germination rate was established at a day temperature of 25°C, a night temperature of 18°C and a photoperiod of 18 hours, so that the crop could be harvested on day 28. Alternatively, Danian Chen et al. [22] have evaluated the effect of $CO_2$ enrichment on lettuce for 30 days following transplanting and found that lettuce height, stem diameter, number of leaves, root length, leaf width, and maximum leaf area were all positively related to the $CO_2$ enrichment. They prove that under double and quadruple the ambient $CO_2$ content (about 400 µmol mol -1) has boosted lettuce morphogenesis, growth rate, has significantly increased biomass accumulation and improved light energy usage in lettuce.

According to André Carrier et al. [23], who have investigated the optimal conditions for lettuce growth in a greenhouse hydroponic system, the most suitable day temperature for growth is of 16°C and the most suitable night temperature is of 10°C, besides an increase in disease risk with the increase in temperature. They have also found that humidity should range between 40% and 85%, that transpiration and growth decrease in a highly humid weather, and that growth is proportional to the amount of light rather than that of heat.

Throughout our proposed approach, where the iterative process is described by the flow chart in Figure 6. lettuce is cultivated in a hydroponic system by first introducing, in the dynamic database, a 16°C of day temperature, 10°C of night temperature, 12 hours of photoperiod, 40% of humidity and 1600 $\mu mol.mol^{-1}$ of $CO_2$. One week after germination, the growth monitoring system (GMS) will increases the regulation setpoints and calculates the growth rate to identify the setpoints values corresponding to the maximum growth rate during a 30-day cycle. At first, the GMS increases the daytime temperature set point by 2°C and calculates the change in the plant growth. If the growth rate improves, the GMS will make a second increment of the daytime temperature and recalculate the growth rate, and if the growth rate decreases, the GMS will take back the previous set point value. However, if the growth rate remains constant the GMS will increase the night-time temperature set point by 2°C and will start again the calculation of the growth rate variation, if the growth rate increases the GMS makes a second increment of the night-time temperature in the dynamic database and repeats calculations, if the growth rate decreases the GMS takes back the previous setpoint value, otherwise the GMS increases the photoperiod by one hour and calculates the growth rate variation and so on until the different growth parameters are covered.

In the case of zero or insignificant growth rate, the GMS indicates a harvest time, but in case of a negative growth rate, an alarm is triggered to indicate an anomaly.

### 4.1. Growth rate calculation

Lingxian Zhang et al [24], have deployed a convolutional neural network (CNN) and used digital images to predict leaf fresh weight (LFW), leaf dry weight (LDW) and leaf area (LA) which are essential indicators to characterize lettuce growth. In the current experiment, we will deploy an algorithm using the opencv library to recognize the plant dimensions in real time, and we will use the values to calculate the growth rate on all 3 sides based on the expression of Eq. 1:

$$GR_{n+1} = \frac{S_{M,n+1} - S_{M,n}}{T_{n+1} - T_n} \tag{1}$$

Where $GR_{n+1}$ denotes the growth rate at the time $T_{n+1}$, witch represents the difference between the average surfaces of two snaps captured at $T_n$ and $T_{n+1}$ divided by time.

$$S_{M,n+1} = \frac{S_{1,n+1} + S_{2,n+1} + S_{3,n+1}}{3} = \frac{1}{3}\sum_{i=1}^{3} S_{i,n+1} \tag{2}$$

Where $S_{M,n+1}$ denotes the average surface of 3 sides of the plant snaped at time $T_{n+1}$.

$$S_{i,n+1} = L_{i,n+1} \times W_{i,n+1} \tag{3}$$

Hence, $S_{i,n+1}$ expresses the generalized expression of average surface, $L_{i,n+1}$ expresses length and $W_{i,n+1}$ expresses width of each side snaped at time $T_{n+1}$.

$$S_{M.n} = \frac{S_{1,n} + S_{2,n} + S_{3,n}}{3} = \frac{1}{3}\sum_{i=1}^{3} S_{i,n} \tag{4}$$

$$S_{i,n} = L_{i,n} \times W_{i,n} \tag{5}$$

Where $S_{M,n}$ denotes the average surface of 3 sides, $S_{i,n}$ the generalized expression of each side, $L_{i,n}$ side length, and $W_{i,n}$ side width snaped at time $T_n$.

Therefore, the generalized expression of growth rate can be defined by Eq. 6.

$$GR_{n+1} = \frac{\frac{1}{3}\sum_{i=1}^{3} S_{i,n+1} - \frac{1}{3}\sum_{i=1}^{3} S_{i,n}}{T_{n+1} - T_n} \tag{6}$$

Then,

$$GR_{n+1} = \frac{\frac{1}{3}\sum_{i=1}^{3}\left(L_{i,n+1} \times W_{i,n+1}\right) - \frac{1}{3}\sum_{i=1}^{3}\left(L_{i,n} \times W_{i,n}\right)}{T_{n+1} - T_n} \tag{7}$$

$$GRD = GR_{n+1} - GR_n \tag{8}$$

Where GRD expresses the difference between the growth rate calculated at Tn+1 and the growth rate calculated at the time of the previous snap.

GR is used to calculate GRD and to determine crop harvesting time, then GRD is used to act on the setpoints values defined in the dynamic database. An example of 3-side-shots of the lettuce snapped at different times during cultivation period is illustrated in figure 5.

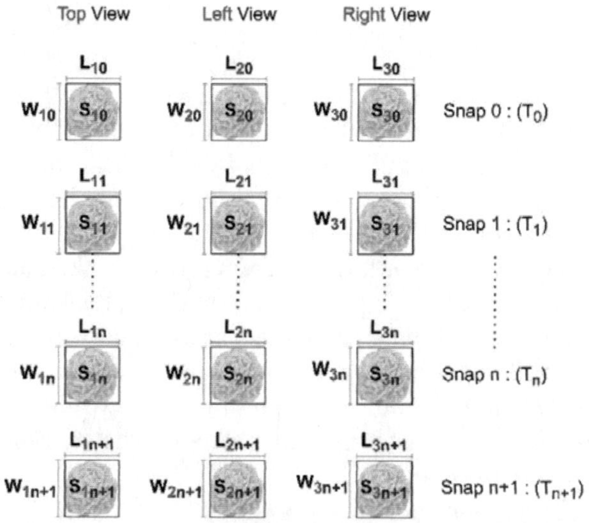


Figure 5. Growth rate mapping

At each time, 3 photos are taken by 3 cameras installed on the top side, on the right side and on the left side of the plant. The machine learning algorithm recognizes the size of each side, and the corresponding values are used to calculate GR and GRD.

### 4.2. Decision Support System

Decision support system shown in figure 6, governs major seven components of the greenhouse namely data acquisition system, data repository, dynamic database, climate monitoring system, nutrient solution monitoring system, growth rate monitoring system and supervisor. Climate monitoring system and nutrient monitoring system are based on a machine learning models able to adjust different actuator states, to provide climate and nutrient solution parameters according to setpoints configured on the dynamic database.

Climate monitoring system displays real time values of climate parameter and provides access to related statistics. It uses external climate parameters values to optimise energy consumption. For example, it can act on windows and exhaust fans to evacuate heat and reduce inner temperature at night-time by using external temperature downhill at sunset time. Nutrient monitoring system displays water temperature, water flow, pH level, nutrient concentration such as $Ca^{2+}$, $Cl^{-}$, $K^{+}$, $Na^{+}$, $NH_4^{+}$, $NO_3^{-}$, $Mg^{2+}$, and acts on water pump, water cooler, water heater, and fertilizer dosing devices. Water system is comprised of two circuits: (i) an external circuit made of a water tank to collect rain and store water reserve to top-up water level in the nutrient solution circuit; the external circuit is equipped with filters and water pump to feed water to the internal tank, in witch nutrient dosing unit add nutrients according to setpoints defined on the dynamic database, and (ii) an internal circuit equipped with water flow pump, water cooler, and water heater to regulate water temperature according to the plant type and germination phases.

An interrupted power supply is installed to provide and manage power generated by photovoltaic panels, wind turbine and solar concentrator. Solar concentrator is used to heat greenhouse climate and nutrient solution.

Growth rate monitoring system displays growth rate values and shows related statistics. It indicates crop time and triggers alarm in case of an abnormal situation.

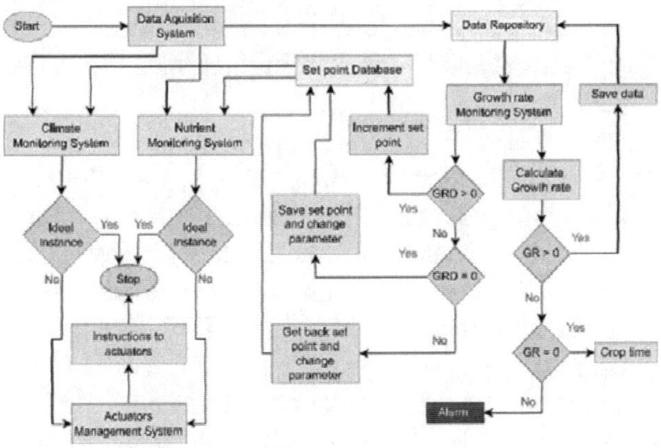


Figure 6. Decision support system workflow

The next phase of this project will be the collection of data from the data acquisition system to be used in the training of machine learning algorithms.

## 5. CONCLUSION AND FUTURE SCOPE

The infrastructure, the whole set of sensors and actuators described in this paper highlight the device layer of the project framework. In addition, we explained the workflow of the proposed decision support system consisting of climate monitoring system, nutrient monitoring system and growth rate monitoring system, which is responsible for automatically adjusting the control setpoints according to the plant growth rate. We also cited some recent related work to place the project in context.

We expect that the currently proposed method allows to determine the optimal values of climatic parameters that enhance the growth of lettuce cultivated in a hydroponic greenhouse. Thus, the data recorded throughout the experimental period can be used to train algorithms that allow to detect plant diseases and undesirable plant growth, as well as to predict thc harvest time according to climatic parameters and nutrient solution parameters, besides estimating energy expenditure and predict the production costs.

## ACKNOWLEDGEMENT

We acknowledge LACS laboratory in which this research is carried out.

We acknowledge ESPRIT school of engineering for financing the project which is built on the fourth floor of IJK building.

## REFERENCES

[1] Burak Ozdogan, Anıl Gacar, Huseyin Aktas, Digital agriculture practices in the context of agriculture 4.0, Pressacademia, 4, 184–191 (2017). doi: 10.17261/pressacademia.2017.448.

[2] Yuwen Liu, Dejuan Li, Shaohua Wan, Fan Wang, Wanchun Dou, Xiaolong Xu, Shancang Li, Rui Ma, Lianyong Qi, A long short-term memory-based model for greenhouse climate prediction, International Journal of Intelligent Systems, 37,135–151 (2022). doi: 10.1002/int.22620.

[3] Pradyumna K. Tripathy, Aditi Agarwal, Ajaya K. Tripathy, Saraju P. Mohanty, IEEE CONSUMER ELECTRONICS MAGAZINE 1 MyGreen: An IoT-Enabled Smart Greenhouse for Sustainable Agriculture, IEEE Consumer Electronics Magazine, 10, 57-62 (2021).

[4] Gabriela Cáceres, Pablo Millán, Mario Pereira, David Lozano, Smart Farm Irrigation: Model Predictive Control for EconomicOptimal Irrigation in Agriculture, Agronomy, 11 (2021). doi: 10.3390/agronomy11091810.

[5] Faisal Jamil, Muhammad Ibrahim, Israr Ullah, Suyeon Kim, Hyun Kook Kahng, Do-Hyeun Kim, Optimal smart contract for autonomous greenhouse environment based on IoT blockchain network in agriculture, Computers and Electronics in Agriculture, 192 (2022). doi: 10.1016/j.compag.2021.106573.

[6] Ya-Hong Wang, Wen-Hao Su, Convolutional Neural Networks in Computer Vision for GrainCrop Phenotyping, Agronomy, 12 (2022). doi: 10.3390/agronomy12112659.

[7] H. Navarro-Hellín, J. Martínez-del-Rincon, R. Domingo-Miguel, F. Soto-Valles, R. Torres-Sánchez, A decision support system for managing irrigation in agriculture, Computers and Electronics in Agriculture, 124, 121-131 (2016). doi: 10.1016/j.compag.2016.04.003.

[8] Jalal Javadi Moghaddam, Ghasem Zarei, Davood Momeni, Hamideh Faridi, Non-linear control model for use in greenhouse climate control systems, Research in Agricultural Engineering, 68, 9-17 (2022). doi: 10.17221/37/2021-RAE.

[9] Usharani Bhimavarapu1, Gopi Battineni, Nalini Chintalapudi, Improved Optimization Algorithm in LSTM to Predict Crop Yield, Computers, 12 (2023). doi: 10.3390/computers12010010.

[10] T. Rumpf, A.-K. Mahlein, U. Steiner, E.-C. Oerke, H.-W. Dehne, and L. Plümer, Early detection and classification of plant diseases with support vector machines based on hyperspectral reflectance, Computers and Electronics in Agriculture, 74, 91-99 (2010). doi: 10.1016/j.compag.2010.06.009.

[11] Prabira Kumar Sethy, Nalini Kanta Barpanda, Amiya Kumar Rath, Santi Kumari Behera, Deep feature-based rice leaf disease identification using support vector machine, Computers and Electronics in Agriculture, 175, (2020). doi: 10.1016/j.compag.2020.105527.

[12] Elisa Kamir, François Waldner, Zvi Hochman, Estimating wheat yields in Australia using climate records, satellite image time series and machine learning methods, ISPRS Journal of Photogrammetry and Remote Sensing, 160, 124-135 (2020). doi: 10.1016/j.isprsjprs.2019.11.008.

[13] Chiara Bersani, Carmelina Ruggiero, Roberto Sacile, Abdellatif Soussi, Enrico Zero, Internet of Things Approaches for Monitoring and Control of Smart Greenhouses in Industry 4.0, Energies, 15, (2022). doi: 10.3390/en15103834

[14] Manas Wakchaure, B.K. Patle, A.K. Mahindrakar, Application of AI techniques and robotics in agriculture: A review, Artificial Intelligence in the Life Sciences, 3, (2023). doi: 10.1016/j.ailsci.2023.100057.

[15] Abia Katimbo, Daran R. Rudnick, Jingwen Zhang, Yufeng Ge, Kendall C. DeJonge, Trenton E. Franz, Yeyin Shi, Wei-zhen Liang, Xin Qiao, Derek M. Heeren, Isa Kabenge, Hope Njuki Nakabuye, Jiaming Duan, Evaluation of artificial intelligence algorithms with sensor data assimilation in estimating crop evapotranspiration and crop water stress index for irrigation water management, Smart Agricultural Technology, 4, (2023). doi: 10.1016/j.atech.2023.100176.

[16] Divyanshu Varshney, Javed Khan, Burhanuddin Babukhanwala, Deepika Saxena, Machine Learning Techniques for Plant Disease Detection, International Conference on Trends in Electronics, and Informatics, ICOEI, 1574-1581 (2021). doi: 10.1109/ICOEI51242.2021.9453053.

[17] Pallepati Vasavi, Arumugam Punitha, T. Venkat Narayana Rao, Crop leaf disease detection and classification using machine learning and deep learning algorithms by visual symptoms: A review, International Journal of Electrical and Computer Engineering, 12, 2079-2086 (2022). doi: 10.11591/ijece.v12i2.pp2079-2086.

[18] KhaledObaideen, Bashria A.A. Yousef, Maryam Nooman AlMallahi, Yong Chai Tan, Montaser Mahmoud, Hadi Jaber, Mohamad Ramadan, An overview of smart irrigation systems using IoT, EnergyNexus, 7, (2022). doi: 10.1016/j.nexus.2022.100124.

[19] Meriem Soussi, Mohamed Thameur Chaibi, Martin Buchholz, Zahia Saghrouni, Comprehensive Review on Climate Control and Cooling Systems in Greenhouses under Hot and Arid Conditions, Agronomy, 12 (2022). doi:10.3390/agronomy12030626.

[20] Abhinav Sharma, Arpit Jain, Prateek Gupta, Vinay Chowdary, Machine Learning Applications for Precision Agriculture: A Comprehensive Review, IEEE Access, 9, 4843-4873 (2021). doi: 10.1109/ACCESS.2020.3048415.

[21] Kyungdeok Noh, Byoung Ryong Jeong, Optimizing Temperature and Photoperiod in a HomeCultivation System to Program Normal, Delayed, and HastenedGrowth and Development Modes for Leafy Oak-Leaf andRomaine Lettuces, Sustainability, 13 (2021). doi: 10.3390/su131910879.

[22] Danyan Chen, Yanhao Mei, Qi Liu, Yongjun Wu, Zhenchao Yang, Carbon dioxide enrichment promoted the growth, yield, and light-use efficiency of lettuce in a plant factory with artificial lighting, Agronomy Journal, 113, 5196-5206 (2021).

[23] André Carrier, Michel Senécal, LES LAITUES ONT CHAUD, Réseau d'avertissements phytosanitaires, Québec (2011).

[24] Haozhe Zhanga, Long Hea, Francesco Di Gioiac, Daeun Choia, Antonio Eliad, Paul Heinemann, LoRaWAN based internet of things (IoT) system for precision irrigation in plasticulture fresh-market tomato, Smart Agricultural Technology, 2 (2022). doi: 10.1016/j.atech.2022.100053.

# An Ontology-based Epidemic Hospital Model Extraction

Zhen Dang[1], Qingping Yang[1], Tao Zhang[1]

[1] *Department of Mechanical and Aerospace Engineering, Brunel University London, Uxbridge, United Kingdom,*

**ABSTRACT**: Since the end of 2019, people have been devastated by the coronavirus. In response to the sudden increase in patients, various countries have built mobile cabin hospitals. It is crucial to deliver projects on time in a short period of time. The traditions have been challenged by novel technologies and approaches which are possible to disrupt the construction industry. In addition to novel established methods such as Building Information Modelling (BIM), BIM is considered an emerging technology in the construction industry and has attracted widespread attention in other industries, which can promote the digitization and knowledge creation of construction. The nature of low digitalization and fragmentation of construction information make construction projects widely criticized, and the procedures are tricky too. To achieve punctuality, accurate and fast information exchange should be prioritized. In this paper, we establish a general epidemic hospital ontology model based on the existing Building Ontology (BOT) model. The layout of the wards in Huoshenshan Hospital and the constraints of the existing site conditions are taken into consideration to accelerate the construction progress. However, the main obstacle is that ifcOWL ontologies contain a large amount of information, which makes processing difficult and time-consuming.

**Keywords**: BIM, Ontology, IFC, Data-exchange.

**Received** January 1, 2023; **In final form** March 31, 2023; **Published** June 2023



**Corresponding author:** Zhen Dang, e-mail: 1613889@brunel.ac.uk

## 1. INTRODUCTION

The world has been devastated by Covid-19 since the end of 2019. During this period, various countries have built resilient hospitals to varying degrees in response to this fast-spreading virus. The most illustrious case is the Huoshenshan modular Hospital in Wuhan, China, which completed the process from design to construction in only 10 days [1]. This example of rapid construction demonst- rates that efficiently delivering project on time is one of the main factors that determine the success. According to the national situation, different countries have adopted different resilient hospital construction models. For example, the United Kingdom constructed seven Nightingale hospitals by rebuilding existing buildings, including one in London Excel that was completed in just nine days [2].

For short and efficient construction projects, a vast amount of information from various aspects, including design, construction, and equipment supply, is involved. In other words, construction activities are driven by information. Those information are often complex and fragmented, because information from relevant building entities is typically obtained through various sources and by different stakeholders across various fields of construction, using various tools, systems, and software. The fragmented information from one source may not be understandable to others, resulting in inadequate interaction and ineffective sharing and exchange of data among different systems [3]. Therefore, efficiently and accurately integrating information is crucial [4]. However, this process is often with high-cost and intensive work [5] [6]. To deal with this challenge, the foundation which requires standard information structure models to support information management and exchange needs to be developed [7] [8].

Ontology as the branch of philosophy deals with the nature of existence and reality. In computer science and information technology, ontology refers to a formal representation of knowledge or concepts in a particular domain. It also could improve the ability to exchange or reuse information, data, and domain knowledge [9].

In this paper, we discuss a partial model extracted from a large BIM model of Huoshenshan epidemic hospital. The Industry Foundation Classes (IFC) standard is used for the formal representation of BIM. The IFC-to-OWL tool, translating the IFC schemas into Ontology Web Language (OWL), transforms this model into an ontology-based model. This way of expressing the elements of a building can be used to code information that is very useful for generating layout, such as the location of elements. A general epidemic hospital ontology model is established based on the existing BOT (Building Ontology) model, introducing existing site conditions, such as location elements, as constraints can facilitate more expeditious construction schedules.

The rest of this paper is structured as follows: Section 2 reviews related research on BIM and ontologies as background for this study. In Section 3, the method to building ontology is outlined. Then, the content of the ontology model and modules, and the details of the obtained maps are covered in Section 4. Finally, Conclusion and future developments are provided in Section 5.

## 2. LITERATURE REVIEW

### 2.1. Overview of BIM

The rapid development of information and communication technology (ICT) has brought about novel changes in construction practices, using the latest development of technologies and management tools [10]. The ICT in the construction industry has undergone major changes. As a new computer-aided design (CAD) paradigm, building information modelling has been widely disseminated in industry and academia [11]. The development of 3D modelling began in the 1970s, based on early computer-aided design (CAD) achievements in multiple industries. Although many industries have developed integrated analysis tools and object-based parametric modelling (as the basic concept of BIM), the construction industry has been limited to traditional 2D design for a long time [12].

Construction projects are becoming more complex and resulting inconvenience for manage. One source of complexity is the interplay between different stakeholders such as architects, engineers, contractors, suppliers and industry [13]. Complex construction projects require inter-organizational cooperations. In order to ensure the success of inter-organizational project, trust between different project partners is considered a key factor for success. Due to the nature of these inter-organizational joint ventures, it is well known that there is a demand for improving the integration, cooperation, and coordination of teams involved in the process [14]. Inter-organizational information system (IOIS) is a possible way to deal with the integration, cooperation and coordination challenges faced by the construction industry. IOIS is also referred to as web-based Project Management (PM) system, Web-Collaborative Extranets (WCEs) or Document Management Systems (DMS). Regar-dless of the terminology used, such systems facilitate accurate and timely sharing of various types of information [9]. Therefore, BIM may be a key method to ensure this integration and move from the document paradigm to the integrated database paradigm.

To cope with the increasing complexity and difficulty of project management, BIM has been developing rapidly and being widely used. BIM is currently the most common phrase for adopting new methods for building design, construction and maintenance. It is defined as "a set of interacting policies, processes and technologies generating a methodology to manage the essential building design and project data in digital format throughout the building's life-cycle" [11]. In addition, BIM is also used for various individual components of smaller projects. The 3D BIM model includes a wide range of data, including the geometry, physical properties, and functional characteristics of each building element. This information can be used to simulate the construction process, optimize building design, and facilitate communication among the different teams involved in a construction project. In addition to the 3D model, BIM also includes other types of information, such as cost estimates, construction schedules, and maintenance information, which can be updated and shared in real-time with all stakeholders. This helps to streamline the construction process, reduce errors, and improve collaboration among architects, engineers, contractors, and building owners. In addition, the public and private sectors in the United States are collaborating to promote the use of BIM [15]. Succar's [11] definition of BIM highlights its integrity, including not only software that allows geometric modelling and information input, but also tools and processes related to project management (PM). Therefore, from the overall perspective of BIM, it firmly places BIM in the field of architectural PM. It can be used for construction project managers to improve collaboration between stakeholders, reduce the time required for project documentation, and produce beneficial project results.

### 2.2. Ontology works on BIM

Ontologies provide a structured way to represent knowledge in particular subject areas, using a precise definition of the concepts and connections between them, a formal representation of concepts and their interrelationships in a particular field of knowledge [16] [17]. The use of ontologies as a formal mechanism to exchange and recycle domain-specific knowledge has gained widespread acceptance in various fields. In the AEC industry, ontology development began in the early 2000s and has emerged as a critical component in enhancing the management of information and knowledge [18]. Unlike traditional conceptual information models, it offers a machine-readable method of formally representing knowledge that can be used on various computer and artificial intelligence (AI) applications. In the construction field, multiple ontologies have been developed, covering various topics to assist orders such as data integration and transfer, and information extraction [9] [18].

Luiten et al. [19] presents an information model for buildings that emphasized essential concepts in construction, such as products, activities, resources, and contracts, along with the inter-conceptual relationships among them. The Industry Foundation Classes (IFC) [20] is widely utilized for the universal information format for sharing data, particularly in the context of Building Information Modelling (BIM). Table 1 shows the elements of the two models.

Table 1. Related Models

| Models | Element |
|---|---|
| Luiten et al. | products, activities, resources, and contracts, |
| IFC | projects, elements, executor , products, objects, resources, and relationships |

## 2.3. Industry Foundation Classes

Projects in architecture, engineering, construction, and facility management (AEC-FM) include numerous specialists from several fields working together to complete a project. The illustration in Figure 1 demonstrates the information flow within construction projects, depicting how professionals from various domains (e.g. estimating, scheduling, supply chain, and fabrication domains) in the construction industry utilize a centralized 3D BIM model to obtain the required information. This information is then utilized to produce data that represents their perspectives of the project. Integrating information related to a building element becomes a cumbersome task when it is stored in multiple file formats. This requires accessing numerous project documents and manually extracting and combining the relevant information.

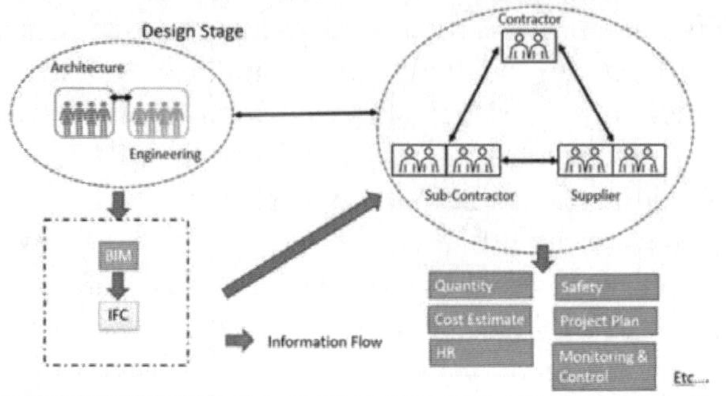


Figure 1. BIM information flow.

The primary objective of creating the IFC format for BIM data was to simplify communication among various AEC-FM software programs. Nevertheless, in order for data to be effectively shared between two applications, both need to be familiar with the IFC schema.

To overcome the limitations of the IFC data model in transmitting information, a user case approach has been established [21]. This approach requires domain experts to develop an Information Delivery Manual (IDM) and a Model View Definition (MVD). To implement this approach, professionals are required to generate an IDM and an MVD that specify the information that must be transferred between two software applications. Although the IDM and MVD methods offer a fixed representation of data that can be exchanged between two applications, they do not offer an automated rule-based process for extracting data from multiple sources. [22].

At present, diverse segments of the AEC-FM sector store project-related information in dissimilar data formats. [22]. To illustrate, BIM data is commonly saved in IFC objects, XML (such as ifcXML or gbXML), or relational ODBC databases. On the other hand, cost estimates and project progress data are typically kept in relational databases, whereas product data from material suppliers are usually accessible in text, HTML, XML, or relational format.

When data from various sources is saved in diverse data formats, computers face difficulty in integrating the data. Several factors contribute to this issue, including:

a. The data source mode is local and not shareable across computer applications over the internet.;
b. Inconsistent vocabulary usage across different data sources may result in referring to the same entities with different terms, or certain words may carry distinct meanings in two databases.;
c. Modifying the database schema dynamically poses a challenge because the data schema is linked to the object model of the computer program that employs it.

Stated differently, each domain creates its unique schema for denoting the domain attributes of a common object. To illustrate, the estimation domain and the scheduling domain utilize two distinct class hierarchies for modelling a particular building element. Consequently, integrating cost and schedule attributes of the same building element becomes challenging.

## 3. METHODOLOGY

Initially, several advanced ontology development methods are reviewed. Since the 1990s, various methods have been established to construct ontologies [18]. The more commonly used methods by timeline for building ontology are Grüninger and Fox method [23], "METHONTOLOGY" system [24], Uschold and Gruninger method [25], and "simple knowledge engineering methodology" (SKEM) [26]. To some extent, these techniques overlap, and the majority of the steps encompass term specification acquisition, conceptual integration, implementation, and evaluation. SKEM furnishes a comprehensive procedure for developing an ontology, covering classes, attributes, and axioms.

In this research, SKEM approach has been used, meanwhile using semantic knowledge of 3D layout from Luca [27]. Luca presented an approach that segregates information regarding objects, spatial relationships, and constraints from the generative process. This enhances the spatial layout in design and planning. Distinguishing between knowledge and practical application is a crucial aspect of semantic technologies, which enable access to a vast quantity of knowledge preserved in formal ontologies.

The various professional drawings of Huoshenshan Hospital are open to access, and the 3D models of partial hospital wards are drawn through Revit based on the 2D drawings. Based on the IFC file of single Huoshenshan resilient hospital ward unit, the IFCOWL ontology was built by the IFC-OWL tool, restricting layout of the existing space through this ontology. Building Topology Ontology (BOT) has been referred as the minimal OWL DL ontology for representing topology relationship between entities. As an extensible baseline, BOT is recommended for use with more domain specific ontologies.

Through the use of a RGB-D camera mounted on a mobile Turtlebot robot, the 3D map of the selected space is acquired.

## 4. PARTIAL WARD ONTOLOGY

Figure 2 shows the partial layout of Huoshenshan hospital, drawing by Revit software, it was the treatment area of Part D of Area 1, and the far right is the preparation area for medical staff. In the case of the NHS Nightingale Hospital

Figure 2. Huoshenshan resilient hospital BIM model

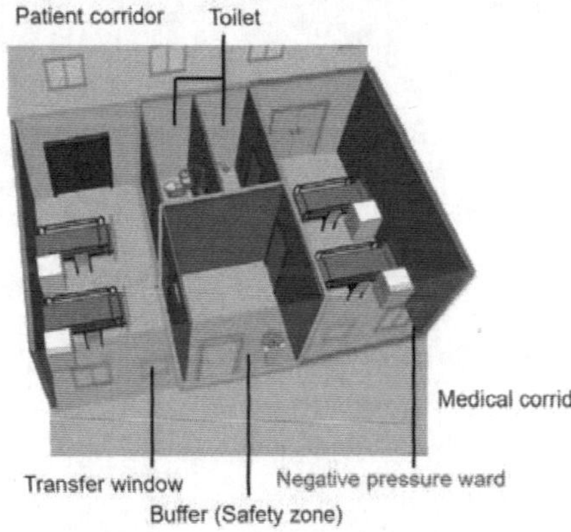


Figure 3. Huoshenshan Ward Unit

conversion, only a single ward unit needed to be extracted.

Figure 3 shows the details inside a ward. The components of the unit chosen for this study were two 6 × 3 meter patient room, a 3 × 3 meter toilet, a 3 × 3 meter buffer zone for medical staff, and two 9 × 3 meter at each end corridor. It is worth noting that the reason for the two corridor modules is that the buffer zone for medical staff is connected to the dedicated corridor for medical staff, patient room attach to patient corridor, which is conducive to the diversion of personnel.

Revit software comes with the export function of IFC type files, which has been converted into

Figure 4. IFCOWL Ontology.

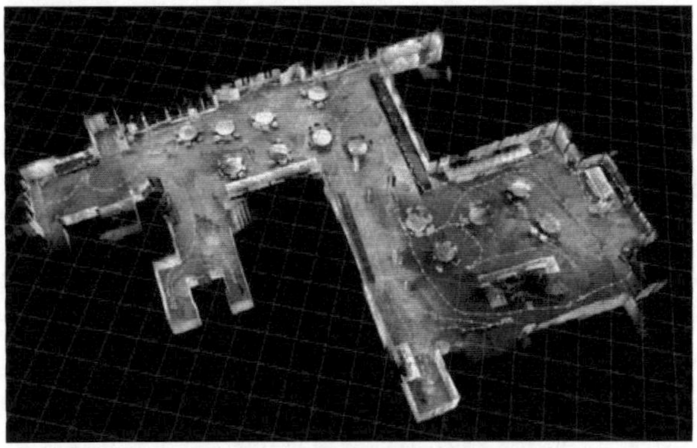

Figure 5. 3d Map of the selected space.

IFCOWL ontology through the IFC-to-OWL tool, as shown in Figure 4.

Figure 5 shows the public space on the ground floor of a university, which is an existing space selected for this study to renovate. The relationship between ward units can be used as constraints to establish the ontology of the space.

The result of the spatial layout is queried through SPARQL, and the result contains 6 ward unit space, which means that 12 beds can be provided for patients. When querying the corridor space, the result contains fifteen corridor spaces, which obviously has redundant corridors. Since the result is not visualized, it cannot generate a floor plan in the traditional sense. It is not friendly to the design and construction personnel without sufficient relevant background information and knowledge, and it is impossible to evaluate the pros and cons of the result, and it is also impossible to determine whether there is a problem with the connection of each unit.

In the process of IFC-to-OWL data conversion, the data structure of the IFC file is not clear due to different data sequences, the ontology generated by the converted data is disordered, and the constraints need to be adjusted manually, which takes a long time and is complicated.

## 5. CONCLUSION AND FUTURE DEVELOPMENTS

### 5.1. Conclusion

The integration of space ontology and ward ontology proves that ontology is beneficial for information reuse. Gathering information from scratch would have been a much longer process. Effectively separating useful information, which is spatial information in this study, is a crucial part of improving efficiency. Automated or assisted means can accelerate the process of obtaining information, which would be advantageous in obtaining more existing ontologies.

In the process of establishing ontology, utilizing formal ontology languages to draft ontologies is necessary for achieving conceptual clarity and unambiguous specifications. Expressing concepts in a formal and explicit manner requires significant expertise, which can make it a time-consuming and inefficient process. In addition, ontologies need to have a level of generalization since they aim to describe general knowledge that can be shared and reused, rather than personal knowledge. This is an important aspect of ontologies, as it justifies the effort put into their creation.

### 5.2. Future Development

There are three parts to the future work envisioned. Firstly, in Luca's project, [27], he generation of images is carried out using SketchUp, a software application that is highly valued for its user-friendly graphical user interface (GUI) and its ease of use in manipulating and editing 3D designs. There should also be related functions in the Revit software, and the next step is to obtain a visual floor plan space diagram. Secondly, assuming some spaces of different shapes and sizes, the ontology is then tested. In the end, the existing ward ontology is for epidemics that require strict control of airborne transmission. Changes to the spatial constraints allow ontology to be applied to the treatment of patients on more occasions, such as earthquakes, tsunamis and other natural disasters caused by large-scale public safety incidents.

# References


[1] M. Zhou, Y. Chen and X. a. A. L. Su, "Rapid construction and advanced technology for a Covid-19 field hospital in Wuhan, China," in *Proceedings of the Institution of Civil Engineers-Civil Engineering*, 174 (1) , pp 29-34, (2020).

[2] J. Wise, "Covid-19: London's Nightingale Hospital will reopen for non-covid cases," *BMJ,* vol. 372, p. n15, 2021.

[3] E. Curry, J. O'Donnell, E. Corry, S. Hasan and M. a. O. Keane, "Linking building data in the cloud: Integrating cross-domain building data using linked data," *Advanced Engineering Informatics,* vol. 27, no. 2, pp. 206-219, 2013.

[4] Y. Zheng and S. a. S. Törmä, "A shared ontology suite for digital construction workflow," *Automation in Construction,* vol. 132, p. 103930, December 2021.

[5] I. Mutis and R. R. Issa, "Framework for semantic reconciliation of construction project information," *Journal of Information Technology in Construction (ITcon),* vol. 17, no. 1, pp. 1-24, 2012.

[6] A. Akinyemi and M. a. G. J. Sun, "An ontology-based data integration framework for construction information management," *Proceedings of the Institution of Civil Engineers - Management, Procurement and Law,* vol. 171, no. 3, pp. 111-125, 2018.

[7] F. Thomas, "Models of Construction Process Information," *Journal of Computing in Civil Engineering,* vol. 10, no. 3, pp. 183-193, 1996.

[8] F. Thomas, "Future directions for IFC-based interoperability," *Journal of Information Technology in Construction (ITcon),* vol. 8, no. 17, pp. 231-246, 2003.

[9] C. J. Anumba, R. R. Issa and J. a. M. I. Pan, "Ontology-based information and knowledge management in construction," *Construction Innovation,* vol. 8, no. 3, pp. 218-239, 2008.

[10] L. Taxén and J. Lilliesköld, "Images as action instruments in complex projects," *International Journal of Project Management,* vol. 26, no. 5, pp. 527-536, 2008.

[11] B. Succar, "Building information modelling framework: A research and delivery foundation for industry stakeholders," *Automation in Construction,* vol. 18, no. 3, pp. 357-375, 2009.

[12] C. M. Eastman, C. Eastman, P. Teicholz and R. a. L. K. Sacks, BIM handbook: A guide to building information modeling for owners, managers, designers, engineers and contractors, John Wiley & Sons, 2011.

[13] S. K. Sears and R. H. a. S. G. A. Clough, Construction project management: a practical guide to field construction management, John Wiley & Sons, 2008.

[14] S. Cicmil and D. Marshall, "Insights into collaboration at the project level: complexity, social interaction and procurement mechanisms," *Building Research & Information,* vol. 33, no. 6, pp. 523-535, 2005.

[15] J. Underwood and U. Isikdag, "Emerging technologies for BIM 2.0," *Construction Innovation,* vol. 11, no. 3, pp. 252-258, 2011.

[16] T. R. Gruber, "A translation approach to portable ontology specifications," *Knowledge,* vol. 5, no. 2, pp. 199-220, 1993.

[17] T. R. Gruber, "Toward principles for the design of ontologies used for knowledge sharing?," *International Journal of Human-*

*Computer Studies,* vol. 43, no. 5, pp. 907-928, 1995.

[18] Z. Zhipeng and Y. M. a. L. Goh, "Overview and Analysis of Ontology Studies Supporting Development of the Construction Industry," *Journal of Computing in Civil Engineering,* vol. 30, no. 6, p. Article 04016026, 2016.

[19] G. Luiten, T. Froese, B. Björk, G. Cooper, R. Junge and K. a. O. R. Karstila, "An Information Reference Model for Architecture, Engineering, and Construction," in *First International Conference on the Management of Information Technology for Construction*, Singapore, 1993.

[20] b. International, buildingSMART International, [Online]. Available: https://www.buildingsmart.org/standards/bsi-standards/industry-foundation-classes/. [Accessed 22 Janurary 2021].

[21] C. Eastman, Y.-S. Jeong and R. a. K. I. Sacks, "Exchange model and exchange object concepts for implementation of national BIM standards," vol. 24, no. 1, pp. 25-34, 2010.

[22] T.-W. Kang and H.-S. Choi, "BIM perspective definition metadata for interworking facility management data," *Advanced Engineering Informatics,* vol. 29, no. 4, pp. 958-970, 2015.

[23] G. Michael and S. F. Mark, "Methodology for the Design and Evaluation of Ontologies," in *Workshop on Basic Ontological Issues in Knowledge Sharing*, Montreal, Canada, 1995.

[24] M. Fernández-López and A. a. J. N. Gómez-Pérez, "Methontology: from ontological art towards ontological engineering," in *AAAI-97 Spring Symposium Series*, California, USA, 1997.

[25] M. Uschold and M. Gruninger, "Ontologies: Principles, methods and applications," *The knowledge engineering review,* vol. 11, no. 2, pp. 93-136, 1996.

[26] N. F. Noy and D. L. McGuinness, "Ontology development 101: A guide to creating your first ontology," Stanford Knowledge Systems Laboratory Technical Report KSL-01-05 and Stanford Medical Informatics Technical Report SMI-2001-0880, california, USA, 2001.

[27] L. Caneparo, "Semantic knowledge in generation of 3D layouts for decision-making," *Automation in Construction,* vol. 134, p. 104012, 2022.

# Monitoring and detection of toothbrushing with smart watches and artificial intelligence

Eduardo Casilari[1], Francisco J. González-Cañete[1]

[1]*Dpto. de Tecnología Electrónica, Universidad de Málaga, Instituto TELMA, 29071 Málaga, Spain, ecasilari@uma.es*

**ABSTRACT**: This work proposes to combine wearables and the use of artificial intelligence techniques to detect manual mobility patterns caused by brushing teeth. Specifically, the article describes and evaluate a system based on convolutional neural networks, able to identify brushing gestures from samples of few seconds of inertial accelerometry signals gathered by wrist-worn devices. The architecture is systematically trained and validated with the signals provided by different public databases which were collected when different experimental subjects executed different manual actions. The results show the effectiveness of the detector, since it reaches a sensitivity and specificity greater than 95% when applied to discriminate brushing from other hand actions. In addition, the system is re-trained and assessed with the real-life samples captured by a smartwatch, where the neural model could be implemented to operate and produce real-time decisions.

**Keywords**: Human activity detection, wearable, accelerometer, convolutional neural network.

**Received** January 1, 2023; **In final form** March 31, 2023; **Published** June 2023



**Corresponding author: Eduardo Casilari, e-mail: ecasilari@uma.es**

## 1. INTRODUCTION

It has been estimated that oral diseases affect close to 3.5 billion people worldwide [1] while, only in the USA, dental services cost 108 billion yearly. [2]. Plaque buildup on the gingiva that is not removed can cause caries, discomfort, and occasionally even tooth loss and infection. This plaque accumulation can be reliably controlled through tooth brushing and other mechanical cleaning techniques, provided that they are performed thoroughly and on a frequent basis. [3]. In this regard, there is a general medical consensus about the benefits of brushing the teeth for two minutes twice a day with a fluoride-containing paste [2]. In spite of the evidence, according to certain surveys in some western countries, the proportion of adults that do not brush their teeth daily may reach almost 50%, with a percentage higher than 64% for those aged over 55 [4]. In this context, aging is clearly linked to a degradation of the oral hygiene Extensive evidence indicates that poor oral health is more common with increasing age [5]. Moreover, older adults or persons in the early stages of dementia may require to be reminded to brush their teeth. Thus, the development of low-cost seamless tools that can automatically track and measure the frequency and duration of this important hygienic habit has received substantial research attention during recent years.

In this ambit, many efforts have been devoted to the implementation of the so-called 'smart toothbrushes', capable of computing not only the brushing duration, but also the brushed areas of the mouth or the applied pressure or the held angle [6]. In some works of the related literature, this smart device is achieved by simply attaching a sensor (usually a bulky inertial measurement unit) equipped with a wireless transmission module to the handle of a conventional toothbrush [7] [8]. In most prototypes, the information collected by this unit is typically sent to an app running in a nearby smartphone so that the oral health behavior (OHB) of the user can be recorded and analyzed.

In some cases, these gadgets are complemented by some type of augmented or virtual reality systems [9]. Thus, a screen representing the evolution of the brushing movements on a two or three-dimensional image of the mouth is offered as a guidance or educational tool to enhance the toothbrushing protocol followed by the user.

To avoid the costs and hardware complexity of these intelligent devices, other studies suggest to track the users' OHB by analyzing the image of external video sequences recorded while brushing their teeth. In some experiments, the camera embedded in a smartphone or a table is utilized for this goal [10] [11]. However, in addition to privacy issues, these image-based detectors present different technical drawbacks, as they can be strongly affected by operative aspects such as lighting, self-shadows or the position or resolution of the employed camera. Furthermore, as analyzed by Marcon et al. in [12], some regular circular movements caused by toothbrushing can be hardly detected through image analysis due to the small displacements of the hands.

A low-cost alternative to OHB monitoring can be accomplished by using hand wearables (such as smartwatches, smartbands or bracelets). Although initially envisaged to track sporting performance, current smartwatches and smartbands have found a relevant field in HAR (Human Activity Recognition) systems, especially in those applications intended to supervise health status and personal well-being. These popular devices, which have been broadly incorporated into the daily life by many users and natively integrate inertial sensors, can be reprogrammed to embed activity recognition applications. Hence, they can avoid the use of a specific monitoring tool (a smart toothbrush or a video camera system) to track toothbrushing.

The idea of leveraging wearables and wrist gestures to analyse oral hygiene routines is not new. There are examples in the literature that employ commercial smartwatches [13] [14] [15] to identify the hand mobility patterns generated by manual toothbrushing. Obviously, for this identification, the smartwatch must be worn on the dominant hand, instead of its more common position in the less occupied (non-dominant) wrist.

In these systems, the recognition process is based on the analysis of inertial signals (usually triaxial acceleration, although there are architectures that also make use of the information from the gyroscope or the magnetometer). Due to the variety and complexity of hand movements during tooth brushing, the proposed detection algorithms rely on supervised learning models.

As the decision 'core' of the detector, almost all these proposals in the literature employ 'classical' machine learning techniques (such as Decision Trees, Support Vector Machines, or Multilayer Perceptrons). These learning models require some pre-processing of the 'raw' sensed data aimed at generating a set of input features (statistics derived from the time-domain or frequency domain analysis of the measured signals) with which the classifier is really trained and fed. Contrariwise, deep learning algorithms minimize the human guidance and hand engineering in the detection process, as they can autonomously extract the most adequate features to discriminate patterns in large datasets.

In this respect, Convolutional Neural Networks (CNNs) are one of the most powerful deep learning models, and have successfully been incorporated into HAR (Human Activity Recognition) systems [16]. CNNs, which are composed of a series of sequential processing layers of adaptable convolutional filters, are capable of discovering hidden patterns in large datasets by learning how to represent the data using various levels of abstraction. CNNs and other deep learning architectures, such as recurrent neural networks (RNN) and long short-term memory (LSTM) networks have already been proposed to recognize hand movements. The work by Zhao et al. in [17] describes a gesture recognition algorithm based on a LSTM network that operates on the inertial signals captured by a wrist band. However, the identification of toothbrushing is not contemplated. In [18], authors successfully employ a CNN for the recognition of hand gestures measured by the embedded inertial unit in a smartphone. Nonetheless, the system is oriented to enable the remote control of home appliances and, obviously, cannot be considered to track OHBs.

In this paper we assess the potential of this type of neural networks to distinguish toothbrushing from other manual activities based on the signals gathered by a wrist-worn device.

## 2. EMPLOYED DATASET

In order to implement the detector, the learning model must be trained with a set of labelled data including mobility samples of different hand movements.

There are various public repositories containing measurements of inertial signals that were captured by a sensor located on the wrist while a group of experimental subjects performed a series of predefined manual activities (see, for example, WISDM [19], HTAD [20], EJUST-ADL [21] or HMP [22] or Multi-sensory [23] databases).

For our study, we selected the PAAL dataset [24], as it is the repository with the highest number of mobility samples (6071, including 227 recordings of manual toothbrushing sessions). In addition, it encompasses a noteworthy variety of activities (24 types of hand motions, ranging from eating or drinking to typing, handwriting or sneezing the nose) executed by a wide set of participants (52 volunteers comprising 26 males and 26 females) selected across a broad age spectrum (18-77 years). The duration of the traces spans from 0.2 to 254.6 s (with a mean value of 7.34 s). During each experiment, the experimental subjects were requested to wear an Empatica 4 (E4) wristband [25] on their dominant hand. To generate the traces, the wearable measured the triaxial acceleration signals with a sampling frequency of 32 Hz and stored the data in its internal memory.

## 3. DEFINITION OF THE CNN

### 3.1. Selection of the input features

In spite of the growing potential of current high end smartwatches, the real-time activity detection algorithm to be deployed on the wearable must take into account the constrains in the computing and processing capabilities of these devices. In this light, one of the key benefits of CNNs is their ability to learn from the internal structure of the input data without requiring to calculate any other input feature. Therefore, we suggest to directly feed the classifier using the measurements obtained by the sensors, avoiding the need of computing arbitrary complex statistics from the time series of the inertial measurements gathered by the transportable sensor.

As the basis for the detection decision, we employ as input features the numerical series containing the measurements captured by the triaxial accelerometer during observation intervals of fixed duration. These patterns are extracted from each movement trace as samples arrays ($M_s$) of three columns in the form:

$$M_S = \begin{bmatrix} A_{x_{i_o}} & A_{y_{i_o}} & A_{z_{i_o}} \\ A_{x_{i_o+1}} & A_{y_{i_o+1}} & A_{z_{i_o+1}} \\ & \cdots & \\ A_{x_{i_o+\lceil T\cdot f_S\rceil}} & A_{y_{i_o+\lceil T\cdot f_S\rceil}} & A_{z_{i_o+\lceil T\cdot f_S\rceil}} \end{bmatrix} \quad (1)$$

where $A_{x_i}$, $A_{y_i}$ and $A_{z_i}$ denote the *x*-, *y*-, and *z*-components of the *i-th* measurement of the acceleration vector of the corresponding trace, and $i_o$ is the index of the first considered sample. This initial index must be chosen in the range:

$$i_o \in [1, N - \lceil T \cdot f_s \rceil] \quad (2)$$

where $N$ represents the total number of measurements of the acceleration in the trace.

In these formulae, $T$ and $f_s$ are the duration of the observation window and the employed sampling rate, respectively, whereas the operator $\lceil x \rceil$ indicates the lowest integer greater than $x$. Consequently, the number of rows in the input feature matrix is $1+\lceil T \cdot f_S \rceil$. For the study, we considered different values for $T$ in a range from 2 to 4 s (also employed in [26]) since the analysed activities do not require actually a longer duration and an interval of 2 s is considered a good compromise between recognition efficiency, data complexity and identification speed in HAR classification systems [27].

In order to compensate strong unbalance between the number of traces corresponding to toothbrushing (227 sessions) and the rest of manual activities in the database (5844 sessions), we obtained up to 15 patterns from each toothbrushing trace, following a sliding window technique. To this effect, we extracted different consecutive observation windows with acceleration measurements from each trace. The step size of the sliding window was set to 8 samples (0.25 s).

Conversely, from each 'non-toothbrushing" traces, this sliding windowing policy is not applied and we derived a single array corresponding to central interval of $T$ seconds within the trace.

In this analysis, all the traces with a duration lower than $T$ were discarded. Similarly, the number of acquired patterns from each toothbrushing trace (up to 15) depended on the particular duration of the session (which varies from just 2.5 s to 41.8 s -with a mean value of 14 s-).

As a result of this procedure, for the window length of 3 s, we generated 3182 and 3237 patterns of toothbrushing and other hand (non-toothbrushing) activities, respectively. A slightly different number of patterns were obtained for the other values of $T$ (2 or 4 s) employed in the study.

Other data augmentation techniques were considered but they produced poorer results.

### 3.2. Configuration of the model

The general structure of the utilized CNN is depicted in Figure 1. As it can be observed, after an initial input layer which simply introduces the data in the model, a sequence of convolutional blocks is in charge of identifying the feature extraction at different time scales. These blocks basically consist of four processing units:

1) a convolutional layer, which apply a certain number of adaptive fixed-size convolutional filters (whose coefficients are adjusted during the training phase to maximize a correct pattern identification)
2) a batch normalizer, which normalizes every mini-batch of data used to speed up and stabilize training.
3) a ReLU (Rectified Linear Unit) Activation Function which introduces an essential non-linearity in the model to adapt to the intrinsically non-linear nature of the data.
4) a Max Pooling layer, aimed at down-sampling and 'summarizing' the features produced by the previous and enlarging the considered time scale for the next convolutional back, by reducing the dimensionality of the input data.

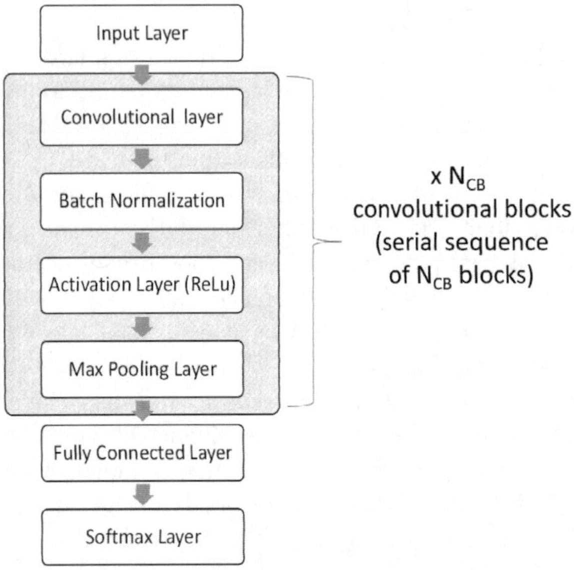


Figure 1. General architecture of the employed CNN

After this feature extraction, a fully connected neural layer (whose weights are also adjusted during training) maps the output of the previous layers into a class probability distribution (a stochastic likelihood characterization of each class). In our architecture, this is achieved through a Softmax activation function, which calculates for every feature combination the probabilities of belonging to the two movement classes (toothbrushing or not). A final cross-entropy loss function produces the final classification decision based on these probabilities.

A typical 5-fold cross-validation procedure was applied to the model for training and evaluation. Hence, the set of patterns was divided into five partitions with an approximately equal number of labelled instances. This trace division is carried out at random although it is guaranteed that each fold roughly contains the same class proportions (toothbrushing and other activities) as in the original set. Then, the CNN goes through five iterations of testing and training. Each iteration uses a different partition (20% of the total patterns) for testing while the remaining four sub-groups are reserved for training (three partitions) and validation (one partition). To prevent overfitting, the validation set is used. Therefore, the training algorithm is progressively applied to the data until the error of the model for the validation patterns starts increasing, which evinces that the network is beginning to overlearn the training data. Besides, L2 Regularization technique is also implemented to mitigate overfitting.

For each iteration, after training the model, the performance of the classifying decision is exclusively assessed with the test data reserved for that fold. After the completion of the five training and testing cycles, the mean values of the performance metrics obtained for the five repetitions are then calculated to characterize the effectiveness of the classifier.

## 4. EVALUATION OF THE DETECTOR AND RESULTS

The CNN was programmed through scripts developed with the Deep Learning Toolbox TM's Matlab framework[28]. Since this toolbox is primarily conceived to process images, the input matrixes were mapped into equivalent "images" with a dimension of $(1 \text{ x } (1+\lceil T \cdot f_s \rceil))$ "pixels" and three "channels" (one for each acceleration axis). As it refers to the feature scaling, we evaluated two policies: 1) the case in which the raw data are not normalized, 2) the case in which the values of the acceleration measurement are z-score normalized before being fed to the classifier.

A massive grid search was applied to determine the optimal configuration of the hyperparameters of the CNN. The combination of hyperparameters with which the best performance is achieved are presented in Table 1, which also indicate those other values that were considered for diverse parameters during to the grid search to tune the model.

Table 1. Hyperparameterization of the CNN

| Parameter | Optimal configuration | Other evaluated values |
|---|---|---|
| **Network dimensioning and structure** | | |
| Number of input per channel (window size) | 97 (3 s) | 65 (2 s)<br>129 (4 s) |
| Input scaling | No scaling | z-score normalization |
| Number of convolutional blocks | 2 | 3,4 |
| Number of filters in each block | 256 | 32,64, 128,256 |
| Filter size | 1x16 | 1x3, 1x4, 1x5, 1x10, 1x12 |
| Size of padding | Same as filter size | |
| Filter stride | 1 | - |
| Pooling size | 1x4 | 1x2, 1x5 |
| Pooling stride | Same as pooling size | |
| **Configuration of the training process** | | |
| Parameter | Optimal configuration | Other evaluated values |
| Training algorithm | Stochastic Gradient Descent Momentum | |
| Mini-batch size | 2 | 1,4,8,16,32,64,128 |
| Maximum number of training epochs | 10 | - |
| Number of validations per epoch | 2 | - |
| Validation patience | 3 | - |
| Initial learning rate | 0.0001 | - |

To assess the overall quality of the classifier decisions after being trained, we computed three performance typically considered in the evaluation of binary detectors:

1) Sensitivity or recall (defined as the ratio between the toothbrushing intervals that are correctly recognized and the global number of toothbrushing patterns used for testing).
2) Specificity (percentage of non-tooth brushing intervals that are adequately identified –i.e. without being misinterpreted as a toothbrushing operation)
3) Accuracy (global ratio between the number of the correctly identified patterns and the total number of test movements).

The metrics achieved with the test data for the best combination of hyperparameters are presented in Table 2. The table shows that the z-score normalization of the input data introduces a very slight (not statistically significant) improvement, although the model can also classify in a satisfactory way the mobility patterns directly based on the raw signal gathered by the accelerometer.

In any case, these results (higher than 96% for both sensitivity and specificity) outperform those obtained by most related works in the literature which use wrist-worn device and other AI classifier to identify toothbrushing activities (see, for example, the systems presented by Cherian [29]or by Akther in [30]).

Table 2. Performance of the CNN for the best combination of hyperparameters when the test set is employed

| Normalization | Sensitivity | Specificity | Accuracy |
|---|---|---|---|
| z-score | **0.96674** | **0.99301** | **0.98006** |
| No normalization | **0.97057** | **0.98244** | **0.97658** |

In the analysis so far, just one observation window (the central one) for each of the movement samples in the database not corresponding to toothbrushing activities has been considered for the training and testing of the classification model. In a second evaluation phase, we proceeded to test the capability of the trained model to avoid false positives (for unnormalized inputs) when the whole duration of all the traces in the repository is employed. To this end, all the possible 3-s observation windows (with a one second overlap between consecutive windows) that can be extracted from the time series of samples were generated. In this way, 16444 windows (containing 1414 intervals of toothbrushing) with triaxial accelerometer inertial measures were obtained and inputted into the classifier. The sensitivity and specificity achieved with this new extended set of patterns were 0.9321 and 0.9715, respectively. The classification model gave a wrong response and thus generated false positives for 428 out of the 15030 windows produced by activities other than brushing teeth.

As a confusion matrix, Table 3 shows the rate and number of errors produced for each type of the manual movements included in the repository. As can be seen, the model only loses effectiveness against very particular movements that involve raising the hand to the face (such as blowing one's nose, brushing one's hair, or drinking water from a glass). In this case, the error could be justified by the fact that toothbrushing may shares similar movements to those activities. The specificity of the detector also seems to deteriorate when very specific activities requiring repetitive and short-trajectory movements are performed (such as washing dishes or washing hands). On the other hand, for the rest of the hand activities, the model behaves in a very adequate manner.

Table 3. Performance of the CNN when the whole dataset is employed as the test set. Confusion matrix for non-toothbrushing manual activities.

| Hand activity | Number of misclassified observation windows | Total percentage of misinterpreted windows |
|---|---|---|
| Blow nose | 30 | 16.85% |
| Brush hair | 33 | 2.68% |
| Drink water | 13 | 5.31% |
| Dusting | 37 | 3.45% |
| Eat meal | 0 | 0.00% |
| Ironing | 11 | 0.67% |
| Open a bottle | 0 | 0.00% |
| Open a box | 0 | 0.00% |
| Phone call | 0 | 0.00% |
| Put on a jacket | 3 | 0.37% |
| Put on a shoe | 21 | 2.49% |
| Put on glasses | 0 | 0.00% |
| Salute | 2 | 10.52% |
| Sit down | 1 | 2.54% |
| Sneeze cough | 0 | 0.00% |
| Stand up | 0 | 0.00% |
| Take off a jacket | 1 | 0.22% |
| Take off a shoe | 2 | 0.33% |
| Take off glasses | 3 | 14.24% |
| Type on a keyboard | 0 | 0.00% |
| Washing dishes | 84 | 4.41% |
| Washing hands | 187 | 11.82% |
| Writing | 0 | 0% |

## 5. CONCLUSIONS AND FUTURE WORK

It has been estimated that oral and dental diseases affect almost half of humanity, largely due to the infrequency with which a considerable proportion of the population brush their teeth (less than twice a day, with a regularity that markedly decreases for older ages). In this context, the automatic monitoring of dental hygiene routines may be of great interest, since it can help promote healthy habits and remind the user (especially older persons or patients in the initial stages of dementia) of the need to brushing her/his teeth after each meal. Smartwatches and similar wrist-worn devices may offer and affordable, non-invasive tool, which is already fully integrated into our daily lives, capable of informing at all times about the evolution of diverse biosignals or health parameters and even generating alerts in case a medical alarm is suspected.

This work has investigated the possibilities of identifying mobility patterns generated by toothbrushing based on the signals captured by a wrist-worn device. Specifically, a deep learning model (a trained convolutional neural network) has been employed to discriminate the acceleration signals of toothbrushing from those generated by other manual movements. Unlike other artificial intelligence techniques, CNNs are capable of producing a classification decision from the raw acceleration measurements, without requiring the choice and calculation of a set of input characteristics. This may notably facilitate the implementation of the model in low-cost and lightweight devices that have relevant hardware limitations for real-time computing.

To evaluate the system, we have utilized a public repository containing the measurements of the inertial signals measured during the execution of 24 different activities by a wide group of experimental subjects monitored by means of a by a smartband located in the dominant hand. The results obtained prove that the accuracy of the network to identify toothbrushing movements from accelerometry signal windows of a few seconds exceeds 95%.

Our ongoing studies are focused on implementing these classifiers in real devices. In particular, the trained network has already been implemented on an Android Wear OS smartwatch with the TensorFlow Lite library and encouraging preliminary results are being obtained.

Besides, our future work will also focus on the use of other databases and on incorporating into the system the ability to distinguish not only manual toothbrushing but also using an electric toothbrush.

.

## ACKNOWLEDGEMENT

This research was funded by Andalusian Regional Government (-Junta de Andalucía- grant

PAIDI P18-RT-1652), Spanish Ministry of Science and Innovation (grant TED2021-130456B-I00) and Universidad de Málaga, Campus de Excelencia Internacional Andalucia Tech.

## REFERENCES


[1] World Health Organization (WHO), "Oral health (Key facts -15 March 2022)." https://www.who.int/news-room/fact-sheets/detail/oral-health (accessed May 19, 2022).

[2] National Center for Chronic Disease Prevention and Health Promotion (U.S.). Division of oral health., "Oral health; preventing cavities, gum disease, tooth loss, and oral cancers: at a glance 2011," *CDC a glance Ser.*, 2011, Accessed: Jun. 16, 2022. [Online]. Available: https://stacks.cdc.gov/view/cdc/11862.

[3] H. Löe, "Oral hygiene in the prevention of caries and periodontal disease," *Int. Dent. J.*, vol. 50, no. 3, pp. 129–139, 2000, doi: 10.1111/J.1875-595X.2000.TB00553.X.

[4] D. Manton *et al.*, "Australia's oral health tracker technical paper: First edition," *Aust. Heal. Policy (Technical Pap. No. 2018-2)*, 2018, [Online]. Available: https://www.vu.edu.au/sites/default/files/australias-oral-health-tracker-technical-paper.pdf.

[5] P. P. Coll *et al.*, "The Prevention of Infections in Older Adults: Oral Health," *J. Am. Geriatr. Soc.*, vol. 68, no. 2, pp. 411–416, Feb. 2020, doi: 10.1111/JGS.16154.

[6] D. Sharma, S. Chandel, V. K. Bhardwaj, A. S. Thakur, P. Jhingta, and N. Negi, "Recent Advances in Oral Healthcare-A Review," *Int. J. Drug Res. Dent. Sci.*, vol. 2, no. 3, pp. 55–63, Aug. 2020, doi: 10.36437/IJDRD.2020.2.3.H.

[7] Z. Hussain, D. Waterworth, M. Aldeer, W. E. Zhang, Q. Z. Sheng, and J. Ortiz, "Do You Brush Your Teeth Properly? An Off-body Sensor-based Approach for Toothbrushing Monitoring," in *2021 IEEE International Conference on Digital Health (ICDH 2021)*, Sep. 2021, pp. 59–69, doi: 10.1109/ICDH52753.2021.00018.

[8] B. Stark and M. Samarah, "Ensemble and Deep Learning for Real-time Sensors Evaluation of algorithms for real-time sensors with application for detecting brushing location," in *IEEE 5th International Conference on Computer and Communications (ICCC 2019)*, Dec. 2019, pp. 555–559, doi: 10.1109/ICCC47050.2019.9064080.

[9] K. Sakuma, H. Li, and L. Jing, "Toothbrush Force Measurement and 3D Visualization," in *International Conference on Human-Computer Interaction*, 2021, vol. 1498 CCIS, pp. 151–158, doi: 10.1007/978-3-030-90176-9_21/FIGURES/9.

[10] A. Flagg, J. Boger, and A. Mihailidis, "An Intelligent Toothbrush: Machines for Smart Brushing," 2011, Accessed: Jun. 17, 2022. [Online]. Available: https://www.semanticscholar.org/paper/AN-INTELLIGENT-TOOTHBRUSH-%3A-Machines-for-Smart-Flagg-Boger/f48280801ede76c9b6ee22ee3f7cb1c30f107d7f.

[11] M. Marcon, A. Sarti, and S. Tubaro, "Toothbrush motion analysis to help children learn proper tooth brushing," *Comput. Vis. Image Underst.*, vol. 148, pp. 34–45, Jul. 2016, doi: 10.1016/J.CVIU.2016.03.009.

[12] M. Marcon, A. Sarti, and S. Tubaro, "Smart toothbrushes: Inertial measurement sensors fusion with visual tracking," *Lect. Notes Comput. Sci. (including Subser. Lect. Notes Artif. Intell. Lect. Notes Bioinformatics)*, vol. 9914 LNCS, pp. 480–494, 2016, doi: 10.1007/978-3-319-48881-3_33.

[13] G. Csizmadia, K. Liszkai-Peres, B. Ferdinandy, Á. Miklósi, and V. Konok, "Human activity recognition of children with wearable devices using LightGBM machine learning," *Sci. Reports 2022 121*, vol. 12, no. 1, pp. 1–10, Mar. 2022, doi: 10.1038/s41598-022-09521-1.

[14] S. Akther, N. Saleheen, M. Saha, V. Shetty, and S. Kumar, "mTeeth: Identifying Brushing Teeth Surfaces UsingWrist-Worn Inertial Sensors," *Proc. ACM Interactive, Mobile, Wearable Ubiquitous Technol.*, vol. 5, no. 2, p. 25, Jun. 2021, doi: 10.1145/3463494.

[15] R. Lutze and K. Waldhor, "Personal Health Assistance for Elderly People via Smartwatch Based Motion Analysis," in *IEEE International Conference on Healthcare Informatics, (ICHI 2017)*, Sep. 2017, pp. 124–133, doi: 10.1109/ICHI.2017.79.

[16] F. Ordóñez, D. Roggen, F. J. Ordóñez, and D. Roggen, "Deep Convolutional and LSTM Recurrent Neural Networks for Multimodal Wearable Activity Recognition," *Sensors*, vol. 16, no. 1, p. 115, Jan. 2016, doi: 10.3390/s16010115.

[17] S. Zhao, H. Cai, W. Li, Y. Liu, and C. Liu, "Hand gesture recognition on a resource-limited interactive wristband," *Sensors*, vol. 21, no. 17, pp. 18–22, 2021, doi: 10.3390/s21175713.

[18] Y. C. Chu, Y. J. Jhang, T. M. Tai, and W. J. Hwang, "Recognition of hand gesture sequences by accelerometers and gyroscopes," *Appl. Sci.*, vol. 10, no. 18, 2020, doi: 10.3390/APP10186507.

[19] G. M. Weiss, K. Yoneda, and T. Hayajneh, "Smartphone and Smartwatch-Based Biometrics Using Activities of Daily Living," *IEEE Access*, vol. 7, pp. 133190–133202, 2019, doi: 10.1109/ACCESS.2019.2940729.

[20] E. Garcia-Ceja *et al.*, "HTAD: A Home-Tasks Activities Dataset with Wrist-Accelerometer and Audio Features," *Lect. Notes Comput. Sci. (including Subser. Lect. Notes Artif. Intell. Lect. Notes Bioinformatics)*, vol. 12573 LNCS, pp. 196–205, Jun. 2021, doi: 10.1007/978-3-030-67835-7_17.

[21] S. Ashry and W. Gomaa, "Descriptors for Human Activity Recognition," in *International Japan-Africa Conference on Electronics, Communications and Computations (JAC-ECC 2019)*, Dec. 2019, pp. 116–119, doi: 10.1109/JAC-ECC48896.2019.9051211.

[22] B. Bruno, F. Mastrogiovanni, A. Sgorbissa, T. Vernazza, and R. Zaccaria, "Analysis of human behavior recognition algorithms based on acceleration data," in *IEEE International Conference on Robotics and Automation (iCRA'2013)*, 2013, pp. 1602–1607, doi: 10.1109/ICRA.2013.6630784.

[23] M. Ruzzon, A. Carfì, T. Ishikawa, F. Mastrogiovanni, and T. Murakami, "A multi-sensory dataset for the activities of daily living," *Data Br.*, vol. 32, p. 106122, 2020, doi: 10.1016/j.dib.2020.106122.

[24] P. Climent-Pérez, Á. M. Muñoz-Antón, A. Poli, S. Spinsante, and F. Florez-Revuelta, "Dataset of acceleration signals recorded while performing activities of daily living," *Data Br.*, vol. 41, 2022, doi: 10.1016/j.dib.2022.107896.

[25] Empatica, "E4 wristband | Real-time physiological signals | Wearable PPG, EDA, Temperature, Motion sensors." https://www.empatica.com/en-eu/research/e4/ (accessed Feb. 17, 2023).

[26] G. Luzhnica, J. Simon, E. Lex, and V. Pammer, "A sliding window approach to natural hand gesture recognition using a custom data glove," in *IEEE Symposium on 3D User Interfaces, (3DUI 2016 )*, Apr. 2016, pp. 81–90, doi: 10.1109/3DUI.2016.7460035.

[27] O. Banos, J.-M. Galvez, M. Damas, H. Pomares, and I. Rojas, "Window Size Impact in Human Activity

Recognition," *Sensors*, vol. 14, no. 4, pp. 6474–6499, Apr. 2014, doi: 10.3390/s140406474.
[28] Mathworks., "Deep Learning Toolbox Documentation." https://es.mathworks.com/help/deeplearning/index.html (accessed Feb. 21, 2023).
[29] J. Cherian, V. Rajanna, D. Goldberg, and T. Hammond, "Did you Remember to Brush?: A Noninvasive Wearable Approach to Recognizing Brushing Teeth for Elderly Care," doi: 10.1145/3154862.
[30] S. Akther, N. Saleheen, S. A. Samiei, V. Shetty, E. Ertin, and S. Kumar, "mORAL: An mHealth Model for Inferring Oral Hygiene Behaviors in-the-wild Using Wrist-worn Inertial Sensors," *Proc. ACM Interactive, Mobile, Wearable Ubiquitous Technol.*, vol. 3, no. 1, pp. 1–25, Mar. 2019, doi: 10.1145/3314388.

# Sentiment Analysis of Public Opinion in Social Media Using SVM

Jing Liu*, Yanmeng Xu, Nadarajah Manivannan, Federico Colecchia

*Brunel Design School, Brunel University London, Kingston Lane, UB8 3PH, Uxbridge, UK*
** Jing.Liu@brunel.ac.uk*

**ABSTRACT**: The social media is a promising channel for gaining insight into public opinion with reference to events and circumstances of societal relevance. Inference of public opinion using social media data can support governments in defining appropriate policies. The COVID-19 outbreak in China was chosen as a case study, and a machine learning model was developed for predicting sentiment trends of social media posts, with a view to revealing a relationship between government actions and public opinion. Social media data relevant to COVID-19 in China have been collected and analysed using a Support Vector Machine model trained as part of this study. This article documents data collection, processing, and analysis, and suggests links between sentiment analysis outputs and government action during the COVID-19 emergency in China.

**Keywords**: Sentiment analysis, public opinion, SVM.

**Received** January 1, 2023; **In final form** March 31, 2023; **Published** June 2023



**Corresponding author:** Jing Liu, e-mail: Jing.Liu@brunel.ac.uk

## 1. INTRODUCTION

The public opinion analysis of public health emergencies can help governments to monitor the evolution of critical situations and to manage the sentiment of the general public. According to the definition of the Chinese Center for Disease Control and Prevention, public health emergencies refer to outbreaks of infectious diseases that could severely endanger public health [1]. The public opinion can help administration departments adjust response measures and policies timely to address emergencies. Appropriate public opinion analysis can increase transparency of the government's work and improve public confidence in the measures implemented.

The social media is a promising channel for collection of data about public opinion. In the past three years, the COVID-19 pandemic, declared a Public Health Emergency of International Concern (PHEIC) in 2020, damaged life, security, and property worldwide. In facing this event, some departments of the Chinese government used social media platforms such as Sina Weibo (a social media platform like Twitter), Chinese TikTok, and Xiaohongshu (a social media platform akin to Instagram) to collect opinions from the general public and to plan responses. For example, government publicity departments in Chinese cities published Against Epidemic Help Platforms through social media [2], which enabled citizens to submit questions and requests about the COVID-19 emergency to government authorities. For example, when citizens encounter problems of the COVID-19, they can submitt their requirements to the officials through these platforms in the social media. Social media therefore played an important role in China throughout the COVID-19 pandemic.

Sina Weibo was used for data collection in the context of this study with reference to the COVID-19 public health emergency. A Support Vector Machine (SVM) model was used for analysing sentiment in Weibo data relevant to COVID-19. First, posts relevant to the target topic were collected from Sina Weibo. The second step was to train a SVM model to predict the sentiment trends using the collected posts. The final step was to use the trained model for detecting public opinion trends in the posts based on sentiment analysis.

## 2. RELATED WORK

The traditional method for public opinion analysis is survey polls. For example, using qualitative and quantitative methods of analysing questionnaires with reference to events of societal relevance can support the detection of trends in public opinion [3]. However, this method also has drawbacks, as questionnaires often reflect opinions of a limited group of participants in the research [4-5], and the limited size of the dataset collected can reduce the value of the research findings. Existing digital technology has enabled efficient ways of collecting data from broader audiences. This has resulted in larger datasets, reduced data collection costs, and increased productivity [6].

The adoption of large-scale digital methods such as those based on analysis of social media data has streamlined the process of analysing larger public opinion datasets. Scholars can use machine learning for analysing people's views, and sentiment analysis of public opinion is an area of active research.

Researchers have been improving the accuracy of sentiment classification based on text data. The N- ram method can build a sentiment classification model by extracting features from the Chinese reviews of newspaper and internet [7]. Kalaivani et al. compared SVM, Bayes classifiers, and k-NN models for sentiment analysis of movie reviews, and it was found that SVM can achieve 80% accuracy [8]. Alsaffar et al. compared three supervised machine learning algorithms for Malay language sentiment classification. SVM achieves the highest accuracy of 87% [9]. Sentiment analysis has also been used on public opinion data. Li et al. used the Bayes algorithm to detect sentiment of social media posts relevant to typhoon disasters [10]. Liu et al. analysed public opinion from Sina Weibo data using SVM, Bayes classifiers, and Random Forest [11]. Based on the above studies, SVM has shown good performance in term of sentiment prediction accuracy. For this reason, SVM has been selected in this study for classifying sentiment of social media posts reflecting public opinions about the COVID-19 outbreak in China.

The correlation between the outcome of the public opinion analysis and the government decision-making and corresponding actions have been considered in the context of this study, , which has not been previously done by other researchers. Although there are some studies about the analysis of public opinion using SVM models or other algorithms, few of them have focused on the relationship between government actions and public opinion during a public health emergency. Nonetheless, studying the above relationship is important as it can generate insights to inform future response strategies of government authorities.

## 3. SUPPORT VECTOR MACHINE

Support Vector Machine (SVM) is a supervised machine learning algorithm often used for classifying text sentiment polarity [12]. Figure 1 provides a schematic representation of how SVM works. In the figure, H represents the optimal hyperplane separating data points corresponding to two different classes. The square dots below H1 and the round dots below H2 are the 'support vectors' [13].

The principles of operation are as follows. If the two classes are linearly separable, the model will find an optimal hyperplane separating the two classes. If the two classes are not linearly separable, the model will first use a kernel function to convert all samples to the linear case, after which the optimal separating hyperplane will be identified. [14].

## 4. EXPERIMENT AND ANALYSIS

This study relied on SVM for predicting the sentiment trends from Sina Weibo posts. Based on sentiment analysis of the posts, meaningful relationships were identified between government actions and public opinion trends during the COVID-19 outbreak in China.

### 4.1. Experiment process

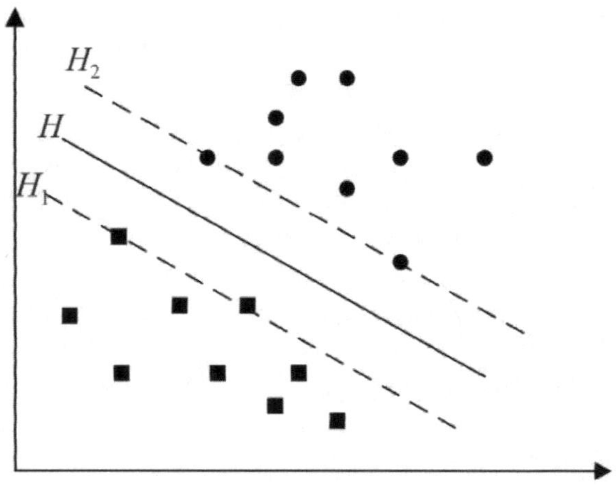


Figure 1 S chematic graph of Support Vector

Machine [13]

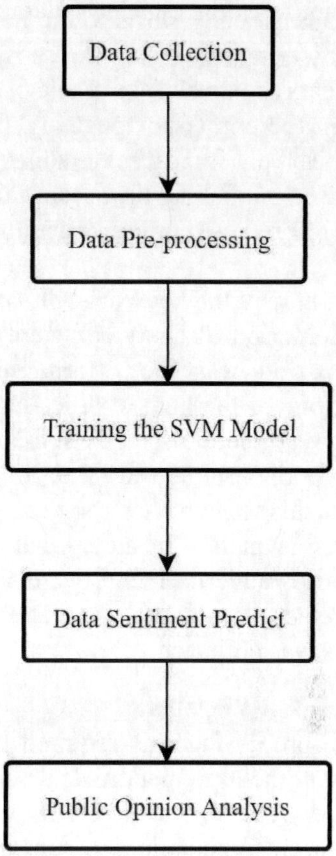


Figure 2. Flowchart of the experiment process.

Figure 2 shows the flowchart of the experiment process. A public online dataset containing 100,000 Weibo posts was downloaded for training the SVM model. After that, the trained SVM model was used for predicting sentiment trends from a separate smaller sample of Weibo posts, collected using a Python script developed for this purpose ('test sample'). This program was developed to crawl the Sina Weibo platform.

Regarding collection of the test sample, existing data collection tool were considered not appropriate due to issues of missing data and related artifacts. For example, some online tools only collected part of the data over a one-day period. The second step was data pre-processing. The SVM model was subsequently trained on the larger Weibo dataset including sentiment analysis labels, and the model was finally used for predicting sentiment on the training dataset. Model training is discussed in Section 4.4. The final step was to analyse the public opinion according to the SVM model output. The relationship between actions by the government and sentiment trends in public opinion was then explored, and meaningful relationships were highlighted.

### 4.2. Data collection

A Python script specifically developed for this study was employed for collecting Sina Weibo posts under the topic of "Shenzhen Covid-19" corresponding to the period 14th March 2022 to 20th March 2022. A total of 7,964 posts was collected. The tool for coding this program is Pycharm (2022.3.1 Community Edition), and the imported libraries and modules are listed in the Appendix. The principle of this program is setting a cyclic function to crawl the corresponding data under the keyword "Shenzhen Covid-19" corresponding to one week from 14th March 2022 to 20th March 2022. To avoid the limitation of Sina Weibo web page crawling, this program also set the time interval of crawling to one hour. For example, the program crawls the data for one hour of the day first and sequentially crawls the data during the next hour of the same day. When data from one web page has been collected, the program automatically shifts to the next page and continuously crawls data. A sample of the collected data is shown in Table 1. It can be clearly seen the content of posts by Weibo users, the number of repost/review/like, and the corresponding publishing time from this table. The trained SVM predicted the sentiment trends of this data set.

Table 1. Sample of the collection data.

| Name | Time | Repost/Review/Like | Posts |
|---|---|---|---|
| A | 2022.3.14 00:56 | 0/0/0 | Shenzhen cheer up! #Shenzhen, Covid-19# |
| B | 2022.3.15 03:27 | 0/1/12 | #Shenzhen Covid-19# I'm confident with Shenzhen, but I really don't wanna NAT test. |
| C | 2022.3.18 18:06 | 15/5/30 | #Shenzhen Covid-19# A super city just stopped because of Covid, but I trust the government and medical treatment… |

The reason why the keyword "Shenzhen Covid-19" and the period of one week were chosen was that this period was the official lockdown of Shenzhen (one of the biggest cities in China), and the local government also took some measures to respond to public opinion in time. In addition, the posts under this topic have strong regionalism and pertinence, which means that irrelevant information or advertisements were few, thus the data collected were more accurate. A total of 7,964 posts was collected.

### 4.3. Data pre-processing

Data pre-processing was required before using SVM for sentiment prediction. The purpose of this stage of the work was to delete useless data and perform word segmentation. A Jupyter Notebook (6.4.12) was developed for this purpose. The imported libraries and modules are listed in the Appendix. Firstly, the collected 7,964 posts were imported to the Jupyter Notebook. Secondly, empty and duplicate data were removed through the drop function in the Pandas library. Subsequently, emojis and other symbols were removed by defining a function in the Jupyter Notebook, because the SVM model was not trained to use non-literal symbols for prediction. Subsequently, information about geographic location in the posts was removed. Inclusion of information about geographic location is encouraged when posts are published in Sina Weibo. However, when the Python script was used for collecting Weibo posts, the location information resulted in spurious characters. For example, if a Weibo user published a post with "Shenzhen" as his/her location, the location information would be shown in the collected data set as "2&%Shenzhen". Following pre-processig, the Jieba Python library (0.42.1) (a Chinese text segmentation library) was used on the text of the posts. A 'stop word' list developed by Harbin Institute of Technology [15] was used to remove stop words. As a result, the remaining posts were reduced to 7,673 in total following pre-processing.

### 4.4. Training process of SVM model

The SVM classifier is a reasonable choice for binary classification. According to related research discussed in Section 2, SVM classification accuracy is on a par with (and sometimes better than) other algorithms like Bayes classifiers and k-NN. Furthermore, sentiment classification for this study was a binary classification task with reference to 'positive' and 'negative' sentiment.

Figure 3 shows the flowchart of the training process for the SVM model.

#### 4.4.1. Choosing Sina Weibo posts

This research used 100,000 unlabeled raw Sina Weibo posts [16] related to COVID-19 topics in China as the data for training the SVM model. Then, a sentiment lexicon was used to label these posts. The 100,000 posts come from an open online data set of Chinese Software Developer Network (CSDN, an open community for developers to learn, share, and collaborate) [17]. This data set was uploaded by an anonymous user with over 1,000 views and obtained a high-quality score evaluated by CSDN. Therefore, this data set was chosen and downloaded directly from the community to train the SVM model. The SVM did not use the 7,673 data of Section 4.3 to train but rather to predict the sentiment trends of this smaller data set. Moreover, the characteristics of the 100,000 dataset are similar to the 7,673 dataset, because they are both Sina Weibo unlabeled raw posts and the 100,000 data was published in October 2021, close to the collected period of the 7,673 data.

After downloading the 100,000 data set, the Jupyter Notebook was used to process the posts.

#### 4.4.2. Text pre-processing

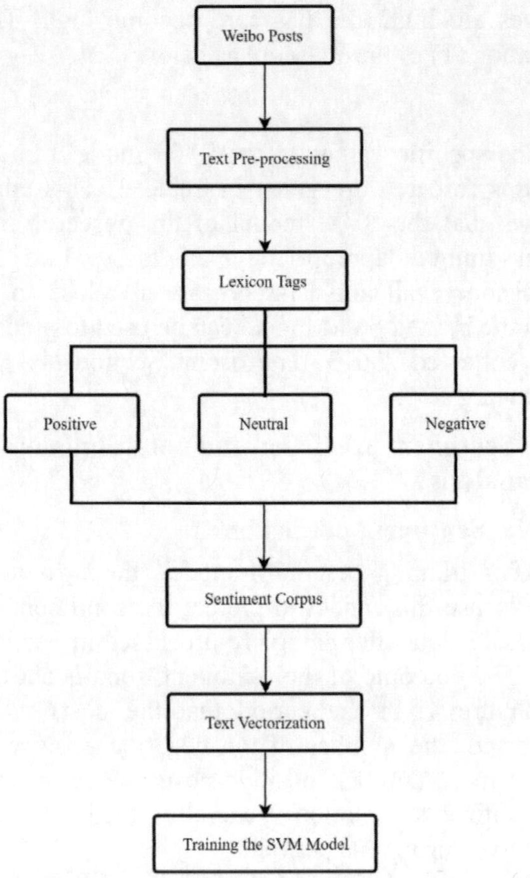


Figure 3. Flowchart of training the SVM model.

The pre-processing work of 100,000 data was similar to the one described in the Section 4.3. According to the characteristics of these data, this research initially chose to remove some meaningless posts which contain "Weibo Questions and Answers". Because the contents of these posts were folded into a link on the Weibo web page, the Python program cannot grasp these contents directly. Some posts of this data set contained reposted information from other users, which affected the recognition of the original meaning of the posts, therefore, these reposted contents have been deleted in the followed processed step. Information about geographic location, spurious symbols, and URLs were also dropped. After that, the Jieba library and the stop word list from Harbin Institute of Technology were used in the same way as described in Section 4.3.

#### 4.4.3. Lexicon tags text

The National Taiwan University Semantic Dictionary (NTUSD lexicon) developed by the researchers from Taiwan University [18] was used to tag the processed data from Section 4.4.2. The NTUSD lexicon was used for comparing every post's content in the data set. The positive and negative words of every post's text were calculated the specific quantity. If the number of positive words was more than the number of negative words in a sentence, the sentiment was defined as 'positive', otherwise as 'negative'. Every post was labelled with corresponding sentiment information using the lexicon, and a sentiment corpus was therefore generated.

The whole labelled process was carried out in the Jupyter Notebook. First, a function was defined to load the NTUSD sentiment lexicon. Next, another function was defined to calculate the word frequency of positive and negative parts in every post's text. Then, the difference between the number of positive and negative words in each post was calculated and estimated the sentimental trend. The final step was to label each post.

#### 4.4.4. Building sentiment corpus

This section explains the generation of the sentiment corpus. After the sentiment trend of every post has been evaluated, this research summarised a sentiment corpus for training the SVM model. The criterion for building this corpus is that the sentence must have apparent sentiment trend. When the difference between the number of positive and negative words in a sentence was three or greater, this sentence was defined to have an evidence of emotional sentiment trend which can be selected as a part of the corpus. In this corpus, the positive and negative posts were labelled separately.

This corpus was vectorized as explained in the next section, and the vectorized data of the corpus was utilized to train the SVM model.

#### 4.4.5. Text vectorization

The next step in the SVM model training process was that the Word2Vec model (an implementation of word embedding) was applied to convert the sentiment corpus into a vector form [19]. The vectorized process was also completed in the Jupyter Notebook, and the import library and modules listed in the appendix. Gholamy et al. think the best outcome can be obtained if the experiment use 70%~80% of the data for training and remain 20%~30% of the data for testing [20]. Therefore, the corpus of the experiment in this research has been randomly split into the training set of 80% and the testing set of 20% by the Sklearn library. The features of the corpus's posts were selected to build the SVM classifier. The Gensim library (an open-source Python library for representing documents as semantic vectors) was used to train the word2vec model and calculate the word embedding. Next, the word embedding of every sentence in the corpus was calculated. Therefore, the whole sentiment corpus could be vectorized.

#### 4.4.6. SVM model training

The final step was training the SVM model in the Jupyter Notebook. The precision value, recall value and F1-score of this SVM have been calculated by the testing data set, which was 20% from the corpus, to evaluate the model.

The precision value, recall value and F1-score are references to evaluate the SVM model [21].The precision value is called positive predictive value. In a classifier, when the precision value is close to 1, it represents this classifier to be ideal. The recall value is known as sensitivity or true positive rate, and if the recall value is close to 1, it also reflects this classifier is good. Therefore, for an ideal classifier, both the precision and the recall values need to be close to 1 [21]. The F1-score is another metric that considers these two values in the meantime. Only when these two values are high, the F1-score become high. The equation (1) of the F1-score as below [22]:

(1)

The specific values of the SVM model trained by this research are given in Table 2. This table shows that the SVM model of this research has been trained appropriately as the values of precision recall and F1-score are all close to 1, thus the trained SVM model can be used to predict the collected 7,673 data from Section 4.3 in following step.

Table 2. Precision Recall and F1-Score

| | Precision | Recall | F1-Score |
|---|---|---|---|
| **0.0 (Negative)** | 0.90 | 0.93 | 0.91 |
| **1.0 (Positive)** | 0.94 | 0.92 | 0.93 |

### 4.5. Sentiment prediction and public opinion analysis

#### 4.5.1. Sentiment prediction

After training the SVM model, the next step was to use this model to predict the sentiment of the 7,673 data after being pre-processed in Section 4.3. The outcome of the sentiment trend is shown in Figure 4. In the period that the posts were collected, the number of the negative posts was much more than the positive posts, which means the citizen's emotion generally tends to be negative during this period.

Because the total number of posts is different on different days, the proportion of negative and positive posts can show sentiment changes over time The comparison of the variation of the positive and negative posts is shown in Figure 5.

The results show that negative sentiment declined over time and positive sentiment grew since the beginning of the COVID-19 pandemic, which suggests a change in people's perception of the emergency.

#### 4.5.2. Analysis and discussion

The reason that caused the variation of sentiment can be found from the public opinion. The 14th and 15th of March have the most amount of negative sentiment posts which are mainly focused on the lockdown policy and the problem

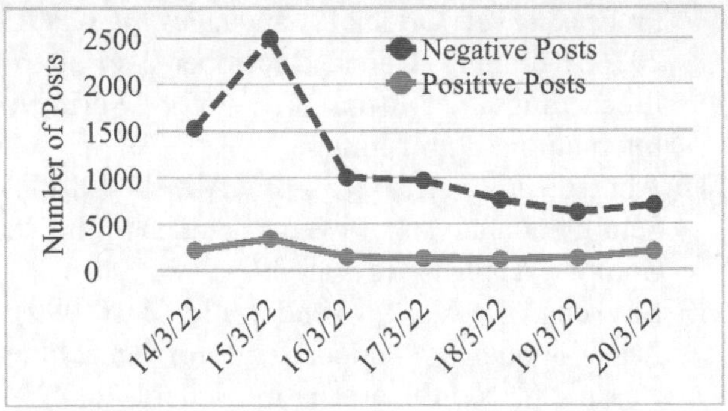


Figure 4. The sentiment variation of collected data.

of nucleic acid testing (NAT). The total number of the posts containing the negative sentiment is always at a higher level from the whole period of 14th to 20th of March compared with posts containing the positive sentiment, however, it can be seen from the comparison results shown in

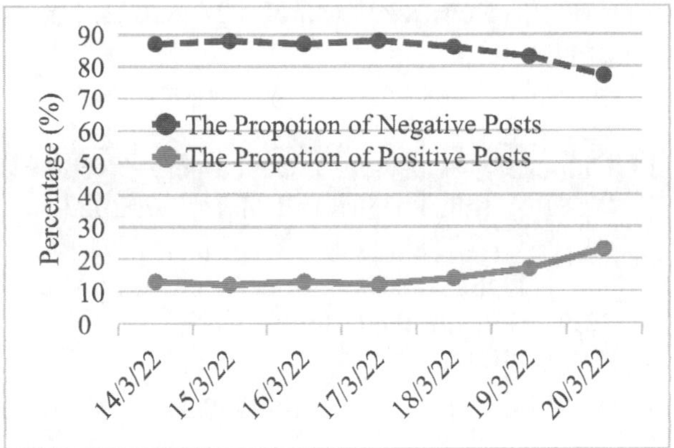


Figure 5. The proportion variation of negative posts.

Figure 5 that the proportion of the negative posts started to decline since the 17th of March whereas the proportion of the positive posts started to increase. This decrease can be associated with response measures put in place by government authorities. For example, food supplies were provided and molecular COVID tests were deployed at community level. The analysis suggests that the implementation of these measures was generally met with approval from the general public, as reflected in Weibo post sentiment. After 17th March, public sentiment estimated using Weibo posts improved. This could be a result of the implementation of the above-mentioned measures, as well as of material support from other cities in China, like the food donation, and subsidy from the local government.

The results highlight the relationship between public sentiment, as reflected in Weibo posts, and the response by the government. The results also suggest that, even when public opinion sentiment is negative, appropriate action by government authorities can at least partially restore positive public sentiment. For example, at the beginning of the COVID-19 pandemic, public sentiment in China, as detected using Weibo posts, was negative, but the trend improved following the implementation of government measures. The SVM model developed for this study showed good performance in detecting sentiment from Weibo posts relevant to the COVID-19 pandemic. The promising results presented in this article have the potential to inform future work on how detection of public sentiment using social media content can support the definition of government strategies in response to public health emergencies.

## 5. CONCLUSION

For this study, established machine learning techniques, combined with sentiment analysis, were used on social media data in order to highlight the relationship between government responses to the COVID-19 outbreak in China and public sentiment as reflected in social media posts.

The results suggest that government actions and policies in response to public health emergencies can influence public sentiment, and that application of machine learning techniques, combined with sentiment analysis, on social media data can provide guidance to government authorities in setting out strategies for dealing with future emergencies.

## REFERENCES

[1] Emergencies. (n.d.). Retrieved March 27, 2023, from Chinese Center for Disease Control and Prevention: https://en.chinacdc.cn/health_topics/emergencies/

[2] Meishan Against Epidemic Help Platforms. (2023). Retrieved March 27, 2023, from Sina

Weibo: https://weibo.com/1990198375/MmKLk4wt1?refer_flag=1001030103_%E3%80%81

[3] McGregor, S. C. (2019). Social media as public opinion: How journalists use social media to represent public opinion. Journalism, 20(8), 1070-1086.

[4] Fishkin, J. S. (2006). Beyond polling alone: the quest for an informed public. Critical Review, 18(1-3), 157-165.

[5] Murphy, J., Link, M. W., Childs, J. H., Tesfaye, C. L., Dean, E., Stern, M., ... & Harwood, P. (2014). Social media in public opinion research: Executive summary of the AAPOR task force on emerging technologies in public opinion research. Public Opinion Quarterly, 78(4), 788-794.

[6] Shaeer, O., & Shaeer, K. (2016). 06 Female Genital Cutting: Prevalence and public opinion among internet users in the Middle East. The Journal of Sexual Medicine, 13(6), S265.

[7] Yang, J., Hou, M., & Wang, N. (2010, August). Recognizing sentiment polarity in Chinese reviews based on topic sentiment sentences. In Proceedings of the 6th International Conference on Natural Language Processing and Knowledge Engineering (NLPKE-2010) (pp. 1-6). IEEE.

[8] Kalaivani, P., & Shunmuganathan, K. L. (2013). Sentiment classification of movie reviews by supervised machine learning approaches. Indian Journal of Computer Science and Engineering, 4(4), 285-292.

[9] Alsaffar, A., & Omar, N. (2014, November). Study on feature selection and machine learning algorithms for Malay sentiment classification. In Proceedings of the 6th International Conference on Information Technology and Multimedia (pp. 270-275). IEEE.

[10] Shaopan, L. I., Fei, Z. H. A. O., Yiqi, Z. H. O. U., Xiangliang, T. I. A. N., & Hong, H. U. A. N. G. (2022). Analysis of public opinion and disaster loss estimates from typhoons based on Microblog data. Journal of Tsinghua University (Science and Technology), 62(1), 43-51.

[11] Liu, L., Feng, S., Wang, D., & Zhang, Y. (2016). An empirical study on Chinese microblog stance detection using supervised and semi-supervised machine learning methods. In Natural Language Understanding and Intelligent Applications: 5th CCF Conference on Natural Language Processing and Chinese Computing, NLPCC 2016, and 24th International Conference on Computer Processing of Oriental Languages, ICCPOL 2016, Kunming, China, December 2–6, 2016, Proceedings 24 (pp. 753-765). Springer International Publishing.

[12] Ahmad, M., Aftab, S., & Ali, I. (2017). Sentiment analysis of tweets using svm. Int. J. Comput. Appl, 177(5), 25-29.

[13] Suykens, J. A., & Vandewalle, J. (1999). Least squares support vector machine classifiers. Neural processing letters, 9, 293-300.

[14] Wentao, W., & Shibao, Z. (2021). Emotion Analysis of Micro-blog Netizens Based on Emotion Dictionary and SVM. Modern Information Technology, (24),24-27+31.

[15] The Stop Word List of Harbin Institute of Technology. (n.d.). Retrieved March 27, 2023, from the Github: https://github.com/goto456/stopwords

[16] Sina Weibo COVID-19 related posts set. (2021). Retrieved March 27, 2023, from CSDN: https://download.csdn.net/download/sanpi329/28732302

[17] Chinese Software Developer Network (CSDN). (n.d.). Retrieved March 27, 2023: https://www.csdn.net/

[18] The NTUSD Lexicon. (n.d.). Retrieved March 27, 2023, from the Github: https://github.com/Shimon-Guo/chinese_sentiment_dictionary

[19] Wallach, H. M. (2006, June). Topic modeling: beyond bag-of-words. In Proceedings of the 23rd international conference on Machine learning (pp. 977-984).

[20] Gholamy, A., Kreinovich, V., & Kosheleva, O. (2018). Why 70/30 or 80/20 relation between training and testing sets: A pedagogical explanation.

[21] Guia, M., Silva, R. R., & Bernardino, J. (2019). Comparison of Naïve Bayes, Support Vector Machine, Decision Trees and Random Forest on Sentiment Analysis. KDIR, 1, 525-531.

[22] Powers, D. M. (2020). Evaluation: from precision, recall and F-measure to ROC, informedness, markedness and correlation. arXiv preprint arXiv:2010.16061.

## APPENDIX

**The libraries and modules of Python program of data collection**

1. The Requests library: 2.28.1
2. The Beautifulsoup4 library: 4.11.1
3. The Pandas library: 1.5.2
4. The OS module

**The libraries and modules of the Jupyter Notebook**

1. The Jieba library: 0.42.1
2. The Pandas library: 1.5.2
3. The Numpy library: 1.23.4
4. The Gensim library: 4.3.0
5. The Sklearn library: 0.0.post1
6. The PyNLPIR library: 0.6.0
7. The Json library: 0.9.6
8. The OS module
9. The Codecs module

# A 3D modelling pipeline based on fringe projection profilometry

Tao Zhang[1], Qingping Yang[1]

[1]*College of Engineering, Design and Physical Sciences, Brunel University London, Uxbridge, Middlesex, UK*

**Abstract:** This paper aims to implement a 3D modelling pipeline using fringe projection profilometry (FPP). A high-precision 3D scanner based on phase-shifting fringe projection profilometry is built with a camera and a projector. After calibrating the intrinsic parameters, distortion coefficients and relative pose between the camera and the projector, the surface within the field of view can be measured by triangulating the deformed fringe images. After calibrating the relative location and orientation between the 3D scanner and a turntable, partial point clouds are captured and then registered into a complete point cloud. The object's surface can then be reconstructed from the point cloud. Finally, the reconstructed surface is post-processed to generate a watertight surface and to simplify the representation. The paper presents some preliminary results, including the calibration results, and measurement results of several samples using the 3D scanner. Quantitative analysis shows the 3D scanner can achieve a precision of tens of micrometres. The proposed method and system have wide applications in various industries.

**Keywords**: Fringe projection profilometry, camera calibration, triangulation.

**Received** January 1, 2023; **In final form** March 31, 2023; **Published** June 2023



Corresponding author: tao.zhang@brunel.ac.uk

## 1. INTRODUCTION

Three-dimensional modelling is increasingly important in many sectors, such as 3D graphics [1], advanced manufacturing [2], robotics [3], among many others. Compared with the traditional contacting methods such as coordinate measuring machine (CMM) which measures by scanning with a contact probe in a point-by-point fashion [4], optical methods have the advantages of being noncontact and nondestructive, and typically features fast measurements [5]. Interferometry, time of flight (ToF) range imaging, stereo vision, and structured light systems are representatives of optical technologies. Interferometry extracts information from the interference of superimposed waves and features high accuracy up to subnanometre level, but can only measure specular surfaces and requires rigorous alignment owing to the numerical aperture issue [5-7]. ToF range imager can simultaneously capture depth and intensity information. It works by emitting a light pulse, and then obtains the depth information using the round-trip time of flight of the light pulse. Albeit moderate accuracy, ToF range imagers find widespread applications in self-driving vehicles and mobile robots owing to the fast measurement and cost effectiveness [5]. The working principle of stereo vision and structured light are similar, both make use of the multiple-view geometry. A stereo vision system comprises two identical cameras, and recovers the height information via the disparity of two different views of a scene captured by the two cameras. The disparity is derived by solving the correspondence problem. However, stereo vision is limited to scenes with salient features, the measurement result is typically sparse and the accuracy is not very good. A structured light system has a similar setup compared to a stereo vision system; the difference is that a structured light system replaces one of the cameras with a projector and simplifies the correspondence problem by actively projecting images with abundant features (such as fringes). The structured light system features high accuracy, high robustness and dense measurement [5]. It is widely used in various industries, attracting extensive research.

## 2. PRINCIPLE OF FRINGE PROJECTION PROFILOMETRY

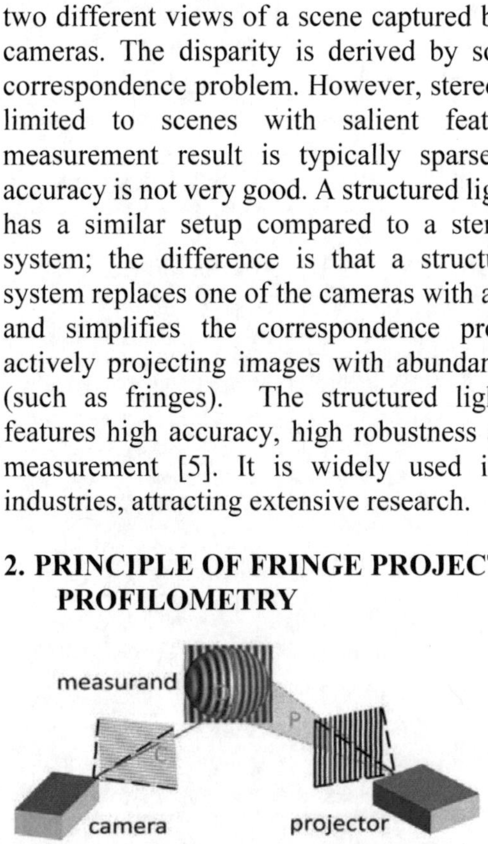


Figure 1. Schematic diagram of FPP.

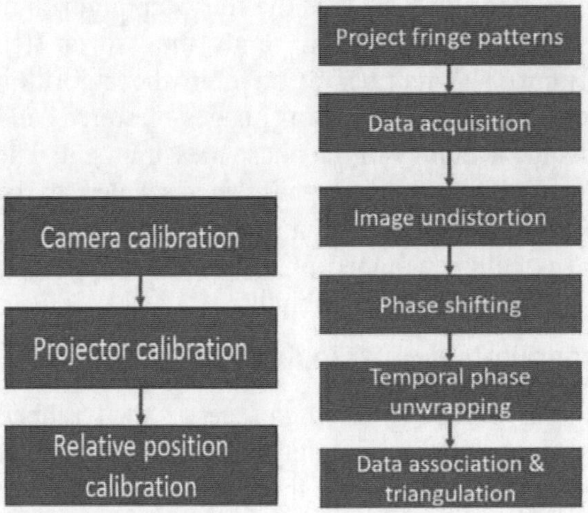


(a) (b)

Figure 2. Working process of FPP. (a). calibration, (b). measurement.

As shown in Figure 1, FPP typically comprises a camera and a projector. The projector projects fringe patterns to the measurand, which is captured by the camera. After the camera and the projector are calibrated, a pixel C in the camera can be unprojected to a ray CO from the centre of projection, and the corresponding fringe in the projector can be unprojected to a plane P, covering the centre of projection, using the intrinsic parameters respectively. The surface point O can be located by calculating the intersection of the ray and the plane, if the locations and orientations of the camera and projector are known. Iterating this process for each and every pixel, the whole surface topography can be obtained. As shown in Figure 2, this section is split into two parts, namely calibration and measurement. The first part includes the calibration of the camera and projector, as well as their relative pose. The latter discusses the measurement process, including data association between the camera and the projector, and the triangulation. The accuracy of the calibration significantly affects the quality of reconstruction. One common solution to the data association problem for FPP is phase-shifting and temporal phase unwrapping, which has higher precision compared to binary/Gray-coded patterns. Triangulation for FPP is to solve the intersection of a ray and a plane to accurately locate the measured surface point of the measurand.

## 2.1. Calibration of FPP

FPP calibration entails calibration of the camera, the projector and their relative pose.

### Camera calibration

This paper uses the Caltech calibration toolbox [8] which was based on Zhang's method [9]. During the calibration, only a planar chessboard was used. After capturing images of the calibration board at several arbitrary poses, homography matrices could be calculated. Decomposing the homography matrices leads to an initial estimation of the intrinsic parameters and poses of the camera. With a bundle adjustment to minimise the reprojection error, camera intrinsic parameters, distortion coefficients and poses of the camera can be refined. Distortion coefficients are later used to undistort the images to reduce the measurement error.

### Projector calibration

The principle of projector calibration is the same as camera calibration, the main difficulty lies in the acquisition of the corresponding pixels in the projector image plane and the feature points in the scene. After that, the calibration process is the same as camera calibration, namely to obtain an initial estimation and then minimise the reprojection error via a bundle adjustment.

Projector calibration is done with the help of a calibrated camera. The projector projects, both vertically and horizontally, fringe patterns to a planar chessboard at several different poses, while the camera captures the images of the calibration board [10]. Centres of the white squares could be used to find out the corresponding pixels and feature points in the scene. Camera image can be used to locate the pixel, and then the corresponding pixel in the projector can be calculated using phase shifting and temporal phase unwrapping algorithm, which will be discussed later in the paper. Coordinates of the feature points in the scene can be easily obtained because the size of the chessboard is known. After extracting the corresponding feature points at several poses, the projector can be calibrated to work out the intrinsic parameters, distortion coefficients and the projector poses. Distortion coefficients can later be used to undistort the projected fringe patterns to reduce the measurement error.

### Calibration of the relative pose

The relative pose of the camera and projector can be obtained simply by viewing at the same scene. However, it is vulnerable to noise. For example, after calibrating the projector, each pose of the calibration board can be calculated in both the camera and projector frame, which can be used to calculate the relative pose of the camera and the projector. However, inconsistency up to ~3 mm exists in these results due to the random noise. One way to aggregate the information is to "take average". Translation can be averaged, however, rotation matrices are converted to quaternions first, and then use the inverse to find out the least squares solution [11].

## 2.2. Measurement process of FPP

During the measurement, FPP uses phase shifting and temporal phase unwrapping algorithm to work out the data association. After that, triangulation can be done to generate a dense point cloud.

### Undistortion for the FPP

Effectiveness of undistortion varies with the apparatus adopted. For example, if a fisheye lens with serious distortion is used, undistortion can significantly improve measurement accuracy.

After the calibration, distortion coefficients of both the camera and the projector are known, so the fringe images can be undistorted. The undistortion process is slightly different for the camera and the projector.

For the camera, undistortion is done after capturing the images using the distortion coefficients, including both the radial and tangential coefficients, which requires computing resources. For the projector, the projected fringe patterns are known before the measurement. The fringe patterns to be projected can be pre-undistorted. So the undistortion does not need any extra computing resources.

### Phase shifting

Phase shifting is the process to recover the phase of pixels via a series of intensity images that are projected with different phase shift $\varphi$.

$$I(x, y) = A + B\cos(2\pi fx + \varphi) \quad (1)$$

The series of images are then processed using phase shifting algorithm to calculate the phase at each pixel corresponding to a point on the object's surface. The phase shifting algorithm uses the intensity of the pixel in each image to calculate the phase [7]. There are several variations of the phase-shifting algorithm, such as the four-step algorithm, the five-step algorithm, and the seven-step algorithm. The number of steps in the algorithm determines the number of images required and affects the accuracy of the phase measurement. The range of the calculated phase is restricted to be within the interval of $[-\pi, \pi)$ with ambiguity, so the signal is called wrapped phase and unwrapping is required to resolve the ambiguity.

### Temporal phase unwrapping

Temporal phase unwrapping processes the wrapped phase to resolve the ambiguity [12], so that the result can unambiguously locate the fringe line to achieve the data association, as shown in Figure 1. For example, the fringes described in Equation (1) is perpendicular to x-axis, the unwrapped phase should be linearly related to x-coordinate. Then the unwrapped phase can be unambiguously mapped back to its x-coordinate for the data association.

### Triangulation

After the data association is achieved, triangulation can be done to work out the measured surface points of the measurand. A minor difference exists between the triangulation of stereo vision and FPP, stereo vision solves the intersection of two rays (or the closest point to the two rays if they do not intersect) [13], but FPP solves the intersection of a ray and a plane. This process is repeated for each pixel of interest in the images.

After phase unwrapping, a pixel in the camera image is associated with a line in the projector image plane. The pixel in the image can be unprojected to a ray originating from the camera centre of projection, and the line in the projector image plane can be unprojected to a plane passing through the projector centre of projection. Because the relative location and orientation between the camera and the projector are known, the intersection of the ray and the plane can be solved by solving a system of linear equations.

The accuracy of the triangulation depends on several factors, including the accuracy of the data association, the accuracy of the calibration including the camera, the projector and the relative pose. For example, the phase-shifting algorithm has higher accuracy than binary/Gray-coded fringe patterns, so phase-shifting FPP typically has higher accuracy than FPP using binary/Gray-coded fringe patterns.

## 3. PRELIMINARY EXPERIMETAL RESULT

The FPP apparatus has been set up. The projector is a Texas Instruments micromirror device (model: DLP4500, resolution: 912 x 1140), the camera is a SVS-Vistek industrial camera (model: evo2050CFLGEA, resolution: 1200x1600). The algorithm was implemented in Matlab.

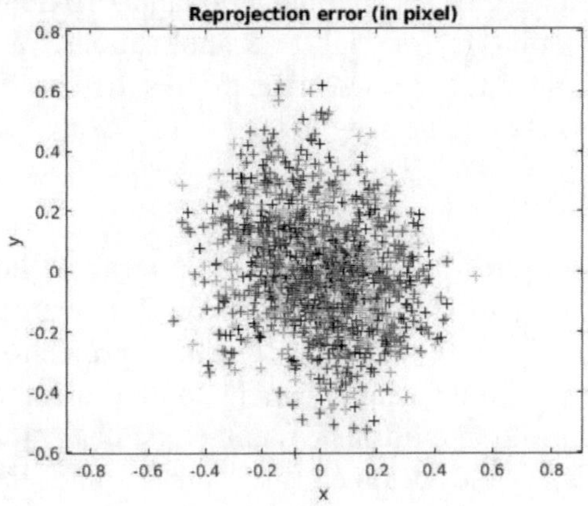


Figure 3. Calibration result of the camera, Reprojection error is 0.05303 and 0.05308 pixel in the horizontal and vertical axis respectively.

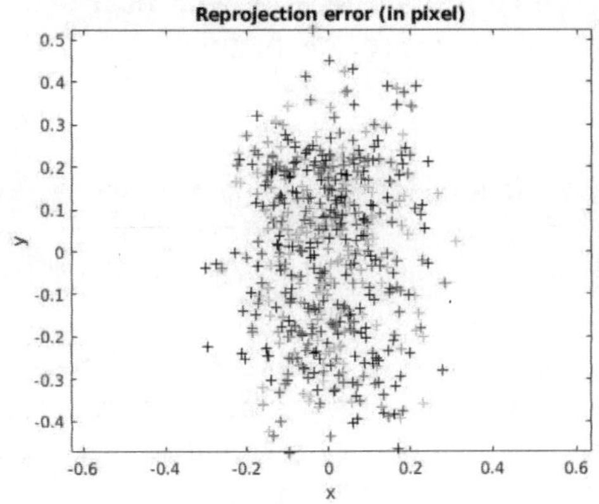


Figure 4. Calibration result of the projector. The reprojection error is 0.11155 and 0.19621 pixel in the horizontal and vertical axis respectively.

Figure 3 shows the camera calibration result, with a reprojection error of ~0.05 pixel, which is a good result.

The projector was calibrated with the help of the camera. Figure 4 shows the results. The reprojection error is 0.11155 and 0.19621 pixel in the horizontal and vertical axis respectively. The result is not as good because all the feature points were extracted from the images captured by the camera using phase-shifting and temporal phase unwrapping algorithms, and the noise would propagate and accumulate.

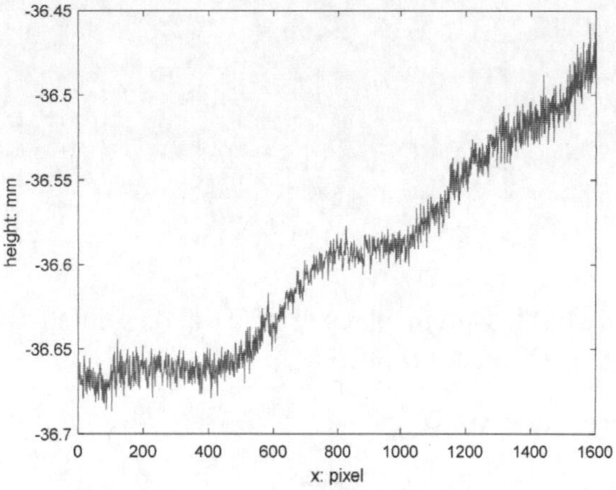


(a)

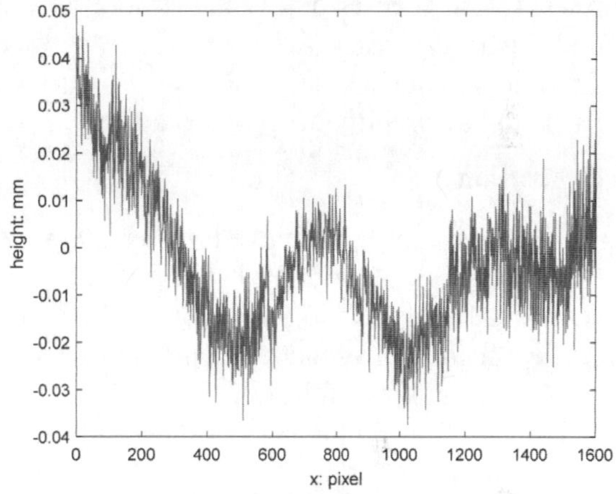


(b)

Figure 5. Measurement result of a profile of a planar board. (a). the raw data. (b). the result after form removal.

A ceramic planar calibration board has been measured, Figure 5(a) shows the raw data of one profile of the measurement result, Figure 5(b) shows the result after form removal, the standard deviation is 14.6 µm.

Some samples have been measured. A 3D printed cat and a ten euro cent coin were measured and the raw results without any post-processing are shown in Figure 6. The texture can be clearly seen.

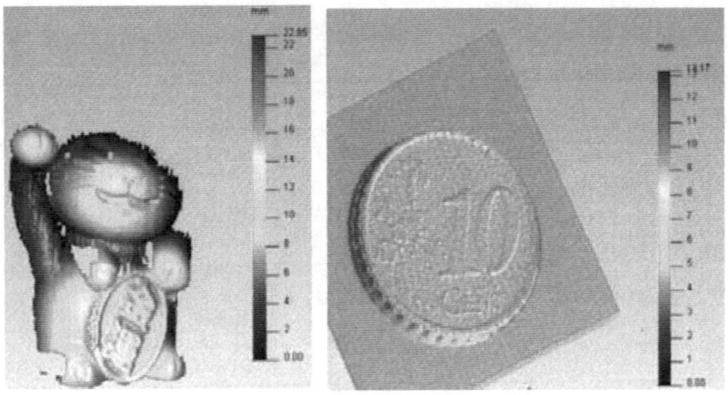

(a) (b)

Figure 6. Measurement result of (a). a 3D printed cat and (b). a ten euro cent coin.

## 4. FUTURE WORK

This paper presents some preliminary work on fringe projection profilometry and much more work continues, which focuses on 3D registration of the acquired partial point clouds and surface reconstruction such as Poisson surface reconstruction to simplify the representation.

### 3D registration

3D registration can be achieved using Iterative Closest Point (ICP) algorithm [14]. Registration is easy if the data association is known, difficulty mainly lies in the correspondence problem. Some plans have been made as follows:

1. If an accurate turntable is used, we only need to calibrate the relative pose of the camera and the turntable, and then the point clouds can be fused together.
2. For each measurement, one extra image can be taken without projecting any fringes, features can then be extracted using feature extractors such as SIFT or ORB etc., and the descriptors can be obtained to find out the associations. Bag of words and RANSAC algorithms can be used to accelerate and improve the accuracy of the matching. The association can then be achieved.
3. ICP algorithm will be explored to refine the registration.

### Surface reconstruction

In many applications such as 3D printing, watertight surface must be used. Poisson surface reconstruction algorithm is a commonly used algorithm to reconstruct the surface and fill in the holes [15]. It can provide a robust and accurate way to create 3D surface models from point cloud data. The technique is based on the Poisson equation, which relates the Laplacian of a function to its source distribution. The solution to the Poisson equation produces a continuous, smooth surface that interpolates the input points. The resulting surface is guaranteed to be watertight. Poisson surface reconstruction has several advantages over other surface reconstruction techniques. It can handle large and noisy datasets, and it produces smooth and continuous surfaces that accurately represent the input points. It is also computationally efficient, making it suitable for real-time applications. We plan to explore this area so that the results can be used in reverse engineering.

## 5. CONCLUSION

This paper aims to implement a 3D modelling pipeline using FPP. A high-precision 3D scanner based on phase-shifting fringe projection profilometry is built with a camera and a projector. After calibrating the intrinsic parameters, distortion and relative pose between the camera and the projector, the surface within the field of view can be reconstructed via triangulation. Quantitative analysis shows the FPP can achieve a precision of tens of micrometres. Future work will focus on 3D registration and surface reconstruction.

## REFERENCES

[1] Y. Ma, S. Soatto, J. Košecká, and S. Sastry. An invitation to 3-d vision: from images to geometric models (Vol. 26). New York: springer (2004).

[2] Y. Liu, L. Blunt, Z. Zhang, H. A. Rahman, F. Gao, and X. Jiang. "In-situ areal inspection of powder bed for electron beam fusion system based on fringe projection profilometry." Additive Manufacturing 31: 100940 (2020).

[3] Guanwu Jiang, Minzhou Luo, Lijuan Lu, Keqiang Bai, Omar Abdelaziz, and Saixuan Chen, "Vision solution for an assisted puncture robotics system positioning," Appl. Opt. 57, 8385-8393 (2018).

[4] R. Hocken, and P. H. Pereira, eds. "Coordinate measuring machines and systems". Vol. 6. Boca Raton, FL: CRC press (2012).

[5] S. Zhang, ed. "Handbook of 3D machine vision: Optical metrology and imaging". CRC press (2013).

[6] Tao Zhang, Feng Gao, and Xiangqian Jiang, "Surface topography acquisition method for double-sided near-right-angle structured surfaces based on dual-probe wavelength scanning interferometry," Opt. Express 25, 24148-24156 (2017).

[7] D. Malacara, M. Servin, and Z. Malacara. Interferogram analysis for optical testing. CRC press (2018).

[8] Bouguet, J.-Y. (2022). Camera Calibration Toolbox for Matlab (1.0). CaltechDATA. https://doi.org/10.22002/D1.20164

[9] Zhang, Zhengyou. "A flexible new technique for camera calibration." IEEE Transactions on pattern analysis and machine intelligence 22, no. 11 (2000): 1330-1334.

[10] Zewei Cai, Xiaoli Liu, Ameng Li, Qijian Tang, Xiang Peng, and Bruce Z. Gao, "Phase-3D mapping method developed from back-projection stereovision model for fringe projection profilometry," Opt. Express 25, 1262-1277 (2017)

[11] Hesch, Joel A., Anastasios I. Mourikis, and Stergios I. Roumeliotis. "Mirror-based extrinsic camera calibration." In Algorithmic Foundation of Robotics VIII: Selected Contributions of the Eight International Workshop on the Algorithmic Foundations of Robotics, pp. 285-299. Springer Berlin Heidelberg, 2010.

[12] C. Zuo, L. Huang, M. Zhang, Q. Chen, and A. Asundi. "Temporal phase unwrapping algorithms for fringe projection profilometry: A comparative review." Opt. and Las. in Eng. 85 (2016): 84-103.

[13] R. Hartley, and A. Zisserman. Multiple view geometry in computer vision. Cambridge university press, (2003).

[14] Besl, P. J., & McKay, N. D. (1992). A Method for Registration of 3-D Shapes. IEEE Transactions on Pattern Analysis and Machine Intelligence, 14(2), 239-256.

[15] Botsch, M., Kobbelt, L., Pauly, M., Alliez, P., & Lévy, B. (2010). Polygon mesh processing. CRC press.

# Enhancing collaboration through centralised terminology resources

Michael Chrubasik[1,*], Chris T.S. Lorch[1], João Gregório[1], Paul M. Duncan[1]
[1] *Informatics, Data Science, National Physical Laboratory, 99 George St, Glasgow G1 1RD, UK, Michael.Chrubasik@npl.co.uk*

**ABSTRACT**: Even in the connected measurement world of today, organisations, national metrology institutes (NMIs), and stakeholders from a wide range of disciplines need their own specialised language to discuss measurements, experiments, and projects. The terminology used is usually guided by pre-existing standards or industry norms, but the overlaps between these standards and the breadth and depth of applied language often create confusing and misinterpretable terminology landscapes. This makes cross-discipline and cross-industry collaboration difficult, especially when companies use their own terminology. This work presents a flat ontology that mimics a glossary to record semantic information in discipline-specific jargon. A REST API and front-end graphical user interface provide access to ontology data. This manuscript describes the requirements for creating and distributing a controlled terminology resource. From vocabulary creation to ontology disclosure via RESTful API, the development process is described. The Medicines Manufacturing Innovation Centre, a UK collaboration between academic, funding, and research institutions and industrial pharmaceutical partners, provided a case study to demonstrate the methodology to demonstrate the methodology. In this use case, communication was enabled between the collaboration partners, building a ground truth terminology resource for their collaborative and pre-competitive online platform.

**Keywords**: Ontology, REST-API, terminology, reproducibility, glossary.

**Received** January 1, 2023; **In final form** March 31, 2023; **Published** June 2023



**Corresponding author:** Michael Chrubasik, e-mail: Michael.Chrubasik@npl.co.uk.

## 1. INTRODUCTION

National Measurement Institutions (NMIs), alongside their partners and other third-party associates, cover a wide range of scientific areas. Each member within these areas applies their own specific language, terminology, and jargon in communicating concepts, which leads to difficulties in inter-industry collaboration. Although institutions and companies have internal and project specific glossaries, the collation and distribution of this information to partners is still cumbersome and inefficient.

Difficulties interlinking company-specific languages arise due to the lack of machine-operable accessibility of the relevant standards and corporations' internal lexica. For this reason, the development of machine-operable and well-established vocabularies has applications in a wide range of industrial, academic, and metrological arenas [3][4]. Without centralised terminology resources that allow for the inclusion of rich semantic information, such as synonyms or sources, translation and miscommunication become significant bottlenecks to large collaborative projects. Ensuring interoperability by removing the ambiguity associated with company-specific vocabulary can boost research output through the smooth exchange of data, reduce costs associated with labour intensive vocabulary mapping [6], and can improve product quality through the identification and pre-emptive correction of errors [5].

The National Physical Laboratory (NPL) has been exploring the use of knowledge bases for domain-agnostic measurement ontologies [**1**] as a method to capture and inform on measurement data within the organisation. These techniques have also been applied externally, with partners at the Medicines Manufacturing Innovation Centre (MMIC), by leading the construction of ontologies for use in pharmaceutical approval processes. The MMIC is a collaborative centre working across major pharmaceutical manufacturers (AstraZeneca, GSK, Pfizer) as well as academic and technological organisations (such as University of Strathclyde and the Centre for Process Innovation) to provide industry-wide innovation [7]. Whereas previously individual companies developed their own solutions, each party works in developing both company and sector-wide solutions. It therefore follows that a centralised terminology resource is essential to allow each member to participate in this collaborative process. NPL is working with the

MMIC to aid in the creation of a dashboard which would control all quality information required to approve the release of pharmaceutical products from clinical trials for human consumption. As the consequences of releasing substandard drugs are extremely severe this is a highly regulated and complex area.

The pharmaceutical industry – mirroring the measurement sciences in this respect – has a plethora of standards and vocabularies to guide the use of terminology. It is clear however, that this abundance of jargon introduces congestion in communication at the inter-organisational and scientific level. This leads to miscommunication issues and subsequent time costs.

We present a framework to record science-area-specific semantic information and idioms within a flat glossary-like ontology and make that information accessible through a Representational State Transfer (RESTful) Application Programming Interface (API), also referred to as a restAPI. The MMIC "Qualified Persons Dashboard" project, a collaborative project involving many pharmaceutical industry partners, organisations, and academic institutions, drives state-of-the-art research and collaboration in the field of digital pharmaceutical manufacturing assurance and compliance. However, as alluded to, communication and collective agreement on terms between parties has been challenging due to terminological ambiguities and harmonisation challenges.

This paper outlines the requirements to facilitate such operations: from generation of a vocabulary, via transformation of said vocabulary into a flat glossary-like ontology, to exposition of the ontology via an API. Furthermore, we present our industry-aligned use case via a dictionary web front-end that shows direct application of the ontology-based REST web service as well as the wider industrial use case. Finally, we discuss future potential applications of this methodology.

## 2. METHODS

Our methodology was based on a four-step process. Steps 1 and 2 pertain to the construction of the glossary and are graphically illustrated in Figure 1, while steps 3 and 4 define the API data link and front-end dictionary application, illustrated in Figure 3.

1. Through guided exposition by domain experts, a centralised glossary was agreed upon and established in a collaborative environment.
2. The glossary was validated by the ontology engineers and programmatically transformed into an ontology format.
3. The resulting ontology was exposed to users through a Python-based API that handles queries and delivers query results in Hypertext Transfer Protocol (HTTP) form to be consumed by any third-party service. This exposed ontology now represents a centralised and controlled vocabulary, essentially delivering terms as a service.
4. A basic web-based dictionary application allows parties to query project terms and understand how organisational terms are related to those through a user-friendly interface. Terms can also be identified as organisation-specific or as grounded in existing standards. Aligning their terminologies allows collaborators to readily navigate ambiguities and communication issues.

### 2.1. Building a glossary

Institutions and organisations operate based on established industry or discipline-specific parlance. As such, creating and maintaining controlled vocabularies is critical for effective communication, particularly when addressing disparities between companies. This becomes paramount when projects include multiple parties in cross-industry collaboration. Glossaries aid in collaborations as they not only include terms and definitions, but also

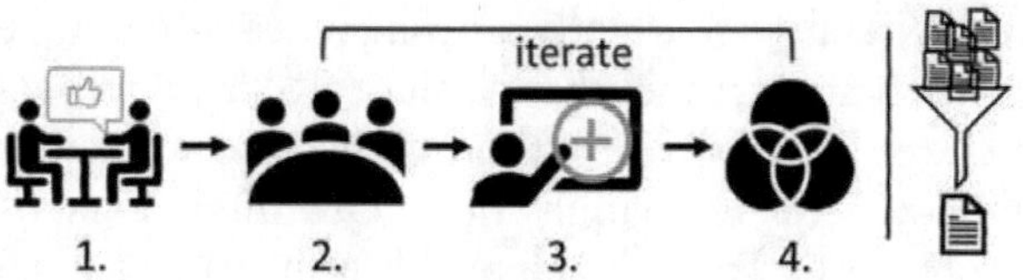


Figure 1. The glossary-building framework method: (1) All parties agree upon the necessity of a centralised vocabulary, identify central themes and nominate a committee of domain experts. (2) Terminology is decided upon by a committee of domain experts based on the central themes. (3) The core terms are approved and appended to the glossary through an iterative process. (4) End-of-iteration harmonisation is performed and additional information, e.g. synonyms and term sources, are added. Iteration terminates once a final consensus is reached.

acronyms, synonyms, term sources, etc. For larger vocabularies, additional questions of governance and stewardship arise concerning responsibilities for upkeep, change and maintenance of the glossary. At this stage a well-organised and planned approach to glossary development was required.

For the purpose of our use case with the MMIC, we followed an iterative framework of collaborative creation with our partners as demonstrated in Figure 1. It is critical not to overextend the vocabulary beyond the central themes and to filter out unnecessary additions.

There are many commercially available glossary creation tools, such as the IBM InfoSphere [11], however, due to time restrictions a basic spreadsheet-based approach was chosen, which would make transfer to an ontological format easier in future steps. Using this approach, each unique term was recorded in a row with its descriptors and metadata being described as columns. Glossary creation is a particularly lengthy process and should be initiated early on in a large-scale project. The fluid nature of vocabularies means changes are to be expected, however even early iterations of the glossary can be useful and highlight significant issues in project communication.

A glossary specification document was generated which identified 10 unique columns to describe terms for the vocabulary, as shown in Table 1.

Applying this specification document and framework allowed us to establish a routine operation for the generation of this glossary. Our early iteration currently encompasses 60 unique terms based on the pharmaceutical drug approval process, largely built on terms that all companies will adhere to within the "Qualified Persons Dashboard". Due to the breadth of pharmaceutical standards involved in this work, harmonisation of identified standards, such as "ISO 11238 (2018) Health informatics"[15], was guided by domain experts.

## 2.2. Creating an "ontology"

Ontologies categorise and represent entities and concepts along with their properties and relations. This work establishes a foundation from which a more formal ontology can be built in the future.

Many highly regarded libraries, e.g SKOS (Simple Knowledge Organization System) [12] and DCTERMS (Dublin Core Metadata Element Set) [13], are available in the knowledge management space that aid in constructing knowledge organisation systems, e.g. vocabularies and taxonomies. Employing these recommendations in aligning and describing metadata and column properties improves access and readability of the vocabulary. Furthermore, transferring to an ontology format enables a less complex presentation of information, simplifying findability and

Table 1. Unique column descriptors for terms in the glossary.

| Column | Description |
|---|---|
| ID | A unique identifier for all available terms in the glossary |
| base term | Agreed base term that will be displayed in the "Qualified Person Dashboard" |
| base definition | Definition for the agreed base term |
| abbreviation | Common abbreviation for the term |
| term source | Source where the term originated from, if known (e.g., standard) |
| related terms | Other terms directly related to the base term |
| category | Descriptive term for usage context |
| stewardship | Descriptor for ownership and responsibility |
| status | Descriptor for whether term has been agreed upon or is under discussion |
| comment | Property allowing parties to raise concerns and comments |
| **+ optional organisation specific terms** | |
| term synonym | Collaborator synonym terms |
| term definition | Synonym term definition |
| term source | Synonym term source |

accessibility of the data and in particular, making it machine operable.

These resources allow us to describe unique terms as classes with their relationships and metadata as properties, building semantic links and increasing richness of the available information.

### 2.3. Creation of a restAPI

A restAPI is an API that adheres to the REST architectural style and enables interaction with RESTful web services. REST is an acronym for Representational State Transfer and embodies a set of architectural constraints [2]. A restAPI obtains resources via commands, using established HTTP protocols such as "GET", which retrieves a resource from the API [2].

The concept of restAPIs is widely regarded as the de facto standard protocol for web APIs due to their ease of use and widespread availability. Open-source frameworks like Swagger [9] exist to greatly alleviate the time-consuming task of building RESTful interfaces. Swagger is a collection of open-source tools, derived from the OpenAPI specification, that assist in the design, development, documentation, and consumption of restAPIs. The Swagger editor allows one to define an API specification that is platform independent and then export the result as a functional server, based on the programming language required.

For our use case, we implemented a Python server, specifically using the Flask Python web framework [14]. Flask offers tools, libraries, and technologies for developing web applications. Once this restAPI server was established, answers to HTTP requests could be served.

In linking the API with the web service, for this application, one must initially stage the ontology using the Owlready2 [9] Python library within the controller file, which is the entry point of a web application/web service or restAPI server, containing the extraction format definition. The controller file was automatically generated through the Swagger editor tool based on the API specification. Then, employing Owlready2 such that term rows and columns can be flexibly translated, the controller file was tailored to a specific use-case. The glossary-translation script was made to dynamically adapt to new iterations of the glossary, thus reducing engineering time spent on validation checks.

### 2.4. restAPI consumption: web application

In technical terms, restAPIs are "consumed" by applications that use their information. To exemplify this functionality of the API a web-application was developed using the Flask web framework which allows for quick deployment as well as flexible and dynamic Python-based web content delivery.

Web pages are typically split into two parts: the back-end service generates quasi-dynamic HTTP requests based on the information requested by the

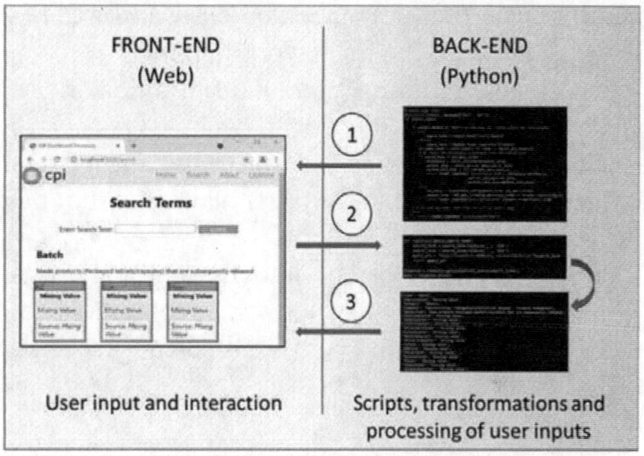


Figure 2. A basic representation of front- vs. back-end: 1. Python-based hosting generating a website and allowing user access. 2. User request for data. 3. Querying of data via Python script and API followed by output of query to website.

user via the front-end application and consumes the API via the available *requests* [10] Python library. Requested information is passed back up the chain to be reformatted for its intended use within the front end. The Front-end application renders information to the user and lets them interact with it. When using Flask, the framework is also responsible for "hosting", i.e. delivering the front-end to the user. A basic representation of this can be found in Figure 2.

## 3. RESULTS

We present our use case in the form of a dictionary web application by applying the accessible method discussed in Section 2. This serves as a prototype to a direct glossary implementation within the "Qualified Persons Dashboard".

Initially, user input is entered on a web service front-end, where it gets translated into a query and transmitted to the back-end of the application. The query is then interpreted by the web application module flask file which translates it into an HTTP request to be consumed by the API.

The restAPI then uses the HTTP request to search for matching information on the Glossary/Ontology layer and retrieve it. That information is then passed, by the restAPI, to the API controller module which communicates it to the flask file. Lastly, the flask file which reformats the retrieved information and renders it on the front-end for user display.

Figure 3 describes the entirety of this process and comprises a visual summation of our results and the interplay between the framework steps.

Implemented through the Flask framework, a small number of functional web pages were established that describe the project and allow users to query and explore the terms contained within the glossary.

Porting of the glossary into the ontology was achieved via a data connector, which took the form of a Python script that converted spreadsheet-like

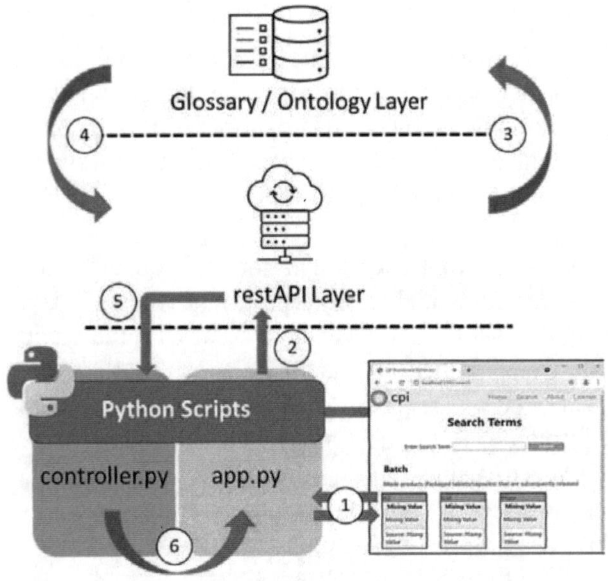


Figure 3. Framework layer interplay. (1) A user input is sent from the web service front-end to the back-end. (2) Based on the query, an HTTP request is generated within the app.py flask file, which consumes the API. (3) The restAPI retrieves the information from the request and passes it back up the chain (4)-(5) as outlined in the API specification. (6) The requested information is finally passed from the controller file to the app where it undergoes a final reformatting before being rendered in the user front end.

data into an ontology digestible format, tailored to our specific use case vocabulary. It is also of note that provenance of terms and versioning issues were encountered at this stage.

In this iteration of work, users are limited to "GET" HTTP requests only. Updating and changing terms within the controlled vocabulary was a privilege only afforded to the maintainer and was achieved through the "data connector" script.

By using this approach, we were able to achieve the level of security required within the use case, and whilst a login feature could later be implemented, it was beyond the scope of this project.

With all required files and connectors established, the Flask API server was shown to serve any third-party application with access to the API and provide users with answers to the available "GET" queries. The exposition of the contained terms through the restAPI permits direct programmatic querying of term information as well as enabling machine-readable and operable interaction with the contents of the ontology.

## 4. DISCUSSION

Throughout development of the restAPI, the usefulness of a more general dictionary-style web application became apparent, not only as a use case for the API but also, as a general tool for future use. For this specific application, the dictionary was designed with the aim of enabling satisfactory querying of the terms within the glossary and highlighting ambiguities, inter-organisational synonyms and other potential problems that could arise from related technical jargon.

While our testing shows that it performs adequately in supplying such information to the end user via the front end, one should also consider that if the underlying glossary was already present and organised in a taxonomy, for example, the same methodology used here could still be applied. This would come with a significant reduction of the work involved in the back-end processes related to porting the glossary into an ontology. The expected result would consist of a direct output of the taxonomy model into the API.

As for the "data connector" script, developed to port the glossary into the ontology, while it was specific to the vocabulary employed in this project, the methodology applied in its development is universally applicable and renders itself useful to similar efforts in the measurement and metrology space currently under way at NPL. This has previously been alluded to in our previous publication on Domain Agnostic Measurement Ontologies [1]. Despite this successful implementation, the encountered versioning issues suggest that a web-ontology tool, such as Web Protégé, might be more suited for future implementations, since it would allow for the bypassing of the porting procedure as already mentioned above.

However, this work still consists of a significant improvement to typical document-based vocabularies as there is a large breadth of exploitation avenues to such available glossaries through direct implementation in applications, such as the "Qualified Persons Dashboard" but also text editors, natural language processors and many more. Furthermore, the base terminology layer represents a great foundation for higher order ontology creation as the "controlled vocabulary" has already been established.

## 5. CONCLUSIONS

We have presented a framework to record science-area-specific semantic information and jargon within a flat glossary-like ontology to then make that information accessible through a RESTful application programming interface.

The proposed ontology-based restAPI-powered centralised vocabulary has the potential to satisfy all project partners and collaborators by providing the most appropriate term via a substitution and/or query interface. This has been exemplified by our industrial use case, which demonstrates the method's potential in providing an avenue into frictionless interoperability.

While the results above focus on a specific use case from the pharmaceutical industry, similar scenarios can occur in any large scientific collaboration. With the advent of digital collaborations and product generation, harmonisation efforts will only increase. Abstracting the presented findings to measurement sciences and the application in interdisciplinary and inter-NMI projects, machine-operable "glossaries and terminologies as a service" could be highly beneficial to increase accessibility to technical and specific jargon. It may also benefit the collaboration of such stakeholders through simplification of jargon-alignment, in particular when projects involve external and international organisations.

## ACKNOWLEDGEMENT

This work was funded by the Department for Business, Energy & Industrial Strategy through the UK's National Measurement System. The authors would further like to thank our collaboration partners at the Medicines Manufacturing Innovation Centre consisting of our partners at CPI, University of Strathclyde, UK Research & Innovation, Scottish Enterprise and founding industry partners, AstraZeneca and GSK. Finally, we would like to acknowledge our colleague Jean-Laurent Hippolyte for his valuable input and discussions on the topic.

## REFERENCES

[1] J-L. Hippolyte, M. Chrubasik, F. Brochu & M. Bevilacqua, "A domain-agnostic ontology for unified metrology data management", Measurement: Sensors, Vol 18, 2021.

[2] Roy Thomas, Fielding. Architectural Styles and the Design of Network-based Software Architectures. Doctoral dissertation, University of California, Irvine, 2000.

[3] Gentile, A.L, Gruhl, D., Ristoski, P. & Welch, S. (2019), Personalized Knowledge Graphs for the Pharmaceutical Domain. In The Semantic Web -- ISWC 2019.

[4] Gansel, X., Mary, M., & van Belkum, A. (2019), Semantic data interoperability, digital medicine, and e-health in infectious disease management: a review. European Journal of Clinical Microbiology & Infectious Diseases, 38. pp 1023-1034

[5] Kaelber, D.C., & Bates, D.W. (2007), Health information exchange and patient safety. J. Biomed. Inform, 40.

[6] Lin, M.C., Vreeman, D.J., McDonald, C.J., & Huff, S.M. (2011) A characterisation of Local LOINC Mapping for Laboratory Tests in Three Large Institutions. Methods Inf. Med. 50(02), pp 105-114.

[7] UK CPI (2019), Medicines Manufacturing Innovation Centre project to deliver Just in Time clinical trials. URL: https://www.uk-cpi.com/news/medicines-manufacturing-innovation-centre-project-reaches-next-stage-in-delivering-just-in-time-clinical-trial

[8] SmartBear Software (2021) Swagger Editor Documentation. URL: https://swagger.io/docs/open-source-tools/swagger-editor/

[9] Lamy, J.B. (2019) Welcome to Owlready2's documentation!, URL: https://owlready2.readthedocs.io/en/v0.36/

[10] Reitz, K. (2019) Requests: HTTP for Humans, URL: https://docs.python-requests.org/en/latest/

[11] IBM InfoSphere Information Governance Catalog, (2022) IBM, URL: https://www.ibm.com/us-en/marketplace/information-governance-catalog

[12] Isaac, A., & Summers, E. (2009), SKOS Simple Knowledge Organization System Primer, URL: https://www.w3.org/TR/skos-primer/

[13] Rühle, S., Baker, T., & Johnston, P., (2022), Dublin Core Metadata Initiative, URL: https://www.dublincore.org/resources/userguide/publishing_metadata/

[14] Pallets, (2010) Flask: Web development one drop at a time, URL: https://flask.palletsprojects.com/en/2.0.x/

[15] ISO 11238 (2018). Health informatics — Identification of medicinal products — Data elements and structures for the unique identification and exchange of regulated information on substances. ISO

# Impact of Supply Chain Risk Management on Supply Chain Performance and Sustainability: Case Study of Moroccan Petroleum Industry

Sara Sarir[1], Mohamed El Oumami[2], Zitouni Beidouri[3],

[1]*LARILE, ENSEM, Hassan II University of Casablanca, El Jadida Road. Km 7, 8118, Oasis-Casablanca, Morocco, sara.sarir@ensem.ac.ma*
[2] *LARILE, ENSEM, Hassan II University of Casablanca, El Jadida Road. Km 7, 8118, Oasis-Casablanca, Morocco,*
[3] *LARILE, ENSEM, Hassan II University of Casablanca, El Jadida Road. Km 7, 8118, Oasis-Casablanca, Morocco,*

**ABSTRACT**: Several academics have emphasized supply chain risk management and are still doing so. They have developed different models and frameworks related to supply chain risks. However, in Morocco, few studies have examined the relationship between risk mitigation strategies and supply chain performance.

For this purpose, we conducted an empirical study based on questionnaires with 75 participants operating in the downstream petroleum sector in Morocco to assess the importance of some risk mitigation strategies and key performance indicators of supply chain. Therefore, this research aims to measure the impact and demonstrate how risk mitigation strategies can enhance the petroleum supply chain's performance. It will also assist managers in implementing proper risk management strategies to better handle the numerous uncertainties they must deal with.

**Keywords**: Risk management, petroleum supply chain, performance, mitigation.



**Corresponding author:** SARA SARIR, e-mail: sarir.sarah@gmail.com.

## 1. INTRODUCTION

In today's increasingly competitive world, companies face numerous challenges, including ensuring the sustainability of their operations, driving profits, and gaining market share. To that end, they choose to improve their products or services as one of the methods for increasing customer satisfaction. But, these enhancements can sometimes lead to significant financial, operational, or technological risks that affect their supply chain [1].

Managers, therefore, incorporate supply chain risk management (SRCM) and adopt specific risk mitigation strategies (RMS) to deal with the various internal and external uncertainties that can adversely affect company performance.

For the petroleum supply chain, there are additional specific risks to consider; that is why most researchers and practitioners have given special attention to SCRM in this field. Risk management is prominent in the oil industry due to the complexity of its processes and infrastructures [2], [3], and the peculiarity of its market [4]. Moreover, uncertainties can arise at different levels, from strategic to operational.

In Morocco, according to the literature, a few studies [5], [6], [7], [8] have focused on supply chain risk management and even fewer in the oil industry.

Thus, this research aims to conduct an empirical study to analyze the relationship between some risk mitigation strategies and supply chain performance. The companies in question are those involved in the import, storage, distribution, and transportation of petroleum products.

The originality of this study is that it investigates the most effective risk mitigation strategies to improve the Moroccan petroleum downstream supply chain performance, particularly for a country that is considered a net hydrocarbon importer by the Energy International Agency [9].

This article is structured as follows: The second section represents a literature review of RMS and the supply chain key performance indicators (KPIs). This part also exposes the research questions. Section 3 describes the research methodology, while Section 4 highlights the study findings. Section 5 is devoted to discussions. Finally, section 6 provides a conclusion and highlights research limitations.

## 2. LITERATURE REVIEW

### 2.1. Literature review

- **Supply Chain Risk Management**

Most studies pointed out that SCRM has four main pillars: the identification, evaluation, mitigation, and monitoring of risks [10] [11] [12] [13]. Indeed, risk identification is the first step in SCRM. Once potential risks are listed, they are analyzed according to their effects and likelihood of occurrence to assess them. Risk assessment allows the decision-maker to judge whether the risk is acceptable or not. In case, it is acceptable, actions must be taken for monitoring the risk. Otherwise, if it's not, risk mitigation is required [14].

Risk mitigation is based on four crucial strategies [15]:

- Information Management
- Supply Management
- Product Management
- Demand Management

However, mitigating risks can generate other risks that need to be analysed. Therefore, risk analysis on mitigating actions proposed is essential for identifying the most critical risks and the optimal trade-offs.

Among the risk mitigation strategies that have attracted the attention of researchers and academicians, we retain in our study:

- Collaboration: [10], [16], [17], [18], [19]
- Contingency planning: [20], [21]
- Flexibility of processes: [18], [21], [22]
- Information sharing: [18],[21],[22],[23]
- Multi-sourcing: [18], [25]
- Responsiveness: [18], [25]
- Technology adaptation: [22], [25]

- **Supply Chain Performance**

The evaluation of supply chain performance has been the subject of several published research projects in recent years. Furthermore, the SCOR model, analytical hierarchy process (AHP), balance scorecard (BSC), data envelopment analysis (DEA), economic value added (EVA), and activity-based costing (ABC) are among the most commonly used chain evaluation methods [26].

Regarding the metrics used by scholars and practitioners to evaluate supply chain performance, which means its efficiency and effectiveness, P.R.C. Gopal & J. Thakkar [26] presented a literature review of those indicators. They highlight that cost, quality, lead time, and flexibility remain among the most important indicators used by companies to measure the performance of their supply chain.

In our research, we have chosen to focus more on the following indicators:

- Time: Total lead time, purchase order lead time, customer order cycle time, supplier lead time, [27]
- Cost: buyer-vendor cost saving initiative [27]
- Quality: delivery reliability,
- Demand forecasting accuracy [27]
- Supply chain flexibility.

### 2.2. Research questions

In this paper, we study the impact of these risk mitigation strategies on supply chain performance by addressing this crucial question:

What mitigation strategies are there to implement to enhance the overall performance of Morocco's supply chain for petroleum products?

Hence, this study relied on two constructs: risk mitigation strategies and supply chain performance indicators.

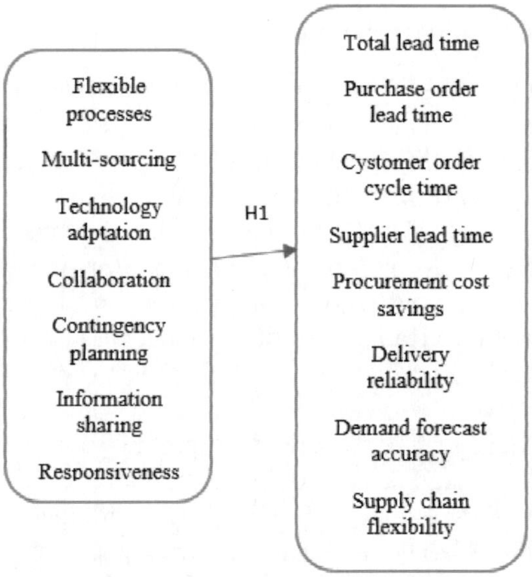


**Figure 1: Research model & Hypothesis**

H1: Flexible processes, multi-sourcing, technology adaptation, collaboration, contingency planning, information sharing, and responsiveness positively impact the total lead time, purchase order lead time, customer order cycle time, supplier lead time, procurement cost savings, delivery reliability, demand forecast accuracy, and supply chain flexibility.

## 3. METHODS

The information for this research was gathered using two methods: a literature review, as described in the previous section, and semi-structured interviews.

The interviews consisted of asking:

(1) Open questions on General company information (Name, location, activities, ISO certifications)

2) Closed-ended and open questions on specific company information (the presence of an entity dedicated to risk management; the presence of an IT tool dedicated to risk management; does this tool integrate identification, assessment, and monitoring of risks); if the answers are yes, for what types of risks does the tool integrate?

(3) Closed-ended questions about the profile's respondent (position held, direction, years of experience, knowledge of the ISO 31000 standard, participation in the risk management process).

(4) Closed-ended questions to evaluate risk mitigation strategies and performance indicators using a 5-point Likert scale; each point corresponds to a degree of importance:

- 1: not important at all
- 2: slightly important
- 3: moderately important
- 4: very important
- 5: extremely important

### 3.1. Data collection tool

First, we started with a sample of 10 participants working in the Moroccan petroleum downstream supply chain to get their opinions and comment on the proposed questionnaire. In light of the interviewees' feedback, we revised the questionnaire. While we omit some useless questions, we change others for better comprehension.

We gave the final questionnaire to 120 employees from different petroleum companies in Morocco from March 2022 to December 2022. We conducted semi-structured interviews with some respondents face-to-face at their workplaces. The sampling was done according to the snowball effect through some respondents' recommendations. The profile of the participants was a criterion to consider in defining the target population. Thus, only responsibles, managers, directors, and some chief operators with more than 10 years of experience responded to the questionnaire. This choice is because this category is the most involved in risk assessment and mitigation.

We also contacted some participants through LinkedIn after conducting research based on two criteria: the company's name and their profile (position held).

As a result, only 75 of the employees contacted agreed to complete the questionnaire, yielding a 62.5% response rate. The interviewees' profiles are described in Table 1.

Table 1: Interviewees' profiles

| **Characteristics of participants** | | **Percentage of sample (%)** |
|---|---|---|
| Gender | Female | 8% |
| | Male | 92% |
| Job position | Responsible | 53,3% |
| | Head of department | 5,3% |
| | Manager | 16% |
| | Director | 20% |
| | Other | 5,3% |
| Year's experience in the company | < 5 years | 12% |
| | 5-10 years | 18,7% |
| | 10-20 years | 33,3% |
| | > 20 years | 36% |

Figure 2: Participant involvement in the risk management process

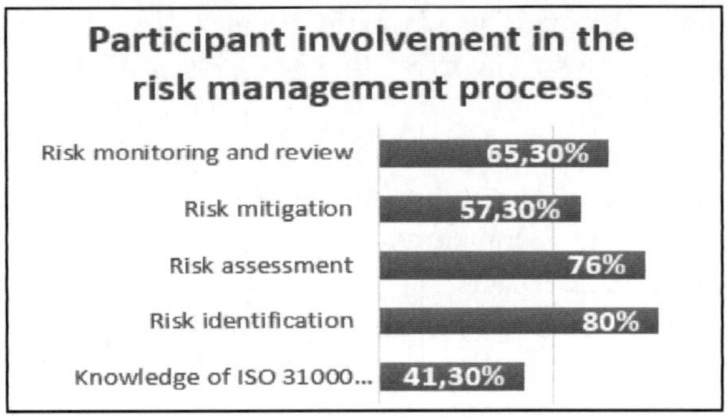


For confidentiality reasons, company's names will be kept anonymous, and replaced with letters from A to M as listed in the table 2.

Table 2: Survey of respondents' company characteristics

| Company code | Nb of employees | interviewees in each company | |
|---|---|---|---|
| | | Frequency | Percentage |
| A | > 500 | 51 | 68% |
| B | > 500 | 5 | 6,7% |
| C | 100-500 | 1 | 1,3% |
| D | 20-100 | 2 | 2,7% |
| E | 100-500 | 2 | 2,7% |
| F | 100-500 | 2 | 2,7% |
| G | 100-500 | 2 | 2,7% |
| H | 20-100 | 2 | 2,7% |
| I | 100-500 | 2 | 2,7% |
| J | 100-500 | 1 | 1,3% |
| K | 100-500 | 2 | 2,7% |
| L | 20-100 | 2 | 2,7% |
| M | 100-500 | 1 | 1,3% |

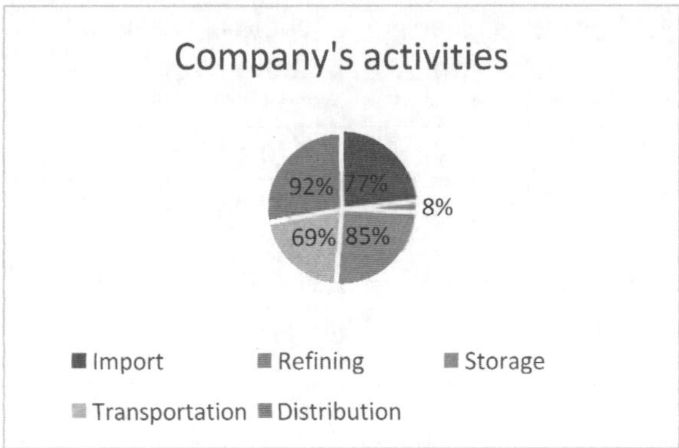


Figure 3: Company's activities

Indeed, the companies where the respondents work operate in several activities of the supply chain; moreover, some manage at the same time the storage, importation, and distribution of petroleum products, as shown in the chart above.

### 3.2. Data analysis

We used IBM SPSS statistics software (version 26) to analyze the data and results. For each RMS and KPI, we ran the skewness and kurtosis statistics to examine the normality of the data. According to the standards set forth by George and Mallory (2010), the usual range for skewness and kurtosis should be between +2 and -2 for normal distribution. In our case, both conditions were satisfied for all variables.

Before assessing the impact of the selected risk mitigation strategies on supply chain performance, we conducted a factor analysis that allowed us to obtain two components for the RMS and two components for the KPI.

Flexible process, multi-sourcing, and technology adaptation represent the first RMS component, while collaboration, contingency planning, information sharing, and responsiveness belong to the second.

We evaluated the internal correlation by measuring the Kaiser-Meyer-Olkin index and applying Bartlett's sphericity test. A KMO index higher than 0.5 and a p-value of Bartlett's test less than 0.05 indicate that the correlation matrix is acceptable for factor analysis [28].

For all variables, the KMO index was higher than 0,6, and the significance through Bartlett's test of sphericity was zero (less than the recommended value of 0,05).

- **Reliability analysis**

Cronbach's alpha was calculated to test the reliability scales of each component. It was higher than 0.7 for all of them. The alpha score between 0.70 and 0.90 indicates high reliability, according to Hinton et al. (2014) [29].

- **Factor analysis:**

We carried out the factor analysis using the principal component analysis (PCA) in SPSS software. The variables were reduced utilizing the rotational method: Varimax with KAISER normalization. The results of this analysis are summarized in the tables below. The loadings range between 0,632 and 0,879, meaning that the variables strongly impact the component.

Table 3: Data analysis of the first construct - RMS-

| | | 1st component of RMS | | | 2nd component of RMS | | | |
|---|---|---|---|---|---|---|---|---|
| | | Process flexibility | Multi-sourcing | Technology adaptation | Collaboration | Contingency planning | Information sharing | Responsiveness |
| Skewness | | -0,471 | -0,074 | -0,540 | 0,030 | -0,548 | -0,418 | -0,453 |
| Kurtosis | | 0,214 | -1,290 | 0,090 | -0,807 | 0,291 | 0,257 | -0,094 |
| KMO Measure | | | 0,674 | | | 0,764 | | |
| Bartlett's test of Sphericity | Approx. $\chi 2$ | | 36,114 | | | 59,103 | | |
| | df | | 3 | | | 6 | | |
| | Sig. | | 0,000 | | | 0,000 | | |
| Loadings | | 0,804 | 0,773 | 0,819 | 0,819 | 0,698 | 0,757 | 0,782 |
| Eigenvalue | | | 1,915 | | | 2,342 | | |
| Total variance explained | | | 63,842 | | | 58,561 | | |
| Cronbach's alpha | | | 0,714 | | | 0,762 | | |

Table 4: Data analysis of the second construct - KPI

| | | 1st component of KPI | | | | | 2nd component of KPI | | |
|---|---|---|---|---|---|---|---|---|---|
| | | Procurement cost savings | Delivery reliability | Demand forecast accuracy | SC flexibility | Total Lead time | Purchase order lead time | Customer order cycle time | Supplier lead time |
| Skewness | | -0,799 | -0,563 | -0,371 | -0,277 | -1,036 | -0,528 | -0,548 | -0,675 |
| Kurtosis | | 0,768 | 0,694 | -0,169 | -0,765 | 0,633 | 0,198 | -0,486 | 0,221 |
| KMO Measure | | | 0,652 | | | | | 0,685 | |
| Bartlett's test of Sphericity | Approx. $\chi 2$ | | 54,906 | | | | | 100,795 | |
| | df | | 6 | | | | | 6 | |
| | Sig. | | 0,000 | | | | | 0,000 | |
| Loadings | | 0,632 | 0,860 | 0,770 | 0,849 | 0,865 | 0,879 | 0,792 | 0,765 |
| Eigenvalue | | | 2,452 | | | | | 2,734 | |
| Total variance explained | | | 61,303 | | | | | 68,361 | |
| Cronbach's alpha | | | 0,761 | | | | | 0,842 | |

## 4. RESULTS

To analyze and measure the degree ofrelationship between the variables, we conducted a linear regression in SPSS. We supposed the following hypothesis for this analysis:

- H01: The first RMS component (process flexibility, multi-sourcing, and technology adaptation) doesn't impact the 1st component of KPI (the procurement cost savings, delivery reliability, demandforecast accuracy, and supply chain flexibility).
- H11: The first RMS component (process flexibility, multi-sourcing, and technology adaptation) positively impacts the first component of KPI (the procurement cost savings, delivery reliability, demandforecast accuracy, and supply chain flexibility).
- H02: The second RMS component (collaboration, contingency planning, information sharing, and responsiveness) doesn't influence the first KPI component (procurement cost savings, delivery reliability, demand forecast accuracy, and supply chain flexibility).
- H12: The second RMS component (collaboration, contingency planning, information sharing, and responsiveness) positively influences the first KPI component (procurement cost savings, delivery reliability, demand forecast accuracy, and supply chain flexibility).
- H03: The first RMS component (process flexibility, multi-sourcing, and technology adaptation) doesn't impact the second component of KPI (total lead time, purchase order lead time, customer order cycle time, supplier lead time).
- H13: The first RMS component (process flexibility, multi-sourcing, and technology adaptation) positively impacts the second component of KPI (total lead time, purchase order lead time, customer order cycle time, supplier lead time).
- H04: The second RMS component (collaboration, contingency planning, information sharing, and responsiveness) doesn't influence the second component of KPI (total lead time, purchase order lead time, customer order cycle time, supplier lead time).
- H14: The second RMS component (collaboration, contingency planning, information sharing, and responsiveness) positively influences the second component of KPI (total lead time, purchase order lead time, customer order cycle time, supplier lead time).

The results of testing the hypotheses are presented in the table below.

Table 5: Results of hypothesis tests

| Hypotheses | Beta | t | Sig. | Accepted? |
|---|---|---|---|---|
| H11 | 0,397 | 2,746 | 0,009 | Yes |
| H12 | 0,261 | 1,803 | 0,080 | NO |
| H13 | 0,239 | 1,595 | 0,119 | NO |
| H14 | 0,332 | 2,216 | 0,033 | YES |

As shown in the table, only H11 and H14 have a p-value less than 0,05, which means that we accepted the hypotheses H11 and H14 and rejected H12 and H13.

Therefore, we can conclude that, on the one hand, process flexibility, multi-sourcing, and technology adaptation have a significant impact on vendor procurement cost savings, delivery reliability, demand forecast accuracy, and supply chain flexibility. On the other hand, collaboration, contingency planning, information sharing, and responsiveness have a significant effect on the total lead time, purchase order lead time, customer order cycle time, and supplier lead time.

## 5. DISCUSSIONS

Risk mitigation strategies are one of the main pillars of risk management strategies. In this paper, we focus more on some of the RMS that have attracted attention from several academics.

The results show that the RMS that could improve the supply chain's performance in terms of lead time, cost, quality, and flexibility are: process flexibility, multi-sourcing, technology adaptation, collaboration, contingency planning, information sharing, and responsiveness. These results confirm the results revealed by Elandaloussi et al.[8], which highlighted the importance of collaboration and flexibility of processes on supply chain resilience. Supply chain resilience is a significant factor in improving supply chain performance [22]. Although the responsiveness also allows for improving the supply chain [22]. Among the limitations of this study is: the size sample which isn't large enough compared to similar analyses in other countries. This issue is because the number of companies operating in the sector is not high enough and because of the strong competitiveness between these companies.

## 6. CONCLUSIONS

This empirical study results from an interviewwith 75 participants operating in the oil and gas field. This research contributes to the supply chain risk management literature by exploring the relationship between risk mitigation strategies and Moroccan downstream petroleum supply chain performance. It analyses the impact of some risk mitigation strategies on supply chain performance. The risk mitigation strategies chosen in this study are flexibility of processes, multi-sourcing, technology adaptation, collaboration, contingency planning, information sharing, and responsiveness. As for supply chain performance, we opted for the following KPIs: procurement cost savings, delivery reliability, demand forecast accuracy, and supply chain flexibility. The findings have shown that collaboration, contingency planning, information sharing, and responsiveness positively influence the total lead time, purchase order lead time, customer order cycle time, and supplier lead time. In addition, we demonstrated that process flexibility, multi-sourcing, and technology adaptation have a significant effect on vendor procurement cost savings, delivery reliability, demand forecast accuracy, and supply chain flexibility.

Hence, we could consider other risk mitigation strategies for a similar analysis, such as agility, pooling, strategic stock, and insurance. Other KPIs for supply chain performance, such as profit, quality, and inventory level, could be investigated. Moreover, a larger sample size than the one chosen in this study and other sectors other than the oil sector could further improve the reliability and validity of this study.

## ACKNOWLEDGEMENT

The authors would like to express their gratitude and acknowledgement to all participants whoagreed to take part in this study for their time and contributions to the field of supply chain risk management.

## REFERENCES

[1] R.Sreedevi, H.Saranga, "Uncertainty and supply chain risk: The moderating role of supply chain flexibility in risk mitigation", International Journal of Production Economics, 193 (2017).

[2] N. M. Nasab, M.R. Amin-Naseri, Designing an integrated model for a multi-period, multi-echelon and multi-product petroleum supply chain, Energy 114, 708-733 (2016)

[3] L. J. Fernandes, A.P. Barbosa-Povoa, S. Relvas, Risk Management Framework for thePetroleum Supply Chain, 20th European Symposium on Computer Aided Process Engineering (2010)

[4] Purvin & Gertz Inc, Overview of the European Downstream Oil Industry, Brussels, Belgium (2009)

[5] L. Oubaouch, G. Paché, "Risk Management in the Supply Chain: Characterization and Empirical Analysis", The Journal of Applied Business Research, Volume 30, Number 2– (2014).

[6] M. El Abdellaoui, Y. M. Moflih, « Analysis of Risk Factors and Events Linked to the Supply Chain: Case of Automotive Sector in Morocco", Journal of Logistics Management, 6(2): 41-51, (2017 ), DOI: 10.5923/j.logistics.20170602.02

[7] T. Benazzouz, A. Charkaoui, A. Echchatbi, "Risks related to the medical supply chain in public hospitals in Morocco: Qualitative study", Le Pharmacien Hospitalier et Clinicien 2019;54:19-29 2211-1042/ß 2018 Elsevier, https://doi.org/10.1016/j.phclin.2018.10.058

[8] Z. Elandaloussi, B. Benbba, H. Ameziane, « The impact of SCRM strategies on supply chain resilience: A quantitative study in the Moroccan manufacturing industry", International Journal of Supply Chain Management, Vol. 6, No. 4, December 2017.

[9] https://www.eia.gov/international/analysis/country/MAR

[10] U. Jüttner, H. Peck, M. Christopher, Supply chain risk management: outlining an agenda for future research, Int. J. Logist. Res. Appl. (2003)

[11] S. Fazli, R. K. Mavi, M. Vosooghidizaji, Crude oil supply chain risk management with DEMATEL-ANP, Int. J. Oper. Res. (2015)

[12] R. Cigolini, T. Rossi, Managing operational risks along the oil supply chain, Prod. Plan. Control (2010)

[13] W. Ho, T. Zheng, H. Yildiz and S. Talluri, Supply chain risk management: A literature review, Int. J. Prod. Res. (2015)

[14] Adhitya, R. Srinivasan, I.A. Karimi, Supply Chain Risk Management through HAZOP and Dynamic Simulation, 18th European Symposium on Computer Aided Process Engineering – ESCAPE18- (2008)

[15] S. Fazli, R. K. Mavi, M. Vosooghidizaji, Crude oil supply chain risk management with DEMATEL-ANP, Int. J. Oper. Res. (2015)

[16] Lavastre, O., Gunasekaran, A. and Spalanzani, A. (2012), "Supply chain risk management in French companies", Decision Support Systems, Vol. 52, pp. 828-838

[17] K.Scholten , P.Sharkey Scott and, B. Fynes, 2014 "Mitigation processes – antecedents for building supply chain resilience", Supply Chain Management: An International Journal, Vol. 19 Iss: 2, pp.211 – 228

[18] Woojung Chang Alexander E. Ellinger Jennifer Blackhurst , (2015),"A contextual approach to supply chain risk mitigation", The International Journal of Logistics Management, Vol. 26 Iss 3 pp. 642 – 656 http://dx.doi.org/10.1108/IJLM-02-2014-0026

[19] Chang, C.H., Xu, J., Dong, J.X. and Yang, Z, "Selection of effective risk mitigation strategies in container shipping operations", Maritime Business Review, Vol. 4 No. 4, pp. 413-431, (2019).

[20] I. Manuj, J.T. Mentzer, « Global Supply Chain Risk Management », Journal of Business Logistics, Vol. 29, No. 1, (2008).

[21] A. Ghadge, S. Dani, R. Kalawsky, « Supply Chain Risk Management : Present and Future Scope », International Journal of Logistics Management, Vol. 23 No. 3, pp. 313-339, (2012)

[22] Y.C .Saglam, S.Y. Çankaya, « Proactive risk mitigation strategies and supply chain risk management performance : an empirical analysis for manufacturing firms in Turkey », Journal of Manufacturing Technology Management, Vol. 32 No. 6, (2021)

[23] Baihaqi, I., and A. S. Sohal. "The Impact of Information Sharing in Supply Chains on Organisational Performance : An Empirical Study." Production Planning & Control 24 (8–9): 743–758 ( 2013).

[24] Xiaojun Wang, Puneet Tiwari & Xu Chen (2017): Communicating supply chain risks and mitigation strategies: a comprehensive framework, Production Planning & Control, DOI: 10.1080/09537287.2017.1329562

[25] J. Roh, P. Hong, H. Min, « Implementation of a responsibe supply chain strategy in global complexity : The case of manufacturing firms », International Journal of Production Economics, (2014)

[26] P.R.C. Gopal, Jitesh Thakkar, "A review on supply chain performance measures and metrics: 2000-2011", International Journal of Productivity and Performance Management, Vol. 61 Iss: 5 pp. 518 – 547, (2012)

[27] S. K. Jakhar, M. K. Barua, « An integrated model of supply chain performance evaluation and decision-making using structural equation modelling and fuzzy AHP, Production Planning & Control : The Management of Operations (2013)
DOI: 10.1080/09537287.2013.782616

[28] https://radiant-rstats.github.io/docs/multivariate/pre_factor.html

[29] Hinton, P. R., McMurray, I., & Brownlow, C. SPSS explained (2nd ed.). Routledge/Taylor & Francis Group (2014). https://doi.org/10.4324/9781315797298

# Measurement Uncertainty Evaluation of Coordinate Measuring Machines Using Web Application and Ontology

*Priyanka Bharti, QingpingYang*

*College of Engineering, Design and Physical Sciences, Brunel University London, Uxbridge, UK*
*priyanka.bharti@brunel.ac.uk, qingping.yang@brunel.ac.uk*

**Abstract -** The ability to evaluate measurement uncertainty is essential for risk analysis and decision-making. Coordinate measuring machines (CMMs) are widely used for dimensional metrology, and the uncertainty evaluation of the measurement processes like CMMs requires a range of data and in-depth knowledge about the measurement process. Some early studies have attempted to develop web-based tools for the evaluation of measurement uncertainty, allowing the user to select the mathematical model and supporting the decision-makingClick or tap here to enter text.. But they are still rather limited in their functionalities with the evaluation process knowledge only implicitly represented, making it difficult to re-use the key information and provide the inference for subsequent usage. Because the sources of uncertainty and their values change over time, the user must investigate and invest time to acquire the data each time the measurement uncertainty is evaluated.

In this paper the author has addressed these existing challenges through the use of an ontological knowledge base to represent the measurement results and additional data obtained for the uncertainty evaluation so that the user can evaluate and update the sources of uncertainty values and relevant information for the uncertainty evaluation and improvement of the measurement process. In this work, Jena Fuseki is used as an ontology server connecting to Python Flask API. The user interfaces for uncertainty evaluation have been developed using Python, HTML, Bootstrap, and AJAX. The user can evaluate the CMM measurement uncertainty using the GUM (Guide to the Expression of Uncertainty in Measurement) Framework, and the results can also be customized and directly added to the ontology with the original ontology expanded and updated dynamically to support further analysis and decision making concerning the measurement and product quality verification.

Keywords: CMM, Ontology, Uncertainty Evaluation, GUM, UML

**Corresponding author:** Bharti Priyanka, *Priyanka.bharti@brunel.ac.uk*

## 1. INTRODUCTION

Measurement uncertainty is an intrinsic part of the measurement process. The ISO Guide to the Expression of Uncertainty in Measurement (GUM) [1] describes measurement uncertainty as a "parameter, associated with the outcome of a measurement, that represents the dispersion of the values that could reasonably be attributed to the measurand". According to the VIM, it is "a non-negative parameter that, according to the data utilised, describes the distribution of the magnitude values assigned to a measurand" [2].

It is necessary to evaluate measurement uncertainty when reporting measurement results. A coordinate measuring machine (CMM) is a widely used measuring instrument for dimensional metrology. A measurement expert can use a variety of methods and software to evaluate measurement uncertainty. When an artefact is measured by a CMM, uncertainty sources include environmental factors, measured artefact, CMM design and its components, operator, procedures, and calibration of references.

The ability to evaluate measurement uncertainty is essential for risk analysis and decision-making. Industries make decisions routinely based on quantitative measurement data. Precise knowledge (metadata) about the measurement procedure is required to evaluate the uncertainty.

In current manufacturing and metrology for Industry 4.0, there is increasing demand to organise relevant metadata and knowledge to present information in a semantically meaningful, reusable, easily accessible, and interoperable form. Up-to-date information on measurement uncertainty is the key to interpreting measurement results and evaluating the quality of the measurement process. Although various technologies from knowledge engineering have been proposed to fulfil this requirement, previous work still needs to address the uncertainty during the measurement process fully.

The results and data from the uncertainty evaluation of CMM measurement process can be represented as knowledge in the form of an ontology so that the user may evaluate and update the sources of uncertainty to improve the measurement uncertainty. An ontology is a formal, expressive explanation of the concepts in an area of discourse, including the classes (or concepts), properties of each concept (also known as slots, roles, or properties), and constraints on slots (or role restrictions). A knowledge base comprises an ontology and a collection of unique instances of classes [3].

The Unit of Measurement and Related Concepts Ontology (OM) is an OWL ontology of quantities and units of measurement that clarifies quantitative research data so that data can be integrated, validated, and reproduced [4]. OM represents essential concepts and relationships in scientific studies. It mainly concentrates on units, quantities, measurements, and dimensions. OWL 2 – Web Ontology Language – is used to develop the ontology of units of measurement.

The work [5] explains the use of semantic web technologies that could contribute standardised measurement data and metadata. The instances given in this paper are machine-actionable explanations of earth observation and bathymetry measurement datasets founded on two ontologies of quantities and units of measurement chosen for their importance in the semantic web. The specified ontologies presented an unprecedented scope of the concepts associated with quantities, dimensions, unique units, and systems of units. However, they demonstrated deviations and voids in the range, absoluteness, and traceability of other metrology concept expressions such as standard uncertainty, expanded uncertainty, combined uncertainty, coverage factor, probability distribution, etc.

A technical report explains the recommendation of ontology expressing the provided Skoda quality control use case [6]. It shows technologies utilised for the suggested ontology and represents the development of the ontology. This work discussed SkodaOnto — an ontology for manufacturing and measuring processes in Skoda Auto.

At present, during the CMM measurement processes, the user/staff of an organisation produces lots of data in a raw or unstructured format. To identify all information associated with a measurement task user must spend lots of time in textual and digital files, which is very time consuming and hectic. This data needs to be synchronised in a structured form. This well-arranged data can help trace the measurement information related to a specific task. For quality measurement results of CMM, uncertainty information should be included in the outcome. The staff can achieve quality measurement results of CMM once the previous information about the measurement task and related uncertainty information is known. The user can compare the results with past experiments, which helps to reduce uncertainty in the CMM measurement results.

The knowledge base is a computer-readable repository of knowledge acquired from human professionals. It is a set of rules and data emanating from human specialists.

This research developed a novel web-based application for evaluating and expressing measurement uncertainty under the GUM uncertainty framework, using an ontology for the CMM measurement process and its measurement uncertainty. This system integrates with Apache Jena Fuseki server, Python, JAVA script, JSON, jQuery and maths.js on the backend. It facilitates saving the results into the web-based ontology for future uncertainty evaluation and update.

This work ensures a quality management framework for digital outputs in metrology in which values can be extracted from the information value chain for primary and secondary re-use. All elements of the chain are qualified, i.e., interoperable, and reproducible. It links from output to a real-world system, which is findable to the user.

## 2. SEMANTIC WEB TECHNOLOGY

The semantic web known as web 3.0 define as web of definitions [7]. Web 3.0 can be progressed from present web 2.0, but both cannot work in parallel [8]. The semantic web opens the door to link the human with machine, which cannot be done by current web system. Ontology is the best technology to achieve this cooperation. Both semantic web and ontology are technologies in artificial intelligence to develop knowledge modelling and inferencing system. Ontology use different knowledge representation languages such as First Order Logic (FOL) , OWL (web ontology language) , RDF (Resource Description Language) and many more. The strength of ontology depends on its capability to model the relationships between concepts or classes and individuals or instances . It enables the inferencing system of knowledge by assigning the properties to these relationships.

### 2.1. SPAQL Query Language

In the context of Semantic Web, query answering is crucial because it provides a tool for users and applications to interact with ontologies and data. Several query languages, including RDQL, SeRQL and, most recently, SPARQL, have been produced for this purpose [9]. SPARQL is the query language and protocol of options for Linked Open Data and RDF databases. Because it was developed to query a broad range of data, it can efficiently extract knowledge hidden in non-uniform data accumulated in diverse structures and origins. The SPARQL Query specification expresses a query analysis technique based on tuple matching [10]. It can be described in terms of the simple entailment association between RDF graphs, this type of query evaluation is also comprehended as simple entailment. SPARQL 1.1 incorporates several entailment rules, including RDFS and OWL, to facilitate more detailed entailment associations, such as those generated by RDF Schema (RDFS) or OWL semantics. Several scientific databases utilize RDF/OWL and SPARQL to explain and link detailed knowledge consistently. In this work, the ontology can answer SPARQL queries with the measurement results.

## 3. PROPOSED WEB APPLICATION FOR CMM MEASUREMENT UNCERTAINTY EVALUATION

In this work, the author has designed a web application for the developed ontology system that uses GUM to evaluate measurement uncertainty. Additionally, this application accesses and updates the ontology's data dynamically.

**Figure 1. Part 1 of web application of uncertainty evaluation**

The input measurement data has been used to evaluate the measurement uncertainty. Using both Type A and Type B evaluation, this case study examines the measurement uncertainty of a 100 mm gauge block using a CMM [11]. The user enters the mathematical model in the equation box in Part 1 of Figure 1. This equation is automatically parsed with the maths.js library. Each parameter of this equation enters Part 2 of the table given in Figure 2.

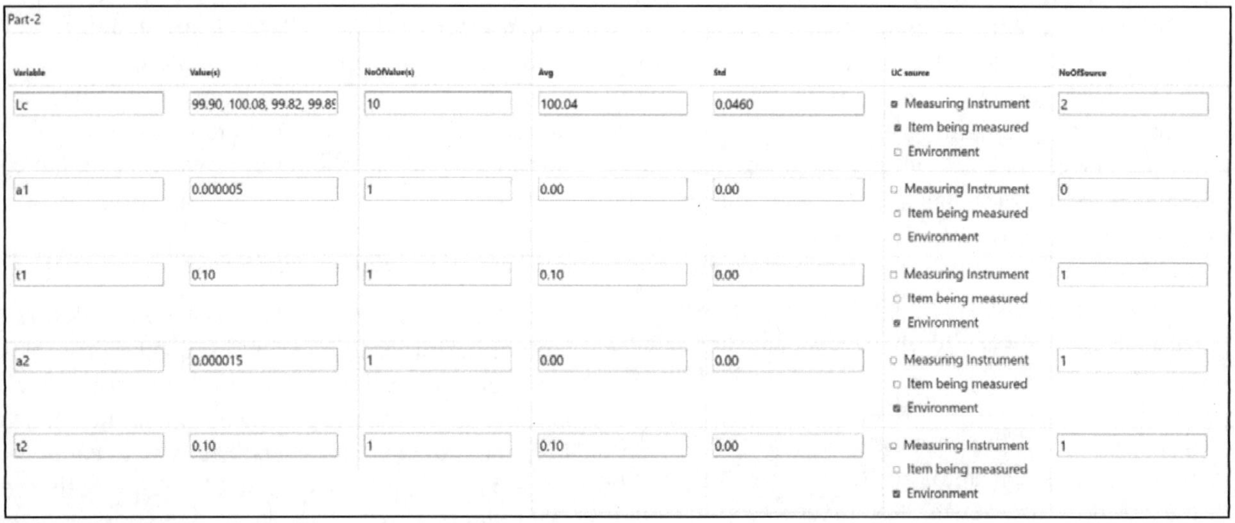


**Figure 2: Part 2 of uncertainty evaluation**

The parsing result of the equation –

$$L_b = L_c(1 + \alpha_c \Delta T_c - \alpha_b \Delta T_b),$$

is $L_b$= $L_c$ + $L_c$ * $a_1$ * $t_1$ - $L_c$ * $a_2$ *$t_2$, where:

$L_b$= Length of gauge block at 20 °C;
$L_c$ = Length of the gauge block measured by CMM;
$a_1$ = Coefficient of thermal expansion of CMM scale;
$t_1$ = Temperature deviation of CMM scale;
$a_2$ = Coefficient of thermal expansion of gauge

block;
$t_2$ = Temperature deviation of gauge block.

The user adds the rows and enters the input values for these parameters in . The system then calculates these variables' mean and standard deviation.

Given the type of uncertainty sources, the user chooses the sources contributing to measurement uncertainty, with the number of uncertainty sources also selected. The $L_c$ has two contributing uncertainties, one from the measuring instrument CMM and the other from the gauge block being measured.

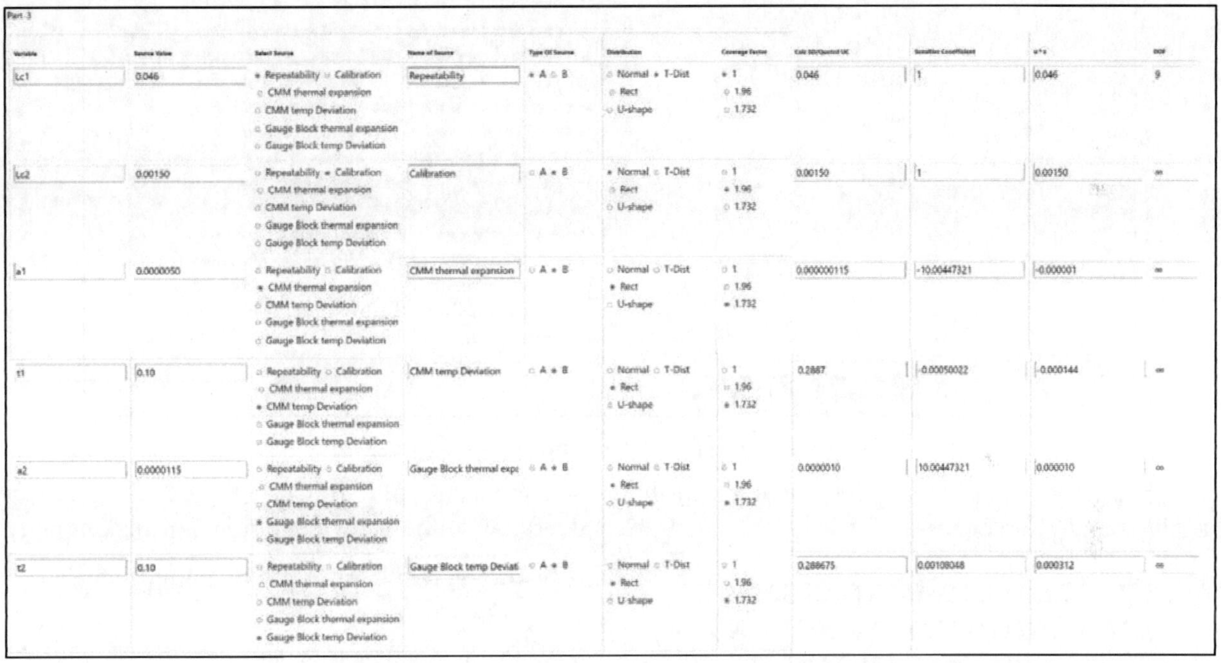


**Figure 3: Part 3 of Uncertainty Evaluation**

In Part 3 of uncertainty evaluation, the selected uncertainty sources are inserted with new rows added illustrated in Figure 3. The value of uncertainty source parameters such as CMM calibration ($L_{c_1}$), repeatability ($L_{c_2}$), coefficient of thermal expansion of CMM scale ($a_1$), temperature deviation of CMM scale ($t_1$), coefficient of thermal expansion of gauge block ($a_2$), and temperature deviation of gauge block ($t_2$) have been entered in Figure 3. In the following columns of Part 3, Type A, or Type B uncertainty evaluation, is selected. Distribution type and coverage factor were also chosen for individual uncertainty sources. After these steps, the functions of evaluating the standard uncertainty and sensitivity coefficient of the given measurement model are executed automatically on the back end of this web application. Apache Jena Fuseki runs as server for this web application. The maths.js library of JavaScript parse the inserted mathematical equation. The functions to execute these functionalities written on PyCharm editor. It executes and interacts with Apache Jena Fuseki. This server provides the response on web page when user enter measurement data and request the add row button.

A function of calculating the degree of freedom is executed and calculated for each parameter. These uncertainty evaluation steps are executed horizontally in all the tables for individual parameters.

In part 4 (Figure 4), the function of combined standard uncertainty calculates the square root of the sum of squared standard uncertainty components of sources, which may be called 'summation in quadrature' or 'root sum of the squares'. Each component is the product of the standard uncertainty and its associated sensitivity coefficient. The coverage factor has been chosen as 2, which is multiplied by the combined standard uncertainty, giving the expanded uncertainty with a confidence level of 95%, as shown in Figure 4. The user can describe these results in natural language,

**Figure 4: Part 4 of Uncertainty Evaluation**

which can be added to the ontology for further analysis and inference.

## 4. ONTOLOGY DEVELOPMENT FOR CMM MEASUREMENT PROCESS INCLUDING UNCERTAINTY OF MEASUREMENT

An ontology for the proposed system has been discussed using the UML knowledge model [12]. It consists of nine main concepts or classes extracted from the enumerated terms. These classes have attributes as properties and relationships. The class name is at the top of the rectangle box, and the attributes are given inside the box, including the data properties of this class. The arrow is used to show the object properties as the relationships between classes. For example, Class "Artefact" has data properties such as "artefactTempDeviation", "artefactThermalCoefficient" etc. The class "User" has a relationship "performTaskFor" with the "Artefact". The relationship name " performTaskFor" means the user performs the measurement of artefact. Figure 5 gives an overview of the knowledge flow for this ontology.

### 4.1. Adding results into the ontology using SPARQL query

With the final output and description given in result box in Figure 6, when the user clicks on the "Add result to the ontology", the result will be dynamically added to the existing ontology. The SPARQL endpoint for this system has been accessed by the SPARQL Wrapper class. This has been imported into the "app.py" file of the system, which is the main file for running all the associated files and functions. A query can then be run to add the result instantly to the existing ontology. The Fuseki is running behind the system, allowing the user to run the SPARQL query on ontology and

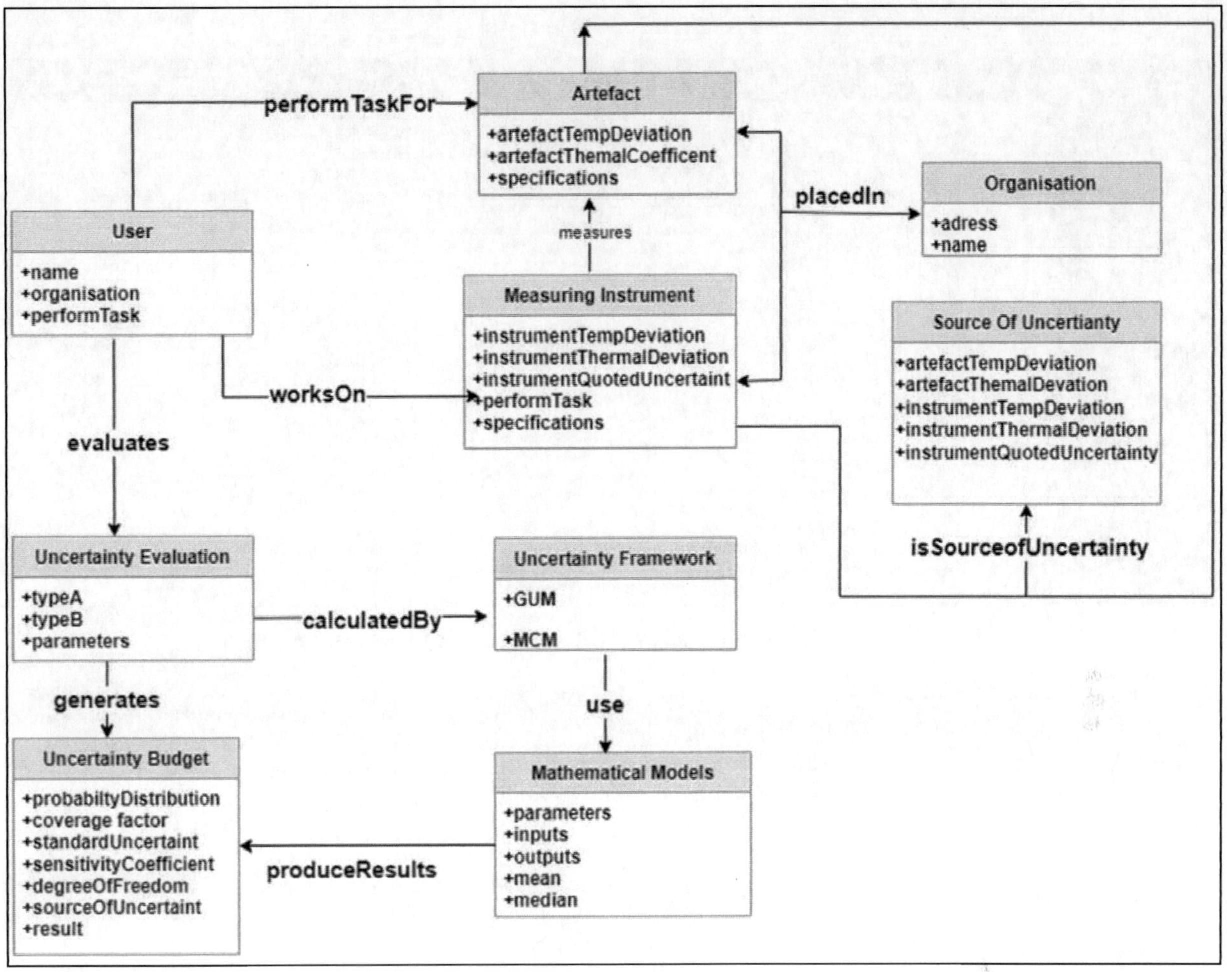


**Figure 5. UML diagram for CMM measurement process ontology**

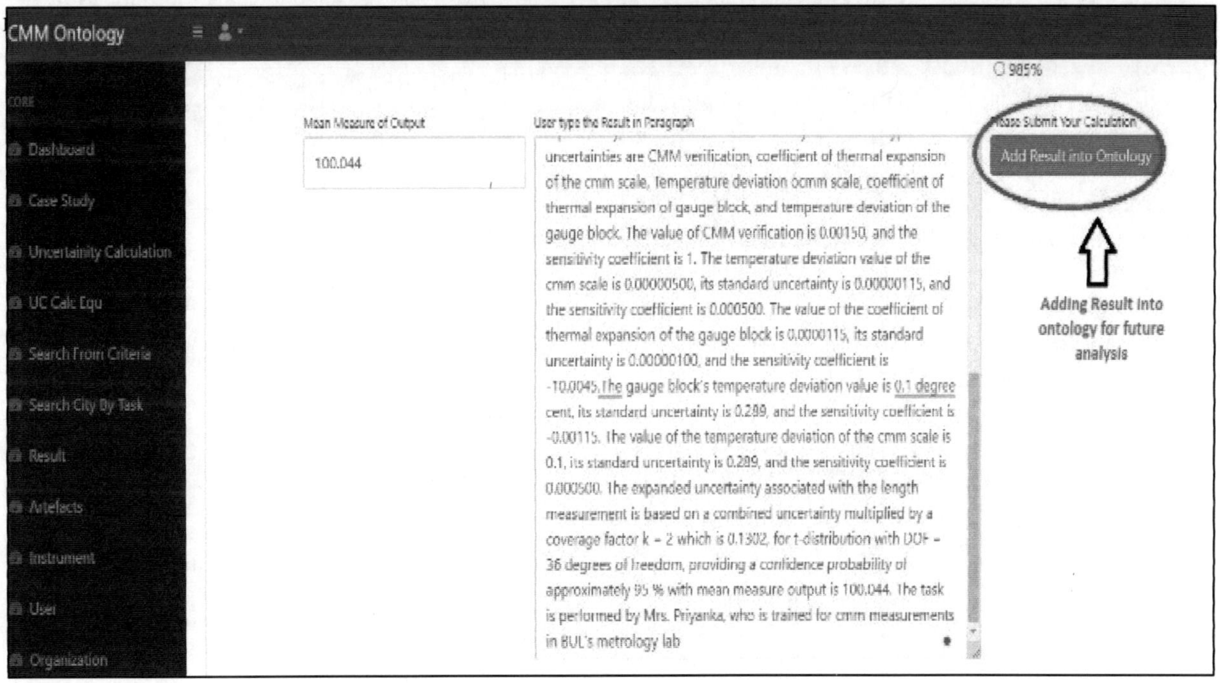


**Figure 6. Saving result into Ontology**

**Figure 7. Displaying added result into result class on web app**

application's user interface.

Figure 6 shows the dashboard of saving the information of the measurement into the ontology and displaying it in Figure 7. This result can be utilised for further measurement data analysis.

## 5. CONCLUSION

A web-based application is developed that integrates the knowledge model and ontology. This web application evaluates the uncertainty of CMM measurement results and makes this data accessible and semantically searchable. This study develops a set of SPARQL query rules in the proposed ontology framework, which helps integrate ontology with the web application. The system provides dynamic functionality to update the uncertainty data. The end user can estimate the measurement uncertainty of CMM measurements remotely at any time using only a Web browser. It performs well in terms of findability, accessibility interoperability, reusability, interoperability, and compatibility. The future work includes the further development of the semantic search and question answering system, which help to perform Create, Read, Update and Deletion (CRUD) operations on measurement data of developed ontology.

## REFERENCES

[1] Joint Committee For Guides In Measurements, "Evaluation of measurement data — Guide to the expression of uncertainty in measurement," *International Organization for Standardization Geneva ISBN*, vol. 50, no. September, 2008, doi: 10.1373/clinchem.2003.030528.

[2] P. de Bièvre, "The 2012 International Vocabulary of Metrology: 'VIM,'" *Accreditation and Quality Assurance*, vol. 17, no. 2. 2012. doi: 10.1007/s00769-012-0885-3.

[3] N. F. Noy and D. L. Mcguinness, "Ontology Development 101: A Guide to Creating Your First Ontology." [Online]. Available: www.unspsc.org

[4] C. Keßler, W. Kuhn, H. Rijgersberg, M. Van Assem, and J. Top, "Semantic Web 0 (0) 1 Ontology of Units of Measure and Related Concepts; one anonymous reviewer", Accessed: Mar. 10, 2022. [Online]. Available: http://www.unitsofmeasure.org

[5] J.-L. and R. M. and B. M. and D. P. and H. S. E. and G. T. F. and P. A.-S. and N. J. Hippolyte, "Using Ontologies to Create Machine-Actionable Datasets: Two Case Studies," *Metrology*, vol. 3, no. 2673–8244, pp. 65–80, 2023.

[6] Petr J˚uza and Martin Maca ̌, "SkodaOnto-Ontology for representation of manufacturing and measuring process," Jan. 2023.

[7] P. Hitzler and K. Janowicz, "Linked Data, Big Data, and the 4th Paradigm," *Semantic Web*, vol. 4, no. 3. 2013. doi: 10.3233/SW-130117.

[8] H. Che, "A Semantic Web primer," *Journal of the American Society for Information Science and Technology*, vol. 57, no. 8, 2006, doi: 10.1002/asi.20368.

[9] I. Kollia and B. Glimm, "Optimizing SPARQL query answering over OWL ontologies," *Journal of Artificial Intelligence Research*, vol. 48, 2013, doi: 10.1613/jair.3872.

[10] E. Prud'hommeaux and A. Seaborne, "SPARQL Query Language for RDF. W3C Recommendation 15 January 2008," *World Wide Web Consortium*, 2008.

[11] P. Bharti, Q. P. Yang, A. B. Forbes, and Y. Koucha, "UML knowledge model for measurement process including uncertainty of measurement," *International Journal of Metrology and Quality Engineering*, vol. 12, p. 26, 2021, doi: 10.1051/IJMQE/2021024.

[12] P. Bharti, Q. P. Yang, A. Forbes, M. Romanchikova, and J. L. Hippolyte, "Ontology development for measurement process and uncertainty of results," *Measurement: Sensors*, vol. 18, Dec. 2021, doi: 10.1016/J.MEASEN.2021.100325.

# The degree of status for executing DDMRP in Moroccan Aerospace firms

Soumaya Idrissi Jazouli[1], Mohamed Ben Ali[2], Otmane Bouksour[3], Ahmed Adri[4], Said Rifai[5]

[1]*ESTC High School of Technology, Industrial department, ENSEM School of Engineering, University Hassan II of Casablanca, Morocco,* Soumaya.idrissijazouli@ensem.ac.ma, soumaya.idrissijazouli-etu@etu.univh2c.ma

[2]*ESTC High School of Technology, Industrial department, ENSEM School of Engineering, University Hassan II of Casablanca, Morocco*

[3]*ESTC High School of Technology, Industrial department, ENSEM School of Engineering, University Hassan II of Casablanca, Morocco*

[4]*ESTC High School of Technology, Industrial department, ENSEM School of Engineering, University Hassan II of Casablanca, Morocco*

[5]*ESTC High School of Technology, Industrial department, ENSEM School of Engineering, University Hassan II of Casablanca, Morocco*

**ABSTRACT**: Demand Driven Material Requirement Planning (DDMRP) is a relatively new idea that focuses on planning, production, and inventory, particularly in a VUCA environment (Volatility, Uncertainty, Complexity, and Ambiguity). It was introduced in 2011 to improve the performance of supply chain planning. Contrary to Material Requirement Planning (MRP), which bases supply chain management on production load, Demand Takes on the Role of Supply Chain Pilot in DDMRP.

In this paper, we propose a technique for assessing the level of DDMRP implementation preparedness among the main Moroccan aerospace businesses. However, there hasn't been any research done on the potential implementation of DDMRP in Moroccan Aeronautical manufacturers. We drew inspiration from the (SAE) to elaborate the proposed model.

**Keywords**: DDMRP, The level of readiness, Uncertainty, Manufacturing firms, VUCA, management, measurement.

**Received** March 30, 2023; **In final form** March 31, 2023; **Published** June 2023



**Corresponding author:** Soumaya IDRISSI JAZOULI, e-mail: Soumaya.idrissijazouli@ensem.ac.ma

## 1. INTRODUCTION

For several years now, and as a result of the continuous evolution of the manufacturing industry and the globalization of markets, we have been observing an increase in the use of Excel files in companies. This practice perfectly reflects the need to compensate for the shortcomings of our current methods and systems. [1]

These deficiencies are also illustrated by a bimodal distribution of stock where we have too much of what we don't need and not enough of what we do need. In the majority of companies, the central planning system remains the MRP. This planning model was conceived in the 1950s, coded in the 1960s, and commercialized in the 1970s, but it has not evolved since then. It is based on the propagation of a signal (in most cases this signal will be a forecast) throughout the product BOM (bill of material) in order to calculate a requirement. This system is perfectly adapted to an environment where demand is higher than supply and in which the use of the industrial tool must be optimized, but it does not meet the current challenges. The norm today is shorter product lifecycles, increasing forecast errors, proliferating products, and globally extended supply. However, customers expect shorter and shorter lead times, which requires new tools and new methods.[2]

Faced with this context defined by the acronym VUCA, (Volatility, Uncertainty, Complexity and Ambiguity) a concept born in the military and recently extended to organizations and the supply chain (Packowski2013; Bennett and Lemoine2014). Carol Ptak and Chad Smith, two practitioners propose a new production management method called DDMRP-for Demand-Driven Material Requirements Planning- [4]-[5]-[9].

DDMRP is an abbreviation for Demand Driven Material Requirement Planning which is a process of planning and executing that allows for end-to-end supply chain management. It focuses on the flow to protect it from fluctuation while keeping it in step with the market. DDMRP is built on a demand-driven flow; if the market isn't ready to acquire what you've got in your flow, you'll only squander resources and product inventories.[15]

And to succeed under these vulnerable conditions, the process must be transparent, and to do this, one of the main keys is: the management of measurement processes [2].William Thomson, known as Lord Kelvin, has a popular statement which is "I often say that when you can measure what you are speaking about, and express it in numbers, you know something about it; but when you cannot measure it, when you cannot express it in numbers, your knowledge is of a meagre and unsatisfactory kind"[3].

Thus, the significance of implementing the DDMRP within our aeronautical supply chain, and to do this and well before, it will be necessary to measure if today our companies are ready to initiate the DDRMP approach at the level of their supply chain, and our study is based on the proposal of a new calculation model that companies can adopt before launching into the implementation of the DDMRP; this specific one remains the first one made and appeared in Morocco.

According to figures 1 & 2 below (SCOPUS), it can be deduced that there has been a significant growth in the interest shown in the DDMRP topic from 2016 until the middle of 2023 in different countries around the world.

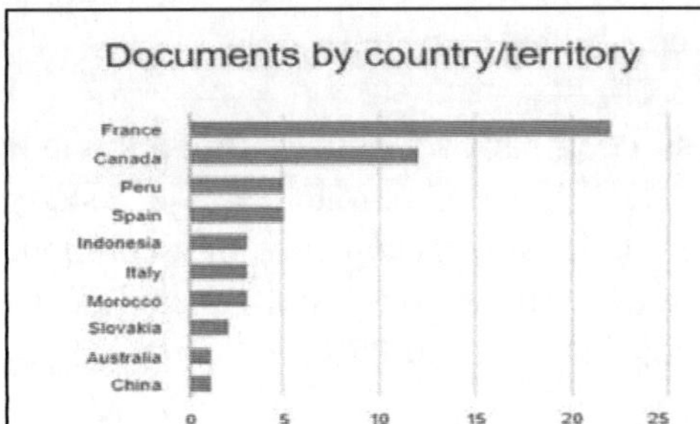


Figure 1. Research document by country (Scopus)

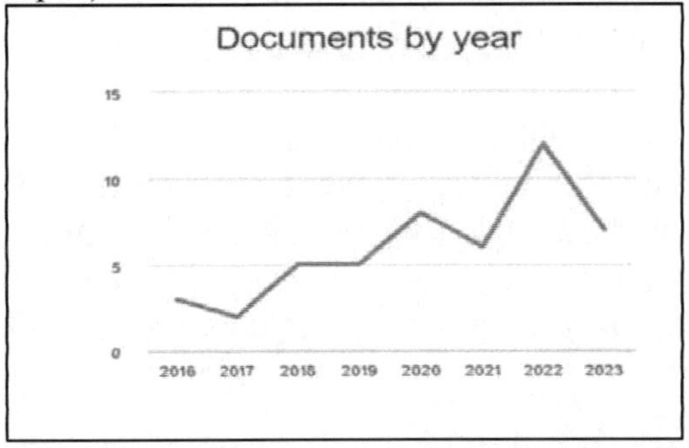


Figure 2. Research document by year (Scopus)

The remainder of this work is organized as follows: an introduction, followed by a section on methodology. The method's application in a contemporary company is then demonstrated through the use of an example, which is presented before the results and discussion, and finally the conclusion.

The current work aims to propose a method for determining how prepared a key aeronautical organization is to implement DDMRP. Our Study was based on the SAE J4000 Standard. [6].

## 2. METHODOLOGY

The following approach is based on a framework where SAE established a method for identifying and measuring best practices for lean deployment in firms SAE J4000- is a tool for identifying and measuring best practices in lean operations deployment in a manufacturing firm. [6]-[7].

The J4000 standard covers six factors for lean implementation, which represent the parts of an organization where lean practices will be evaluated. The recommended procedure provides a number of components for each aspect in order to measure the extent of adoption in an organization. These are instructions that are intended to highlight the pertinent lean implementation components for each issue under examination. This assessment is carried out by finding four possible responses to every single one of the statements below: Level 0 (L0) indicates that an element does not exist or that its implementation is inconsistent; Level 1 (L1) indicates that the element exists but its adoption has minor inconsistencies; Level 2 (L2) indicates that the element is almost entirely implemented; and Level 3 (L3) indicates that the element is completely implemented. [7]-[8].

As a result, the information needed to figure out is which of the four levels L0, L1, L2, or L3 most effectively illustrates what is happening with this component is gathered in order to determine the level of execution of a component in an organization. As a result, if the specialist determines that L1 is the explanation that best shows what is happening in the organization during the assessment, it can be determined that L1 will be the explanation in this specific element of the degree of implementation. This identical process is duplicated for each of the SAE J4000 standard's 52 components. [9].

As previously stated, this study was adopted as the foundation for the modification of the model to measure readiness degree as SAE Standard 'J4000/4001' [6]. Each component of the first SAE standard is related to a recognized DDMRP invention to accomplish this. As a result, the approach (element DDMRP) possesses a grouping of "n" criteria that are linked to the sections of the SAE standard. the approach (element DDMRP) possesses a set of "n" prerequisites connected to the SAE standard's sections. As a result, according to SAE J4000, the level of acceptance of these criteria is classified into four distinct levels: Level 0 signifies that the component does not exist in the examined company; Level 1 indicates that the requirement exists but is only partially implemented; Level 2 indicates that the requirement exists but is only partially implemented; and Level 3 indicates that the requirement is fully realized. [7]-[8]-[9].

However, in order to determine the level of preparation, it is necessary to assess how widely this approach is used in a given organization. As a result, our study examined the current literature to identify the prerequisites. This search revealed that there were at least six and up to eight criteria. This investigation used a rating system with seven points to eliminate the most irrelevant norms.

Nonetheless, the seven prerequisites have chosen for the approach were: 1) The company is familiar with DDMRP and its three steps? 2) The company have the previous awareness of how to constitute the inventory/stock Buffers in order to constitute the decoupling point? 3) The company have a clear strategy about defining the ADU (average daily usage), variability, lead-time and Minimum order quantities (MOQ) for manufactured, purchased and distributed items? 4) The company have the ability to readjust dynamically the buffers (initially configured)? 5) The company have the financial capacity to train the supply chain Team in case of implementing DDMRP Approach in production planning? 6) The company have a clear strategy to move toward making stocks (be aware of increase of WCR)? 7) The company have a previous mitigation strategy to deal with that risk (Implementation of DDMRP)?[10]-[11]-[12]-[13].

## 2.1. Example

e.g. DDMRP Approach (The element)

e.1. The company has the previous knowledge of DDMRP and its 3 steps (prerequisite 1)

- L0. The company does not have a previous knowledge of DDMRP and its 3 steps
- L1. The company has a medium previous knowledge of DDMRP and its 3 steps.
- L2. The company has an almost the previous knowledge of DDMRP and its 3 steps.
- L3. The company has the previous knowledge of DDMRP and its 3 steps.

e.2. The company have the previous awareness of how to constitute the inventory/stock Buffers in order to constitute the decoupling point? (prerequisite 2)

- L0. The company does not have the previous awareness of how to constitute the buffers stock.
- L1. The company has a medium previous awareness of how to constitute the buffers stock.
- L2. The company has an almost the previous awareness of how to constitute the buffers stock.
- L3. The company has the previous awareness of how to constitute the buffers stock.

To assess a company's readiness for applying this Element (DDMRP Approach), we suggest establishing its level of acceptance of a component utilizing a model proposed by researchers Lucato et al, and Athos Paulo Tadeu Pacchini (2019). [9]

In fact, to assess the adoption of a prerequisite, this work recommends assigning a point value to each implementation level, as follows: L0 - 0 point, L1 - 1 point, L2 - 2 points, and L3 - 3 points.

therefore, Günther and Lucato et al. (2017) calculated the degree of preparedness of a given company "Gn" by dividing the total number of points collected in the analysis by the sum of the highest number of points possible for the element.

Thus:

$$g_n = \frac{\sum \text{point gathered as a result of evaluation of components/prerequesities of The Element (DDMRP)}}{\text{Maximum points possible}}$$

Consider the following element, which has seven prerequisites, as an illustration of the suggested calculation as we named them, "components": A.1–L0, A.2–L0, A.3–L1, A.4–L0, A.5–L0, A.6–L1, and A.7–L0. The degree of readiness (g) for a particular company A can be determined as follows:

$$g_A = \frac{0+0+1+0+0+1+0}{3+3+3+3+3+3+3} = \frac{2}{21} = 0{,}095 \; or \; 9{,}5 \;\%$$

The calculation describes that the degree of readiness of the approach enabler (DDMRP) for a given company A is equal to 0,095 out of maximum of 1.0000 (such as: L3 for all four components).

It is also possible to express that, in relation to that approach, the firm gathered only 9,5 % of the required prerequisites-components.

Now, it remains to be seen how prepared the major Moroccan aerospace businesses are to implement the DDMRP Approach; the perspective degrees of adoption of the perquisites have been identified; they can be named as: $g_A$, $g_B$, $g_n$.

In the above:

$$D_R = \frac{g_A + g_B + \cdots + g_n}{n} = \frac{\sum_1^n g_n}{n} \quad (2)$$

Here:

Dr = degree of readiness of the main Moroccan aerospace companies;

ga= degree of adoption of the approach for the company (A).

gb = degree of adoption of the approach for the company (B).

And gn = degree of adoption of the approach for the company n.

In order to assess the extent to which Moroccan aviation companies are prepared for DDMRP in their supply chain, we have referred to the International Organization for Standardization (ISO)/International Electrotechnical Commission (IEC) standard 15504-5 [14] as a reference, which proposes six levels of consecutive and cumulative measures.

They are presented in Table 1.

Table 1. Readiness degree status [6].

| Degree of Readiness ($D_R$) - % | Status | Characteristics |
|---|---|---|
| $0 \leq D_R < 10$ | Embryonic | The company has some superficial knowledge of a small number of enabling technologies (if any). |
| $10 \leq D_R < 25$ | Initial | The company has some knowledge of some technologies but may not know all of them. |
| $25 \leq D_R < 50$ | Primary | The company has a good knowledge of all technologies, but not all of them have already been adopted. |
| $50 \leq D_R < 75$ | Intermediate | The company has full knowledge of all technologies and all them have already begun to be adopted. |
| $75 \leq D_R < 90$ | Advanced | The company has full knowledge of all technologies and all them have a high degree of adoption |
| $90 \leq D_R \leq 100$ | Ready | The company has practically all the enabling technologies in full degree of maximum adoption. |

## 3. RESULTS AND DISCUSSION

A case study was created to demonstrate how the proposed approach could be employed in a real-world setting, the Moroccan aeronautical companies chosen for this study were 10 out of approximately 100 companies existed in Morocco according to the Moroccan Ministry of Industry, Trade and Investment and the Digital Economy. The number of responses gathered was 10 responses which represent only 10% of the selected companies.

The survey contained several questions about the existing of each component (in total there were 7 components) of that approach in a given company. an example of the obtained results for a given company is shown in Table 2 after that we calculated the degree of readiness of each company using equation 1, consequently, we conclude the degree of readiness of the Moroccan Aerospace companies as a whole using equation 2, then defining the degree of adoption of each enabler component of DDMRP in the Moroccan aeronautic companies, the results are presented in table 3.

Table 2: An illustration of the responses for companies

| Company | e.1. Does the company have the previous knowledge of DDMRP and its 3 steps? | e.2. Does the company have the previous awareness of how to constitute the inventory/stock Buffers in order to constitute the decoupling point? | e.3. Does the company have a clear strategy about defining the average daily usage (ADU), variability, lead-time and Minimum order quantities (MOQ) for manufactured, purchased and distributed items? | e.4. Does the company have the ability to readjust dynamically the buffers (initially configured)? | e.5. Does the company have the financial capacity to train the supply chain Team in case of implementing DDMRP Approach in production planning? | e.6. Does the company have a clear strategy to move toward making stocks (be aware of increase of WCR)? | e.7. Does the company have a previous mitigation strategy to deal with that risk (Implementation of DDMRP)? |
|---|---|---|---|---|---|---|---|
| **A** | L2 | L2 | L2 | L2 | L2 | L2 | L2 |
| **B** | L0 | L0 | L0 | L0 | L0 | L0 | L0 |
| **C** | L1 | L1 | L2 | L1 | L2 | L2 | L2 |
| **D** | L2 | L3 | L3 | L2 | L3 | L2 | L2 |
| **E** | L2 | L2 | L3 | L2 | L3 | L2 | L2 |
| **F** | L1 | L1 | L2 | L2 | L2 | L1 | L1 |
| **G** | L2 | L2 | L3 | L2 | L3 | L2 | L2 |
| **H** | L0 | L1 | L2 | L1 | L3 | L2 | L3 |
| **I** | L0 | L0 | L1 | L0 | L0 | L1 | L0 |
| **J** | L2 | L2 | L2 | L2 | L2 | L2 | L2 |

Table 3. Result of the degree of readiness in Moroccan Aerospace Companies

| | The degree of adoption of each component (eq.1) | | | | | | | | |
|---|---|---|---|---|---|---|---|---|---|
| **Company** | **e1** | **e2** | **e3** | **e4** | **e5** | **e6** | **e7** | **gn (eq.1)** | **%** |
| A | 2 | 2 | 2 | 2 | 2 | 2 | 2 | 0,666666667 | 67% |
| B | 0 | 0 | 0 | 0 | 0 | 0 | 0 | 0,00000000 | 0% |
| C | 1 | 1 | 2 | 1 | 2 | 2 | 2 | 0,523809524 | 52% |
| D | 2 | 3 | 3 | 2 | 3 | 2 | 2 | 0,80952381 | 81% |
| E | 2 | 2 | 3 | 2 | 3 | 2 | 2 | 0,761904762 | 76% |
| F | 1 | 1 | 2 | 2 | 2 | 1 | 1 | 0,476190476 | 48% |
| G | 2 | 2 | 3 | 2 | 3 | 2 | 2 | 0,761904762 | 76% |
| I | 0 | 1 | 2 | 1 | 3 | 2 | 3 | 0,571428571 | 57% |
| J | 0 | 0 | 1 | 0 | 0 | 1 | 0 | 0,095238095 | 10% |
| H | 2 | 2 | 2 | 2 | 2 | 2 | 2 | 0,666666667 | 67% |
| **DR= The degree of readiness of the Moroccan Aerospace Companies (eq.2)** | | | | | | | | **0,533333333** | **53%** |

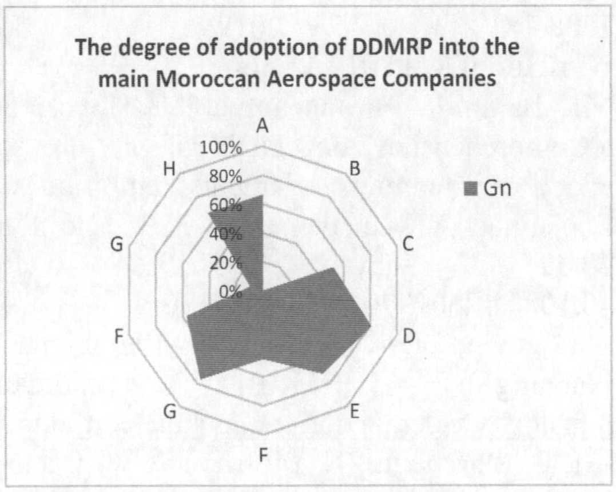


Figure 3. A graphical representation of the level of readiness of Moroccan Aerospace Companies

Regarding the results shown in Table 3 and Figure 3, the degree of readiness of the Moroccan aerospace companies is 0,5333, or 53%. This means that these companies have 53% of the components in place that are required to achieve a suitable implementation of DDMRP in their supply chain.

The number of DDMRP practices that have been adopted by the investigated companies is not taken into account in this estimate. Is an organization ready to begin or prepare a new process? is the question it answers. Furthermore, the Oxford Dictionary (Stevenson, 2010) defines maturity as "the state, fact, or period of being mature" and readiness as "the state of being fully prepared for something." [8]

Additionally, we discuss the readiness of an organization to complete a task (component or prerequisite) in our study.

The goal of our study—the degree of readiness—is to determine the proportion of each prerequisite for that strategy that is present in these firms. The percentage of DDMRP requirements that have thus far been satisfied is 53%, as determined. As a result, Moroccan aerospace firms are in the process of integrating the DDMRP Approach into their supply chain.

Finally, this study served as an analogy to the suggested methodology to determine the readiness of Industry 4.0 in the automotive industry.

## 4. CONCLUSION

The suggested framework has theoretical and practical applications. On the one hand, this research provides a new technique for assessing the level of readiness to implement DDMRP in a specific industry sector that has never been investigated. In terms of application, the model gives executives a tool to assess how the business is set up to use the DDMRP Approach.

This study also has several limitations. The largest and most renowned Moroccan aerospace companies were the initial targets of the investigation. Future research could look at a variety of aeronautic businesses for better outcomes. The current study also relies on seven critical elements gleaned from the literature; however, other researchers may choose to consider more. To match this situation, the offered model is easily adaptable.

The results of this work can be applied in the future to create a conceptual model for this type of study and the successful integration of DDMRP into the Moroccan aerospace industry's supply chain.

## REFERENCES

[1] « Méthodologie d'amélioration de l'agilité des chaînes logistiques - application à une Othmane Dayi 2019.pdf ». J. Abadie, E. Piat, S. Oster, M. Boukallel, Sens. Actuat. A **173**, 227–237 (2012)

[2] R. Schmitt, J. Lose, et M. Harding, « The management of measurement processes – key to robust and cost optimal production of high quality products », Int. J. Metrol. Qual. Eng., vol. 1, no 1, Art. no 1, 2010, doi: 10.1051/ijmqe/2010010

[3] W. Thomson, Electrical Units of Measurement, Popular Lecture an Addresses, Vol. I (Macmillan, London, 1883), p. 73

[4] B. Bahu, L. Bironneau, et V. Hovelaque, « Compréhension du DDMRP et de son adoption : premiers éléments empiriques », Logistique & Management, vol. 27, no 1, p. 20-32, janv. 2019, doi: 10.1080/12507970.2018.1547130

[5] N. Bennett et G. J. Lemoine, « What a difference a word makes: Understanding threats to performance in a VUCA world », Business Horizons, vol. 57, no 3, p. 311-317, mai 2014, doi: 10.1016/j.bushor.2014.01.001

[6] A. P. T. Pacchini, W. C. Lucato, F. Facchini, et G. Mummolo, « The degree of readiness for the implementation of Industry 4.0 », Computers in Industry, vol. 113, p. 103125, déc. 2019, doi: 10.1016/j.compind.2019.103125

[7] « J4000_202104: Identification and Measurement of Best Practice in Implementation of Lean Operation - SAE International ». https://www.sae.org/standards/content/j4000_202104

[8] A. Schumacher, S. Erol, et W. Sihn, « A Maturity Model for Assessing Industry 4.0 Readiness and Maturity of Manufacturing Enterprises », Procedia CIRP, vol. 52, p. 161-166, déc. 2016, doi: 10.1016/j.procir.2016.07.040

[9] W. C. Lucato, A. P. T. Pacchini, F. Facchini, et G. Mummolo, « Model to evaluate the Industry 4.0 readiness degree in Industrial Companies », IFAC-PapersOnLine, vol. 52, no 13, p. 1808-1813, 2019, doi: 10.1016/j.ifacol.2019.11.464

[10] B. Bahu, L. Bironneau, et V. Hovelaque, « Compréhension du DDMRP et de son adoption : premiers éléments empiriques », Logistique & Management, vol. 27, no 1, p. 20-32, janv. 2019, doi: 10.1080/12507970.2018.1547130

[11] « Demand Driven Material Requirements Planning (DDMRP) », ddmain. https://www.demanddriveninstitute.com/ddmrp

[12] M. E. Marzougui, N. Messaoudi, W. Dachry, H. Sarir, et B. Bensassi, « DEMAND DRIVEN MRP: LITERATURE REVIEW AND RESEARCH ISSUES », p. 11, 2020.

[13] A. Azzamouri, P. Baptiste, G. Dessevre, et R. Pellerin, « Demand Driven Material Requirements Planning (DDMRP): A systematic review and classification », *JIEM*, vol. 14, n° 3, p. 439, mai 2021, doi: 10.3926/jiem.3331.

[14] « ISO/CEI 15504 », Wikipédia. 16 juin 2021. Disponible à : https://fr.wikipedia.org/w/index.php?title=ISO/CEI_15504&oldid=183854649

[15] A. Azzamouri, P. Baptiste, G. Dessevre, et R. Pellerin, « Demand Driven Material Requirements Planning (DDMRP): A systematic review and classification », *JIEM*, vol. 14, n° 3, p. 439, mai 2021, doi: 10.3926/jiem.3331.

# Blockchain-based IoT for Industry 4.0: Exploring Opportunities and Applications

Dorcas Dachollom Datiri[1], Maozhen Li[2]

[1]*College of Engineering, Design and Physical Sciences, Department of Electronic and Electrical Engineering, Brunel University, Kingston Lane, Uxbridge, UB8 3PH, London, United Kingdom, dorcas.datiri@brunel.ac.uk*

[2]*College of Engineering, Design and Physical Sciences, Department of Electronic and Electrical Engineering, Brunel University, Kingston Lane, Uxbridge, UB8 3PH, London, United Kingdom*

**ABSTRACT**: Internet of Things (IoT) a societal opulence that has brought about automation of day-to-day activities, and blockchain (BC) a trustless technology that facilitates security are Industry 4.0 enablers. The merging of these paradigms - IoT and BC, births Blockchain based Internet of Things, a concept that has increasingly gained popularity owing to its applicability in versatile scenarios. Blockchain based Internet of Things is an avenue for better provisioning of Quality of Service (QoS), Quality of experience (QoE) and security features to industrial settings. Industry 4.0, the digital transformation of processes within industry and manufacturing/production is plagued with multiple complexities that make it inaccessible for small businesses; specific requirements such as low latency, scalability and security have proven to be the bane of its existence. In this article the thriving BC based IoT which offers potential solutions to security issues such as integrity, privacy, authentication, authorization, accountability, confidentiality, and trust is reviewed and harnessed to develop an approach suitable for Industry 4.0. Considering the advantages as well as lapses of the BC based IoT, concepts such as edge computing (EC) and adaptive algorithms are further explored for the furtherance of Industry 4.0's optimization techniques, thus setting it apart from Industry 4.0's current state of the art. Consequently, the proposed study aims to generate a framework necessary for incorporation of resource optimization techniques and security features in Industry 4.0. In the first phase of the methodology, several works are scrutinized, extracting key features that need addressing to come up with the second phase of the methodology: a framework suitable for reasoning about the algorithmic theories appropriate for resource optimization and security for industry 4.0. Finally, the effectiveness of the framework in bringing about QoS, QoE, security and resource optimization is presented.

**Keywords**: Internet of Things (IoT); Industry 4.0; Blockchain (BC); Edge Computing (EC); Security; Resource Optimization.

**Received** XXX, XXX; **In final form** March 31, 2023; **Published** June 2023



**Corresponding author:** Dorcas Dachollom Datiri, e-mail: dorcas.datiri@brunel.ac.uk

## 1. INTRODUCTION

Internet of things (IoT), the umbrella word for extending the internet beyond smartphones and computers to a whole range of things such as appliances, smart sensors, cars, and traffic lights, requires effective management for supreme efficiency [1]. IoT, which allows accessibility from place at any time has brought a revolution in the current century by enabling ubiquitous and exponential connectivity of billions of devices [2]. The current IoT's applicability extends to all aspects of life; businesses and industries included. In addition to helping industries increase operational efficiency with the convergence of Information Technology (IT) and Operational Technology (OT), Industrial IoT (IIoT) is further bringing an evolution in the manufacturing process by withstanding the mission-critical requirements as compared to IoT [2]. Industry 4.0 (I4.0) also referred to as the fourth Industrial Revolution 4.0 is the digital transformation of processes within industry and manufacturing/production that create value. I4.0 is made up of three (3) core components: firstly, the Cyber-Physical systems (CPS) which is an industry 4.0 enabled environment for manufacturing, consequently providing real-time data collection and analysis; secondly, IoT, a large amount of digital and analog components alongside usage of internet and data communication technology [3]; and finally, IIoT a vital element that harnesses the power of smart machines and real-time analysis to bring about return of investment. The work of [4] gives a summary indicating that Industry 4.0 $\subset$ IIoT $\subset$ IoT and Industry 4.0 = IIoT $\cap$ CPS, however, a more appropriate synopsis for industry 4.0 is the one given by [2] stating that the convergence of IoT, IIoT, and CPS form the Industry 4.0 component.

I4.0 is achieving new heights in the current industrial revolution and marking the beginning of ubiquitous connectivity and expansion of industrial networks.

The concept behind Industry 4.0 is to create new and interlinked industrial systems that can share, use data, and analyse data to drive intelligent actions in the physical world [3]. In the work of [2], the difference between IoT and IIoT is presented, with emphasis on IIoT's requirement for high scalability, interoperability, reliability, and security. Ref. [4] reiterates the need for interoperability, scalability and security arising from the heterogeneous nature of Industry 4.0 components. With the advances in the Industrial Internet of Things (IIoT), cloud computing, extended cloud, and machine-to-machine communications [5], Industry 4.0's prospects for revolutionizing production are immense; thus, manufacturing companies are increasingly integrating innovative technologies including but not limited to blockchain (BC) technologies, machine learning, and big data for more efficient and secure outputs [4].

The fourth Industrial revolution 4.0 is driven by increased connectivity, digitization, and automation. Autonomy of manufacturing assets triggers strong optimization perspectives, new businesses as well as a handful of new threats which need to be properly addressed [6]. Major characteristics of Industry 4.0 resulting in massive data production include: large scale networks and applications, devices and networks heterogeneity, vast number of connected devices, dynamic devices states and measurements [4]. Data generation from Industry 4.0 is extensive owing to the use of devices such as sensors and actuators, thus, in the absence of a robust and secured architecture, I4.0 is susceptible to threats that could hamper its integrity and confidentiality. Threats that could impede the efficiency of the system include Address Resolution Protocol (ARP), network congestion, manipulation from third unauthorised parties and many more [3]. Data mining and data management are important components of I4.0 as they enable well governed data access and extraction, through intelligent methods, as well as effective analysis and decision making for scientific, industrial, or operational use. Decisions are based on both data, and the ability to retrieve the significant data at the relevant time, in appropriate formats, accessible to the specific operators [7]. The huge data generation usually stored in the cloud, the naturally preferred storage technology [5] are prone to latency and bandwidth issues due to the cloud's model which is not realistically developed to handle the variety, volume and velocity of data coming from the I4.0 system [5]. Considering that the key concern of I4.0 is efficient and secure manufacturing which is majorly governed by data management and data mining in real time, this paper:

1. Explores and presents optimization problems of the I4.0.
2. Explores and presents security challenges associated with I4.0.
3. Presents a three-tiered Blockchain-based IoT solution for the I4.0 environment.

In Section two (2), the context of the work is presented, pointing towards potential applications through a synopsis of related works. Section three (3) describes the optimization and security problems associated with I4.0, section four (4) on the other hand delivers a three-tiered blockchain-based IoT, showing its relevance in the I4.0's environment, finally, the conclusion summarizing the work is given in section five (5).

## 2. THEORETICAL BACKGROUND

Industry 4.0, a maturing paradigm that marries advanced manufacturing techniques with the IoT [3] aims at creating the "smart industry" – an integration of complex physical machinery and devices with networked sensors and software, to predict, control and plan for better business and societal outcomes. I4.0 is extending to other application contexts [2] [8], where each context further has its own approach. This therefore suggests that a general framework functional for all industrial contexts and approaches of the fourth industrial revolution 4.0 is near non-existent.

Smart industry, the output of I4.0 can be further defined as an industry in which every element of the system communicates and cooperates with each other as well as humans in real time, through the internet of services [7]. There is therefore an increasing need for the fourth Industrial revolution 4.0 to lean towards a user-centred approach, with the aim of guaranteeing a flawless and natural interaction of the user with the technological systems [8]. In Industry 4.0 as oppose its predecessor Industry 3.0, the products are part of the network, functions are distributed throughout the network structure, and the participants can communicate with each other irrespective of the system hierarchy [2]. I4.0 comes with many advantages to the manufacturing industry, on a business level, its benefits include improved competitiveness, presentability, efficiency, threat mitigation and cost effectiveness. However, owing to its youthful stage Industry 4.0 still has several challenges associated with it. Challenges that plague the burgeoning I4.0 include data security and data leveraging as well as trained human resource and team support [3] [5] [7].

IoT the connection of various devices communicating with each other to bring about automation of daily activities and BC a trustless database used for decentralised transactions are highly effective technologies [3], as well as industry 4.0 enablers. In the industrial sector, IoT aims to make the control and maintenance systems of most industrial processes autonomous and intelligent [9], BC on the other hand is more concerned with creating immutable documentation of all production services, consequently, BC based IoT systems are able to effectively proffer solutions for optimization and security problems associated with the budding Industry 4.0. There are increasing works on industry 4.0, however many of such works are domain-specific with extraordinarily little focus on delivering a general I4.0 framework, aimed at efficiency and security applicable to all industry 4.0 contexts. For instance, the work of [7] focuses on Industry 4.0 in the application context of smart cities, [8] accentuates on industry 4.0 in the application perspective of health, and [9] emphasizes on Indusrty 4.0 in the context of Multimeasurement Wireless sensors to ensure accurate data. It is to this effect that this article aims to provide a framework applicable to all sectors of I4.0.

## 3. INDUSTRY 4.0 OPTIMIZATION AND SECURITY PROBLEM

Industry 4.0's increasing popularity and applicability is ladened with optimization and security problems. For better understanding of the challenges associated with Industry 4.0, this section, is divided in to three (3) subsections, the first subsection examines I4.0's optimization problem, the second presents I4.0 security problem, finally, the third surveys the current solutions for I4.0 optimization and security problem.

### 3.1. Industry 4.0 Optimization Problem

Optimization, the process of finding the best solution from a set of feasible solutions, thus improving a system's performance by realising better efficiency owing to optimal management of resources, is an important requirement for the emerging I4.0. Industry 4.0's optimization problem which stems from IoT's current centralized topology [1] [10] is a deterring factor that necessitates prompt confrontation. The I4.0's optimization problem hinges on several factors, with scalability and heterogeneity being predominant.

Scalability a vital issue in IoT [1] [10] requires standardized distributed and dynamic network models and topologies in addition to communication protocols [4], otherwise a myriad of complexities arise. IoT's current centralized topology gives rise to increased scalability complexities, with just an increase, in the form of an added node [1]. This scalability problem spill over into the Industry 4.0 environment, thus adequate measures need to be taken in order to mitigate arising complexities.

Heterogeneity an equally important problem of the fourth industrial revolution 4.0 requires adequate management for efficacy. In the IoT context, heterogeneity, owing to the varying range of devices combined to form a unit, equates to the implementation of different communication protocols, data formats, and technologies [1] [4] [10]. The I4.0 environment which is a proper subset of IoT equally has an array of heterogeneous devices functioning together to digitally transform processes in the industry. These devices usually follow different protocols and syntaxes, and an improper merger can produce even greater intricacies. The heterogeneity of the fourth industrial revolution 4.0 necessitates satisfactory consideration when developing solutions.

### 3.2. Industry 4.0 Security Problems

Secure access, reliable technology, and data protection become a core part of what companies sell; trust is becoming a critical component of commercial interaction [11]. Owing to several factors such as multiple user entry points, cultural and social factors affecting work habits, intellectual and data property share amongst partners, and network interconnections, securing a company one hundred percent (100%) is virtually impossible in this distributed and integrated I4.0 context [11].

The security problems associated with I4.0 can be considered from an infrastructure and data level viewpoint. In both cases, limiting Industry 4.0 security issues to defending organizational perimeters such as unauthorized access to devices within the network is insufficient, rather, approaching the security issue through the lens of cyber resilience and risk management is more pragmatic. In the industry 4.0 environment, the potential damage of cyberattacks is substantial in terms of continuity of business operations, theft of confidential information, and reputational harm [11].

### 3.3. Current Implementation

Industry 4.0 can be organised into different layers; the sensing layer, network layer and application layer [4]. Current I4.0 implementations have multiple variations hinging on the layer of focus.

Implementations based on the heterogeneous sensing layer is plagued with limited resources and computational functionality due to the differing devices and devices' varying capabilities. Research focusing on the sensing layer promote technologies for reducing power consumption and optimizing resource allocation.

Functions focusing on the second layer – the network layer, produce topological adjustments that encourage efficiency, subsequently improving power consumption and transmission bandwidth. The network layer structures the findings to revolve around heavy resources consumption algorithms for data mining and retrieval for making smarter decisions [4].

Finally, implementations structured around the application layer - most of daily life applications, are steered towards friendly interfaces (Graphical User Interface) for users and RESTful APIs for machine to ease information sharing [4].

[4] in their work portray several methods associated with improving the optimization problem that bedevils I4.0. The attempts provided solutions for I4.0's optimization problem based on the factor of concern; scalability or heterogeneity. The approach tackling the optimization problem, focussing on scalability issues integrates data fusion in ubiquitous environment and integrating cloud and IoT. Confronting the optimization problem from the heterogeneity perspective on the other hand uses different techniques, such techniques include a semantic interoperability model; an architecture for fusing heterogeneous data from multiple sources by generalizing common metadata in datasets; implementing semantics and applying seamless integration and interoperability for solving protocols' heterogeneity; and Bluetooth Low Energy profile adaptor for solving communication interoperability.

Security in the Industry 4.0 context is primarily about strategy and managing of trust through enhanced security features which companies can use to upgrade their competitive positioning as additional revenue streams might be generated through cybersecurity-related services [11]. An array of approaches from a variety of research conducted on the infrastructural and data levels for securing better the IoT and consequently IIoT include technologies for device identification and communication as well as data fusion [4]. The authors of [3] propose a blockchain based Industrial IoT for securing IIoT processes. Several frameworks and standards suggesting an array of cybersecurity methodologies, techniques, checklists, and assessment tools include ISO/IEC 27001, ANSI-ISA-62433 and ETSI TS 103 645 [11].

Table 1. Differences between the Industrial Internet Reference Architecture and Proposed Topology.

| Tier | Industrial Internet Reference Architecture [2] | Proposed Topology |
|---|---|---|
| First | ***Edge Tier*** | ***Edge Layer*** |
| | Varying devices connected to Edge Gateway | Clustered varying devices connected to Cluster Heads |
| | - | User interaction |
| Second | ***Platform Tier*** | ***Dew Layer*** |
| | Performs data transformation, operation, and analytics | Performs data transformation, propagation, offloading and data security measures |
| | Sends information to Enterprise Tier via service network | Resource allocation |
| | - | Load balancing |
| Third | ***Enterprise Tier*** | ***Cloud Layer*** |
| | User performs monitoring and controlling under the domain applications | Data repository |
| | Sends controlling commands to platform tier | - |

## 4. THREE-TIERED FRAMEWORK AND RELEVANCE

This section first summaries the differences between the existing Industrial Internet Reference Architecture (IIRA) and the proposed topology. Thereafter, it details the proposed framework by giving the system's description and detailing its application. The section ends with a representation of the proposed model's prospects in the I4.0 environment.

### 4.1. Standard vs Proposed Topology

According to [2], the Industrial Internet Reference Architecture (IIRA) adapted from the ISO/IEEE/IEC 42010 standards, comprising of three tiers: edge tier, platform tier, and enterprise tier can address the change in industrial control systems by increasing local collaborative autonomy and system optimization through global orchestration. On the other hand, the general architecture of a blockchain based industrial IoT systems (IIoT), a component for industry 4.0 as depicted by [3] has nine core elements: light-weight node; full node; partial hash (Blockchain); local storage; Gateway or base station; Blockchain connector; Cloud storage; Blockchain network and Cloud network. These nine (9) elements work together to ensure a secure blockchain network that tracks orders, payments, accounts, production and many more [3]. Leveraging on the existing reference architecture and BC's general architecture the proposed topology is three-tiered, made up of Edge layer, Dew layer and Cloud layer.

Table 1 summarises the differences between the IIRA and the proposed topology. The proposed model taking into consideration the IIRA and indulging the attributes of the BC is better able to bring about added efficiency and security. From Table 1, it can be deduced that the proposed model puts the user more in control of the activities, further bringing about effective load balancing that translates into resource optimization and better system efficiency.

### 4.2. Proposed Implementation

In a quest for optimal efficiency and security, the intended model labelled PSOR2B-BC (**P**article **S**warm **O**ptimization, **R**ound Robin, **R**esource **B**ased – **B**lock**C**hain) mitigates the previous mentioned problems by adding resource optimization and security features to the current fourth industrial revolution 4.0's environmental setting. Usually, for effective optimization three major steps are necessitated: first, an appropriate model is required, where the objectives, variables and constraints are identified and expressed; second, a determination of the problem type from a range of types – whether continuous or discrete, deterministic, or stochastic, constrained, or unconstrained; and finally, a selection of software appropriate for the selected optimization technique – be it a solver or a modelling software. To this effect, the PSOR2B-BC is a non-deterministic solver with the objective of solving the optimization and security issues associated with the I4.0. The Proposed model places high importance on all I4.0 layers as it is concerned with reducing power consumption, bringing about resource optimization, enabling smarter decision making, and, improving QoS and users' QoE.

The IIoT architectures with centralized controlling mechanisms are being targeted by various security attacks [2], thus the intended topology decentralizes controlling mechanism and enhances security by implementing a distributed topology via the amalgamation of Edge Computing (EC), BC paradigms, in addition to an adaptive algorithm comprising a hybrid algorithm made up of the static Round Robin (RR) and dynamic Resource Based (RB) tagged RR-RB, as well as the Particle Swarm Optimization (PSO) clustering algorithm. This merger aims to bring about resource optimization in addition to security features that will enable the extenuating the attacks common to the current centralized I4.0 topology. The intended framework as depicted in figure 1, consists of three layers: Edge layer (first layer), Dew layer (second layer) and Cloud layer (Third layer).

At the first layer, the concepts of clustering and EC are adopted. The EC paradigm which enables processing of data at greater speed and volume owing to its attribute of processing data closer to where it is generated, plays a key role in minimizing latency and improving security. Clustering on the other hand provides a conducive environment that fosters the advancement of Industry 4.0. The clustering of nodes in the PSOR2B-BC is governed by the Particle Swarm Optimization (PSO) algorithm, which was selected over other clustering algorithms because of its efficiency and ability to work with fewer parameters [1]. The parameter used for clustering in the proposed topology is the Euclidean distance where nodes are clustered based on their proximity to the Cluster Head (CH), which in turn is selected pending two prevailing factors: its proximity to edge servers and its computational and storage capacity. PSO further improves latency and ensures optimal efficiency as it guarantees minimal energy consumption, thus prolonging the battery life of nodes, especially sensor nodes. Furthermore, at this layer, the RR-RB algorithm brings about ideal resource optimization by placing equal importance on resource scheduling and resource allocation [1] [10].

The second layer consisting of the CHs and edge servers is the hub for the BC activities, where authentication, authorization and validation take place to ensure the criterions accountability, confidentiality, integrity, privacy, and trust are met. Fulfilling the previous mentioned criterions implies improved Quality of Service (QoS) and consequently improved Quality of Experience (QoE). The generated blocks are propagated amongst the CH peers ensuring that all records are up to date, thereby eliminating fraudulent activities that may undermine the security of the system. The BC selected for this purpose is the Hyperledger fabric, it was selected over others owing to its efficiency and attribute of allowing predefinition of participants [1].

The third layer consisting of the cloud servers which acts as a repository also propagates blocks amongst participating cloud servers, ensuring that all records are up to date. Retrieval and offloading of blocks from the cloud layer by the peers in the dew layer and vice versa is made seamless by the Hyperledger fabric BC incorporated in the CHs.

In the context of data manipulation, Figure 2 further illustrates the model's functionality at the network layer. At the edge layer, the different nodes in form of devices, sensors, control systems and assets are clustered and connected to the CH via wireless or wired connections in the access network. The CH found in the dew layer is incorporated with the BC technology, thereby enabling it to perform several functions, including and not limited to device management, data management, data propagation, securing data, resource allocation and load balancing. Excess data are offloaded to the cloud layer via the service network. The cloud layer acts as a repository for the excess data generated by the CHs.

The BC incorporated in the CH found at the dew layer governs the offloading, retrieval, and consumption of data from and to the cloud layer, At the edge layer, the user performs the monitoring and controlling under the domain application and sends the controlling commands to the Dew layer through the control flow process. The CH then sends the information as well as best route and appropriate resource to the device in the edge layer to ensure efficient performance of the relevant tasks.

The current IIoT architectures based on BC are subject to scalability, latency, and computational resource issues [1] [2] [10], therefore, incorporating aspects of edge computing as well as clustering ensures that the model is scalable with improved latency. Further incorporation of the hybrid algorithm eliminates bottleneck and latency issues as well as enabling the obtaining of complex real-time and isolated data with low processing time. The BC in the proposed model makes the processing chain secure, traceable, and transparent, thus addressing security and privacy challenges by establishing trust between participating nodes (CH). The CHs incorporated with the BC technology communicate as peers and all transactions are only accessible to permissioned peers. CHs further ensure the detection, computation, and processing of security vulnerabilities to ensure optimal privacy.

Sensors' limited storage and computation capacity is managed by the EC paradigm and clustering technique. The merger reduces the computational and storage requirement of the sensor nodes, thereby mitigating quick death of nodes, subsequently improving efficiency.

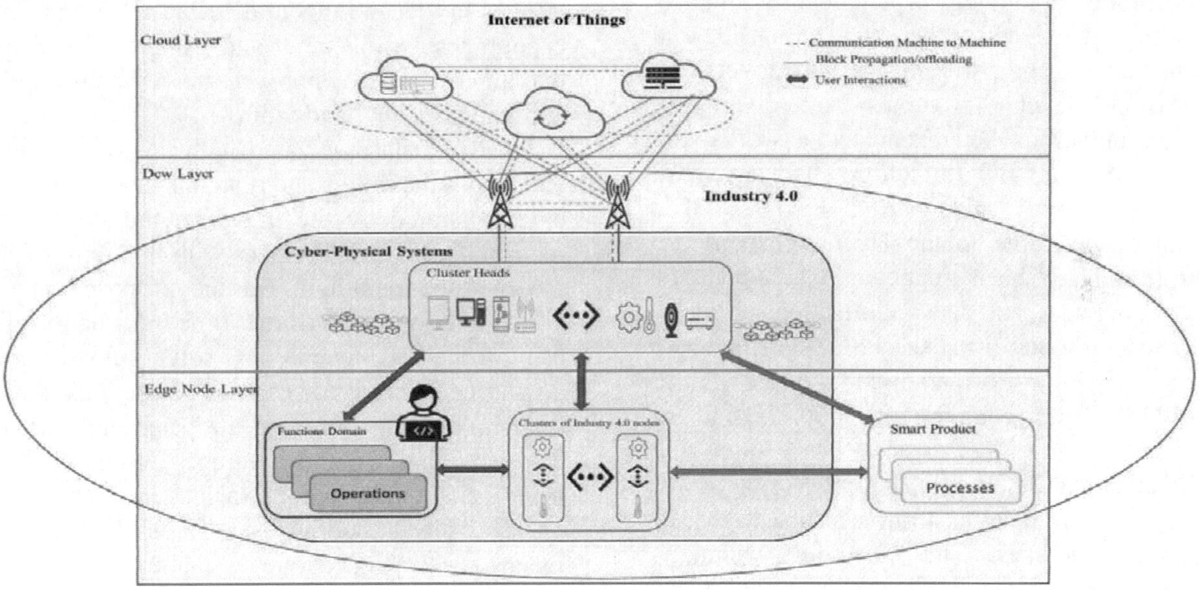


Figure 1. System Model

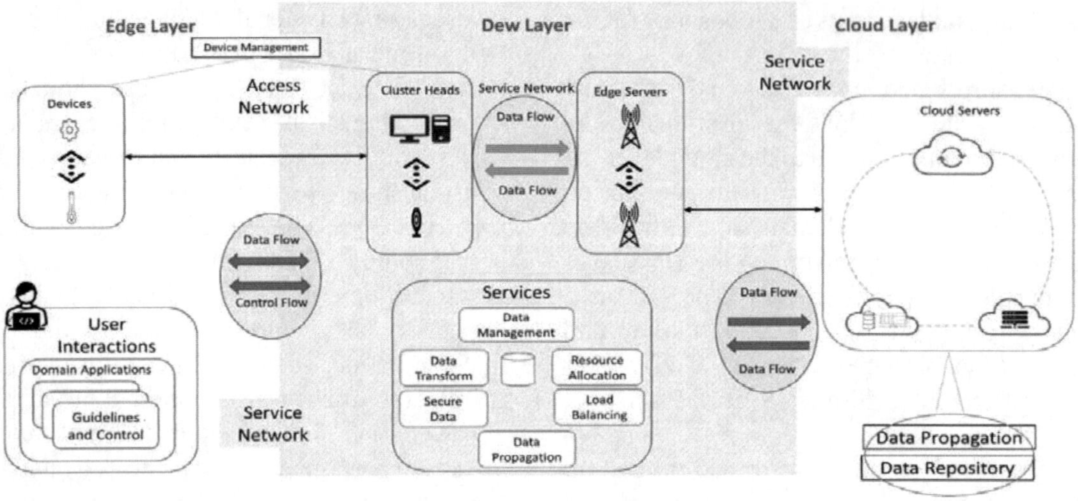


Figure 2. Topology application

### 4.3. PSOR2B-BC Relevance

The proposed topology which focuses majorly on the first two layers of the I4.0 - the sensing and network layers, and partly on the third layer - the application layer, promotes interoperability between numerous heterogeneous networks and devices. PSOR2B-BC's topology enables overall system efficiency, additionally, PSOR2B-BC's relevance applicable to the layers of focus are multiple and have been grouped into three contexts - device, network, and data optimization.

Devices grouped using the PSO algorithm, are governed by the EC paradigm and the hybrid algorithm. This promotes the optimization of resources within the system, by improving communication, battery life, and processing power of all devices, ranging from sensors to heavy industrial machines. The clustering technique further enhances scalability by easing complexities associated with additional devices to the network whereas the EC paradigms enables the reduction of response time and improved fault tolerance. The hybrid algorithm plays a critical role in load balancing by placing equal importance on resource scheduling and resource allocation.

Network optimization is possible via the PSO algorithm, EC paradigm, BC technology and cloud layer. These concepts work together to achieve a distributed system that favours all device types, mobility of devices, interoperability, low latency, and improved scalability. The change in topology implies a decentralized distributed system that encourages efficiency and smarter decision-making owing to improved power consumption and transmission bandwidth.

Finally, Data associated with the system, be it data about the things and domains in the system or data generated by the things in the system, are managed and transformed with the aid of the incorporated paradigms in the proposed model, allowing easy access of real-time information. The use of the BC technology solves cloud server downtime due to its distributed nature; this implies that single point failure is mitigated and efficient data regulation and storage from multiple heterogeneous sources is achieved, thus easing retrieval by abating issues associated with inconsistent, inaccurate, quality and time sensitivity. Moreso, BC enhances security, ensuring that all data is tamper resistant and traceable. BC, a shared distributed ledger manages the data, thereby achieving efficiency,

## 5. CONCLUSIONS

Motivated by Industry 4.0's ability to bring about smart industrial settings within industry and manufacturing/production, this paper sought to bring about efficient business and financial implications by enhancing resource optimization, security, and adequate interoperability amongst machines. Industry 4.0's impeding attributes that are magnified with just an addition of a device, equates immense data generation, heterogeneity, scalability, and latency concerns. The delicacy of Industry 4.0 necessitates adequate optimization, privacy, and security measures in place for efficiency. BC based IoT, a concept which has proven to improve Industry 4.0's security and optimization concerns is inculcated and further advanced by means of the proposed PSOR2B-BC. PSOR2B-BC, hinging on the IoT paradigm is a three-tiered topology that ensures Industry 4.0's equipment with all necessary functionalities for high Quality of Experiences (QoE) and Quality of Service (QoS). PSOR2B-BC, an amalgamation of different concepts and attributes - EC, PSO clustering, BC, and a hybrid algorithm comprising of the static Round Robin (RR) and dynamic Resource Based (RB) algorithms, allows for the framework's flexibility in varying contexts. Industry 4.0's current state of the art's implementation which is dependent on Industry 4.0's layer of focus is domain-specific with no generalized framework for all application scenarios, the proposed PSOR2B-BC on the other hand provides a framework applicable for all application contexts; not only does it stimulate interoperability and optimize resources, but it also provides the much-needed privacy and security measures necessary for an efficient, robust, and secure Industry 4.0. In closing, this paper illustrates PSOR2B-BC's relevance in three contexts – device, network, and data optimization.

## REFERENCES


[1] D. D. Datiri and M. Li, "Effects of Particle Swarm Optimisation on a Hybrid Load Balancing Approach for Resource Optimisation in Internet of Things," *Sensors (Basel, Switzerland),* vol. 23 , no. 4, p. 2329, 2023.

[2] A. A. Mirani, V.-H. Gustavo, A. Awasthi and W. Joseph, "Key Challenges and Emerging Technologies in Industrial IoT Architectures: A Review," *Sensors (Basel),* vol. 22, no. 15, p. 5836, 4 August 2022.

[3] D. Aarju, T. Aditya and W. G. W., "A survey of cyber attacks on blockchain based IoT systems for industry 4.0," *IET blockchain,* pp. 1-15, 27 October 2022.

[4] Y. Mina, H. H. Essam, E. Mohamed and A. A. Abdelmgeid, "Challenges and recommended technologies for the industrial internet of things: A comprehensive review," *Measurement : journal of the International Measurement Confederation,* vol. 151, p. 107198, February 2020.

[5] G. Gemini and M. T. Sabu, "Combinatorial Analysis for Securing IoT-Assisted Industry 4.0 Applications From Vulnerability-Based Attacks," *IEEE Transactions on Industrial Informatics,* vol. 18, no. 1, pp. 3-15, January 2022.

[6] A. Bécue, Y. Fourastier, I. Praça, A. Savarit, C. Baron, B. Gradussofs, E. Pouille and C. Thomas, "CyberFactory#1 – Securing the Industry 4.0 with cyber-ranges and digital twins," in *4th IEEE International Workshop on Factory Communication Systems (WFCS),* Imperia, Italy, 2018.

[7] G. Dinardo, L. Fabbiano and G. Vacca, "A smart and intuitive machine condition monitoring in the Industry 4.0 scenario," *Measurement : journal of the International Measurement Confederation,* vol. 126, pp. 1-12, 2016.

[8] A. Pasquale, D. B. Egidio and D. Luigi, "Design, implementation, and metrological characterization of a wearable, integrated AR-BCI hands-free system for health 4.0 monitoring," *Measurement: journal of the International Measurement Confederation,* vol. 177, p. 109280, June 2021.

[9] M. Alex, M. Hatem and P. Asvin, "Implementation of a reliability test protocol for a multimeasurement sensor dedicated to industrial applications of the Internet of things," *Measurement : journal of the International Measurement Confederation,* vol. 152, p. 107312, 2020.

[10] D. D. Datiri and M. Li, "Load Balancing for Resource Optimization in Internet of Things (IoT) Systems," *Computing and Informatics,* vol. 41, no. 6, pp. 1425-1445, 2022.

[11] G. Culot, F. Fattori, P. M. and M. Sartor, "Addressing Industry 4.0 Cybersecurity Challenges," *IEEE Engineering Management Review,* vol. 47, no. 3, pp. 79-86, 2019.

# *Integration of Industry 4.0 Services and Features in the Banking Sector: Overview and Feasibility*

Samar AOUN[1,3], Roy ABI ZEID DAOU[2,3,*] and Yves DUCQ[1]
[1] Bordeaux Univeristy, Lab IMS, Group Productic, Talence, Bordeaux, France
[2]Université La Sagesse, Faculty of Engineering, Mechatronics Department, Furn Al Chebbak, Lebanon– email: Roy.abizeiddaou@prof.uls.edu.lb
[3] MART Learning, Education and Research Center, Chananir, Lebanon

*Abstract*— **The banking sector and the industry have been closely linked due to the vast advancement in technology. Thus, the evolution of the industry always led to a development in the banking sector in order to be able to satisfy the demands of merchants and customers. The fourth industrial revolution takes digitalization and hyper-connectivity as a starting point to transform the structure of organizations in order to reduce their costs and increase their profits. Hence, Industry 4.0 is characterized by the total integration of all information between the physical world and the digital world within the framework of production processes. The huge amount of data, collected for interconnected technology, is getting smarter and is at the heart of this industrial revolution. Although the banking sector has adopted lots of features developed for Industry 4.0, mainly through the digital and the neo banks, it still lacks lots of achievements that could help customers satisfy their needs in a faster and easier process. Thus, this paper presents the main features of Industry 4.0 and shows how to integrate them, if not realized so far, in the banking business by considering the strategic and the operational tasks that must be satisfied.**

*Keywords*— **Industry 4.0; Banking sector; services and features; Smart systems**

## I. Introduction

The evolution of the industry since the middle of the 18th century was not matched with an evolution of the banking sector. Although this latter is so old (some references reveal that the first banks appeared four millenniums ago [1]), the evolution of this active sector did not follow the advances realized in the industrial sector. Added to that, as both sectors are complementary, in particular after launching Industry 4.0, the integration of new features in the banking sector are more than required [2].

Thus, this paper will present, on one hand, the industrial developments through the four industrial revolutions while focusing on the fourth one. The main technological tools will be shown in Industry 4.0. On the other hand, the different types of modern banks will be presented while comparing the features, the advantages and the limitations of each type.

At a third stage, the features of the industry 4.0 that are not implemented so far in the banking sector will be presented and a model will be proposed to implement them. Note, at this level, that there is no interest in implementing all technological features of Industry 4.0 in the banking sector. A detailed technical presentation will be delivered at this level to validate our choices.

Back to the state of the art, a very reduced number of papers couples the industrial and the banking sectors together. This is visualized at the level of publications where both keywords are present. Thus, when looking at *ScienceDirect* database, one can identify 377 papers regrouping both keywords (*banking sector* and *industry*) whereas more than 2 million papers are found when searching for *industry* and 800,000 when searching for *banking sector* alone. The same results are obtained when going through Ebsco database (it shows papers published between 1995 and 2022) where 111 papers result when searching for both keywords, more than 127,000 papers contain the *industry* keyword and 88,000 have the *banking sector* keyword.

As for the papers dealing with both sectors, one can list the contribution of ***Javaid et al.*** who published a study on the relationship between Industry 4.0 and environmental sustainability. The authors demonstrated the capabilities of Industry 4.0 in dealing with environmental aspects. One of the essential applications is related to the banking sector; in fact, digital platforms and services offer banks the opportunity to simplify their processes, recognize repetitive and tedious activities, and discuss automation solutions with their range of technology partners. Added to that, blockchain banking makes transfers faster and cheaper [3].

In addition, ***Adam et al.*** propose two modeling methods to define corporate risk management of the industry towards the banks: the ERM (Enterprise Risk Management) model for the banking sector and the CAMELS model to assess the performance of banks [4].

Finally, ***Karakaya et al.*** published an article showing the role of banks entering the market on the growth of the manufacturing sector in the states where they invest. The results found show that the incrementation of certain industry types is positively correlated with the banks that offer credit for these industries in the appropriate states [5].

So, based on the above, the novelty of this work will be to correlate the features and services offered by the industrial sector, mainly Industry 4.0, along with the banking services in order to integrate high-end technological features to banks' customers in such a way to facilitate their daily operations.

To sum up, this paper will be divided as follow: in section II, the different revolutions of the industry will be presented while focusing on the main features of Industry 4.0. Section III will present the different types of banks and show a comparison between the features they present. Section IV will propose the new technological tools implemented in the banking sector whereas section V will present a model of the updated bank proposed in this paper. At the end, a conclusion and some future works will be proposed in section VI.

## II. Industry 4.0 Features

Industry 4.0 or the fourth industrial revolution (also called connected or smart industry) integrated first digitalization and hyper-connectivity to transform the organizations' structure in order to reduce their costs and increase their profits [6].

It is characterized by the incorporation of all information between the physical and the digital world within the processes production framework. The huge amount of data, collected for interconnected technology, is getting smarter and is at the core of the fourth industrial revolution.

Intelligent industry reveals the ease of defining market demand and the flexibility of satisfying those demands with respect to parameters' fluctuation. In addition, the transition between the different stages of production and the need for resources and raw materials is also satisfied and correlated.

So far, four generations of the industry have been developed. A brief definition of each generation is provided:

- The first industrial revolution, known as *industrial revolution*, began in England at the end of the 18th century. It was generated following the invention of the steam engine and the mechanization of the textile industry;
- The second industrial revolution appeared at the end of the 19th century in Germany and United States. It is characterized by mass production. The extraction of oil and the invention of electricity made it possible to adapt fashionable materials (steel and aluminum) to cutting-edge industries;
- The third industrial revolution was launched towards the end of the 20th century in the United States and Japan. Industries have moved to the use of computers and the development of information technologies. In addition, nuclear-generated electricity motivated research, bringing out revolutionary materials and participates in the creation of the internet;
- The fourth industrial revolution goes further – it did not only transform production methods, but also changed the basics of distribution, storage and the way customers come into contact with companies.

Figure 1 shows the evolution of the services offered by the industry from industry 1.0 to industry 4.0.

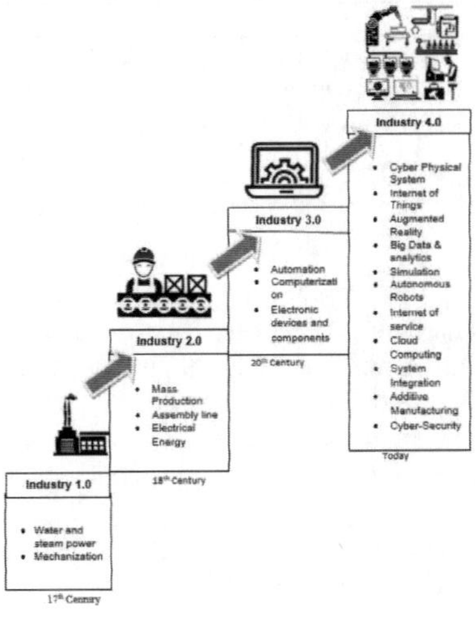


**Figure 1.** Evolution of the services offered by the different generations of industry

Regarding Industry 4.0, Figure 2 shows its particularities as well as the main characteristics and technological tools necessary for this type of industry.

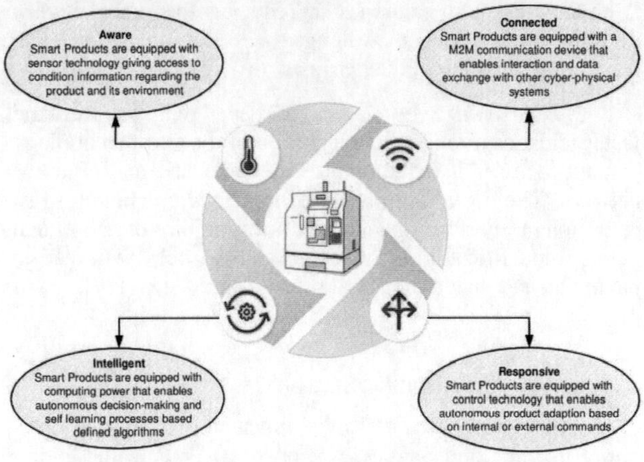


**Figure 2.** Main characteristics and features of Industry 4.0

From the above, it is clear that technology plays a primary role in the evolution of the industry and the creation of Industry 4.0. Thus, network connectivity, speed of response, product monitoring and quality of decisions are key factors in the success of the process. Added to that, to satisfy these factors, technological tools such as the Internet of Things, Big Data, system autonomy, autonomous systems and many others are essential. In the rest of this paragraph, these tools will be further discussed. Thus, the most important features of Industry 4.0 can be summarized by the following thematic:

- ***Internet of Things (IoT):*** it represents the technology used to simultaneously connect physical and virtual objects between them using the Internet or a cloud platform. The IoT is used to limit human intervention and optimize data flows in order to achieve the required service [7]. In 2019, 12% of the industry invested in at least one IoT solution or service. A projection in 2024 shows that the IoT will constitute 25% of the services offered by the industrial sector [8];
- ***Big Data:*** it allows cross-checking and predicting analysis and evaluation of the products and the requests, prospecting analysis (climatic, and environmental), risk management (insurance, commercial, industrial) and decision-making, in different industry types. Big data allows the improvement of the "customer experience" by making it more personalized and contextualized. The diversity of these applications already gives rise to a real economic ecosystem [9] [10] [11];
- ***Artificial Intelligence:*** it represents the set of techniques applied in implementing machines designed to respond referring to human intelligence. Industry 4.0 incorporates one of the richest backgrounds for artificial intelligence [12] [13];
- ***Augmented and virtual reality:*** virtual reality allows a person to isolate himself from the world around him whereas augmented reality carries new fundamentals to the world around him. Virtual reality activates the main senses of the user whereas augmented reality allows a user to build what he sees,

using virtual tools, to obtain the objects that he imagines in a proper environment [14] [15];

- *Digital twins:* It represents the virtual clone of the physical system through the creation of a model coupled to that object (product, machine, process, supply chain) being copied. Digital twins help industries in reducing the time between designing the product, waiting for data acquisition, and generating the final product [16];

- *Blockchain:* It consists of developing smarter and faster logistics through the integration of the latest technology in the processes it requires to create a reliable and effective network. The network aims to include cloud computing in its operations to perform management, traceability of action and helps in identification of goods; all these aspects will lead to having an automated industrial process and system [17].

## III. BANKING SECTOR OVERVIEW

The first prototypes of banks appeared around 2000 BC, mainly in India and Samaria. It consists of merchants giving grain loans to farmers and traders transporting goods between villages. These banks evaluated in ancient Greece, in the Roman Empire, in ancient China and in India at the same era [18].

Having briefly presented the birth of the banking sector, the rest of this section will be reserved for the presentation of the different versions (or type) of banks and a comparison between the services, the features each type offers.

- *Traditional bank:* it is a bank with physical branches offering bank accounts, bank cards, loans, savings, etc;
- *Online banking:* it represents the set of services offered by banks that can be performed online without the physical presence of the customer in the branch. These services are offered either on the bank website or via an application installed on the customer phone;
- *Digital banking:* it represents the set of services that the online bank offers, but this time using a more professional application. This application allows interaction with the bank employees and support center in a fully automated way. Usually, the application is a high-tech system that answer most of the customers needs and accelerates the transactions they ask for. The services of digital banking regroup viewing the account balances, the last transactions, and activating essential teller services (*i.e.,* money exchange, transfers between accounts), paying bills, setting up automatic payments, and managing credit/debit cards;
- *Neo-banking:* it reduced the gap created between the services of the traditional banks and the changes required by customers in this digital age. Neo-banks are financial institutions (that do not have banking licenses and must be partners with other traditional banks in order to operate) offering a cheaper solution for customers (instead of traditional banks). They are almost equivalent to digital banks with no physical branches. They offer services and features that are not provided by traditional banks as personalized solution for each customer and relay mainly on AI to implement these services.

As for the main advantages and limitation presented by these banks (online banks not shown as digital banks became an advanced version of these banks), they are illustrated in table 1.

**Table 1.** Advantages and limitations of the different types of banks

| Advantage 1 | Advantage 2 | Advantage 3 | Limitation 1 | Limitation 2 | Limitation 3 |
|---|---|---|---|---|---|
| **Traditional banks** | | | | | |
| More secure transactions due to the physical presence of customers | Availability of customer service for technical assistance and advice | Customer, especially elders, not required to be high-tech users | Need to open several branches | Cost of running branches and salary of employees | Services available during well-defined hours |
| **Digital banks** | | | | | |
| Service available 7 days / 24 hours | No fees to rent high number of branches or agencies | Relatively small number of jobs compared to traditional banks | Securing customer accounts and transactions | High cost of installing/maintain-ning servers and security programs | Problems of use by the elderly that require technical assistance |
| **Neo banks** | | | | | |
| Relatively low cost | Speed of opening accounts, making transactions… | Convenience like services are offered through an app | Regulatory barriers | Can't operate alone without the presence of traditional/online banks | Need for continuous update and information data to perform AI algorithms |

## IV. EVOLUTION OF THE BANKING SECTOR

The industrial revolution, mainly with the creation of Industry 4.0, has many impacts on the banking sector. These impacts have manifested themselves in many ways, such as:
- the commercial organization model;
- the product offers;
- the work related to safety;
- the external factors of the banking sector;
- the crisis management.

Elaborating manually on all these requirements is severely difficult due to the presence of several parameters and the continuous changes of their values. Thus, a mathematical model representing and validating this system is so complicated.

For that, the use of some features already developed for the industrial sector, mainly for industry 4.0, seems so interesting. Among the six main features shown in section II (*i.e.,* IoT, big data, AI, virtual and augmented reality, digital twins and block chain), one could identify four features that are already implemented, either fully or partially.

The IoT feature is used on a large scale in the banking sector through the integration of security (cameras, alarms,…), the real-time monitoring of accounts, the detection of fraud through the messages received by the customers after each transaction, the display of dashboard representing the account transactions in real time, and the cardless transaction (as linking the account to the customer smart watch).

The big data feature is also widely used on banks due to the needs of processing a hug number of transactions daily. Searching within the database and storing data without applying any advanced computational techniques will not get to an end and will require huge time. Thus, big data algorithms have been implemented in the banking sector since longtime to help manipulating and storing data (most importantly customers and transactions records).

As for blockchain, this concept is extensively applied in finance although the cryptocurrency. Its applications in banks started in 2019 with IBM and some US banks. It mainly helps in currency trading, securing loans, and processing payments [19]. However, this technology, although being so secured, it is still not found in the banking sector.

Finally, the artificial intelligence feature is broadly applied in banks although lots of application paths may still be conquered in this sector. Securing data, proposing dashboard and identifying VIP users while logging in into their accounts are the most applied tools relying on AI.

One should note that the security tools applied in the banking sector are very advanced in comparison to the tools used in the industrial domain due to the damages that could be done if hackers or third-party manipulators login in an illegal way to the system or the database.

In the next section, a general idea of how to integrate technologies, already developed by the industrial sector, in the banks will be presented.

## V. Banks New Perspectives

As already proposed in the previous section, the banking sector still lacks lots of technological tools when being compared to Industry 4.0 although this sector is relatively new compared to the banking sector.

The two tools that are not so far implemented in the bank are the virtual and augmented reality and digital twins. Starting by the digital twins and the virtual reality, their implementations in the banking sector seem not interesting as both features deal with visualizing objects or designs during the phase of design or execution.

However, when it comes to augmented reality, it can be widely used and below are some examples:

- Scanning credit cards while using the bank mobile app can help in delivering all required information regarding the accounts;
- Taking a photo of a new car or new house price can yield to generate the maximum allowed credit that the customer can benefit from, and the monthly payment that results;
- Showing a holiday picture can result in calculating the needed fees and doing the savings whenever the salary of the customer is credited to his account.

As for the AI, although being implemented in banks through the features listed in the previous section, lots of applications can still be improved or even integrated in this sector. The following ideas are proposed:

- Implementing advanced chatbots that can help the customers get answers to their questions or help the employees in being up to date with the new norms and procedures applied at the bank or with new security measures required;
- Generating advanced analytics to customers showing their depends by category (fuel, food, clothing, restaurants, activities…) and presenting weekly, month and yearly budgeting in order to help them in managing their expenses and showing the required income that they have to get in order to fulfil their needs. At this level, some propositions may be generated in order to reach the target.

After presenting the main fields of actions, the modelling can be represented through three different axes (as shown in figure 3):

- strategic, showing how important this feature is for the banking sector;
- tasks, representing the list of requirements that must be fulfilled for the implementation;
- operation, showing a step-by-step procedure needed to implement it.

| **Industry 4.0** | Augmented Reality | Artificial Intelligence |
|---|---|---|
| Strategic | | |
| Tasks | | |
| Operations | | |

| **Digital Banks** | Augmented Reality | Artificial Intelligence |
|---|---|---|
| Strategic | | |
| Tasks | | |
| Operations | | |

**Figure 3.** Modeling the transformation of industry 4.0 services to the banking sector

## VI. Conclusion and Future Works

As a conclusion, this paper has presented the main features of industry 4.0 and digital banks. It had pointed out at the need of technology in order to reach the level of service it delivers nowadays. Concerning the technology in use, computational algorithms and fast communication are the most recurrent tools. As for the comparison between both sectors, the baking sector still far from using all features present in Industry 4.0. Some propositions were made in order to accelerate the investment in this field. A modelling regarding the strategic, tasks and operations was proposed in order to switch between the services offered for both fields.

As a future work, lots of ideas can be proposed:

- Implementation of two AI-based chatbots, one to help the customers in answering their queries and needs and the other to keep the employees informed about the new rules and regulations at the bank;
- Modelling completely the digital banks by including the existing and the proposed features and showing the main risk management items that can affect the banks' activities.

## VII. REFERENCES


[1] N. Ferguson, The Ascent of Money, London: Penguin Books, 2009.

[2] R. Arjun, A. Kuanr and K. R. Suprabha, "Developing banking intelligence in emerging markets: Systematic review aand agenda," *nternational Journal of Information Management Data Insights,* vol. 1, 2021.

[3] M. Javaid, A. Haleem, R. Singh and R. Suman, "Understanding the adoption of Industry 4.0 technologies in improving environmental sustainability," *Sustainable Operations and Computers,* vol. 2, pp. 203-217, 2022.

[4] M. Adam, A. Soliman and N. Mahtab, "Measuring enterprise risk management implementation: A multifaceted approach for the banking sector," *The Quarterly Review of Economics and Finance,* 2021.

[5] N. Karakaya, T. Michalski and E. Ors, "Banking integration and growth: Role of banks' previous industry exposure," *Journal of Financial Intermediation,* 2022.

[6] Y. Liang, Q. Xu and L. Jin, "The effect of smart and connected products on consumer brand choice concentration," *Journal of Business Research,* pp. 163-172, 2021.

[7] L. Atzori, A. Iera and G. Morabito, "Understanding the Internet of Things: definition, potentials, and societal role of a fast evolving paradigm," *Ad Hoc Networks,* vol. 56, no. 1, pp. 122-140, 2017.

[8] Talsom, "Définition: qu'est ce que l'Internet des Objects (IoT)?," Talsom, Montréal, 2019.

[9] P. Delort, "Big Data : un ADN utilisateur séquençable pour moins de 1000 $," *lesechos,* 2012.

[10] L. Rodríguez-Mazahua, C. A. Rodríguez-Enríquez, J. L. Sánchez-Cervantes, J. Cervantes, J. L. García-Alcaraz and G. Alor-Hernández, "A general perspective of Big Data: applications, tools, challenges and trends," *The Journal of Supercomputing,* vol. 72, p. 3073–3113, 2016.

[11] R. Addo-Tenkorang and P. Helo, "Big data applications in operations/supply-chain management: A literature review," *Computers & Industrial Engineering,* vol. 101, pp. 528-543, 2016.

[12] X. Yao, J. Zhou, J. Zhang and C. Boer, "From Intelligent Manufacturing to Smart Manufacturing for Industry 4.0 Driven by Next Generation Artificial Intelligence and Further On," in *5th International Conference on Enterprise Systems (ES),* Beijing, 2017.

[13] M. Poissard, "L'industrie représente l'un des terreaux les plus fertiles pour l'intelligence artificielle," *NeoVision,* 2021.

[14] M. Borel, "La Réalité Augmentée industrielle au service de l'Industrie 4.0," Audros, Saint-Priest, 2020.

[15] L. Damiani, M. Demartini, G. Guizzi, R. Revetria and F. Tonelli, "Augmented and virtual reality applications in industrial systems: A qualitative review towards the industry 4.0 era," *IFAC-PapersOnLine,* pp. 624 - 630, 2018.

[16] T. Uhlemann, C. Lehmann and R. Steinhilper, "The Digital Twin: Realizing the Cyber-Physical Production System for Industry 4.0," *Procedia CIRP,* pp. 335 - 340, 2017.

[17] J. Barata, "The fourth industrial revolution of supply chains: A tertiary study," *Journal of Engineering and Technology Management,* vol. 60, 2021.

[18] A. Beattie, "The Evolution of Banking Over Time," Investopedia, 2021.

# Machine learning for combined predictive strategies in an industrial 4.0 context: a systematic literature review

Jihen Issaoui[1], Nadia Bahria[2], Imen Harbaoui[3]

[1]*University of Tunis El Manar, National School of Engineers of Tunis, LR11ES20 Laboratory Analysis, Design and Control of Systems, 1002, Tunis, Tunisia, jihen.issaoui@enit.utm.tn*

[2]*University of Tunis El Manar, National School of Engineers of Tunis, LR19ES17 Laboratory Optimization and Analysis of Industrial and Service Systems, Tunis, 1002, National School of Engineers of 05 Ave Taha Hussein, 1008, Tunis, Tunisia,nadia.bahria@enit.utm.tn*

[3]*University of Tunis El Manar, National School of Engineers of Tunis, LR11ES20 Laboratory Analysis, Design and Control of Systems, University of Carthage, National Institute of Applied Sciences and Technology, 1080, Tunis, Tunisia, imen.harbaoui @insat.ucar.tn*

**ABSTRACT:** Predictive maintenance (PdM) enabled by machine learning is an integral technology of industry 4.0 that has received considerable attention in recent years. It has led to the emergence of promising tools to support real-time decision making among modern production systems. To benefit from the full potential of this technology, researchers have directly combined PdM with either production scheduling, quality control, or both of those processes. As a result, combined predictive strategies have been introduced in numerous research works under the aim of jointly predicting and optimising manufacturing processes while taking into account the interrelationship between quality, production, and maintenance. The main goal of this paper is to provide a comprehensive review of the combined predictive strategies, to outline the key contributions of researchers, and the future research areas.

**Keywords:** Industry 4.0, Combined predictive strategies, Predictive maintenance, Quality control, Production scheduling, Machine learning.

**Received** January 1, 2023; **In final form** March 31, 2023; **Published** June 2023



**Corresponding author:** Jihen Issaoui, e-mail: jihen.issaoui@enit.utm.tn

## 1. INTRODUCTION

The fourth industrial revolution, known as Industry 4.0 (I4.0), aims to give industries technologically creative ways to handle new business challenges [1]. In this context, companies have devoted significant attention to the concept of I4.0 and its technologies (e.g. Big data, AI, IOT…), to boost their productivity, profitability, and process flexibility. Artificial intelligence (AI) is one of the disruptive techniques of I4.0 that have revolutionised the industrial sector. In fact, through its popular subfield named Machine Learning (ML), it has consistently proven its value in driving intelligence within manufacturing operations, and providing manufacturers with solutions to make real-time decisions. PdM is a key I4.0 innovation that has greatly benefited from the application of ML. In fact, through the analysis of real and historical data, it becomes easier to foresee equipment failure, which can lead to a substantial increase in machine availability [2]. Hence, PdM empowered by ML, has become an attractive innovation for both industrial practitioners and academic researchers. As a result, many literature studies have been carried out to optimise PdM policy through the utilisation of ML methods [3]-[5]. Despite the promising results demonstrated by the above attempts, PdM has always been an effective way for high-performance processes in the context of intelligent systems, while it is directly merged either with production scheduling [12], [16], [10], [17], with quality control [28], [29], or with both processes [35]. In this context, and dealing with the *"prediction and manufacturing"* philosophy, new combined predictive strategies (CPS) have been investigated in order to optimise processes while considering the substantial connection between the three operational pillars. As the prior literature reviews have mostly addressed PdM decision models, but have not examined CPS, this paper addresses this gap, it focuses mainly on a systematic literature review of recent studies related to the different CPS. The remainder of this paper is organised as follows: section 2 describes relevant research methodology; a literature review related to the three CPS and the technologies that can support them are outlined in section 3; section 4 presents a discussion and provides a future research area. Finally, section 5 concludes this paper.

## 2. METHODOLOGY

The selection approach adopted in this paper is based on the search method described by B. Kitchenham et al. in [6]. A manual search process of specific journal papers was proceeds as followed: the available papers were gathered from the academic online sources while using the mentioned keywords illustrated in table.1. All relevant articles were reviewed and broken into three layered categories as follows: (1) PdM-IPS strategy; (2) PdM-IQC; and (3) (PdM-IPS&QC) strategy. Then, the collected papers were organised, cleaned according the inclusion and exclusion criteria. Finally, the remaining papers were reviewed and analysed.

Table1: Literature review process

| | |
|---|---|
| **RESEARCH QUESTION** | - Highlighting deployed application of machine learning for combined predictive strategies in an industrial 4.0 context |
| **KEYWORDS** | (1) PdM integrated production scheduling (PdM-IPS) strategy; (2) PdM integrated quality control (PdM-IQC) strategy; and (3) PdM integrated production scheduling and quality control (PdM-IPS&QC) strategy, (4) Industry 4.0, (5) Artificial intelligence AI, (6) machine learning ML |
| **INCLUSION CRETERIA** | -Academic papers and review written in English.<br>- Journal papers published since 2015. |
| **EXCLUSION CRETERIA** | -Papers non refereed and outside the research area. |
| **ONLINE SOURCES** | -Science direct and Google scholar |
| **LIMITATION** | -The selection process may disregard useful papers which can enrich this work. |

## 3. PREDICTIVE COMBINED STRATEGIES

### 3.1. Predictive maintenance integrated production scheduling (PdM-IPS) strategy

Production scheduling (PS) is defined as the way in which the duration of tasks can be arranged while assigning needed resources to accomplish them. It is a key part of production systems [7]. PdM has emerged as a novel idea in intelligent manufacturing systems, replacing the time-based maintenance. Unlike traditional maintenance methods, PdM can provide many benefits by increasing machine availability and performance [8], and strengthening the business model of companies [9]. These two concepts have been widely examined independently in previous works. However, numerous studies have found that addressing them separately cannot match with the real industrial world [7], [10],[17]. In fact, frequent maintenance activities that are not taken into account in the production plan can cause production disruption and machine unavailability and therefore lead to bad decision-making [10]. To address this, a new PdM-IPS strategy has been properly established with the aim of ensuring optimal production scheduling by predicting and preventing equipment failures. This strategy has been defined in the literature as " *production scheduling with availability constraints* ". Researchers have made attempts to investigate this strategy in a dynamic and deterministic environment, where maintenance operations can be performed only when they are required, based on the information collected from a Prognostic Health Management (PHM) module [12]. PHM has turned into an unavoidable deterministic feature especially with the advent of the I4.0 concept [2], as it provides the access to the current and future health state of a system [13], and the indicators to pilot and maintain production and equipment [25]. In this context, an integrated prognostic based on integrating PdM information extracted from PHM outputs in the scheduling of several jobs on a single multifunctional machine has been presented in [12] with the objective of minimising the total maintenance cost. To solve the combined PdM flow shop scheduling problem and to obtain the best interpretation of PHM results an integrated prognostic genetic algorithm (GA) has been developed. Within the same scope, [14] has proposed a Mixed Integer Linear Programming model and a new prognostic-based GA to cope with the process uncertainty while solving the PdM-IPS problem. Another study investigating the permutation flowshop scheduling as a restricted version of the flowshop problem under availability constraints was carried out in [15]. A hybrid of variable neighbour search and fuzzy logic algorithm has been used to model PHM outcomes and to obtain near optimal integrated solution. Following a similar approach to that used in the previous research, a Fuzzy logic method has been proposed in [7], as well as an improved GA solving the fuzzy permutation flowshop scheduling problem with PdM interventions. A tailored GA has been presented in [16] to solve this problem under the objective of minimising makespan. The previous models were extended to include another production systems typology which is Jobshop. For instance, a new joint conceptual framework of PdM-IPS has been introduced in [17], in which machine deterioration, as well as operation specific stress equivalents, were taken into account. With the same regard, a new decision- making approach has been presented in [10], where prognostics information and available resources are combined to obtain the optimal PS and maintenance decisions, while considering the health status and the dummy age subjected to machine degradation. Furthermore, the joint job shop production and PdM problem has been studied also in [11] and [18], with the aim of predicting and preventing the machine failure and making the best decision at each time. Recently, I4.0- enabling technologies have shown their promise in dealing with the new operating requirements and the decreasing complexity of modern manufacturing systems. More specifically the accelerated growth in the area of AI and ML based solutions have significantly affected both production and maintenance activities and the manner in which they are scheduled and implemented. Thus, comprehensive CPS created with and for industrial data and taking advantage of these technologies, have become a necessity to cope with actual industrial practices [19]. As a result, the existing CPS have been strengthened by ML algorithms in order to deliver promising results in terms of predictive performance, computation effort, and interpretability [8]. From this perspective, a holistic framework has been established in [19], in which an extended version of the PdM integrated flexible Job Shop problem has been investigated. A generative deep learning approach based on the conditional variational autoencoder has been employed to calculate the machine health condition and a two–stage GA was used to solve the mathematical model. The previously described work has been extended in [20] through the development of a subsequent solution of the problem while using a novel two-stage GA based mainly on the interaction of the PdM-IPS problem and the PHM module. A PdM & Schedule approach has been proposed in [21], and several models based on deep neural networks (DNN) and recurrent neural networks (RNN) have been tested in this paper. Additionally, a novel framework which includes PdM constraints in a dynamic flow-shop PS, while using ML-assisted simulation approach has been introduced in [22]. The development of this framework was aided by the use of two software tools capable of avoiding the hard coding which are Microsoft Azure and Flexim. In addition, reinforcement learning (RL) has made a significant contribution to the development and optimization of the PdM-IPS strategy. In this context, a RL approach has been developed in [23], in order to determine the optimal policies that jointly optimise production and maintenance cost. A decision approach based on the combination of the Markov chain model and approximate dynamic programming has been used while taking into account the bottlenecks machines. Other I4.0-enabling technologies have been utilised in this field. For example, a cloud based cyber-physical system for adaptive shop-floor scheduling and CBM has been provided in [13], in order to enable robust and resilient digitalization and to ensure businesses' cost-effectiveness. In the same context, the potential of digital twin in the combination of maintenance plans and production planning control in a prescriptive way has been highlighted in [24], also a new paradigm known as prescriptive maintenance which is able not only to estimate equipment health condition but also to prescribe automatic, or manual solutions has been presented in this paper. The above works have demonstrated that the PdM-IPS strategy supported by I4.0 enabling-technologies become essential in the process of decision-making.

### 3.2. Predictive maintenance integrated quality control (PdM-IQC) strategy

In this strategy, PdM is primarily focused on maintaining the quality of the product by predicting and preventing defects in the manufacturing process. Numerous studies have been conducted with the aim of minimising machine failures and raising quality assurance. However, these models didn't take into account the real-time and future machine conditions which could result in earlier or later interventions. For that, PdM-IQC strategy has been developed in the context of *"prediction and manufacturing"*. Indeed, in order to study the causality relation between machine monitoring and product quality, an innovative approach has been presented in [25] with the objective of anticipating part quality deviations and providing a set of machine health indicators. From this perspective, an integrated strategy of product quality and machine reliability has been proposed in [26]. As well, a model in which the product quality level and PdM decision-making were integrated has been investigated in [27]. SPC, or statistical process control, is touted as a widely used method for measuring and keeping track of quality by carefully examining a specific production process [28]. It has been demonstrated in [28], [29], that the combination of this method with PdM can produce more value than when used separately. For example, the integration of PdM and SPC has been treated in [29] and the X-bar control chart has been selected as an appropriate graphical tool to monitor the process of quality control under the real-time machine health condition. To create more sophisticated proactive policies based on SPC, online-quality monitoring should be used [30]. In this context, the viability of a different sort of control chart, the CUSUM chart, in PdM-IQC strategy has been expanded upon in [28], also Naive-Bayes and other ML techniques have been utilised to assist decision-making. Whereas the prediction of RUL, known as the equipment time before failure, has been the focus of [29], the prediction of tooling-component degradation monitored via real-time online sensors has been investigated in [31]. Through the use of a data driven-dynamic model, the deterioration of product quality and machine reliability was predicted to establish the dynamic cost rate function. The potential of PdM empowered by I4.0-enabling technologies has been explored in [32], through the development of a PdM platform. The proposed platform aims not only in fault prediction, but also in product design and lifecycle management. While these studies have considered PdM as an effective way to identify and eliminate quality deviation and machine failure, continuous quality control has been recognized in [33] as an additional indicator for maintenance needs as it can provide input to online PdM in situations where there are no outward indications of maintenance issues. In conclusion, PdM-IQC strategy has shown a significant contribution in the improvement of quality control and machine availability.

### 3.3. Predictive maintenance integrated production scheduling and quality control (PdM-IPS&QC) strategy

For this strategy, PdM emphasizes both preserving product quality and streamlining the production schedule, in order to meet production targets and best product quality. For instance, a job shop system with fused deposition modelling machine unavailability constraints due to PdM tasks and with good-quality has been established using the ant-colony optimisation algorithm in [34]. An optimisation problem has been formulated as a Markovian decision process in [35], in order to derive the optimal PdM-IPS&QC strategy that contributes to the cost-effectiveness and the profitability of the manufacturing system. The optimal joint policy has been derived by ML, more specifically RL technique.

## 4. DISCUSSIONS

PdM-IPS strategy has gained more attention in literature studies followed by the PdM-IQC strategy, however a few studies have been done regarding the PdM-IPS&QC strategy as shown in Figure.1. I4.0 enabling-technologies have greatly supported these strategies and give them the potential to be more useful in industrial area. ML techniques used to address each class vary depending on the specific focus, in fact for the PdM-IPS strategy, neural network models in notably CAVE and LSTM were the most utilized machine learning techniques. In recent years, RL has drawn increased attention for both PdM-IPS and PdM-IPS&QC strategies. However, Naïve bayes classifier and deep RL algorithm [28] have served to the optimization of PdM-IQC strategy. As a result of this paper which is the first part of our research, two significant gaps are revealed, shown first of all by the few existing papers especially on the PdM-IPS&QC strategy and secondly is the implementation of these strategies within the industrial IT-landscape is remains missing.

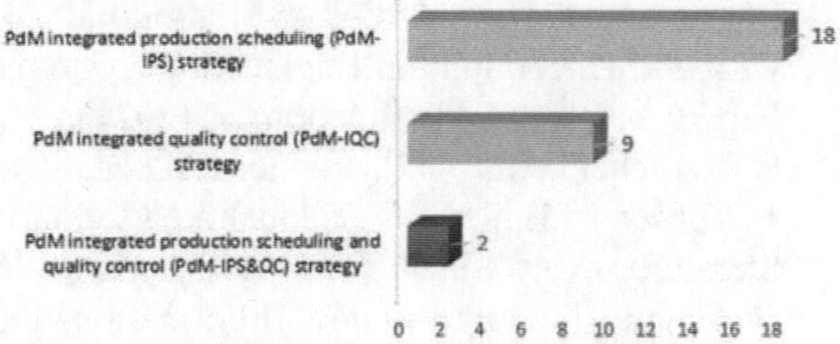


Figure1: Literature papers classification

## 5. CONCLUSIONS

This paper is the first part of our research, it aims to provide a general overview about the following CPS: (1) PdM-IPS strategy, (2) PdM-IQC strategy, and (3) PdM-IPS&QC strategy, established to improve manufacturing performance while focusing on the potential contribution of the I4.0 enabling technologies in supporting these strategies.

**ACKNOWLEDGEMENT**

No potential conflict of interest was reported by the author(s)

**REFERENCES**

*[1]* O.Cardin, F.Ounnar, A.Thomas, D. Trentesaux Future industrial systems: best practices of the intelligent manufacturing and services systems (IMS2) French Research Group, IEEE Trans. Ind Inform. 13, 704-713, (2017). *DOI: 10.1109/TII.2016.2605624.*

*[2]* Z.M.Cenar,A.A.Nuhu, Q.Zeeshan, O.Korhan, M.Asmael, B.Safaei, Machine learning in predictive maintenance towards sustainable smart manufacturing in industry 4.0, MDPI Sustainability, 12, 1-42, (2020). *DOI:10.3390/su12198211*

*[3]* E.Florian, F.Sgarbossa, I.Zennaroa, Machine learning-based predictive maintenance: A cost-

oriented model for implementation, I. J of Production_Economics, 236, (2021). *DOI:10.1016/j.ijpe.2021.108114*

*[4]* K.T.P. Nguyen ,K.Medjaher, A new dynamic predictive maintenance framework using deep learning for failure prognostics,Reliability Engineering and System Safety,13, 251-262, (2019). *DOI: 10.1016/j.ress.2019.03.018*

*[5]* Y. Ren,Optimizing Predictive Maintenance With Machine Learning for Reliability Improvement,The ASCE-ASME Journal of Risk and Uncertainty in Engineering Systems, Part B: Mechanical Engineering,7, (2021).

*[6]* B. Kitchenham, O.P.Brereton, D.Budgen, M.Turner, J.Bailey, S.Linkman, Systematic literature reviews in software engineering – A systematic literature review, Information and Software Technology,7–15, (2009), Doi:10.1016/j.infsof.2008.09.009

*[7]* A.Ladj, F.Benbouzid-Si Tayeb , C.Varnier, A.A Dridi, N.Selmane, Improved Genetic Algorithm for the Fuzzy Flowshop Scheduling Problem with Predictive Maintenance Planning, IEEE, 1301-1305, (2019). *DOI : 10.1109/ISIE.2019.8781464*

*[8]* E.Azeb, M. Nafea, L.A.Shihata, M.Mashaly, A Machine-Learning-Assisted Simulation Approach for Incorporating Predictive Maintenance in Dynamic Flow-Shop Scheduling, Appl.Sci. 11, 1-17, (2021). *DOI: 10.3390/app112411725*

*[9]* M.Calabrese, M.Cimmino, F.Fiume, M.Manfri n, L.Romeo, S.Ceccacci, M.Paolanti, G.Tosca no, G.Ciandrini, A.Carrotta, M. Mengoni, E. Frontoni, D. Kapetis, SOPHIA: An Event-Based IoT and Machine Learning Architecture for Predictive Maintenance in Industry_4.0, MDPI, 11, 117, (2020). *DOI:10.3390/info11040202*

*[10]* Q. Liu a, M. Dong b, F.F. Chen, Single-machine-based joint optimization of predictive maintenance planning and production scheduling, Robotics and computer-integrated-manufacturing, 51, 238-247, (2018). *DOI:10.1016/j.rcim.2018.01.002*

*[11]* G.Bencheikh, A.Letouzey, X.Desforges, An approach for joint scheduling of production and predictive maintenance activities, J.Ofmanufacturing systems, 64,546-560, (2022). *DOI: 10.1016/j.jmsy.2022.08.005*

*[12]* A. Ladj, C. Varnier, F. Benbouzid-Si Tayeb, IPro-GA: an integrated prognostic-based GA for scheduling jobs and predictive maintenance in a single multifunctional machine, IFAC, 49, 1821-1826, (2016). *DOI:10.1016/j.ifacol.2016.07.847*

*[13]* D.Mourtzis, E.Vlachou, A cloud-based cyber-physical system for adaptive shop-floor scheduling and condition based maintenance, Journal of Manufacturing Systems, 47, 179-198, (2019). *DOI: 10.1016/j.jmsy.2018.05.008*

*[14]* A.Ladj, C.Varnier, F.B.Si Tayeb, N.Zerhouni, Exact and heuristic algorithms for post prognostic decision in a single multifunctional machine, International journal of prognostics and health management, 8, 1-15, (2017). *DOI: 10.36001/ijphm.2017.v8i2.2620*

*[15]* A.Ladj, C.Varnier, F.B.Si Tayeb, A.A.Dridi, N.Selmane,A Hybrid of Variable Neighbor Search and Fuzzy Logic for the permutation flowshop scheduling problem with predictive maintenance, Procedia computer science,112, 663-672,(2017). *DOI:10.1016/j.procs.2017.08.120*

*[16]* A.Ladj, F.B.Si Tayeb, C.Varnier, Tailored Genetic Algorithm for Scheduling Jobs and Predictive Maintenance in a Permutation Flowshop, IEEE, (2018). *DOI: 10.1109/ETFA.2018.8502462*

*[17]* S.Zhai, A.Riess, G.Reinhart, Formulation and Solution for the Predictive Maintenance Integrated Job Shop Scheduling Problem,IEEE, (2017). *DOI: 10.1109/ICPHM.2019.8819397*

*[18]* C.Fitouri, N.Fnaiech, C.Varnier, F.Fnaiech, N.Zerhouni, A Decison-Making Approach for Job Shop Scheduling with Job Depending Degradation and Predictive Maintenance, IFAC, 49, 1490-1495, (2016). *DOI:10.1016/J.IFACOL.2016.07.782*

*[19]* S.Zhai, B.Gehring, G.Reinhart, Enabling predictivemaintenance integrated production

scheduling by operation-specific health prognostics with generative deep learning, Journal of manufacturing systems, 61, 830-855,(2021). *DOI: 10.1016/j.jmsy.2021.02.006*

*[20]* S.Zhai, M.G.Kandemir, G.Reinhart, Predictive maintenance integrated production scheduling by applying deep generative prognostics models: approach, formulation and solution, Production engineering,16,1-24, (2021). *DOI: 10.1007/s11740-021-01064-0*

*[21]* Z.Tiago, C.A.D.Costa, F.A.Zeiser, R.D.R.Righi, A predictive maintenance model for optimizing production schedule using deep neural networks, Journal of manufacturing systems,62,450-462, (2022). *DOI: 10.1016/j.jmsy.2022.08.005*

*[22]* E.Azab, M.Nafea, L.Shihata, M.Mashly, A Machine-Learning-Assisted Simulation Approach for Incorporating Predictive Maintenance in Dynamic Flow-Shop, Appl Sci, 11, 1-17, (2021). *DOI:10.3390/app112411725*

*[23]* M.FENG,Y.LI, Predictive maintenance decision making based on reinforcement learning in multistage production systems, IEEE ,10, 18910-18921, (2022). *DOI: 10.1109/ACCESS.2022.3151170*

*[24]* A.Padovano, F.Longo, L.Nicoletti, L.Gazzaneo, A.Chiurco, S.Talarico, A prescriptive maintenance system for intelligent production planning and control in a smart cyber-physical production line, Procedia CIRP, 104, 1819-1824, (2021). *DOI:10.1016/j.procir.2021.11.307*

*[25]* A.Voisin, T.Laloix, B.Lung, E.Romagne, Predictive Maintenance and part quality control from joint product-process-machine requirements: application to a machine tool, Procedia manufacturing, 16, 147-154, (2018). *DOI: 10.1016/j.promfg.2018.10.166*

*[26]* C.Gu, Y.He, X.Han, Z. Chen, Integrated predictive maintenance strategy for manufacturing systems by combining quality control and mission reliability analysis,I.J. of production and research, 55, 5841-5862, (2018). *DOI: 10.1080/00207543.2017.1346843*

*[27]* Y.He, C.Gu, Z. Chen, X.Han, Product quality oriented predictive maintenance strategy for manufacturing systems, IEEE, (2017). *DOI: 10.1109/PHM.2017.8079213*

*[28]* C.Saidy, K.Xia, A.Kircaliali, R.Harik, A.Bayoumi, The Application of Statistical Quality Control Methods in Predictive Maintenance 4.0: An Unconventional Use of Statistical Process Control (SPC) Charts in Health Monitoring and Predictive Analytics, Springer, 1051-1061, (2017). *DOI: 10.1007/978-3-030-57745-2_87*

*[29]* Y.Li, E.Pan, Z.Chen, Considering Machine Health Condition in Jointly Optimizing Predictive Maintenance Policy and X-bar Control Chart, IEEE, 328-337, (2017). *DOI: 10.1109/GSIS.2017.8077727*

*[30]* M.Colledani, A.Yemane, A.Tognetti, M.Analysis of In-line Quality-oriented Assembly Strategies in the Production of Electric Drives, Procedia CIRP, 50, 784-789(2016).*DOI: 10.1016/j.procir.2016.05.032*

*[31]* B.Lu, Z.Chen, X.Zhao, Data-driven dynamic predictive maintenance for a manufacturing system with quality deterioration and online sensors, Reliability engineering and system safety, 212, (2021). *DOI: 10.1016/j.ress.2021.107628*

*[32]* C.Saidy, S.P.Valappil, R.M.Matthews, A.Bayoumi, Development of a Predictive Maintenance 4.0 Platform: Enhancing Product Design and Manufacturing, Smart Innovation, Systems and technologies,166, 1035-1049, (2021).*DOI: 10.1007/978-3-030-57745-2_86*

*[33]* J.Lindstrom, H.Larsson, M.Jonsson, E.Lejon, ,Towards intelligent and sustainable production: combining and integrating online predictive maintenance and continuous quality_control, Procedia CIRP, 63, 443-448, (2017). *DOI: 10.1016/j.procir.2017.03.099*

*[34]* I.Paprocka, W.M.Kempa, Model of Production System Evaluation with the Influence of FDM Machine Reliability and Process-Dependent Product Quality, Materials, 14, 1-25, (2021). *DOI: 10.3390/ma14195806*

*[35]* P.D.Paraschos,G.K.Koulinas,D.E.Koulouriotis, Reinforcement learning for combined production-maintenance and quality control of a manufacturing system with deterioration failures, J.of manufacturing systems, 56, 470-483, (2020). *DOI:10.1016/j.jmsy.2020.07.004*

# Analysis of Research Trend and Detection Technology of Hydrogen Damage in Metallic Materials

ChenXi Zhu[1], Qin Hu[1], Haiting Zhou[1], Qiang Wang[1], Dongdong Ye[2], Muda Jin[3]

[1] *College of Quality and Safety Engineering, China Jiliang University, Xueyuan street, No. 258, 310018, Hangzhou, China*
[2] *School of Artificial Intelligence, Anhui Polytechnic University, Beijing Middle Road, No. 8, 241004, Wuhu, China*
[3] *Zhejiang Academy of Special Equipment Science, Taixuan Road, No. 211, 310009, Hangzhou, China*

**ABSTRACT**: The development of the hydrogen energy industry has put forward higher requirements on material properties, and it is urgent to investigate the effects of hydrogen on metallic materials. In order to summarize the research status of hydrogen damage and provide a reference for future researchers, this paper selected the relevant literatures collected in the core journals from Web of Science from 2008 to 2022 as samples, and made statistical analysis in terms of the number of published articles, detection methods and research hotspots. In recent years, authors and institutions have paid more and more attention to the field of hydrogen damage, but have not yet forms close cooperation. The current research focus is mainly on the micro level to study the mechanism of hydrogen damage, and various testing techniques are used to determine the impact of hydrogen damage on the properties of metallic materials. Tensile testing has always occupied the dominant position of destructive testing, and ultrasonic testing has gradually replaced acoustic emission testing, beginning to occupy the important position of non-destructive testing. Researchers have noticed the necessity of extensive cooperation, and the research focuses mainly on the exploration of hydrogen damage mechanism and prediction of hydrogen damage degree.

**Keywords**: metallic materials; hydrogen damage; VOSviewer; bibliometrics; detection methods

**Received** January 1, 2023; **In final form** March 31, 2023; **Published** June 2023



**Corresponding author:** Haiting Zhou, e-mail: zhouhaiting@cjlu.edu.cn

As far back as 1817, it was discovered that pickling could reduce the ductility of steel. With the onset of the industrial revolution and the rising demands for metal materials in the early 20th century, scholars began a systematic investigation into the effects of hydrogen on metal materials. Hydrogen damage refers to the harm caused to metal or alloy by hydrogen during production, processing, and use. The root cause of such damage lies in the degradation of metal material performance due to the ingress of hydrogen, typically resulting in decreased plasticity and increased brittleness. Researchers at this stage primarily categorize hydrogen damage as hydrogen embrittlement, hydrogen bubble, hydrogen-induced crack, hydrogen corrosion, and so forth [1]. Metal hydrogen damage can lead to catastrophic accidents and result in significant economic losses and even casualties. It is a subject of great importance in engineering practice and has received widespread attention in recent years. With the increasing use of high-strength steel in modern industry, the problem of metal hydrogen damage has become more acute, and its detection methods have continued to develop, improve, and innovate. Both destructive and non-destructive detection techniques have been widely employed.

Existing literature reviews on hydrogen damage often focus on its mechanisms[2, 3], practical applications[4], and protective measures[5]. For instance, Laadel, NE[6] provides a summary of the mechanism and contributing factors behind hydrogen embrittlement, while Professor Xie[7] of Xi'an Jiaotong University concentrates on the effects of hydrogen on the behavior of micro-defects in materials, such as vacancies, dislocations, and interfaces. Mohtadi-Bonab, MA[8] has studied methods for improving steel's resistance to hydrogen-induced cracking. However, there are few studies that use bibliometric analysis to statistically analyse hydrogen damage detection technology.

To gain a comprehensive understanding of the research topic of hydrogen damage and the recent advancements in its detection technology, this paper utilizes bibliometric analysis. The visual tool VOSviewer is employed to conduct cooperative network analysis, co-citation analysis, co-occurrence analysis, and other relevant techniques to show the relationships between documents in a visual format. This approach enables researchers to quickly and efficiently comprehend the current research status and future development trends in the field of hydrogen damage, ultimately promoting a better understanding of hydrogen damage monitoring and detection technology.

## 1. RESEARCH OBJECT AND DATA SOURCE

### 1.1. Research object

In many cases, the mechanical and anti-corrosion properties of various metals and alloys are compromised by hydrogen during smelting and usage. This poses a significant threat to the safety of metal materials in the machinery manufacturing, infrastructure, and energy industries[7]. The penetration of hydrogen atoms or molecules into metal can cause different types of damage, such as hydrogen embrittlement, hydrogen bulging, hydrogen cracking, and more. To explore the research hotspots, future trends, and detection methods related to investigating the behaviour of hydrogen damage in metals and alloys, this study focuses on different types of hydrogen damage using the VOSviewer software for analysis and summary. The outcomes of this analysis can provide valuable insights and references for researchers in the field of hydrogen damage.

### 1.2. Data source

This study utilized the core collection of Web of Science as the primary data source, with a focus on retrieving relevant literature from various disciplines using the subject field. The retrieval formula used was "hydrogen damage" and (test* or detection*) and (steel* or alloy*), covering all years. A total of 572 articles were initially retrieved. The specific deletion and selection steps are shown in Figure 2, Web of Science categories were used to exclude six categories of literature that were not relevant to the research topic, including "Microbiology", "Dentistry Oral Surgery Medicine", "Medicine Research Experimental", "Oncology", and "Veterinary". This resulted in a total of 566 articles being included in the analysis. The source types of these literature are shown in Figure 1, with the majority coming from the fields of materials science, metallurgical engineering, and engineering machinery.

During the analysis process, the title and abstract of each literature were examined to determine whether they should be excluded based on two criteria. Firstly, the research object of the literature must be related to the hydrogen damage behaviour of metal materials. Secondly, the literature must involve the use of one or more hydrogen damage detection methods. A total of 291 literatures were excluded based on these criteria, leaving 275 available literatures, including 55 conference papers and 220 journal papers. The literature covered a period from 2008 to 2022.

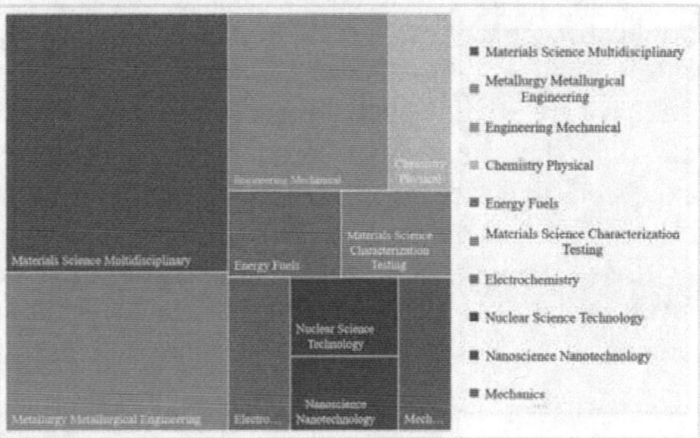


Figure 1. Top 10 Types of Literature Sources.

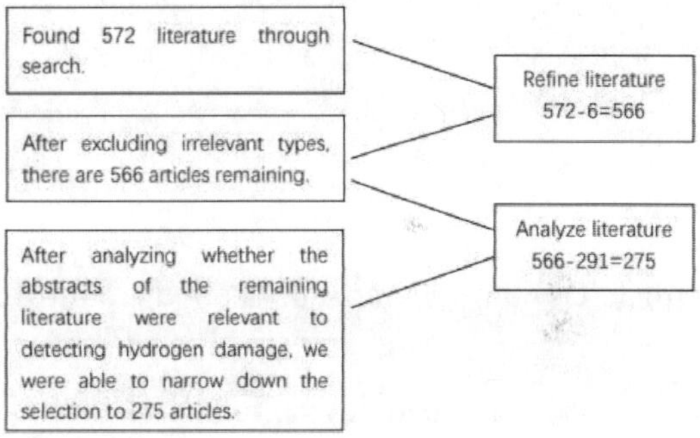


Figure 2. Paper selection process.

## 2. RESULTS AND ANALYSIS

### 2.1. Temporal distribution analysis

To some extent, statistics on the number of papers published each year can illustrate the evolution of a field. To examine the development of hydrogen damage detection, we collected and analysed relevant literature published between 2008 and 2022. Using this data, we created a line chart that maps the number of published documents against the year to provide a visual representation of the field's annual changes.

Figure 3 illustrates the overall upward trend in the number of published papers on hydrogen damage detection of metal materials from 2008 to 2022. During the period from 2008 to 2014, the growth rate remained relatively stable, with a notable fluctuation in 2010. The highest number of published papers, 22, was recorded during these six years. From 2015 to 2019, the number of published papers showed a rapid increase, with four consecutive years (2018-2021) surpassing 25 publications each year. Due to the August 2022 cutoff for data collection, the number of papers in 2022 was relatively small. Overall, the total number of published papers after 2015 significantly exceeded that before 2015, indicating that more experts and scholars have shown interest in hydrogen damage detection of metal materials since 2015.

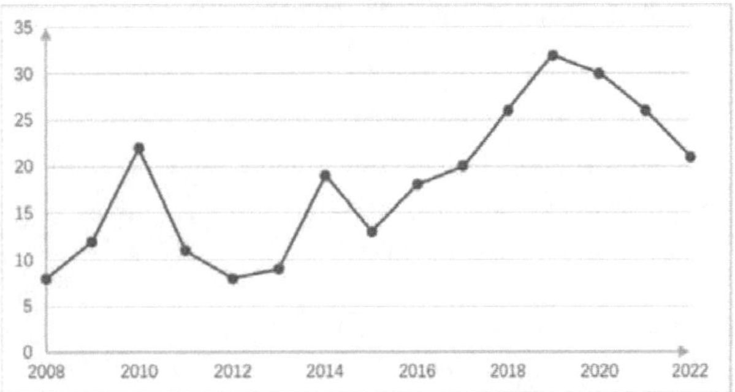


Figure 3. Trend of Annual Publication Count Chart.

### 2.2. Analysis of countries/regions and their cooperation

Based on a statistical analysis of 275 literature author sources, the authors represented 41 countries/regions, as shown in figure 4. The top five countries in terms of the number of published articles were China, Japan, the United States, France, and Germany. China ranked first with 60 publications, followed by Japan and the United States with 34 and 32 papers respectively. France and Germany ranked fourth and fifth with 31 and 27 papers respectively.

Using VOSviewer to analyse the cooperative relationships between the countries/regions represented by the authors, we selected the 21 countries/regions with 4 or more publications. As shown in the figure 5, Chinese authors had the largest number of publications; however, their collaboration with other countries was less extensive than that of the United States and Japan. The most intensive cooperation between countries occurred after 2014. France was the first country to collaborate with other countries in studying hydrogen damage (before 2014), followed by the United States and Japan. Cooperation between China and other countries mainly occurred after 2018. Since then, China has actively conducted research and discussions on metal hydrogen damage detection, gradually building close cooperative relationships with other countries in the field.

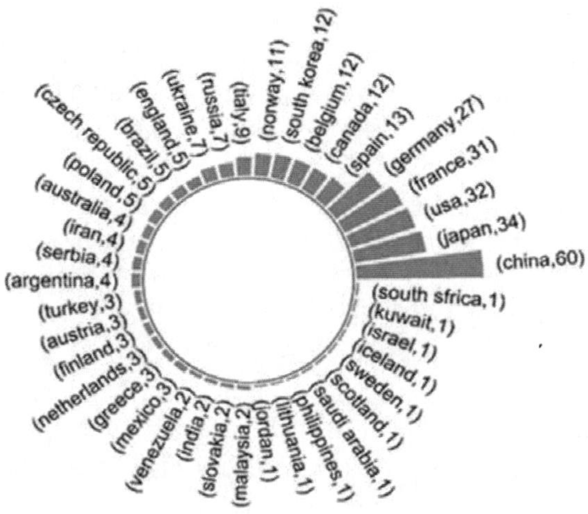


Figure4. Number of publications per country/region.

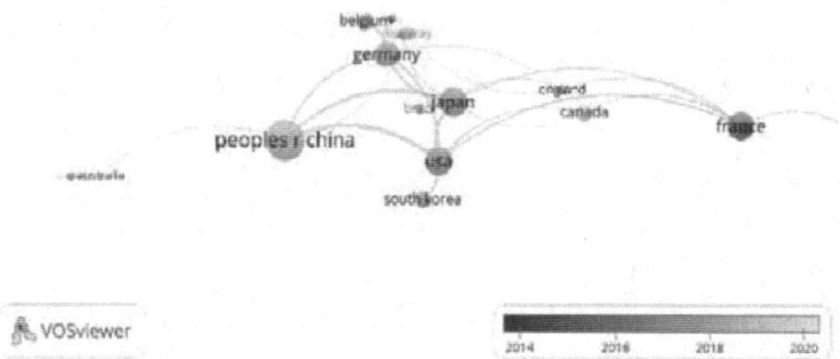


Figure 5. Author Source and Country/Region Collaboration Map.

### 2.3. Analysis of authors and their collaborations

The analysis of author cooperation involved over 1000 authors in total across 275 publications. Table 1 provides statistics on the top 10 most cited authors based on the number of citations of their articles.

Despite ranking first in terms of the number of publications, Koyama Motomichi had only 75 citations and did not make it to the top 10 list. The author with the highest number of citations was K. Verbeken from the University of Ghent in Belgium, with a total of 280 citations for his seven published articles.

The analysis of scientific research institutions showed that Kyushu University and Northeastern University in Japan have a long history of close cooperation with institutions in other countries. The Max Planck Institute in Germany, the Massachusetts Institute of Technology in the United States, and the University of Ghent in Belgium have established a solid research foundation in the field of metal hydrogen damage detection. In China, research primarily comes from teams at Xi'an

Table 1. Top 10 Most Cited Authors in the Literature.

| Serial number | Author | Documents | Citations |
|---|---|---|---|
| 0 | motomichi,K | 8 | 75 |
| 1 | verbeken,K. | 7 | 280 |
| 2 | idrissi,H. | 3 | 147 |
| 3 | kenichi,T | 3 | 137 |
| 4 | depover,T. | 5 | 132 |
| 5 | yameng,Q | 5 | 129 |
| 6 | shuqi,Z | 5 | 129 |
| 7 | andrieu,E. | 3 | 122 |
| 8 | blanc,C. | 3 | 122 |
| 9 | briottet,L | 3 | 122 |
| 10 | moro,I | 3 | 122 |

Jiaotong University, China University of Petroleum, Beijing University of Science and Technology, and East China University of Science and Technology. However, there are few research links among domestic universities, and joint research is not yet common. Research institutions in China are often independent and isolated, with relatively few international contacts. Only Xi'an Jiaotong University has established close cooperation with institutions such as MIT and Northeastern University in Japan, but the duration of these collaborations has been limited.

## 2.4. Analysis of Detection Methods

Destructive testing is an important tool in the research of metal hydrogen damage, as it allows for the evaluation of the mechanical properties of materials under different conditions. The most commonly used destructive tests in this field are tensile tests, which can also involve torsion, small punch, and fatigue tests. In the study of hydrogen embrittlement, tensile tests and scanning electron microscopy are often utilized to assess the damage. Conversely, in the investigation of hydrogen-induced cracking, researchers generally measure the changes in mechanical properties to characterize the extent of damage, and destructive tests are typically simpler and more widely used than non-destructive methods.

By analysing the detection methods involved in the abstracts of the literature, the number of each type of detection method in the 275 papers was counted. The different detection techniques were organized based on their detection principles and the classification of non-destructive testing by the National Aeronautics and Space Administration

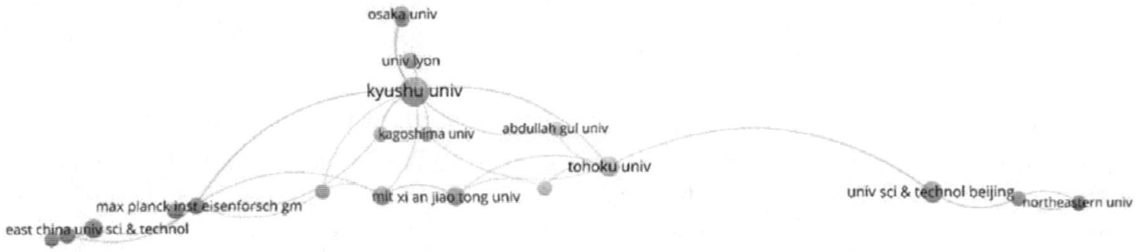


Figure 6. Author Affiliation and Collaboration Map.

(NASA). Over 10 types of destructive testing methods were identified, while 7 types of non-destructive testing methods were found [9, 10]. Among the destructive testing methods, tensile testing is the most commonly used for measuring mechanical properties. Fatigue testing and impact testing are also commonly used. In addition to conventional tensile testing, the slow strain rate tensile testing (SSRT) is a popular choice among many authors, with 17 papers using this method. The use of cyclic tensile testing, single-edge notched tensile testing, and in-situ tensile testing has also gradually increased in recent years.

To explore the frequency of use of various types of non-destructive testing (NDT) technology, statistical data is presented in Figure 9. It shows that ultrasonic testing has the highest frequency of use, accounting for 36.1%, followed by acoustic emission testing at 29.5%. The ultrasonic diffraction time difference method (TOFD) has the lowest frequency of use, while magnetic particle testing and penetrant testing are also relatively low. In industrialized countries, TOFD testing has evolved into a special non-destructive testing technology that offers good reliability and high quantitative accuracy. However, there are challenges, such as blind spots in testing and deficiencies in defect identification[11, 12]. Moreover, TOFD flaw detectors are expensive and require operators with strict qualifications. In terms of the limitations of testing methods, penetrant testing and magnetic particle testing are complex in operation and have low measurement sensitivity. It is difficult to quantify damage and cracks, and magnetic particle testing cannot be used for non-magnetic materials and austenitic stainless steel. In comparison, ultrasonic testing and acoustic emission testing have a broader scope.

Figure 8 displays the usage frequency of various NDT methods in each year. Acoustic emission testing was the most commonly used method in literature from 2008 to 2014. However, since 2015, the use frequency of ultrasonic testing has gradually increased, making it the most important NDT technology in the experimental process. In recent years, ultrasonic testing has been continuously developing due to its high safety, fast speed and low cost advantages[13], and several ultrasonic testing technologies have been derived, such as the total focusing method (TFM), advanced velocity ratio (AVR) measurement, advanced ultrasonic backscatter technology (AUBT), and the time-of-flight diffraction method using ultra-low angle ultrasonic sensor (TULA) [14]. The development of medical ultrasonic testing has also driven the development of industrial ultrasonic testing. Industrial phased array ultrasonic testing originated from medical B-ultrasound, and its progress in ultrasonic digital signal processing, ultrasonic equipment research and development, etc., has been empowered by the continuous development of medicine, which is driving the intellectualization and automation of industrial ultrasonic testing technology.

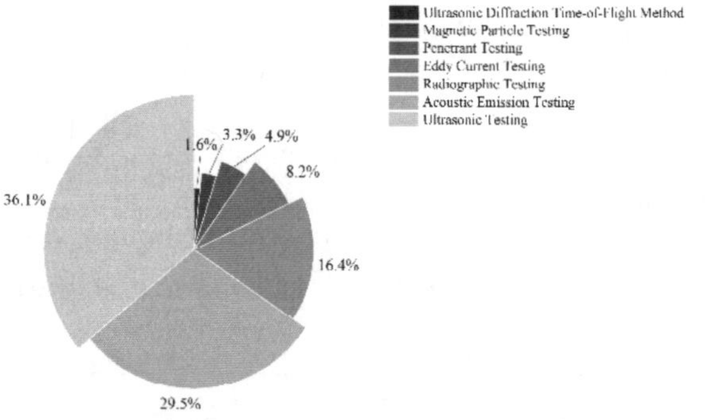


Figure 7. Proportion of usage of various types of non-destructive testing methods in the literature.

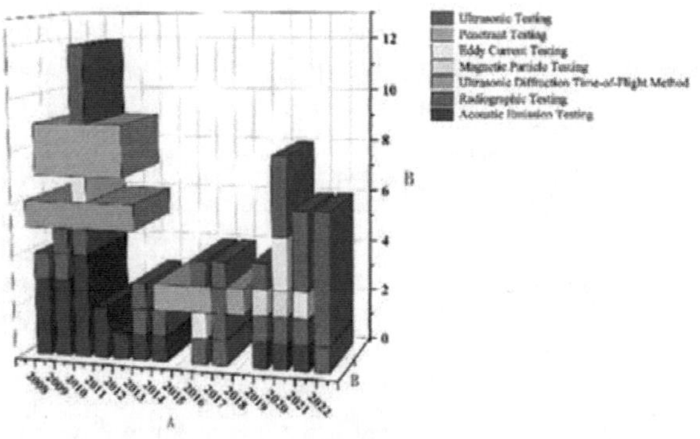

Figure 8. Frequency of usage of various types of non-destructive testing methods from 2008 to 2022.

## 2.5. Analysis of Research Hotspots

Among the selected documents, four papers have been cited more than 100 times, two of which are from the journal *ACTA MATERIALIA*, which has an impact factor of 9.2. Both of these papers concentrate on the issue of hydrogen embrittlement and explore the hydrogen embrittlement sensitivity of steel materials from a microscopic perspective.

The other two papers are from *ENGINE FAILURE ANALYSIS* and *INTERNATIONAL JOURNAL OF HYDROGEN ENERGY*. These studies analyse the impact of hydrogen on the mechanical properties and fracture mechanisms of metals using methods such as tensile tests and hardness tests.

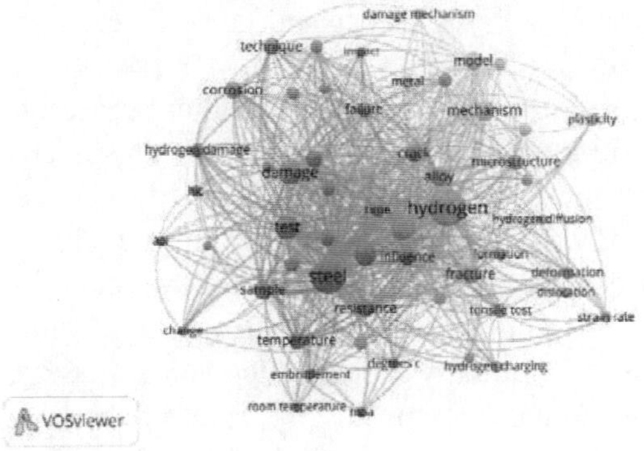


Figure 9. keyword map.

Cluster analysis will be performed on keywords with 20 or more occurrences, and thicker connecting lines between keywords indicate a stronger relationship between them. By setting a minimum correlation strength of "16", unimportant lines will be reduced to simplify the overall picture. The size of the marks in the figure represents the frequency of the keywords. It can be seen that 'hydrogen' (606 occurrences) and 'steel' (531 occurrences) have significantly higher frequency than other keywords and are located at the center of the map. Analysis of the research hotspots in the field of metal hydrogen damage detection reveals that the problem of hydrogen embrittlement is particularly prominent. The fracture characteristics and hydrogen-induced crack propagation behaviour can be explored after the brittle fracture of materials is more likely to occur in the hydrogen environment. The diffusion law of hydrogen in metals can be studied to further understand the mechanism of hydrogen embrittlement and find ways to alleviate the problem [15].

Although 'steel' and 'alloy' are both keywords used in the literature collection process, it can be observed from the figure that 'steel' is significantly more frequently identified than 'alloy', suggesting that research on hydrogen damage in alloys is still limited. Most of the research has focused on high-strength steel. It is generally believed that the higher the strength of steel, the more susceptible it is to hydrogen embrittlement [16]. High-strength steel has consistently been a primary area of research in the field of hydrogen damage. Hydrogen charging and testing are the two main experimental methods employed in the literature. Electrochemical hydrogen charging is the predominant laboratory method used for hydrogen charging. The tensile test has emerged as the most widely used testing method, with the slow strain rate tensile test being the most frequently employed. In recent years, the development of big data has prompted the use of machine learning and other methods to construct prediction models, which have become a leading research trend since 2017.

Using VOSviewer to create a map of key words changing with time, it is observed that keywords such as 'mechanical properties', 'thermal destruction spectrum', 'enhanced localized plasticity', 'induced cracking', 'grain boundary', 'tensile steel', 'model', and 'tense' have gradually emerged after 2019. In terms of research materials, the focus has shifted from carbon steel, alloy, and stainless steel to X80

Table 1. highly cited papers.

| Serial number | Document | Journal | Citations |
|---|---|---|---|
| 1 | Hydrogen embrittlement of ferritic steels: Observations on deformation microstructure, nanoscale dimples and failure by nano voiding | ACTA MATERIALIA | 202 |
| 2 | Hydrogen damage of steels: A case study and hydrogen embrittlement model | ENGINEERING FAILURE ANALYSIS | 151 |
| 3 | Sensitivity of pipelines with steel API X52 to hydrogen embrittlement | INTERNATIONAL JOURNAL OF HYDROGEN ENERGY | 110 |
| 4 | The predominant role of strain-induced vacancies in hydrogen embrittlement of steels: Overview | ACTA MATERIALIA | 104 |

pipeline steel and martensitic steel for exploring hydrogen damage. Regarding detection technology, traditional fracture experiments have been increasingly replaced by thermal desorption spectroscopy, electrochemical impedance spectroscopy, and other measurement methods[17, 18]. From a research direction perspective, more and more scholars are inclined towards seeking the fundamental causes of hydrogen damage and its impact on mechanical properties. This is mainly divided into two directions: fundamentally relieving the impact of hydrogen on metal materials, and detecting, monitoring, and predicting hydrogen damage behaviour in practical applications. Additionally, with the development of computers and the rise of big data analysis, the focus of research on hydrogen damage behaviour has gradually shifted from experiments to simulations, and the assessment of hydrogen damage severity has moved from detection to prediction.

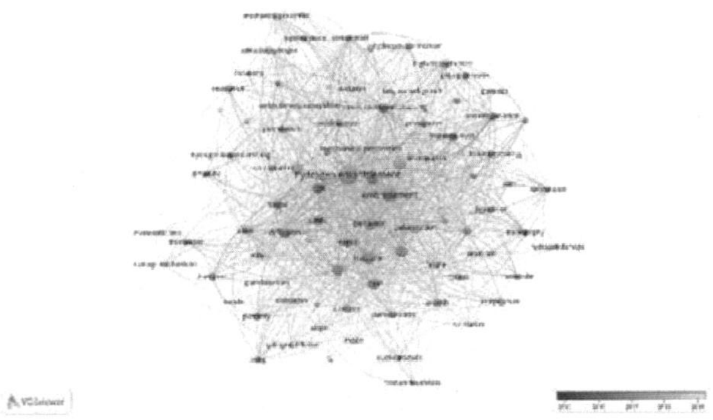

Figure 10. temporal keyword map.

## 3. CONCLUSIONS

Using VOSviewer software, a quantitative analysis was conducted on the annual publication volume, research hotspots, and detection methods of 275 research articles included in the Web of Science core database from 2008 to 2022. The following findings were obtained:

1. The total number of publications after 2015 was significantly higher than before 2015, indicating that more and more people are paying attention to the field of hydrogen damage in metallic materials. There are many researchers in this field, but there are significant differences in publication volume. Currently, there are only a few core author groups that have established close collaborations. In the future, scholars should strengthen cooperation to achieve more breakthroughs.
2. China started late in the field of hydrogen damage, but is now making efforts to catch up with the world. The number of publications in recent years has gradually surpassed other countries. However, there is relatively little cooperation among various domestic research institutions. Therefore, it is necessary to strengthen cooperation with other research institutions while conducting their own research.
3. In destructive testing methods, tensile tests were frequently used, with the slow strain rate tensile test becoming more common in recent years. In terms of non-destructive testing, ultrasonic testing has gradually replaced acoustic emission testing and has become an important method.
4. In recent years, research on hydrogen damage has mainly been divided into two different directions. One is to explore the essence of hydrogen damage from a microscopic level, while the other is to use various types of detection methods to judge and predict the degree of hydrogen damage in actual production applications. Currently, there is no unified and clear answer to these two research directions, and they may become the key points for future development, worth further investigation by scholars.

## ACKNOWLEDGEMENTS

This work was supported by the [Zhejiang Provincial Natural Science Foundation of China] under Grant [number Q21E050068]; [National Key Research and Development Plan Young Scientists Project] under Grant [number 2021YFF0603400]; [Zhejiang Provincial Market Supervision Bureau "Eagle Plan" Cultivation Project] under Grant [number CY2022220]; and [Key Research and Development Projects in Anhui] under Grant [number 2022a05020004]
.

## REFERENCES

[1] LIU Y W. Discussion on hydrogen damage of pressure vessel in wet hydrogen sulfide environment [J], Chemical Management. 09, 154-155, (2020).

[2] X. F. Li, J. Yin, J. Zhang, Y. F. Wang, X. L. Song, Y. Zhang, and X. C. Ren, Hydrogen embrittlement and failure mechanisms of multi-principal element alloys: A review, JOURNAL OF MATERIALS SCIENCE & TECHNOLOGY. SEP 20. 122, 20-32, (2022).

[3] M. Koyama, C. C. Tasan, E. Akiyama, K. Tsuzaki, and D. Raabe, Hydrogen-assisted decohesion and localized plasticity in dual-phase steel, Acta Materialia. May. 70, 174-187, (2014).

[4]M. B. Djukic, G. M. Bakic, V. S. Zeravcic, A. Sedmak, and B. Rajicic, Hydrogen Embrittlement of Industrial Components: Prediction, Prevention, and Models, Corrosion, Jul. 72, 7, 943-961,( 2016).

[5]H. Li, X. W. Cao, Y. Liu, Y. B. Shao, Z. L. Nan, L. Teng, W. S. Peng, and J. Bian, Safety of hydrogen storage and transportation: An overview on mechanisms, techniques, and challenges, ENERGY REPORTS. NOV. 8, 6258-6269, (2022).

[6]N. E. Laadel, M. El Mansori, N. Kang, S. Marlin, and Y. Boussant-Roux, Permeation barriers for hydrogen embrittlement prevention in metals- A review on mechanisms, materials suitability and efficiency, INTERNATIONAL JOURNAL OF HYDROGEN ENERGY, SEP. 47, 76, 32707-32731, (2022).

[7] XIE Degang, LI Meng, SHAN Zhiwei. Review on Hydrogen-Microstructure Interaction in Metals [J]. Materials China. 37, 03, 215-223, (2018).

[8]M. A. Mohtadi-Bonab, and H. Ghesmati-Kucheki, Important Factors on the Failure of Pipeline Steels with Focus on Hydrogen Induced Cracks and Improvement of Their Resistance: Review Paper, METALS AND MATERIALS INTERNATIONAL. SEP.25, 5,1109-1134, (2019).

[9]B. Wang, S. C. Zhong, T. L. Lee, K. S. Fancey, and J. W. Mi, Non-destructive testing and evaluation of composite materials/structures: A state-of-the-art review, Advances in Mechanical Engineering. Apr. 12, 4, 28, (2020).

[10] ZHANG Yuanliang, ZHANG Hongchao, ZHAO Jiaxu, et al. Review of Non-destructive Testing for Remanufacturing of High-end Equipment [J]. Journal of Mechanical Engineering. 49, 07, 80-90, (2013).

[11]R. C. Mayworm, A. V. Alvarenga, and R. P. B. Costa-Felix, A metrological approach to the time of flight diffraction method (TOFD), Measurement. Jan .167, 10, (2021).

[12]H. Q. Jiang, D. Y. Yang, Z. L. Zhi, Q. Z. Jing, J. M. Gao, C. Y. Tao, and Z. X. Cheng, A normal weld recognition method for time-of-flight diffraction detection based on generative adversarial network, Journal of Intelligent Manufacturing. 17,(2021)

[13]J. Brizuela, J. Camacho, G. Cosarinsky, J. M. Iriarte, and J. F. Cruza, Improving elevation resolution in phased-array inspections for NDT, Ndt & E International. Jan. 101, 1-16,(2019).

[14]R. J. Kazys, L. Mazeika, V. Samaitis, R. Sliteris, P. Merck, and Z. Viliunas, Comparative Analysis of Ultrasonic NDT Techniques for the Detection and Characterisation of Hydrogen-Induced Cracking, MATERIALS. JUL. 15, 13, (2022).

[15]D. Asari, S. Mizokami, M. Fukahori, and K. Takai, Microscopic defects formed during crack incubation, initiation and propagation processes causing hydrogen-related fracture of dual-phase steels, MATERIALS SCIENCE AND ENGINEERING A-STRUCTURAL MATERIALS PROPERTIES MICROSTRUCTURE AND PROCESSING. APR. 780, 7, (2020).

[16]J. Venezuela, T. Hill, Q. J. Zhou, H. X. Li, Z. M. Shi, F. T. Dong, R. Knibbe, M. X. Zhang, M. S. Dargusch, and A. Atrens, Hydrogen-induced fast fracture in notched 1500 and 1700 MPa class automotive martensitic advanced high-strength steel, Corrosion Science. Aug. 188, 17, (2021).

[17]L. X. Cai, G. Q. Bai, X. F. Gao, Y. Li, and Y. F. Hou, Experimental investigation on the hydrogen embrittlement characteristics and mechanism of natural gas-hydrogen transportation pipeline steels, MATERIALS RESEARCH EXPRESS. APR. 9, 4, (2022).

[18]H. L. Huang, and W. L. Yang, Corrosion behavior of AZ91D magnesium alloy in distilled water, ARABIAN JOURNAL OF CHEMISTRY. JUL. 13, 7, 6044-6055, (2020).

# Assessing the knowledge and compliance of Quality Management practice among Ghanaian Construction Organisations

Hilary Osei-Bonsu[1], Nuhu Braimah[1], Muhammad Shafique[1]

[1]*College of Engineering Design and Physical Sciences, Department of Civil Engineering, Brunel University, Kingston Lane UB8 3PH, London, United Kingdom, Hilary.Osei-Bonsu@brunel.ac.uk*

**ABSTRACT**: Construction organisations are using Quality Management Systems (QMS) increasingly as a strategy to address issues with quality in their sector to satisfy end-user requirements. Unfortunately, construction projects in Ghana constantly face lack of quality management practices. This study aimed to evaluate perceived benefits, knowledge about QMS practice and compliance among professionals in the Ghanaian Construction Industry. A cross-sectional quantitative approach was adopted involving the administering of an online questionnaire, which yielded 142 responses from respondents who occupy mid-level and senior level positions in the construction industry. It was found out that the respondents had a satisfactory knowledge of QMS practice and its importance. They demonstrated their knowledge by admitting that certain quality drivers such as teamwork and quality education as well as quality measures such as delivering projects within a specified time frame indicate a successful QMS implementation. Finally, organisations' compliance to QMS standards based on participants responses were assessed. It was established that about 65 percent of participants were reported to be compliant. Even though this proportion is appreciable, client satisfaction may be compromised in project delivery.

**Keywords**: Quality, Quality Management System, Construction Project, Construction Organisation, Standards and Compliance

**Received** January 1, 2023; **In final form** March 31, 2023; **Published** June 2023



**Corresponding author:** Hilary Osei-Bonsu, Hilary.Osei-Bonsu@brunel.ac.uk

## 1. INTRODUCTION

Quality has remained at the forefront amongst the factors used to determine the degree of success or failure of a project. Quality is a key success criterion that supports a project delivery process which any organisation renders to its clients [1]. Harris et al. [2] described quality as always interconnected with customer satisfaction and improvements in services or products which makes its implementation process a major influence in satisfying the required needs of the customer. Hence, the idea of quality management is to influence the need to plan and ensure that all projects are of the right standards as required [3].

Quality management systems (QMS) consist of guidelines required to monitor quality control, process improvement, and quality assurance to ensure the effectiveness of its implementation process on projects [4]. Talking about projects, QMS is literally indispensable in the operations of the construction industry.

Construction projects require satisfactory quality management to facilitate quality assurance within the industry [5]. Under project construction, the most vital factors that the client takes into consideration are time, quality, and cost [6].

Pheng and Teo [5] stated that the adoption of quality management by construction organisations can provide several benefits such as increased market shares through the provision of high-quality services to its clients. Despite the high importance of quality management systems, there has been, however, a high incidence of inadequate practices of quality management system at construction sites which often results in severe project delays, reworks, and other undesirable risks [7].

Buildings and other civil infrastructures are in high demand in Ghana. It is thus critical for its construction industry to effectively implement quality management practices to help reduce the recurrent deficits of poor performance, poor job quality, and a lack of creativity or professionalism which often leads to building collapses, injuries, and high construction costs [8].

According to Adusa-Poku and Anokye [9], one of the main issues faced by most Ghanaian construction companies is how to effectively implement quality management systems to satisfy client needs without incurring extra debts at the end of the project lifecycle.

Osei-Asibey et al. [10] confirmed that quality management is still a major challenge in the Ghanaian construction industry, where majority of the construction companies promise to ensure that quality works are implemented, however, they fail to attain the necessary standards that meets the clients' expectations.

As part of efforts to address this challenge, this current study seeks to evaluate perceived benefits, knowledge about QMS practices and compliance among professionals in the Ghanaian construction industry.

## 2. METHODS

This study employed cross-sectional quantitative research methods wherein primary data was collected from key relevant stakeholders of the Ghanaian construction industry via questionnaire survey. The participants of the survey were sampled from Architectural, Construction, Consulting, and Project Management firms operating in the Ghanaian Construction Industry.

### 2.1. Sampling of Study Respondents

A purposive sampling technique was adopted to select the respondents from the afore-listed construction organisations. The respondents who participated were mid-level to senior staffs who have appreciable knowledge and experience to give accurate responses.

***Sample Size Calculation***

Since the population of employees in the Ghanaian construction industry is unknown, Cochran equation was adopted to yield a representative sample for this study.

(1)

$n_o$ is the sample size, e is the desired level of precision (e=0.05), p is the estimated proportion of mid to top level employees (0.1) that is present in the population and q is 1-p (0.9). The value of the standardised score (z=1.96) is found in statistical tables, which is represented by area under the normal distribution curve.

$\approx 138$

To accommodate for possible data errors in entry of missing entry, an additional 4 responses were collected, resulting in a final sample size of 142.

### 2.2. Methods of Data Analysis

The data collected was first edited, coded, transcribed, and then cleaned. It was then grouped based on measures such as ordinal, nominal, and scalar. The data was then coded by attaching numerical value to every categorical data.

Before any statistical analysis was done, a reliability test was conducted to validate the consistency in participants' response of items in ordinal scale ('strongly disagree' to 'strongly agree'). Cronbach's alpha was computed for this test. Cronbach's Alpha >= 0.50 indicates high reliability/ consistency.

Statistical Package for Social Science (SPSS) was used to analyse data using both inferential and descriptive statistics. To examine the relationship between each item of participant's demographics, compliance and knowledge level, Chi Square Test of Independence was used. P-values <0.05 was considered to indicate statistical significance.

### 2.3. Data Interpretation

In this survey, compliance to QMS standards were assessed using four questions encompassing statements about QMS that are required to operate in the construction industry. Respondents who chose "Yes" were given a score of 3, and "Maybe" or "No" response were given a score of 0. Therefore, maximum possible score is 12. Thus, the total score ranged from 0 to 12 points. Compliance was categorised using the median score. Respondents who had a median score or above were classified as compliant, whilst those below the median scores were classified as non-compliant.

The central tendency measures, mean and standard deviation were adopted to draw a conclusion or take sides on various questions in sections that were subjected to a 5-point Likert scale with levels of agreement ranging from 'strongly agree' to 'strongly disagree'. With this scale, a calculated mean of '0.5-1.49' corresponds to 'strongly disagreement' responses to the questions. A mean of '1.5-2.49' corresponds to 'disagreement' and a mean of '2.5-3.49' corresponds to neither 'agreement' nor 'disagreement' (i.e., neutral). For the positive side of the scale, a mean of '3.5-4.49' corresponds to 'agreement' responses whilst a mean of '4.5-5' corresponds to 'strongly agreement' responses.

## 3. RESULTS

Demographic variables of participants and perceptions of QMS practice included in the study were examined using descriptive statistic measure.

### 3.1. Reliability Test

For sections such as importance, perception, and measures for success of QMS practice which had items subjected to an ordinal scale ('strongly disagree' to 'strongly agree'), the computed Cronbach's Alpha was greater than 0.5 which is an indication of some degree of consistency in participant's responses.

**Table 1: Reliability Statistics**

| Cronbach's Alpha | Cronbach's Alpha Based on Standardized Items | N of Items |
|---|---|---|
| 0.837 | 0.840 | 30 |

### 3.2. Demographic Characteristics

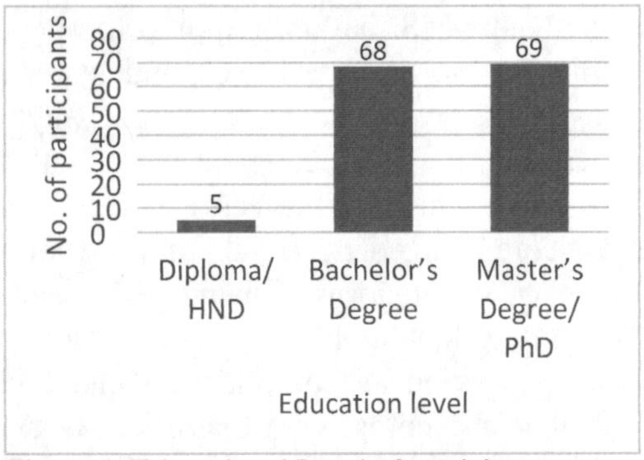


**Figure 1: Educational Level of participants**

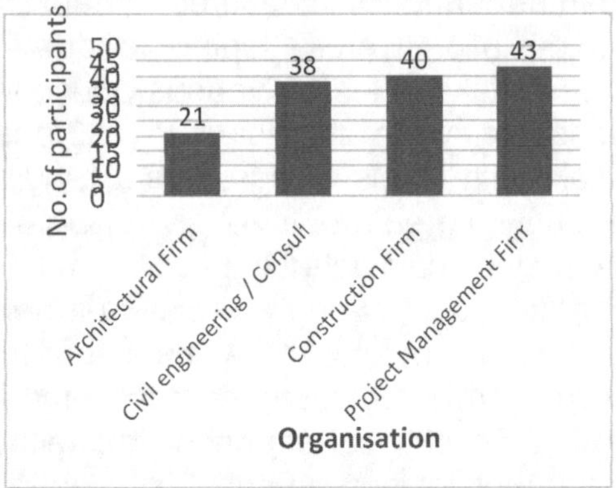


**Figure 2: Participating firms**

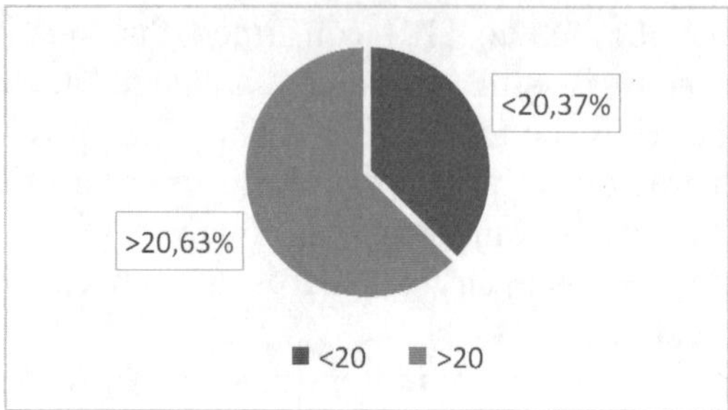


**Figure 3: Organisation size of participants**

This section presents the participants' demographic analysis. The results from the descriptive statistics showed a total of 142 participants. For the educational level, 69(48.6%) have Master's/PhD, 68(47.9%) have Bachelor's degree and 5(3.5%) have Diploma/HND. The number of participants who undertook this survey include construction firms (40), architectural firms (21), consulting/civil engineering firms (38) and project management firms (43). For the organisational size, majority of participants work in firms with more than 20 memberships (N=89, 62.7%) whilst the rest (N=53, 37.3%) responded that their firm membership size was less than 20.

### 3.3. Evaluation of knowledge of QMS practice

Participants were asked to rate using a 5-point Likert scale ('strongly disagree' to 'strongly agree') on issues such as perceptions, drivers, and measures for QMS success in an organisation. The following tables present the results of the responses obtained from the participants.

A. Perception about QMS

**Table 2: Descriptive statistic of perception on QMS**

| Indicators | Mean | Std. Deviation |
|---|---|---|
| QMS can improve client satisfaction | 4.44 | 0.525 |
| QMS provides the right guidelines which always ensures quality | 4.44 | 0.539 |
| QMS reduces re-works on projects | 4.55 | 0.540 |
| QMS focuses on continuous improvement | 4.41 | 0.535 |
| Practicing QMS provides high profits for organisations | 4.54 | 0.554 |
| **OVERALL** | **4.48** | **0.539** |

B. Drivers of QMS implementation

**Table 3: Descriptive statistic of drivers of QMS practice**

| Indicators | Mean | Std. Deviation |
|---|---|---|
| Quality Education | 4.46 | 0.514 |
| Teamwork | 4.54 | 0.514 |
| Employees' Involvement | 4.33 | 0.530 |
| Communication between top managers and employees | 4.57 | 0.511 |
| Organisational culture | 4.45 | 0.527 |
| **OVERALL** | **4.47** | **0.519** |

C. Measures for QMS implementation Success

**Table 4: Descriptive statistic of measures for QMS implementation success**

| Indicators | Mean | Std. Deviation |
|---|---|---|
| Products must meet the acceptable standards | 4.73 | 0.448 |
| Delivering projects within a specified timeframe, cost effective and high-quality standard | 4.79 | 0.410 |
| Achieving projects of high project sustainability | 4.75 | 0.434 |
| Head of Works visits site to check that materials being used are of approved quality and standards | 4.66 | 0.504 |
| **OVERALL** | **4.73** | **0.449** |

With reference to Table 2, Table 3, and Table 4, the respective computed overall mean (Mean> 4.0) suggests that the participants agree with the various statements which is a good indication of an appreciable knowledge about drivers of QMS practice and measures for successful implementation and its importance to project success.

### 3.4. Assessment of QMS effectiveness

Participants' responses to the effectiveness of QMS practice in their respective organisations are presented in the table below. Responses suggest that averagely, QMS practice is effective because of certain measures put in place such as quality reporting structure.

**Table 5: Descriptive statistic of QMS practice Effectiveness**

| Indicators | Mean | Std. Deviation |
|---|---|---|
| Your organisation has an effective quality reporting structure | 4.57 | 0.525 |
| The adopted QMS method is implemented effectively | 4.59 | 0.548 |
| Organisation has a process for effectively managing quality documents | 4.67 | 0.487 |
| Your organisation keeps records of previous work | 4.73 | 0.479 |
| **OVERALL** | **4.64** | **0.510** |

### 3.5. QMS standards Compliance

**Table 6: Response on QMS standards Compliance**

| **Response** | Frequency (N=142) | Percentage (100%) |
|---|---|---|
| **Does your organisation have an adopted QMS in practice?** | | |
| No | 7 | 4.9 |
| Yes | 130 | 91.5 |
| Maybe | 5 | 3.5 |
| **Does your organisation have an approved quality strategy/plan designed by the top management?** | | |
| Yes | 140 | 98.6 |
| Maybe | 2 | 1.4 |
| **Is your organisation's QMS certified in accordance with ISO 9001 international standard or any other standard?** | | |
| No | 23 | 16.2 |
| Yes | 93 | 65.5 |
| Maybe | 26 | 18.3 |
| **Is your organisation's QMS certificate still valid?** | | |
| No | 31 | 21.8 |
| Yes | 69 | 48.6 |
| Maybe | 42 | 29.6 |

| Overall Compliance score | | |
|---|---|---|
| Non-Compliant | 50 | 35.2 |
| Compliant | 92 | 64.8 |

Table 6 presents an assessment of organisations' compliance to key requirements/ standards for QMS implementation. More than half of participants responded in affirmative "Yes" to 3 out of 4 questions posed. With regards to the question on "Is your organisation's QMS certificate still valid?", majority of participants posited "No" or "Not sure".

### 3.6. Chi square Test of Independence

This test was conducted to evaluate the relationship between participants' educational level, organisation, and organisation size and QMS compliance measure.

**Table 7: Pearson Chi Square Test**

| Demographics | | Value |
|---|---|---|
| Educational Level | Chi-square | 3.480 |
| | df | 2 |
| | P- value | 0.176 |
| Participating Firms | Chi-square | 2.570 |
| | df | 3 |
| | P- value | 0.463 |
| Organisation Size | Chi-square | 0.236 |
| | df | 1 |
| | P- value | 0.627 |

The null hypothesis (Ho) was formulated that there is no relationship between a paired categorical variable, while the alternate hypothesis (Ha) states that there is a relationship between the paired categorical variables. P-values computed less than or equal to the alpha level of 0.05 implies rejecting the null hypothesis hence the conclusion that there is a significant relationship between the paired parameters of interest. P-values greater than the alpha level of 0.05 implies accepting the null hypothesis hence the conclusion that there is an insignificant relationship between the paired parameters of interest. In Table 7, it is evident that none of the demographic features has a significant relationship with compliance to QMS standards, thus, whether an organisation is compliant or not, is independent of these features.

## 4. DISCUSSIONS

One of the main goals of this study was to investigate the perceptions and knowledge of participants towards QMS practice. This issue is critical for research to identify the necessary interventions, as projects may not yield the intended success if employees do not have sufficient knowledge.

Wang et al. [11] posits that a consumer weighs the benefits against the cost of adoption, and if the perceived benefit outweighs the perceived cost, consumers are more likely to adopt the product or service. In this study, participants were assessed on the perceived benefits of QMS practice.

Taken together the responses on perceived benefits of QMS practice, "QMS reduces re-works on projects" had the highest average score (mean = 4.55; SD =0.55) while the least item score came from "QMS focuses on continuous improvement" with a mean of 4.41 and SD of 0.54. All the indicators on perceived benefits had an average score higher than 4.40 which was above the median of 3. This signifies that averagely respondents agree

that QMS practice is of importance to project success.

Considering the responses on drivers of QMS practice, "Communication between top managers and employees" had the highest average score (mean = 4.57; SD =0.51) while the least item score came from "Employees' Involvement" with a mean of 4.33 and SD of 0.53. All the indicators on drivers of QMS practice had an average score higher than 4.40 which was above the median of 3. This signifies that averagely respondents agree that all factors proposed are drivers. This finding correlates with study conducted by Kaziliūnas [12] titled: "Implementation Of Quality Management Systems In Service Organisations". He concluded that top management acts as a driver of the implementation of quality management systems. Another study by Pheng and Teo [5] also revealed that employee involvement and empowerment as well as top management commitment are essential in implementing QMS practice.

Considering the responses on measures that indicate QMS successful implementation, "Delivering projects within a specified timeframe, cost effective and high-quality standard" had the highest average score (mean = 4.70; SD =0.11) while the least item score came from "Head of Works visits sites to check that materials being used are of approved quality and standards" with a mean of 4.66 and SD of 0.50. All the indicators on measures of QMS success had an average score higher than 4.50 which was above the median of 3. This signifies that averagely respondents strongly agree that all factors proposed are indicators of successful implementation of QMS. Findings from Joubert [13] posit that measures for successful QMS implementation in the construction industry, including the fact that contractors are expected to deliver products of certain standards (embodied in specifications) within extremely tight time constraints.

Lastly, compliance to QMS standards in organisations was evaluated based on responses by participants. The median score of the QMS standards compliance among participants was 9 (3–12). Overall, about 65% of respondents showed compliance whilst 35% showed non-compliance towards QMS standards/ requirements which establishes that majority of the respondents acknowledge and implement QMS practices. Al-Ani and Adhmawi [14] in their study entitled: "Implementation of Quality Management Concepts in Managing Engineering Project Site" reported that requirements for compliance should cover three main points: Quality Assurance Program, Suitable Organisation, and Necessary Quality Assurance Documents.

## 5. CONCLUSIONS

Construction companies should understand that achieving successful project completion takes time and it requires an organisation to adapt, grow, and learn. There is the need for organisations to adopt and meet all requirements of quality management to ensure successful project completion. Employees must be well equipped with the necessary knowledge and skills through training and provided with a conducive working environment to be complaint with QMS standards. The responses analysed indicated that there are still some respondents whose organisations do not fully adhere to QMS standards. Construction companies should create a flexible and conducive organisational culture to encourage the development and implementation of quality management practices in the construction industry.

## ACKNOWLEDGEMENT

I am grateful for the remarkable efforts and guidance from my supervisors, Dr. Nuhu Braimah and Dr. Muhammad Shafique.

## REFERENCES

[1] D. Van Der Westhuizen and E. P. Fitzgerald, 'Defining and measuring project success', in *Proceedings of the European Conference on IS Management, Leadership and Goverance 2005*, Academic Conferences Limited, 2005, pp. 157–163.

[2] F. Harris, R. McCaffer, and F. Edum-Fotwe, 'Modern Construction Management . Garsington Road'. Oxford, UK, 2013.

[3] M. Bell and V. Omachonu, 'Quality system implementation process for business success', *Int. J. Qual. Reliab. Manag.*, 2011.

[4] D.-E. Lee, T.-K. Lim, and D. Arditi, 'An expert system for auditing quality management systems in construction', *Comput.-Aided Civ. Infrastruct. Eng.*, vol. 26, no. 8, pp. 612–631, 2011.

[5] L. S. Pheng and J. A. Teo, 'Implementing total quality management in construction firms', *J. Manag. Eng.*, vol. 20, no. 1, pp. 8–15, 2004.

[6] Y. Rosenfeld, 'Cost of quality versus cost of non-quality in construction: the crucial balance', *Constr. Manag. Econ.*, vol. 27, no. 2, pp. 107–117, 2009.

[7] S. K. Ansah, C. Aigbavboa, and W. D. Thwala, 'Total quality management implementation in the Ghanaian construction industry: A tool for improving construction productivity', *ARCA*, p. 362, 2015.

[8] N. Androwis, R. J. Sweis, A. Tarhini, A. Moarefi, and M. Hosseini Amiri, 'Total quality management practices and organizational performance in the construction chemicals companies in Jordan', *Benchmarking Int. J.*, vol. 25, no. 8, pp. 3180–3205, 2018.

[9] N. Adusa-Poku and R. Anokye, *Proposed Framework for Applying Total Quality Management in Construction Industry in Ghana*. 2020. doi: 10.5923/j.ijcem.20200903.02.

[10] D. Osei-Asibey, J. Ayarkwa, A. Acheampong, E. Adinyira, and P. Amoah, 'An examination of causes of accidents and hazards in the Ghanaian construction industry', 2021.

[11] S. Wang, J. Fan, D. Zhao, S. Yang, and Y. Fu, 'Predicting consumers' intention to adopt hybrid electric vehicles: using an extended version of the theory of planned behavior model', *Transportation*, vol. 43, no. 1, pp. 123–143, Jan. 2016, doi: 10.1007/s11116-014-9567-9.

[12] A. Kaziliūnas, 'The implementation of quality management systems in service organizations', 2014.

[13] W. Joubert, J. H. Cruywagen, and G. A. J. Basson, 'Will the implementation of a total quality management system benefit South African construction companies?', *South Afr. J. Ind. Eng.*, vol. 16, no. 1, pp. 29–40, 2005.

[14] R. Al-Ani and F. I. Al-Adhmawi, 'Implementation of quality management concepts in managing engineering project site', *Jordan J. Civ. Eng.*, vol. 159, no. 2979, pp. 1–18, 2011.

# Assessment methodology of building energy performance measurements - EPC RECAST Project

Yousra Laaroussi [1], Ugo DE FILIPPIS[1], Lilia GALAI DOL [1], Olivier GRESLOU[1], Rofaida LAHRECH[1]

[1]*CSTB MLV, 84 Avenue Jean Jaurès, 77420 Champs-sur-Marne, France, yousra.laaroussi@cstb.fr*

**ABSTRACT**: This research is a part of a European project H2020 "EPC RECAST", that consists in improving the reliability of EPC (Energy Performance Certificate), and in the emergence of the next generation of EPC by developing a new toolbox to assess the building energy performance and its retrofit needs "www.epc-recast.eu". The project's impact is highly essential in the field, especially that a monitoring approach is adopted to test and evaluate the EPC RECAST developments. Several pilot projects have been identified where the measurements of interior conditions and energy consumption have been implemented. However, after the implementation of smart measurement systems with different levels of monitoring, the subsequent scientific issue is the verification of the collected measures' quality. In this research, the aim is to represent the adopted approach of monitoring activity (sampling and measuring process) in the context of EPC RECAST project, and to highlight the application of TSAR (a developed tool by CSTB) for the data assessment of EPC RECAST project in addition to the representation of some results of its application. The tool contributes clearly on the verification of the effective operation of the sensors, and the continuous analysis of databases. It is an open tool where various functions could be added/adapted for the data assessment to perform a reliable data set ready for the concerned exploitation.

**Keywords:** monitoring approach, data reliability and assessment, Energy Performance Certificate (EPC), residential buildings.

**Received** January 1, 2023; **In final form** March 31, 2023; **Published** June 2023



**Corresponding author:** Yousra.laaroussi@cstb.fr

## 1. INTRODUCTION

The Energy Performance Certificate (EPC) was introduced by the Energy Performance of Building Directive (EPBD) in 2002 as a tool for the assessment of the building energy efficiency (energy consumption and CO2 emissions) and the development of renovation strategies and financing schemes [1]. Despite its potential, the building energy certification tool is largely underutilized due to various factors that affect the confidence and the reliability of the certification process.

Few et al. [2] suggested in her literature research different contributing causes that affect the reliability of Energy Performance Certificate such as: the shortcomings in the regulated energy use calculation methods, the inaccuracies in the quality of the input data and the differences between real and modelled occupant behavior. These factors contribute clearly to the Energy Performance Gap (EPG) between the simulated (predicted) and real (measured) building energy performance [3][4]. To respond to this gap, the monitoring approach was adopted for the assessment of the real energy use & consumption in buildings to better understand, predict, manage the building energy consumption, and improve the reliability of the EPC. The monitoring approach, especially the in-situ long-term measurement is considered as a valuable tool to:

-Provide accurate data about the actual energy performance of a building which is very needed to enhance the reliability of EPC.

-Identify the energy consumption patterns, especially by adopting long term measurement for developing more targeted recommendations [5].

-Evaluate the effectiveness of the various strategies employed in the buildings to develop future energy recommendations.

In this context, EPC RECAST project [6] contributes to the improvement of the EPCs in residential buildings by proposing a new harmonized methodology across different countries in Europe. This methodology will increase the accuracy of the data collection, the building energy performance simulation method, and the final indicators of an EPC. In this research, we will represent the monitoring approach adopted by EPC RECAST and how the measured data were assessed. This process is performed by using TSAR: Time Series Analysis Routines. It is a tool that was initiated in its first version by Antoine BREITWILLER, research engineer in CSTB. This tool is based on the time series analysis which is a useful technique for analyzing data that fluctuates over an interval of time or affected by time. The usefulness of this technique resides in its capacity to provide descriptive & exploratory analysis, forecasting models, pattern classification and anomalies detection [7]. The study discusses the outcomes of applying TSAR in some cases studies monitored in the project. Furthermore, the practical exploitation of the measurements after the performed data assessment will be highlighted.

## 2. METHODS

As presented in figure 1, the innovative process of EPC RECAST consists of three main phases. The input layer that includes the process of collecting building's data with the innovative tools proposed in EPC RECAST to improve the quality of the collected data that will be used for energy performance assessment. Secondly, the evaluation layer that focuses mainly on the evaluation of the EPC RECAST methodology to perform a precise calculated indicator. And finally, the recommendation layer that provides an EPC form with a global overview about the energy characteristics and proposes roadmaps of renovation solutions to the users.

It's expected that the major developments carried out to produce the EPC RECAST process for a reliable EPC will be tested and evaluated. In this context, the monitoring approach was defined as one of the important tools to assess the EPC reliability. The main objective of the monitoring approach is to develop a consistent database for the assessment and validation of the methodology proposed by EPC RECAST. Accordingly, various pilots were selected to be monitored in different countries across Europe.

Figure 1. EPC RECAST global scientific framework.

Hence, it is necessary to implement an evaluation strategy for measured data to ensure its quality prior to its use in the testing and evaluation phase of the EPC RECAST process. For this purpose, three case studies implemented in France were selected to present the performed work of the data assessment. To respond to this part of the research, TSAR will perform the necessary assessment of the collected data. TSAR is based on specific functions developed in Python that represent time series analysis and could be adapted/added according to each project goal. The aim from developing the tool is to support the researchers in the preparation of their final data. TSAR was developed before EPC RECAST but adapted to the context application of EPC RECAST. Three main steps were identified for TSAR utilization: 1) The selection of the case studies, measures, and periods to analyze, 2) the definition of the targeted indicators to evaluate, and 3) the analysis and interpretation of the results. The final output of this assessment is to provide a cleaned database to be used directly in the phase of EPC RECAST evaluation.

In the context of EPC RECAST project, two indicators were defined to assess the reliability of the data: 1) availability and 2) validity. The availability focuses on verifying the actual efficiency of the sensors and acquisition systems to determine the percentage of data available during the specified measurement period. However, the availability of data does not mean directly a coherent data. For this reason, the verification if the data are valid is necessary.

The following sections will describe the monitoring approach developed in EPC RECAST, the results of TSAR application and finally, the designed scientific approach to validate the new generation of EPC.

### 2.1 The monitoring approach: EPC RECAST

A long-time measurement was adopted for the monitoring activity in this project to assess longer periods of energy uses. In the context of our study, long-term measurement is defined by collecting data over a minimum duration of one year.
The energy use is influenced by several factors such as: seasons, building's characteristics, occupants' behavior, and other operating conditions. The selection of the number of pilots to recruit and the parameters to measure was based on the context of the measure's exploitation and EPC evaluation goals. In Total, 56 dwellings were adopted for long-time measurement across Europe (figure 2), and the energy consumption, interior and exterior temperature are the targeted parameters in EPC RECAST project.

The selection of these pilots was based on the variety of typology, systems, occupancy, location, and year of construction. In addition, the identification of the collaborators (inhabitants) that allow their houses to be monitored was a crucial factor in the monitoring implementation.

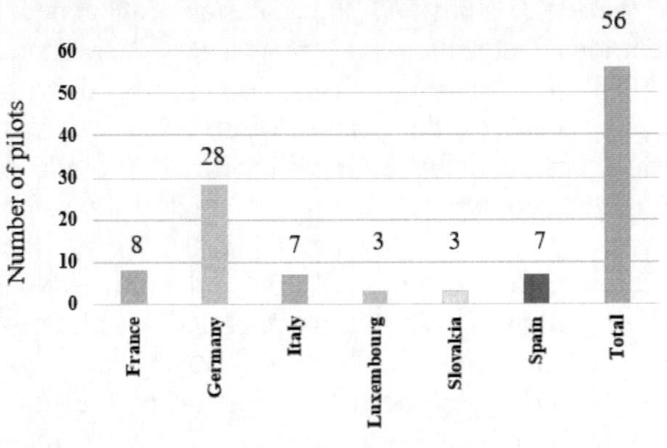


Figure 2. Long-term measurement of EPC RECAST project.

The access to the measurements of energy consumption depends on the type of the generation system in the analyzed building. As shown in figure 3, three different typologies were identified according to the generation system: 1) Single house with independent system, 2) apartment in a multifamily building with independent system, and 3) apartment in a multifamily building with centralized (shared) system. The first adopted approach for buildings with independent systems is the utility meter based on the measurement of the energy flow delivered to the building (e.g., gas/electric utility meter). Regarding the buildings with centralized energy production, the use of sub metering devices was adopted to measure the energy flow absorbed for each dwelling [7].

The choice of the sensors was based on the types of the monitored systems at each pilot site, on the ease of installation, on the adaptation of these sensors to be used for a long-time measurement but also on the feedback of other monitoring activities performed in CSTB. All the collected data are sent via router to the EPC RECAST monitoring platform through a dedicated LoRaWan network.

## 2.2 The targeted case studies in this research

After the implementation of the monitoring approach and the collection of the data, the assessment process of data becomes crucial to provide clean and complete data for the exploitation. In this regard, three different pilots were selected to illustrate the assessment process in this research.

In the individual house (id:A), two years of measures were collected for the analysis, with a time step of one hour for interior temperature and gas consumption. The general consumption in this case study has no defined time step. The case study B represents measures of lighting, heating, and total energy consumption with a time step of 24h, and the interior temperature and thermostat with a time step of one hour. Regarding the case study C, electricity consumption, interior temperature and exterior temperature were measured with a time step of one hour. The case study A and C are situated in the northern region of France and considered as the coldest zone in the country (H1a). The case study B is in the western part of France, where winters are more temperate (H2b). The energy used for the targeted pilots is gas.

| | | |
|---|---|---|
| | *Id* | A |
| | *Typology* | Individual house |
| | *Year of construction* | 1967 |
| | *Climate* | H1a |
| | *Systems* | Individual |
| *Measured parameters* | Interior temperature, gas consumption, general electricity consumption | |

| | | |
|---|---|---|
| | *Id* | B |
| | *Typology* | Apartment |
| | *Year of construction* | 2021 |
| | *Climate* | H2b |
| | *Systems* | Individual |
| *Measured parameters* | Interior temperature, heating consumption, lighting consumption, general consumption | |

| | | |
|---|---|---|
| | *Id* | C |
| | *Typology* | Apartment |
| | *Year of construction* | 2015 |
| | *Climate* | H1a |
| | *Systems* | Collective |
| *Measured parameters* | Interior temperature and humidity, general electricity consumption, heating consumption | |

Figure 3. The targeted case studies for the data assessment.

## 3.RESULTS & DISCUSSIONS

### 3.1 Data assessment Indicators

The first step of the assessment is the evaluation of the **availability** of the expected data. This evaluation is very important to define the operating status of the sensors, and which period could be exploited. Based on this analysis, a general overview is provided to define the percentage of the data available per month and per day. Accordingly, the periods where the measures were not sufficient were detected.
In the case where the monitoring didn't end yet, this verification is also useful to perform a regular checking to ensure the continuity of the measuring process by checking if the sensors :1) work normally, and 2) have missing data. Furthermore, TSAR also proposes a function that highlight the missing data (or the hole) that we cannot easily detect in the raw data set.

The total period of measures acquisition is different for each sensor. For the case study A, over the two years of measures, the availability analysis shows that the measures of interior temperature are complete except the sensors installed in the bedroom with only 3% of available data. The measures of gas consumption represent an availability of 93%, and complete acquisition was detected for electricity consumption. The percentage of data available in the case study B varies from 79% to 90% with a significant missing data during March 2022 to May 2022 as shown in the figure 4. For the case study C, the availability of data analysis shows a complete acquisition of the measures during the period of one year.

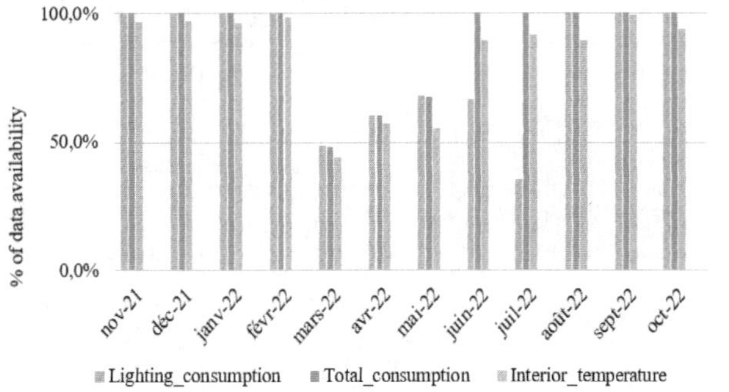


Figure 4. Example of data available in the case study B.
The second step after the global analysis of the data availability is to assess the ***data validity.*** Based on the available data, a selected period with available measure is identified. Thereafter, it is crucial to verify if all the data were measured according to the defined time step to ensure the homogenization of the measures by the re-indexation of the data. An interpolation function proposed by TSAR will be used to complete the missing data.

In the case study A, the measures of general electricity consumption represent a random acquisition with no defined time step and with missing data. For that matter, we selected different time steps to analyze. It will help to provide a homogenized data set, and the analysis of time step sensitivity. The following table 1 shows the percentage of the re-indexation and interpolation performed by TSAR for the targeted time steps. For the time step of 1 hour and 30 minutes few interpolations were performed instead of the time step of 1 minute that represent 27% of total interpolation. TSAR could also provide an overview of the validity of the data as shown in figure 5. The identified mean value of the time step is 4 min and 49 sec. For this reason, the time step of 5 min is recommended. In the context of EPC RECAST, the utilization of a time step of one hour is sufficient.

Table 1. Percentage of re-indexation and interpolation for different time steps (general consumption, Id:A)

| **ΔT** | **1h** | **30 min** | **5 min** | **1 min** |
|---|---|---|---|---|
| **Re-indexation** | 99,7% | 99,5% | 92,5% | 72,8% |
| **Interpolation** | 0,3% | 0,5% | 7,5% | 27,2% |

Other functions are proposed in TSAR to explore the validity of the data such as the "Frozen sensor". This function aims to detect if there's a measure with no significant evolution. The users must define threshold that indicates if this variation is considered as a normal acquisition or as a Frozen sensor. The threshold varies according to the type of the evaluated parameter and according to the time step of the measures. As an example, the user defines a threshold where if the temperature measures do not change by 0.01 °C for four hours (4 complete acquisition), consequently, the function "Frozen sensor" will highlight these measures as invalid. In this case, we can consider two possibilities:

1) Acquisition interrupted by a temporary technical problem related to the sensors or other factors
2) Absence of occupancy especially in the energy consumption measures.

By this fact, this function would be very useful to estimate the scenario of the occupant's presence and absence, and this is one of the important information to collect from the measured data to enhance the accuracy of the EPC RECAST simulation and calibrate the new methodology proposed by EPC RECAST project.

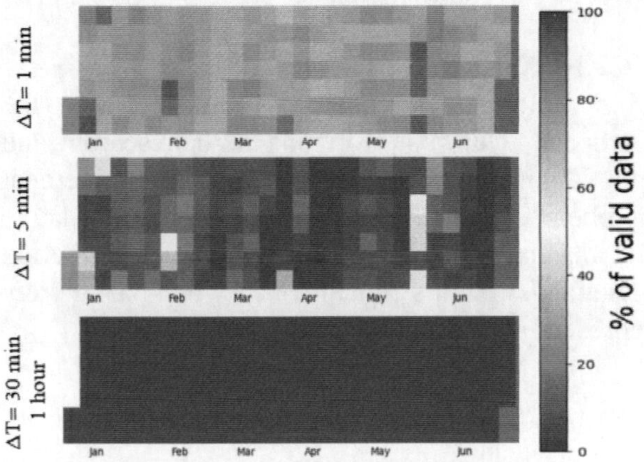


Figure 5. Percentage of valid data for different time steps (general electricity consumption, Id:A)

TSAR contributes also on the detection of values anomalies. In this context, the tool presents to check if there's a high or low value anomalies and high or low derive anomalies. These functions aim to verify the coherence and the compatibility of the measured data by specifying threshold according to the type of the physical variable measured.
One of the important strengths of the tool is the **visibility** that TSAR could provide. A table that summarizes the percentage of functions employed for each analyzed physical variable is important to check the global process of data cleaning (Table 2). It also offers different types of graphs that highlight the position of these functions and identify the quality of the assessed data. As shown in figure 6, the users could easily detect the assessment of the raw data. The cleanup status indicates the used function. For example, the status 100 corresponds to the detected hole in the raw data.
At the end of the data assessment, TSAR generates a final cleaned data set for further utilization.

### 3.2 Long-term measurement's exploitation

The approach adopted for the evaluation of the whole EPC RECAST process will include both quantitative and qualitative aspects. It addresses many different aspects (reliability of some indicators of the EPC, mainly those related to energy consumption, User friendliness of EPCs in terms of clarity and accuracy, Cost effectiveness, Enhanced user awareness, etc.)

Table 2. A summary of the functions employed for data assessment of lighting consumption ( Id:B)

| | % of functions employed | Status in the graph |
|---|---|---|
| **Re-indexation** | 76,25% | 1 |
| **Base interpolation** | 0,39% | 2 |
| **Hole** | 0,58% | 100 |
| **Frozen sensor** | 16,99% | 110 |
| **Linear interpolation** | 5,79% | 10 |

The exploitation of long-term measurement in the context of the EPC RECAST project is divided into two main perspectives:
**1.**The evaluation of the EPC energy consumption indicator reliability. The long-term measurement will allow the comparison of the measured energy consumption and the calculated energy consumption. It could be a comparison of total energy consumption, or system energy consumption depending on the measure's availability. This comparison requires a reliable series of measurement (subject covered in this article) and substantial preliminary work to allow comparisons under similar conditions which raises many questions: which period to consider in the comparison process? The use of TSAR responds clearly to this question. And how to define uses scenarios (set-point temperature, internal gains due to equipment, due to occupants, window openings, etc.) from the measured data? Further analysis will be developed in this regard.
**2.** The development of a method to reduce the gap between predicted and measured Energy Performance, based on the long-term measurement. This method will be used to improve the

interpretability and the accuracy of the EPC RECAST calculation model.

The described work above contributes to the operational rating of EPC RECAST methodology. The long-term measurement represents an important tool for the evaluation of EPC reliability, but a minimum level of building's monitoring could also help in this evaluation.

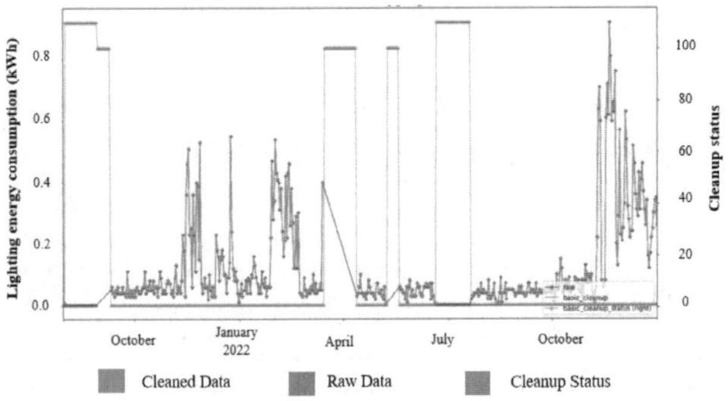


Figure 6. Assessment of energy lighting measures (Id:B)

## 4.CONCLUSION

In the context of EPC RECAST project, the in-situ measurement was selected as an essential tool for accurately analyzing the energy performance gap between the simulated and the real energy use. However, the verification of the data quality is crucial to ensure that the results obtained from the in-situ measurement are reliable and could be exploited for further energy performance improvements, which was the core of our research.

In-situ long measurement was developed across six countries in Europe, and about 56 dwellings were monitored to contribute to the EPC RECAST evaluation process. To guarantee the efficiency of the monitoring approach, CSTB recommends the exploitation of the tool TSAR for the data quality assessment.

According to TSAR approach, a data set with a verified quality signify a data set with available and valid measures. The tool is based on the time series analysis and various functions were proposed by TSAR to:

1. Verify the data's completeness
2. Specify the periods to consider for the data exploitation
3. Complete the missing data (this function has specific conditions)
4. Indicate the non-evolution of the measures
5. Validate the compatibility of the measured data.

By analyzing the data quality with TSAR, the results could represent a successful implementation of in-situ measurement and data acquisition as the case study C. Otherwise, the analysis could reveal several errors and different level of data quality which make this process necessary.

Future work will include the assessment of the data quality of all the measured data in the EPC RECAST project. Other functions could also be developed to meet the targeted goals of the EPC RECAST evaluation process.

## ACKNOWLEDGEMENT

This project has received funding from the European Union's Horizon 2020 research and innovation program under the grant agreement number 893118. The European Union is not liable for any use that may be made of the information contained in this document, which is merely representing the authors' view.

## REFERENCES

[1] Directive 2002/91/CE of the European Parliament and of the Council of 16 December 2002 on the energy performance of buildings, Official Journal of the European Communities,2002.

[2] Few Jessica et al. The over-prediction of energy use by EPCs in Great Britain: A comparison of EPC-modelled and metered primary energy use intensity. Energy and buildings,2023.

[3] Pieter de Wilde. The gap between predicted and measured energy performance of buildings: A framework for investigation. Automation in Construction,2014.

[4] Kirsten Gram-Hanssen et al. Energy performance gaps: promises, people, practices. Building Research & Information,2017.

[5] Marta Maria Sesana, Graziano Salvalai. review on Building Renovation Passport: Potentialities and barriers on current initiatives. Energy and Buildings,2018.

[6] EPC recast website (www.epc-recast.eu)

[7] Robert H. Shumway& David S. Stoffer. Time Series Analysis and Its Applications. Springer,2016.

[8] D3.2. Preliminary testing, measurement and verification of EPCRECAST approach on selected demo cases. EPC RECAST project,2022 (confidential report).

# Data Fusion for Uncertainty Evaluation in Extreme Electrical Metrology

Marija Cundeva-Blajer[1]

[1] *Ss. Cyril and Methodius University in Skopje, Faculty of Electrical Engineering and Information Technologies, ul. Rugjer Boskovic br. 18, 1000 Skopje, Republic of North Macedonia, mcundeva@feit.ukim.edu.mk*

**ABSTRACT**: Many decisions especially in quality assurance are based on the measurement data. Poor data will produce poor models, incorrect results and finally wrong decisions. Different data processing may be deployed if evaluation methodology is essential, as is the measurement results uncertainty evaluation. Through data fusion, greater quality of information for a specific purpose is obtained, by exploiting the synergy of data gathered from different sources of uncertainty. In metrology it is crucial not only to fuse data obtained from multiple sensors, but also to assess threats and risks, i.e. to identify the sources of measurement uncertainty. Data fusion in uncertainty evaluation is based on experimental data from sensing devices and on information obtained by other means (e.g. a priori knowledge, experience, and model application). In the paper a case study of application of data fusion in the process of uncertainty evaluation in the area of calibration of instruments of extreme electrical quantities, will be presented, more concretely in a decision making process of conformity assessment for acceptance of calibration results of instruments for electrical inductance of high values. This is essential for the validation and accreditation of a novel calibration method in the accredited University calibration Laboratory for Electrical Measurements.

**Keywords**: data fusion, uncertainty evaluation, electrical metrology, calibration of inductance meters, best calibration and measurement capabilities in high electrical inductances

**Received** January 1, 2023; **In final form** March 31, 2023; **Published** June 2023



**Corresponding author:** Marija Cundeva-Blajer, e-mail: mcundeva@feit.ukim.edu.mk

## 1. INTRODUCTION

Many decisions especially in quality assurance are based on the measurement data, [1]. Poor data will produce poor models, incorrect results and finally wrong decisions [2], [3]. The revival of measurement and data science is caused by the revolution of sensory devices and the emerging data transmission, storage and processing capabilities available and variously deployed. Several classes of data science problems for which techniques might be developed and evaluated across different domains in metrology are: anomaly detection, cleaning, alignment, data fusion, identification and classification, regression, prediction, knowledge base construction, density estimation, joint inference, [2]. Data science involves ranking, clustering, and transcription, [4]. Additional classes of problems rely on algorithms and techniques that apply to raw data at an earlier "pre-processing" stage, [2]. Different data processing may be deployed if evaluation methodology is essential, as is the measurement results uncertainty evaluation according to the Guide to the Expression of Uncertainty in Measurement (GUM), [5]. The methods for uncertainty assessment may include the frequentist, Bayesian, and fiducial statistical paradigms, [6]. In this context, the ultimate idea underlying data fusion is to obtain greater quality of information for a specific purpose by exploiting the synergy of data gathered from different sources of uncertainty. Data fusion is the process of combining data or information to estimate or predict entity states, [7]. In metrology it is crucial not only to fuse data obtained from multiple sensors, but also to assess threats and risk, i.e. to identify the sources of measurement uncertainty. Data fusion increases robustness, reliability and reduces the vulnerability of the system supporting the decision, allowing decision-making even in absence of some sources of uncertainty information. It provides a better and larger coverage of space and time, reduces ambiguity, as information of higher quality provides better discrimination between available hypotheses. Data fusion in uncertainty evaluation is based on experimental data output by sensing devices and on information obtained by other means (e.g. the user as a data source for a priori knowledge, experience, and model application). Data fusion involves addressing: data from sources with different quality levels (e.g. different accuracy), non-independent data, too much information, leading to computational problems, and need to change the context of the observation (e.g. from time to frequency domain) or to extract features or attributes, as issues of data-processing type, [7].

In the paper a case study of application of data fusion in the process of uncertainty evaluation for purposes of relevant decision making in the area of calibration of instruments of extreme electrical quantities, will be presented, in concrete in the calibration of instruments for high electrical inductance. The data fusion uncertainty evaluation is for the purposes of validation and further accreditation scope extension with a novel calibration method in the already accredited calibration Laboratory for Electrical Measurements (LEM) at the Ss. Cyril and Methodius University in Skopje, according to the international standard ISO 17025:2017, [8].

## 2. DATA FUSION IN LABORATORY DECISION MAKING PROCESSES BASED ON EVALUATION OF UNCERTAINTY IN CALIBRATION

The goal of every measurement is to obtain as accurate as possible measurement result, and to provide its adequate interpretation. Beside the numerical representation of the results, the calibration laboratories are supposed to declare accurate statement of conformity for the specified calibration results, in compliance to standards and specification which are to be fulfilled and by applying a prescribed decision making rule, as a requirement of the international standard ISO 17025:2017, [8]. The ILAC-G8:09/2019, [9] provides guidelines to define the procedure to issue a statement of conformity of the results. The procedures established by the international ILAC-G8 guideline, include the measurement uncertainty estimated by the laboratory as one of the main inputs when defining the main parameters of the laboratory's decision rule, such as the tolerance interval, the acceptance limit, rejection interval, guard band, etc. [9]. When performing a measurement and subsequently making a statement of conformity, for example, in or out-of-tolerance to manufacturer's specifications or Pass/Fail to a particular requirement, there are two possible outcomes, [9]: a) a correct decision is made regarding conformance to specification, or b) an incorrect decision is made regarding conformance to specification. Each measured value has an associated measurement uncertainty, which is the main source of risk for delivery of wrong decision.

## 3. DATA FUSION OF UNCERTAINTY EVALUATION FOR STATEMENT OF CONFORMITY IN CALIBRATION OF INSTRUMENTS FOR MEASURING ELECTRICAL INDUCTANCE

An example of data fusion will be presented for uncertainty estimation of the calibration results applied in deriving decision rule and statement of conformity in calibration of an electrical inductance meter. The case study is for calibration of a LCR-meter in one extreme measurement point of 10 H (very high electrical inductance).

Table 1. Decision rule according to ILAC G8.

| Decision rule | Guard band w | Specific risk |
|---|---|---|
| 6 sigma | 3 U | < 1 ppm PFA |
| 3 sigma | 1.5 U | < 0.16% PFA |
| ILAC G8:2009 | 1 U | < 2.5% PFA |
| ISO 14253-1:2017 [10] | 0.83 U | < 5% PFA |
| Simple acceptance | 0 | < 50% PFA |
| Uncritical | -U | < 2.5% PFR |
| Customer defined | r U | Customers may define arbitrary multiple of r to have applied as guard band. |

The analysis is conducted for various decision rules given in Table 1, as in the ILAC-G8:2019, [9].

### 3.1. Best measurement and calibration capabilities of the field of extreme values of electrical inductance

The metrological infrastructure for calibration in the field of electrical inductance is relatively underdeveloped in comparison to the calibration and measurement capabilities (CMC) of other electrical quantities, and, if metrological improvement in the calibration of instruments for electrical inductance is demonstrated, it can be considered as a contribution to the extreme electrical metrology. Furthermore, most of the National Metrology Institutes and accredited calibration laboratories in their published CMCs comprise the scope of electrical inductance ranges in [mH] level, while the ranges of [H] level are rarely present, [11]. The current state-of-the-art in the field of metrology of electrical inductance is presented bellow through the comparison of the best CMCs at international level and at regional level of South-Eastern Europe, where the LEM laboratory is located. In Figure 1 a comparison of the best CMCs at international level and in Figure 2 the best CMCs at regional level of South-Eastern Europe for electrical inductance of 10 H are presented, based on the data in the KCDB database of BIPM, [11]. The electrical inductance of 10 H is a rather high value, thus belonging to extreme electrical quantities, which introduce challenges in the process of calibration and the number of National Metrology Institutes (NMIs) and accredited calibration laboratories which perform the calibrations at this measurement range is rather low.

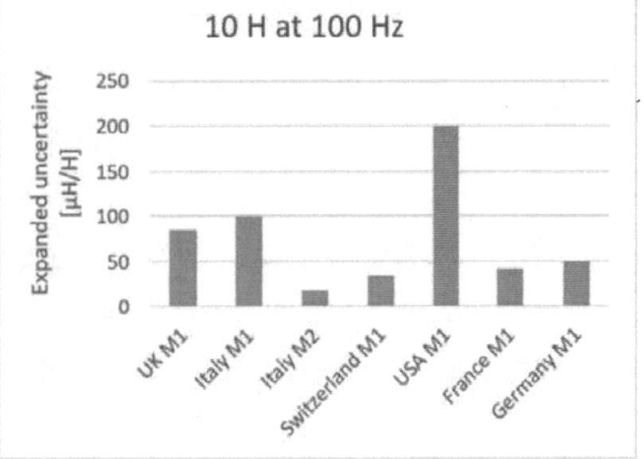


Figure 1. Expanded measurement uncertainties of electrical inductance of 10 H at 100 Hz at the international NMIs level

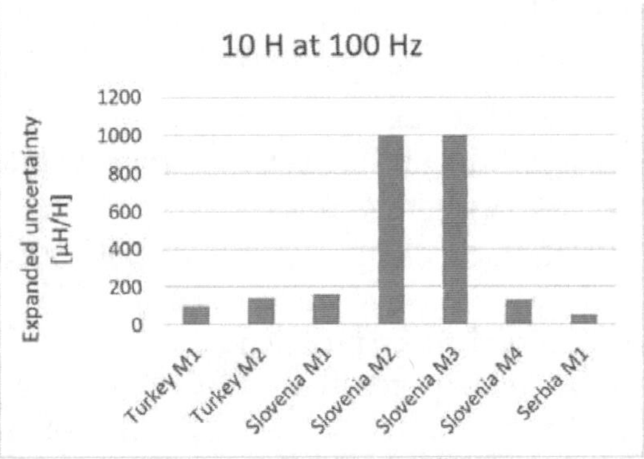


Figure 2. Expanded measurement uncertainties of electrical inductance of 10 H at 100 Hz at the regional NMIs level

The LEM laboratory is an accredited calibration laboratory for instruments for electrical quantities according to ISO 17025:2017 since 2015, but the calibration of instruments of electrical inductance is out of its accreditation scope. LEM develops a new calibration procedure for calibration of instruments for electrical inductance, [12]. It has recently acquired a reference standard for electrical inductance, the Transmille 4015 Multifunctional Calibrator with the option IND for inductance calibration presented in Figure 3, with technical specification as in [14] and in Table 2, all at frequency of 1 kHz.

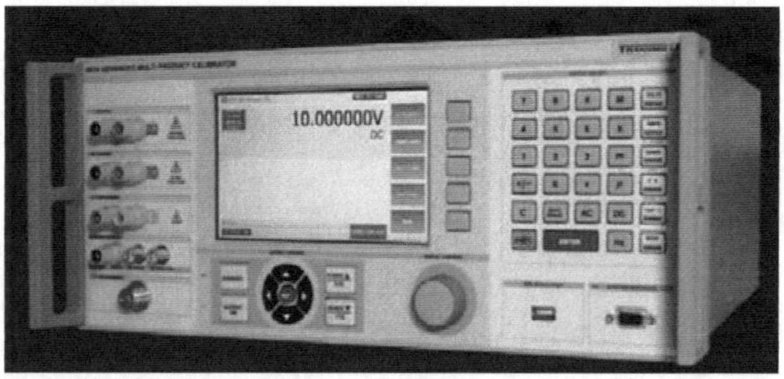


Figure 3. LEM reference standard multifunctional calibrator Transmille 4015 with inductance calibration option

Transmille 4015 is calibrated in the electrical inductance measurement range at the producer's accredited calibration laboratory with established measurement traceability to national and international primary reference standards, with accompanying calibration certificate.

Table 2. Technical specification of the reference standard for electrical inductance of LEM

| **Multifunctional Calibrator Transmille 4015** | | | |
|---|---|---|---|
| **Supplement for calibration of instruments for inductance with specifications for 1 kHz and accuracy of ± 50 μH Transmille IND** | | | |
| **Technical Specifications:** | | | |
| Electrical Inductance | Q-factor | Display resolution | Best annual accuracy: |
| 1 mH | 1 | 100 nH | 0.5 % |
| 10 mH | 2.8 | 1 μH | 0.5 % |
| 19 mH | 3.8 | 1 μH | 0.5 % |
| 29 mH | 4.7 | 1 μH | 0.5 % |
| 50 mH | 6.1 | 1 μH | 0.5 % |
| 100 mH | 8.6 | 10 μH | 0.5 % |
| 1 H | 29 | 100 μH | 0.5 % |
| 10 H | 110 | 1 mH | 0.5 % |

As the presented results bellow are for the case study of calibration at 10 H electrical inductance, some additional technical specification of the reference standard are: maximum current 10 mA, DC resistance 950 Ω, Q-factor 110, display resolution 1 mH. The recommended measurement method in the range from 1 H to 10 H is $L_p$ – parallel reference impedance modelling [14].

### 3.2. LEM calibration test set-up for inductance

The national metrology institutes and the calibration laboratories in the field of electrical quantities develop diverse calibration methods for instruments for impedance i.e. electrical inductance measurement, [15-22]. However, most of the published metrology researches are on reference standards are in the field of low to medium range of electrical inductance, such as 1-100 mH, [15], [16], [19], [20] and [24]. In [18], a transportable multi-value inductance standard built on the basis of circuits of electronic equivalents of inductance with switched capacitors, is described, with inductance range of the standard is 1 mH-1000 H, frequency range is 20 Hz-10 kHz, the uncertainty is 0.02-0.1%. The proposed calibration methods, foremost based on different bridges realization are in the same measurement scope, [17], [21], [22] and [23].

In this case study the Laboratory for Electrical Measurements (LEM), develops a calibration procedure of LCR bridges i.e., more precisely a calibration procedure of meters for electrical inductance. Therefore, a calibration procedure of the electrical inductance measurement range of a LCR-meter is conducted. The unit under test (artefact of calibration) is ROHDE & SCHWARZ HM8118 - Programmable LCR-Bridge, with the main technical specification in [13]. The reference standard in the calibration procedure is a Transmille 4015 Multifunctional Calibrator with the option IND for inductance calibration. The IND option is a built-in black box option of the Transmille 4015 Multifunctional Calibrator and there is no publicly available information on the physical system of the realisation of the inductance reference standard [14].

### 3.3. Calibration procedure

The calibration was performed in the LEM laboratory. For each measurement point 10 repeated measurements are performed for the following measurement points: 1 mH, 10 mH, 20 mH, 30 mH, 50 mH, 100 mH, 1 H, 10 H. The measurement starts by turning on both instruments and connecting them in a suitable way. The LCR meter has BNC connectors to connect to probes on the calibrator's voltage range, as in Figure 4.

Figure 4. Artefact of calibration-connecting of the RCL bridge meter to the calibrator

### 3.4. Data fusion for estimation of uncertainty in calibration of instrument for inductance

The uncertainty budget is built by fusing data from a component of type A and components of type B, as in GUM, [5]. The uncertainty of type A $u_A$ is calculated from the experimental data subjected to statistical processing, i.e. the mean value $L_{mean}$ and the standard deviation of the measurement $s_A$, as in:

$$s_A = \sqrt{\frac{1}{n-1}\sum_{i=1}^{n}(L_{icor} - L_{mean})^2} \quad (1)$$

where

$$L_{mean} = \frac{1}{n}\sum_{i}^{n} L_{icor} \quad (2)$$

$$L_{icor} = L_i - L_{ref} \quad (3)$$

$L_i$ is the measured value in the particular point and $L_{ref}$ is the reference value from the calibrator.

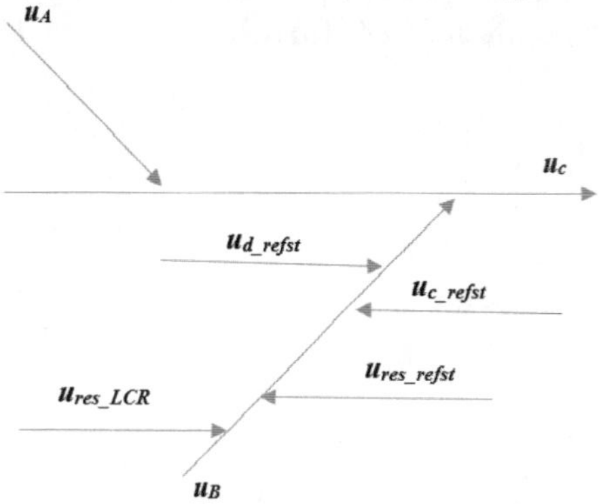


Figure 5. Ishikawa fishbone diagram of data fusion of components in the combined uncertainty budget in calibration of instrument for inductance

The following uncertainty components are fused in the uncertainty budget of type B, $u_B$:

$u_{res\_LCR}$ – uncertainty due to LCR-bridge resolution

$u_{res\_refst}$ – uncertainty due to reference standard resolution

$u_{d\_refst}$ – uncertainty due to reference standard drift
$u_{c\_refst}$ – uncertainty from the calibration certificate of the reference standard (calibrator)

The combined uncertainty of type B is:

$$u_B = \sqrt{u_{res_{LCR}}^2 + u_{res\_refst}^2 + u_{d\_refst}^2 + u_{c\_refst}^2} \tag{4}$$

The total combined uncertainty is:

$$u_c = \sqrt{u_A^2 + u_B^2} \tag{5}$$

The expanded uncertainty deployed in the particular rules for conformity of statement is:

$$u = 2 \cdot u_c \tag{6}$$

The data fusion in the delivery of the combined uncertainty is shown in the Ishikawa (Fishbone) diagram in Figure 5.

The results of the calculation by deploying the data fusion concept at the measurement point of 10 H is as follows in Table 3, with all values in H:

Table 3. Data fusion inputs for calculation of combined uncertainty budget

| $L_{ref}$ [H] | $L_{mean}$ [H] | $u_A$ [H] | $u_{res\_LCR}$ [H] | $u_{res\_refst}$ [H] | $u_{d\_refst}$ [H] | $u_{c\_refst}$ [H] |
|---|---|---|---|---|---|---|
| 10.336 | 10.4996 | 0.0002 | 0.0001 | 0.001 | 0.0362 | 0.006 |

The derived combined uncertainty is:

$$u_c = 0.037 \text{ H} \tag{7}$$

and the expanded uncertainty is:

$$u = 0.073 \text{ H} \tag{8}$$

### 3.5. Comparison of approaches in issue of statement of conformity

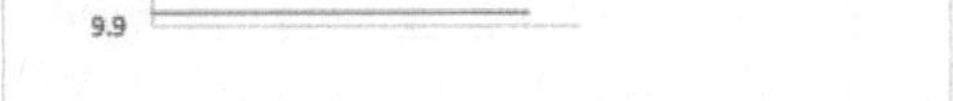


Figure 6. Comparison of the measurement result with the expanded uncertainty to the specification limits within simple acceptance criterion

The uncertainty derived by applying data fusion is an input in the various criteria for delivery of conformity statements of the derived calibration result in the measurement point of 10 H. In Figures 6-12, the results of the calibration are compared to the specifications and to the acceptance limits posed according to different approaches for decision delivery.

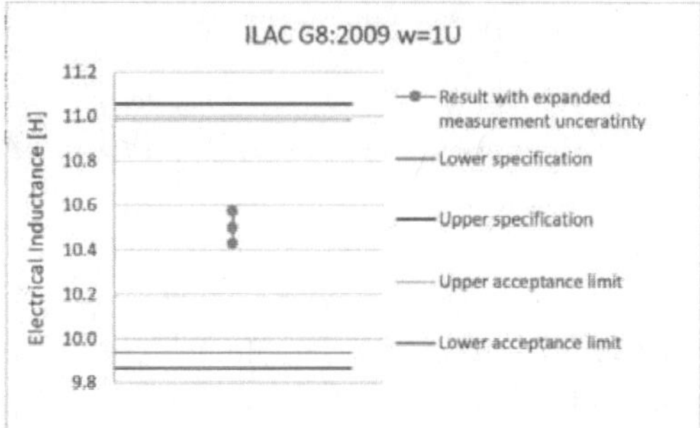


Figure 7. Comparison of the measurement result with the expanded uncertainty to the specification limits with band guard of one expanded uncertainty according to the acceptance criterion of the previous edition of the guideline ILAC G8:2009

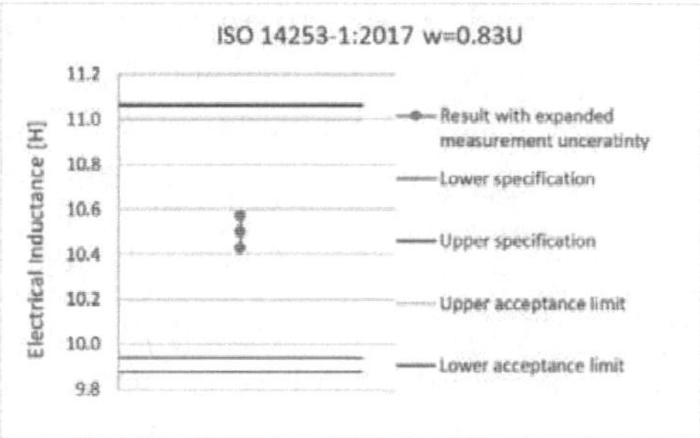


Figure 8. Comparison of the measurement result with the expanded uncertainty to the specification limits with band guard of 0.83 of the expanded uncertainty according to the acceptance criterion of the international standard ISO 14253-1:2017[10]

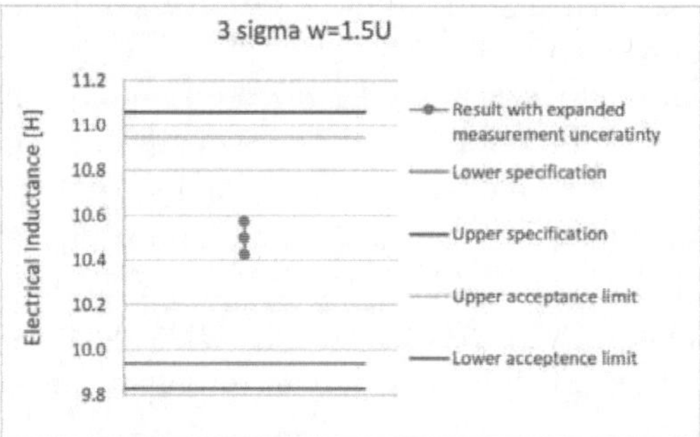


Figure 9. Comparison of the measurement result with the expanded uncertainty to the specification limits with band guard of 1.5 of the expanded uncertainty of both sides according to the acceptance criterion of 3-Sigma.

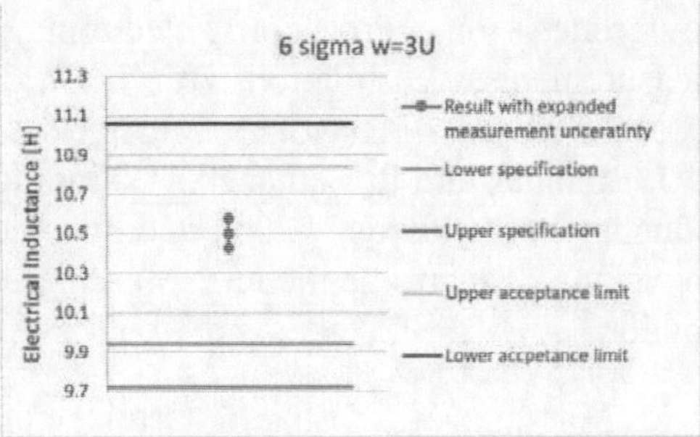


Figure 10. Comparison of the measurement result with the expanded uncertainty to the specification limits with band guard of 3 times of the expanded uncertainty of both sides according to the acceptance criterion of 6-Sigma.

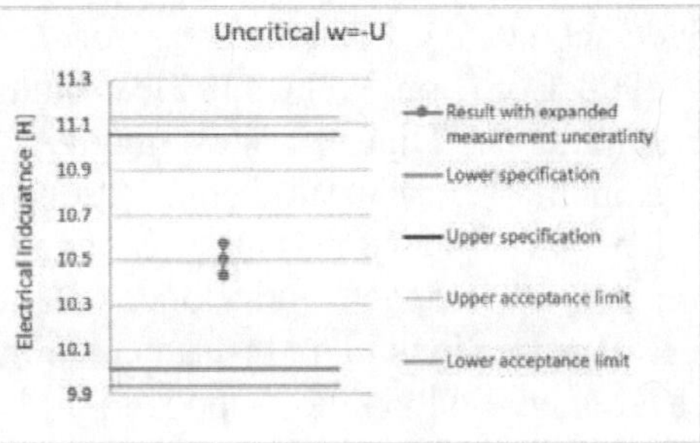


Figure 11. Comparison of the measurement result with the expanded uncertainty to the specification limits when the measurement result is rejected if the measured value is greater than the specification plus the expanded uncertainty-uncritical criterion.

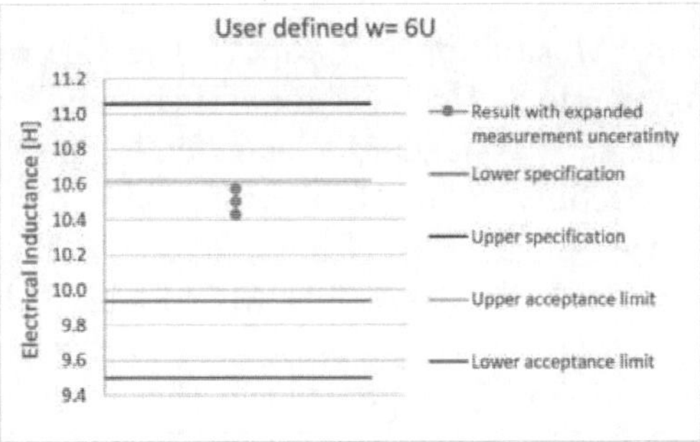


Figure 12. Comparison of the measurement result with the expanded uncertainty to the specification limits when the band guard is defined by the user, (example for r=6 times to the expanded uncertainty)

## 4. DISCUSSION OF THE RESULTS

Based on the presented results, the calibration in the concrete measurement point of 10 H of the LCR-meter in all presented decision making approaches is within the specifications and the tolerance limit interval. According to the ILAC G8:2019, [9], the statement of conformity can be expressed as binary statement with or without guard band (PASS/FAIL) or non-binary statement with guard band (PASS/ Conditional PASS/ Conditional FAIL/ FAIL). For the presented case study, according to all approaches, the measurement results PASS.

## 5. CONCLUSIONS

In the paper an original data fusion approach in the estimation of uncertainty for the purposes of establishment of decision rule and statement of conformity of calibration results is presented. The overall methodology is illustrated by a case study of calibration of instrument for extreme electrical quantity, i.e. calibration of LCR-bridge meter in the range of high electrical inductance. On the basis of the fused data in the budget of the measurement uncertainty, the derived measurement result and the accompanying uncertainty are used as input data in the next level of data fusion, i.e. the delivery of the statement of conformity. Due to the robustness of the data fusion approach in thc two levels of calculation the stated conformity assessment is with very low risk level in issue of wrong statement. The presented data fusion approach uncertainty evaluation for purposes of delivery of statement of conformity in extreme electrical metrology, is universal and can be applied to other cases of conformity assessment.

## ACKNOWLEDGEMENT

This research is conducted in the framework of the scientific project "Development and Upgrade of Laboratory Resources for Research and Introduction of New Analytical Methods in Electrical Metrology", Contract No. 15-15590/22, 22.11.2021, financed by the Ministry of Education and Science of Republic of North Macedonia.

## REFERENCES

[1] M. Cundeva-Blajer, Data Science for Testing, Inspection and Certification, Proceedings of the IMEKO TC11 & TC24 Joint Conference, 17–19 October 2022, Dubrovnik-Croatia, ISBN 978-953-7124-13-7.

[2] K. Cunha, R. Santos. The Reliability of Data from Metrology 4.0. Int. J. on Data Science and Technology. Vol. 6, No. 4, 2020, pp. 66-69, https://doi.org/10.11648/j.ijdst.20200604.11

[3] B. J. Dorr, C.S. Greenberg, C.S., Fontana, P. et al. A new data science research program: evaluation, metrology, standards, and

community outreach. Int. J. Data Sci. Anal. 1, 177–197, 2016, https://doi.org/10.1007/s41060-016-0016-z

[4] Bengio, Y., Goodfellow, I.J., Courville A.: Deep learning. 2015, http://www.iro.umontreal.ca/bengioy/dlbook

[5] "Evaluation of measurement data — Guide to the expression of uncertainty in measurement", JCGM 100:2008 GUM

[6] W. F. Guthrie, H. Liu, A. L. Rukhin, B. Toman, J. C. M. Wang, N. Zhang "Three Statistical Paradigms for the Assessment and Interpretation of Measurement Uncertainty", ed. F. Pavese, A. Forbes "Data Modeling for Metrology and Testing in Measurement Science", Birkhauser Boston, Springer, LLC 2009, pp. 71-116

[7] P. S. Girao, O. Postolache, J. M. D. Pereira "Data Fusion, Decision-Making, and Risk Analysis: Mathematical Tools and Techniques", ed. F. Pavese, A. Forbes "Data Modeling for Metrology and Testing in Measurement Science", Birkhauser Boston, Springer, LLC 2009, pp. 205-254

[8] EN ISO/IEC 17025 "General requirements for the competence of testing and calibration laboratories", Cenelec, Brussels, 2017

[9] ILAC-G8: 09/2019 Guidelines on Decision Rules and Statements of Conformity

[10] ISO 14253-1:2017, Geometrical product specifications (GPS) – Inspection by measurement of workpieces and measuring equipment – Part 1: Decision rules for verifying conformity or nonconformity with specification.

[11] www.bipm.org (retrieved on: 30.03.2023)

[12] M. Cundeva-Blajer, G. Dimitrovski, V. Sapundziovski, V. Dimcev, K. Demerdziev "Infrastructure Development for Extreme Electrical Metrology", Journal of Electrical Engineering and Information Technologies, Vol. 7, No. 2, pp. 101–109, (2022), DOI: https://doi.org/10.51466/JEEIT2272201101chb

[13] Rohde&Schwarz, "HM8118 LCR-Bridge User Manual", Rohde&Schwarz, München, Germany, 2016

[14] Transmille, "Transmille 4015 Multiproduct Calibrator Extended Specifications", Transmille, United Kingdom, 2022

[15] N. Sakamoto, "Long-term calibration results of 10 mH and 100 mH standard inductors using a reactance compensation method," 2012 Conference on Precision electromagnetic Measurements, Washington, DC, USA, 2012, pp. 582-583, doi: 10.1109/CPEM.2012.6251063.

[16] J. Bohacek and R. Sedlacek, "Calibration of Inductance Standards," 2004 Conference on Precision Electromagnetic Measurements, London, UK, 2004, pp. 37-38, doi: 10.1109/CPEM.2004.305408.

[17] M. Marzano, V. D'Elia, M. Ortolano and L. Callegaro, "Primary Realization of Inductance and Capacitance Scales with a Fully Digital Bridge," IEEE Transactions on Instrumentation and Measurement, vol. 71, pp. 1-8, 2022, Art no. 1503008, doi: 10.1109/TIM.2022.3214498.

[18] P. M. Yegorov, "A transportable multivalue inductance standard for the range of 0,1-1000 H," 1998 Conf. on Precision Electromagnetic Measurements Digest, Washington, USA, 1998, pp. 38-39, doi: 10.1109/CPEM.1998.699748.

[19] Han Jun Kim, Rae Duk Lee and Y. P. Semenov, "Compact inductance standard," IEEE Transactions on Instrumentation and Measurement, vol. 54, no. 2, pp. 546-549, April 2005, doi: 10.1109/TIM.2004.843333.

[20] T. Skubis, A. Met and K. Musiol, "Coherence of Comparison Results for 10 mH Inductance Standards," IEEE Instrumentation & Measurement Technology Conference IMTC 2007, Warsaw, Poland, 2007, pp. 1-3, doi: 10.1109/IMTC.2007.379060.

[21] K. Musioł and T. Skubis, "The Use of 1:1 Comparator Bridge for 10:1 and 1:10 Inductance Standard Transfer," in IEEE Transactions on Instrumentation and Measurement, vol. 63, no. 12, pp. 3019-3026, Dec. 2014, doi: 10.1109/TIM.2014.2322711.

[22] M. Ortolano et al., "A Comprehensive Analysis of Error Sources in Electronic Fully Digital Impedance Bridges," in IEEE Transactions on Instrumentation and Measurement, vol. 70, pp. 1-14, 2021, Art no. 1500914, doi: 10.1109/TIM.2020.3034115.

[23] F. Overney, B. Jeanneret, "Impedance bridges: From Wheatstone to Josephson," Metrologia, vol. 55, no. 5, pp. S119–S134, 2018.

[24] O. Velychko, S. Shevkun, M. Dombrovskyi, V. Dovhan "Interlaboratory comparisons of calibration results for electrical capacity measures and inductance measures", Measurement Infrastructure Vol. 4, 2022, https://doi.org/10.33955/v4(2022)-021

# Detecting night opening of windows in summer: a case study

Valentin Hoyet[1,2], Mathieu Bouville[2], Maxime Robillart[2], Marie-Lise Pannier[1]

[1]*Univ Angers, LARIS, SFR MATHSTIC, 49000 Angers, France*

[2]*Kocliko, 74 cours Aristide Briand, 33000 Bordeaux, France*

**ABSTRACT**: One consequence of climate change is that summer heat waves increase in frequency and intensity, and so do uncomfortably hot summer nights. One effective way to counter this effect is night ventilation. As connected temperature sensors are growing more common, they provide easily accessible data, from which nocturnal window openings can be inferred. Machine or deep learning algorithms, common in the literature, tend to require many labelled data. This article instead proposes an algorithm relying on expert rules and knowledge of the thermal behaviour of the building. It detects night openings or closings based, respectively, on a decrease or increase of indoor temperature. In our case study of an apartment equipped with connected window and temperature sensors, the algorithm is able to estimate the number of hours of night ventilation to within ±15%. It was more reliable in the hot summer of 2022 than in the cooler summer of 2021: the hypothesis of an effect of opening on temperature was then more realistic. This knowledge will eventually be used to quantify the potential temperature decrease from opening windows during summer nights, so as to provide residents with personalised advice on their window management.

**Keywords**: building energy simulation, night ventilation, summer thermal comfort, temperature sensors, window openings, rule-based algorithm.

**Received** January 1, 2021; **In final form** January 31, 2021, **Published** June 2021



**Corresponding author:** Marie-Lise Pannier, e-mail: marie-lise.pannier@univ-angers.fr

## 1. INTRODUCTION

A comfortable and healthy environment is essential for the well-being and health of humans in buildings. Nevertheless, it can be difficult to make a home thermally comfortable in all seasons. In summer, it can be especially challenging in areas with high temperature and humidity levels. Night ventilation —opening windows and allowing cooler outside air to circulate throughout a building— can contribute to reducing indoor temperatures and to creating a more comfortable sleeping environment during hot summer nights. It is also a free complement to energy-intensive air conditioning.

By automatically detecting when windows are open, building automation systems can adjust heating and cooling, and thus reduce energy waste and cost. Moreover, knowing people's window-opening habits makes it possible to give feedback to inhabitants on good practice toward a better thermal comfort in summer.

### 1.1. Background

Several methods have been proposed to detect human behaviour in buildings, such as window opening. In their review article, Carlucci *et al.* [1] split these methods into three categories: stochastic, data-driven and rule-based.

#### 1.1.1. Stochastic models

Stochastic methods estimate an outcome by assuming a probabilistic relationship with one or more variables (e.g. probability that an occupant open a window if he enters the room between 8 and 8:15 a.m.). Specifically, they focus on the probability that a window event will occur, using algorithms such as Bernoulli [2] or Markov [3] processes. The Bernoulli approach takes into account only the current situation, thereby ignoring the dynamic process that leads the occupant to open a window. Markov processes correct this shortcoming by making each prediction dependent on the prediction of the previous time steps. While these processes can provide accurate predictions, they only predict the opening of the window and not the closing.

#### 1.1.2. Data-driven models

Data-driven models are a common recent extension of stochastic models. They find a relationship between the input data and the probability of the window state using a statistical model that can learn and adapt without following explicit instructions.

Some of these studies, based on logistic regressions, focus on understanding thermal comfort and the environmental triggers of window opening. The coefficients of a logistic regression show that the indoor $CO_2$ level is the most important variable explaining the opening of windows, and outdoor temperature is the main driver for their closing [4]. A statistical analysis based on logistic regressions found that characteristics of the dwelling area of the residence or home insulation have a strong impact on window opening behaviour: large dwellings (> 93 $m^2$) and those with recent insulation are more likely to have their window open [5]. This study also found that adding variables pertaining to physical characteristics of the dwelling, such as on which floor it is or which direction it faces, improved the prediction.

Another study aimed at improving thermal dynamic simulations, by improving the modelling of human behaviour in residential buildings, in order to obtain a more accurate prediction of the energy performance of a building. The study used XGBoost to reach 80% precision for detecting whether a window was open or shut [6].

Li and coworkers [7] propose a logistic regression that predicts window opening probability, in order to study its impact on the energy consumption of the building.

One limit to data-driven models is that they are specific to the environment they were trained in and will not be able to provide accurate results in a new environment unless they are specifically recalibrated for it [8].

#### 1.1.3. Neural networks increase the variety of input

De Rautlin de la Roy *et al.* [9] use outdoor and indoor air temperatures, outdoor and indoor relative humidity and indoor $CO_2$ concentration to predict the state of a window. They show that neural networks such as long-short-term-memory (LSTM) and gated recurrent unit (GRU) work slightly better than more traditional machine learning such as linear discriminant analysis (LDA) or support vector machine (SVM) models.

More complex sorts of variables can also be used to detect window openings, but these require more specialized methods. For instance, recent studies used real-time images of the outside façade of buildings and convolutional neural network (CNN) to detect whether a window was open [10, 11]. (This may not work at night, which would be an issue for us.)

Audio signal record has also been passed through LSTM-CNN classification to predict events in a residence, including window opening [12]. A microphone is placed in a non-echoing room. When an audio signal is detected, it is first converted into a grey scale image that is then classified by CNN as an event such as shower audio or window opening.

#### 1.1.4. Rule-based models

Rule-based models use a set of expert rules based on schedules or profiles to predict human behaviour. This category is by far the least common. A study [13] predicts the probability of windows being open in offices using outdoor temperature: the higher the outdoor temperature the higher the probability of windows being open, reaching 80% at an outside temperature of 33°C.

### 1.2. Aim of the study

#### 1.2.1. Those who open windows and those who do not

Our goal is to be able to know which occupants in a building open their windows at night in the summer. Such information would enable us to let those who do not, know of potential improvement to their comfort in summer by opening windows. And we could do so without disturbing those who already regularly open their windows.

Our long-term objective is to provide personalized advice to residents, by suggesting to them useful times when to open their windows. This will in addition require to quantify the effect of performing the suggested action and communicate it to the users (e.g., "opening your windows for 2 hours will decrease indoor temperature by 2 °C").

To the best of our knowledge, no study has so far been dedicated to night ventilation in summer.

#### 1.2.2. A rule-based model

Many models aim at establishing the general probability of some window being open given its environment [2, 3, 6, 7, 13]. The goal of the present article is instead to know whether a given window is open at a given time.

We rely on (indoor and outdoor) temperatures as input, because connected sensors are growing in number anyway: their data can be used for our purpose without extra cost (unlike for instance installing opening sensors for this sole aim).

Although less common in the literature, a rule-based approach is a good option since detecting the window opening itself becomes a deterministic problem. It requires smaller amounts of hard-to-obtain labelled data than data-driven methods. The latter also have as a drawback that they are trained in a specific environment and may not be portable to other buildings. To overcome this difficulty, we use building-specific physical information (such as insulation and inertia) to root our work in the specifics of the dwelling we study, as do [5, 14].

## 2. METHODS

### 2.1. Detecting whether a window is open

Since the focus is on summer night ventilation, the method seeks to detect window openings based on a significant drop in indoor temperature. Conversely, the window is deemed shut again when the indoor temperature rises back. This relies on two variables, indoor and outdoor temperatures, measured every 30 minutes, room by room.

Assuming that there is no internal heat gain, it is possible to approximate the evolution of the room temperature $T_{room}$ at night by:

$$C\frac{dT_{room}}{dt} = U \times S \times (T_{out} - T_{room}), (1)$$

with:

- $C$: heat capacity, in W.h/K, of the air and light walls;
- $U$: heat transfer coefficient per surface area of wall in contact with the outside, in W/(m².K);
- $S$: area, in m², of the surface in contact with the outside.

A window opening is deemed to take place when the temperature decreases more than would be expected from Eq. (1):

$$\left|\frac{\Delta T_{room}}{\Delta t}\right| > \left|\frac{1}{\tau} \times (T_{out} - T_{room})\right|, (2)$$

with $\tau = \frac{C}{U \times S}$ the characteristic time in hours of the apartment.

A deep knowledge of the building is needed to compute this constant as it depends on the heat capacity ($C$) and heat transfer coefficient ($U$). The time constant $\tau$ for the apartment of the case study (§ 3) has been estimated at 21 hours using a model of dynamic thermal simulation [15].

The algorithm takes as input the indoor and outdoor temperatures (as well as the aforementioned constants) and returns a classification: the window is open (output of 1) or closed (0).

### 2.2. Algorithm

2.2.1. Logic for the algorithm

The algorithm contains two parts. First, it detects an opening event using the criterion of equation (2). To be taken into account, the temperature drop must be greater than 0.1 K (the sensor resolution).

Then, for each opening found, the algorithm infers the closing of the window according to the condition: indoor temperature has risen by 0.1 K (again, the sensor resolution) either in the last 30 minutes or compared to the lowest temperature reached during the opening.

2.2.2. Algorithm

Here is the algorithm used for the detection, a description is proposed in 2.2.1.

```
FOR EACH i IN temp_in
  derivative_in[i] = temp_in[i] − temp_in[i−1]
  delta_temp = temp_out[i] − temp_in[i]
  IF derivative_in[i] < min_drop
  AND abs(derivative_in[i]) > abs(delta_temp) / tau
    open_estimated[i] = True
FOR EACH i IN open_estimated
  IF open_estimated[i] == True
  AND open_estimated[i−1] == False
    j = i + 1
    temp_min = temp_in[i]
    delta_temp = derivative_in[j]
  WHILE delta_temp < min_rise
    IF temp_in[j] >= temp_min + min_rise
      BREAK
    ELSE IF temp_in[j] < temp_min
      temp_min = temp_in[j]
      open_estimated[j] = True
      j = j + 1
      delta_temp = derivative_in[j]
```

Algorithm 1: Window opening detection

2.2.3. Variables

All variables are floats (or 1D arrays thereof), except *open_estimated* which is a 1D array of Booleans. The input takes the form of two 1D arrays:

- *temp_in*: indoor temperature.
- *temp_out*: outdoor temperature.

These and other 1D arrays hold one value per timestep (every 30 minutes).

To ensure that the data used are accurate and do not include any errors (e.g. outliers or gaps in the data) arising either from the sensor itself or from a problem during data collection, both temperature time series are run through multiple layers of data analysis detailed in annex.

Two local variables are 1D arrays:

- *derivative_in*: first derivative of *temp_in* over 30 minutes.
- *open_estimated*: is the window open? (Boolean).

There is also a float local variable:

- *temp_min*: lowest temperature reached during a given opening, initialized to the first temperature of the opening.

The algorithm also uses three float constants:

- *tau*: characteristic time (see above).
- *min_rise*: minimum temperature increase to consider a closing of the window; set to 0.1 K.
- *min_drop*: minimum drop of temperature to consider an opening; set to 0.1 K.

## 3. CASE STUDY

This algorithm was tested on a 4-room apartment occupied by 2 people and located on the fourth floor of a building near Bordeaux, France (Figure 1) during the summers of 2021 and 2022. The apartment comprises a living room, a kitchen, a study, and a bedroom, as shown in Figure 2. It does not have air conditioning.

Figure 1: Photograph of the apartment, highlighted in red, from the street.

The living room and kitchen face south; bedroom and study, west. The bedroom and the study have a window each; the living room and the kitchen each have a French window, which can be opened to give access to the balcony. The windows are equipped with opening sensors (green dots in Figure 2): they provide a list of the times when their state changes.

The apartment is also equipped with temperature sensors (red dots). They were positioned carefully following technical recommendations: 1.5 m above the floor and away from direct radiation. In this instance, they were installed on furniture or doors, lest the tenants drill holes in the walls.

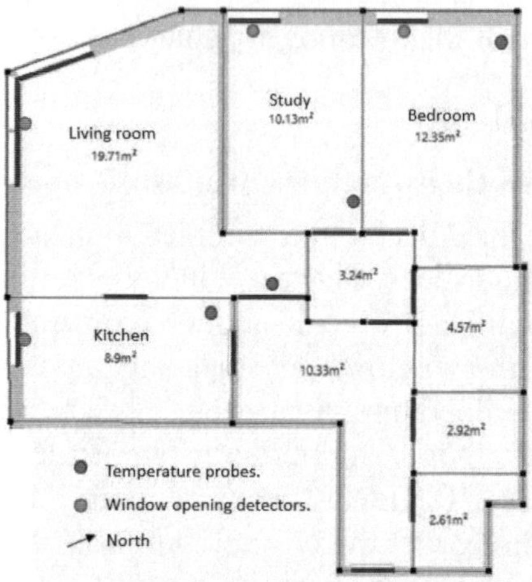


Figure 2: Floorplan of the apartment

These measure indoor temperature every 30 minutes. Since the measurements may not be in phase, the temperature is resampled. For example, the temperature given as 10:30 represents the measure that happened between 10:01 and 10:30. Although the sensors allow a higher frequency, (i) the focus of the study is specifically on night ventilation, so the risk of missing short openings is not a costly one, and (ii) the endgame being to apply the algorithm on a larger scale, it is important to reduce the frequency, and thus the cost, of battery replacement (including manpower and the trouble of entering peoples' homes) through a higher timestep.

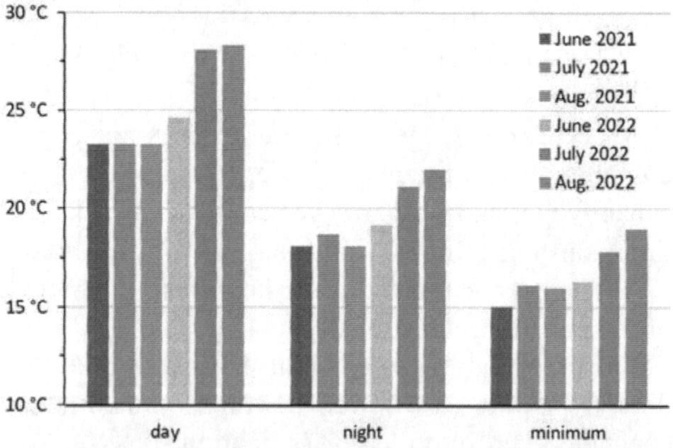


Figure 3: Outdoor temperature, by month, in the summers of 2021 and 2022. Day: 10 a.m. to 8 p.m.

Table 1: Window openings room by room, and month by month in the summers of 2021 and 2022. For each room, left column: total number of openings, centre: total duration [hours], right: median duration per opening [hours]. The last row is the tally over the six months.

| room → | living room | | | kitchen | | | bedroom | | | study | | |
|---|---|---|---|---|---|---|---|---|---|---|---|---|
| ↓ month | nb. | hours | med. | nb. | hours | med. | nb. | hours | med. | nb. | hours | med. |
| June 2021 | 44 | 125 | 0.6 | 24 | 87 | 1.0 | 35 | 38 | 0.8 | 28 | 48 | 0.8 |
| July 2021 | 32 | 98 | 1.3 | 12 | 64 | 9.8 | 13 | 18 | 1.2 | 17 | 38 | 0.6 |
| Aug. 2021 | 6 | 18 | 3.8 | 4 | 17 | 8.5 | 5 | 8 | 0.3 | 5 | 8 | 0.6 |
| June 2022 | 40 | 104 | 1.2 | 19 | 111 | 3.8 | 34 | 45 | 1.0 | 20 | 29 | 1.2 |
| July 2022 | 28 | 199 | 5.3 | 23 | 188 | 6.7 | 25 | 47 | 1.6 | 18 | 36 | 1.1 |
| Aug. 2022 | 30 | 176 | 4.6 | 27 | 149 | 5.3 | 32 | 29 | 0.6 | 27 | 57 | 0.8 |
| 6 months | 180 | 720 | 1.5 | 109 | 616 | 5.1 | 144 | 185 | 0.8 | 115 | 216 | 1.0 |

For the case study, no outdoor sensors were used. (They should face north to avoid direct sunlight, which is easier to achieve at the scale of a building than a single apartment, especially one facing south and west.) The outdoor temperature is thus retrieved from a weather station with a frequency of one hour. This is interpolated linearly down to 30 minutes to be in phase with indoor temperatures. The station being outside the city, by the airport, it is likely to have a lower average temperature and less inertia, thus underestimating temperature (especially in the evening). In future, both indoor and outdoor temperature sensors should be available, and thus the local temperature.

Figure 3 shows, month by month in the summers of 2021 and 2022, the average day and night outdoor temperatures. It also shows the lowest temperature in the morning (specifically the median of these 30 or 31 values for the month). These latter two numbers hint respectively at the possibility to open the windows overnight and at the efficiency of opening them in the morning. Clearly, on all three criteria, July and August of 2022 are hotter than the other four months. Table **1** quantifies window openings, room by room and month by month. It shows that there are far more openings in July and August of 2022 (by number and total duration), which are also the hottest months of the study (Figure 3). August 2021 will not be used hereafter because the residents, being away on holidays, did not open windows.

Living room and especially kitchen tend to have their windows open all night long, whereas bedroom and study have mostly hour-long openings. Residents explain this difference (especially for the bedroom) by the fact that the bedroom and study overlook a noisy street.

When a window is open, it takes on average one to two hours for the temperature to decrease by 1 K. The bedroom and study cool down a little faster because (i) they are smaller and (ii) their openings are shorter, and an opening twice as long will not reduce the temperature twice as much.

## 4. RESULTS

The algorithm checks, at each time step (every 30 minutes), if the window in the room is open ('positive') or closed ('negative'). Comparing to actual state gives rise to four possible outcomes. For example, if the algorithm deems the window closed, and the window is closed, then the classification is a true positive, TP. A false positive, FP, sees open a window which is in fact closed. A false negative, FN, conversely calls shut an open window.

Figures 4 to 7 show night openings over the same week in August 2022 for each of the four rooms. The openings predicted by the algorithm are compared to those identified by the sensors using coloured strips: green for true positive, yellow for false positive and red for false negative. The white background is the default: the window is closed and the algorithm predicts so (true negative). As stated before, the algorithm tries to detect an opening for every time step.

All times are given in local time (GMT + 2 hours). Since the present study focusses on night ventilation, openings during the day (10 a.m. to 8 p.m.) are ignored; these would not be about cooling but for instance simply to go out onto the balcony.

### 4.1. Living room

Figure 4 shows results for the living room. Five night-long openings are correctly detected (green strips). There is often a false negative (in red) in the evening or a false positive (orange) early in the morning. Evening false negatives indicate that the algorithm tends to lag actual window openings. This is sometimes due to the fact that openings do not trigger an immediate drop of temperature in the room and thus cannot be detected right away by the algorithm (for instance, on the evenings of the 7th, 8th, 9th and 10th).

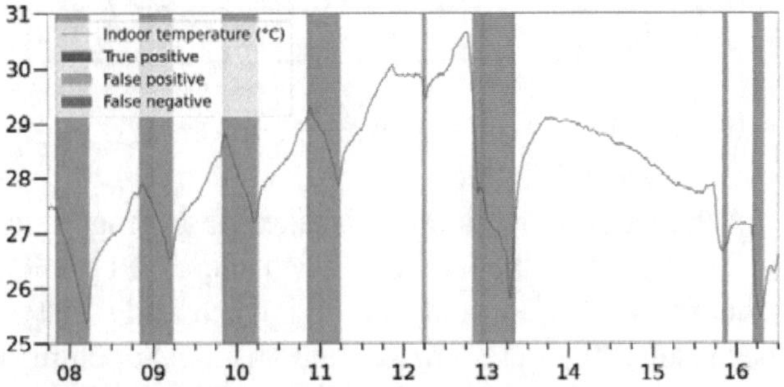


Figure 4: Indoor temperature (line) and predictions (colour strips) for the living room for one week in August 2022.

During the last night in the figure, there is a double opening: the window is open in the evening of the 15th and in the morning of the 16th, but closed during the night itself. The algorithm detects this pattern correctly.

In the morning of the 12th a false positive follows a false negative. It thus seems that the algorithm misses the opening completely (no true positive). But it is in fact a timing error rather than an outright miss: there is a short opening (less than 30 minutes) of the window which is detected a little late and then the opening lingers in the prediction after the window has been actually closed: false positive follows false negative, but the opening has nonetheless been spotted.

### 4.2. Kitchen

Figure 5 indicates that, as in the living room, the algorithm tends to predict openings later than they actually happen in the kitchen when these openings start with a rise of temperature in the room.

The algorithm detects two unlabelled openings in the kitchen, on the 10th and 13th. These drops in temperature are quite visible, but arise from openings in the living room (Figure 4), not the kitchen.

In the morning of the 12th an opening is missed by the algorithm. This opening lasting less than 30 minutes (the period between temperature measurements) makes it hard for the algorithm to spot.

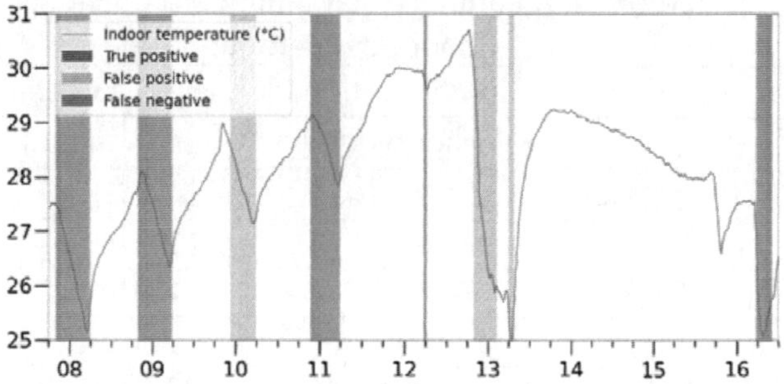


Figure 5: Indoor temperature (line) and predictions (colour strips) for the kitchen for one week in August 2022.

There appears to be a temperature drop in the evening of the 15th. But since it took place unusually early (between 5:30 and 7:30 p.m) it was not deemed *night* opening.

### 4.3. Bedroom and study

Unlike the living room and the kitchen, the bedroom and the study rarely have night-long openings. Figure 6 highlights openings in the bedroom missed by the algorithm on the first five mornings.

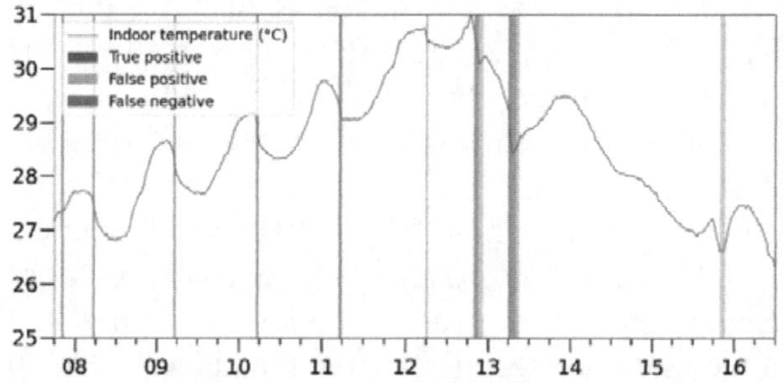


Figure 6: Indoor temperature (line) and predictions (colour strips) for the bedroom for one week in August 2022.

This comes from the details of the criteria used by the algorithm to call an opening, equation (2). On the 10th, for instance, the largest temperature drop occurs between 5:00 and 5:30 a.m.: −0.34 K in half an hour. Calling this an opening would have required a decrease by −0.35 K: the false positive is due to missing the threshold by a mere 0.01 K.

One must bear in mind that openings lasting far less than 30 minutes (the period of the measurements) are bound to result in seemingly small effects on the temperature. A temperature drop of 0.34 K in 10 minutes (2 K/hr) is thus treated as a drop of less than 0.7 K/hr. It makes it difficult to measure their impact on the temperature of the apartment.

In the study, Figure 7, the openings are generally short. However, they are deep enough for the algorithm to identify them. The problem here is the false positive which follows in the morning. The condition for the algorithm to consider a closing of the window is not sensitive enough.

The algorithm misses a big opening on the 16th. This is because after an initial drop the temperature bounces back, which the algorithm interprets as a closing. The temperature does start dropping again later, but not enough for the algorithm to consider an opening.

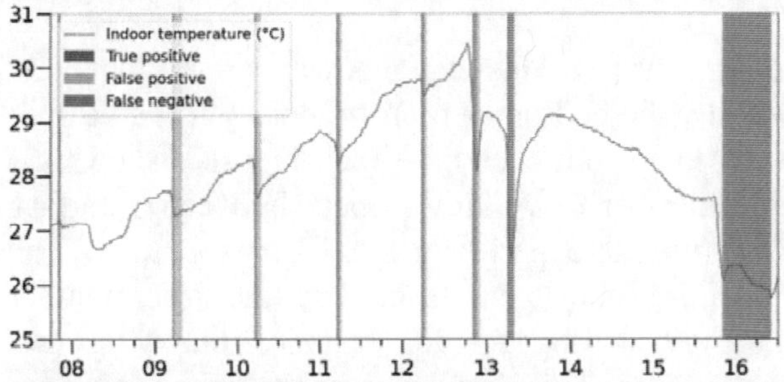


Figure 7: Indoor temperature (line) and predictions (colour strips) for the study for one week in August 2022.

Table **1**) showed that the windows of the living room and kitchen often remained open all night long, unlike in the bedroom and the study (even though the number of times the windows were open is similar).

Table 2 measures the capacity of the algorithm, for each of the four rooms, to detect an opening at a given time step thanks to two metrics, precision and recall. In the definitions, 'TP' is the number of true positives, 'FP' that of false positives and 'FN' false negatives.

*Precision*, $\frac{TP}{TP+FP}$, is the probability that the algorithm be right when it makes a positive prediction (predicts that a window is open). A high precision corresponds to few false positives: predicted openings are likely to be genuine.

Conversely, *recall* normalizes based on windows which are actually open rather than on windows predicted open: $\frac{TP}{TP+FN}$. A high recall means few false negatives: we miss few openings.

The living room and kitchen have better results in July and August 2022 with an average precision of 89% and recall of 81% than in June (respectively 66% and 64%) and 2021 (55% and 63%).

### 4.4. Overall results

Table 2: Results for the four rooms, by month, in the summers of 2021 and 2022. For each room, the columns are: precision (%), recall (%). The last row is the average over the five months.

| room → | living room | | kitchen | | bedroom | | study | |
|---|---|---|---|---|---|---|---|---|
| ↓ month | Pr. | Rec. | Pr. | Rec. | Pr. | Rec. | Pr. | Rec. |
| June '21 | 56 | 66 | 64 | 70 | 44 | 35 | 34 | 46 |
| July '21 | 51 | 57 | 49 | 58 | 22 | 31 | 48 | 47 |
| June '22 | 61 | 74 | 72 | 54 | 37 | 26 | 56 | 56 |
| July '22 | 97 | 79 | 87 | 79 | 57 | 41 | 65 | 57 |
| Aug. '22 | 86 | 83 | 85 | 84 | 29 | 34 | 49 | 57 |
| average | 70 | 72 | 71 | 69 | 38 | 33 | 50 | 53 |

Figures 4 to 7 (and

The overall performance of the other two rooms is poor. This is probably due to the openings being short (possibly shorter than the period of the temperature measurement) and thus hard to identify.

Precision is more sensitive to temperature than recall. The former doubles between July 2021 and July 2022 while the latter increases by only a third. Figure 8 shows that, on a hot month, precision is better than recall (fewer false positives than false negatives) — the converse is true for the cooler month.

Figure 8 : Precision minus recall for the four rooms in Julies of 2021 and 2022.

Table 3: Relative error of the predictions. Left column for each room: the number of times the windows are predicted open divided by the number of times the windows are actually open, minus 1. Right column: same based on the total duration of the openings, rather than on their number.

| room → | living room | | kitchen | | bedroom | | study | | average | |
|---|---|---|---|---|---|---|---|---|---|---|
| ↓ month | number | duration | number | duration | number | duration | number | duration | number | duration |
| June 2021 | − 22% | + 19% | + 12% | + 9% | − 60% | − 21% | − 24% | + 36% | − 23% | + 13% |
| July 2021 | − 5% | + 11% | + 40% | + 18 % | − 34% | + 37% | − 8% | − 3% | − 2% | + 13% |
| June 2022 | − 33% | + 22% | 0% | − 26% | − 71% | − 28% | − 40% | 0% | − 36% | − 7% |
| July 2022 | − 20% | − 18% | + 9% | − 8% | − 56% | − 28% | − 34% | − 12% | − 25% | − 15% |
| Aug. 2022 | 0% | − 3% | + 8% | − 1% | − 67% | + 14% | − 18% | + 16% | + 8% | + 1% |

## 5. DISCUSSION

Table 3 shows the capacity of the algorithm to estimate the number of times or of hours the windows have been open for each month, in each room. For the summers of 2021 and 2022 the algorithm could estimate the duration of night ventilation with errors better than ±15% at the scale of the entire apartment. The number of openings is less reliable, especially the short openings typical of the bedroom and study.

### 5.1. Criteria for success

Success depends on the goal sought — especially its temporal and spatial scales. If it is crucial to know exactly in what room the window is open then the contagion between rooms is a genuine problem. On the other hand, if the question is just whether some ventilation is taking place, getting the window wrong is unimportant so long as the algorithm can tell that some window is open (if not which).

Likewise, if the aim is knowing when windows are open (for instance in real time), a delay in detection is troublesome. But if the purpose is more statistical —how often (and/or how long) are windows open—, a pure offset (delay of the same length to detect when the window is opened and when it is closed again) has no impact.

### 5.2. Wrong room

Figure 5 shows that two night-long openings are detected in the kitchen, when the window is in fact closed. This is a form of contagion: when one window is open (here, in the living room) the temperature also drops elsewhere in the apartment. This leads the algorithm to believe that windows in other rooms are also open, hence the false positives (orange strips). This explains why some rooms (especially the bedroom) perform poorly in Table 3.

To factor out such an effect, Figure 9 shows the total number of windows open (between 0 and 4), over the same period as in Figures 4 to 7. The algorithm (purple curve) may get the exact number (in blue) wrong — for instance believing that windows are open in all four rooms when some are in fact closed. Yet, it is far less likely to confuse the case of all windows closed with that of (at least) some windows open (sum ≥ 1).

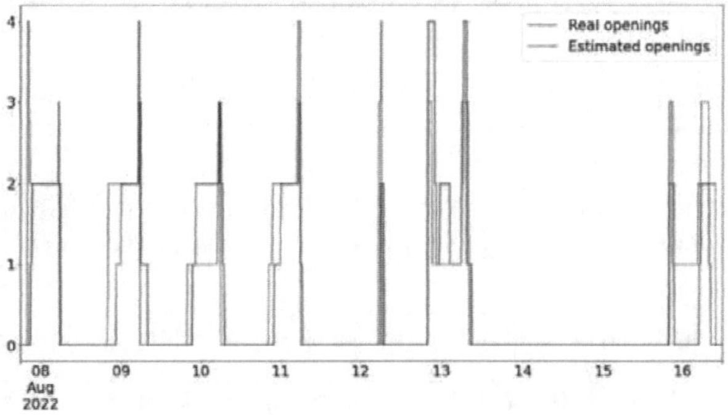


Figure 9: Number of windows open

### 5.3. Wrong time

Figure 10 shows, for August 2022, statistics at the scale of the apartment as a function of the time of day: the average number of windows which are open (top) and the probability that at least one window be open (bottom). It indicates that openings take place mostly between 8 p.m. and 7 a.m. (The solid lines correspond to the periods when the algorithm was applied.)

Overall, the algorithm detects the correct number of openings. But the bottom of Figure 10, especially, shows a clear delay in the prediction (purple curve). This offset explains the frequent succession of false negatives and false positives in Figures 4–7.

In some cases, like in Figure 4, the delay in detecting the opening comes from the fact that the temperature initially rises after the window gets opened. This kind of opening is not considered a plausible one for ventilation and thus cannot be detected by the algorithm. However, there is no symmetric reason for the delay in detecting the closing.

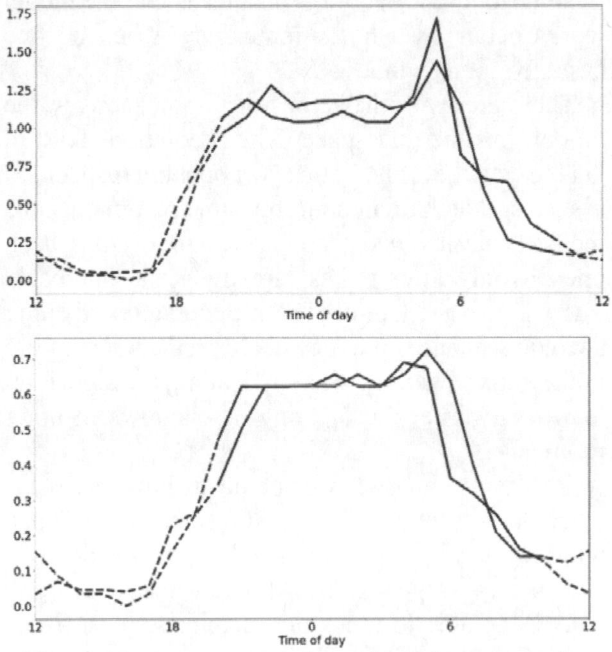


Figure 10: Average number of windows open in the apartment (top) and probability of at least one window open (bottom) by time of the day for August 2022. Blue: real, purple: prediction.

One possibility for fixing this problem could be to have an approximation of the expected temperature evolution while the window is open — the same way equation (2) provides an approximation of the temperature evolution when the window is closed. From this, it would be possible to define more precisely the conditions for the closing of the window. That said, such an approximation would require more knowledge on the environment to be realistic. For example, wind would have a major impact on temperature evolution when the window is open.

A very pragmatic way of improving predictions is: cheating. Since the algorithm consistently delays the detection of events by at least 30 minutes, then one can simply offset all predictions by this amount. When the algorithm says that the opening of the window took place at 9:00, one can improve this raw prediction by turning it into a post-processed prediction of 8:30.

## 5.4. Comparing cool and hot months

Figure 11 compares the probability of at least one window being open in July 2021 (top) and July 2022 (bottom). (August cannot be used for this purpose because the inhabitants were on holiday in August 2021.)

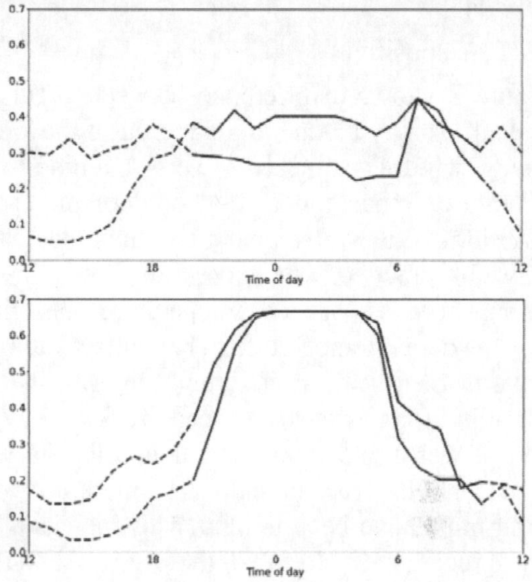


Figure 11: Probability of at least one window open by time of the day. Top: July 2021, bottom: July 2022. Blue: real, purple: prediction.

July 2022 shows a sharp difference between night and day: the windows are opened late in the evening and closed early in the morning. In cool July 2021 the policy is more relaxed than in hot July 2022, with one third fewer openings at night (these are unnecessary) and, conversely, regular openings throughout the day (since it is cool outside, opening a window is not punished by an inflow of hot air).

### 5.4.1. Useful night ventilation

Clearly, the model (blue lines) is less accurate for the cool summer of 2021 than for the hot summer of 2022. Since regulating the temperature was less crucial in 2021, fewer openings were directly intended to cool the apartment than in 2022. (In particular, the apartment of the case study having a balcony, another possible purpose of opening the living room French window is to access it, regardless of the temperature.)

The overarching philosophy of the algorithm makes it capable of detecting only *useful* night ventilation, i.e. a night window opening associated with a significant drop of temperature in the accommodation. In July 2021, the algorithm (blue curve) enforces a pattern that does not actually exist.

The model still has possible improvements which will be the focus of future work. The natural first step was to treat the rooms separately, but correlations between rooms (convective contagion) could come next. However, it depends very much on the configuration of the apartment, so this may be hard to automate.

5.4.2. False positives

Figure 8 shows a difference between precision and recall. It may be due to the inertia of the walls. Opening windows quickly lowers the indoor air temperature. When indoor and outdoor air are at equilibrium, the wall temperature then decreases slowly. In practice, one closes windows in the morning because outside temperature has risen above inside air temperature. The walls which are still warm then heat up the indoor air. But in July 2021, this effect must have been weak: the walls were less warm (closer to thermal equilibrium with the air) and the rise in indoor temperature after closing must have been limited. This increases the delay to recognize a closing of the window, and thus the risk of false positive. We plan on adding the effect of the inertia of the walls to future versions of the model.

## 6. CONCLUSION

Night ventilation can decrease indoor temperature in summer — a need which will only grow in importance as climate change unfolds. This article proposed an algorithm based on expert rules and the thermal behaviour of the building to evaluate night ventilation in summer. It has the advantage of requiring fewer labelled data than the machine or deep learning algorithms which are more common in the literature. It relies on indoor and outdoor temperatures, which are growing more readily available as the number of connected temperature sensors itself grows: no need to install dedicated equipment. The method also uses characteristics of the specific dwelling, such as its insulation and inertia.

In our case study of an apartment equipped with connected window and temperature sensors, the algorithm estimated the number of hours of night ventilation to within ±15% at the scale of the entire apartment for the months of the summers 2021 and 2022.

Overall, the model works better with night-long openings than for short ones (especially shorter than the time increment of half an hour). But these are the ones which really contribute to cooling in any case.

Openings and closings are identified based, respectively, on a drop and increase of indoor temperature between two consecutive time steps — it explicitly assumes that either event will have an impact on temperature and thus the thermal comfort. We necessarily miss windows opened for a few seconds to let the cat out. This means that the model works better on a hot summer day, when no one casually opens windows.

There are two other types of imprecisions in the model: in time and space. The predictions tend to lag the actual events. For a short opening (especially if shorter than half an hour, our time increment), the method may even detect that a window has been opened only after it has already been shut back. There is also a risk of convective contagion: opening a window in one room may decrease the temperature in the entire dwelling, thereby leading the algorithm to wrongly infer the opening of windows in other rooms.

On the bright side, we intend to now use these results to tell, in a building, who seems not to open windows at night. Instead of telling all residents in a blanket message that they should ventilate at night, we will be able to focus on inhabitants most likely to need such advice. And, since this is at the scale of the dwelling rather than the room and averaged over a summer rather than hour-by-hour, our method is certainly reliable enough for our purpose.

A survey is also currently being designed to find patterns in people's behaviour. For instance, is it the same high up in the building and on ground or low floors (where noise and the risk of burglary are greater)? There may also be a policy of opening in the west in the morning and on the east side in the evening. Such information may be included in the model in a Bayesian fashion: what is the probability of the window facing east being opened on the fourth floor in the morning given the temperature?

## ACKNOWLEDGEMENT

This work was performed within the frame of the research project CoLoC (Comfort of Connected Dwellings), granted by the "France Relance" plan for the preservation of R&D employment.

## REFERENCES


[1] Carlucci, Salvatore, *et al.* 2020. "Modeling Occupant Behavior in Buildings". *Building and Environment* 174 (May): 106768. https://doi.org/10.1016/j.buildenv.2020.106768.

[2] Schweiker, Marcel, Frédéric Haldi, Masanori Shukuya, and Darren Robinson. 2012. "Verification of stochastic models of window opening behaviour for residential buildings". *Journal of Building Performance Simulation* 5 (1): 55-74. https://doi.org/10.1080/19401493.2011.567422.

[3] Andersen, Rune, Valentina Fabi, Jorn Toftum, Stefano P. Corgnati, et Bjarne W. Olesen. 2013. "Window Opening Behaviour Modelled from Measurements in Danish Dwellings". *Building and Environment* 69 (November): 101-13. https://doi.org/10.1016/j.buildenv.2013.07.005.

[4] Haldi, Frédéric, and Darren Robinson. s. d. 2012. "A Comparison of Alternative Approaches for the Modelling of Window Opening and Closing Behaviour". https://www.researchgate.net/publication/242108226.

[5] Shi, Shanshan, Hongjian Li, Xue Ding, and Xin Gao. 2020. "Effects of Household Features on Residential Window Opening Behaviors: A Multilevel Logistic Regression Study". *Building and Environment* 170 (March): 106610. https://doi.org/10.1016/j.buildenv.2019.106610.

[6] Mo, Hao, Hejiang Sun, Junjie Liu, and Shen Wei. 2019. "Developing Window Behavior Models for Residential Buildings Using XGBoost Algorithm". *Energy and Buildings* 205 (December): 109564. https://doi.org/10.1016/j.enbuild.2019.109564.

[7] Nan Li, Juncheng Li, Ruijuan Fan, and Hongyuan Jia. 2015. "Probability of Occupant Operation of Windows during Transition Seasons in Office Buildings". *Renewable Energy*, Sustainable Development in Building and Environment (SuDBE) 2013, 73 (January): 84-91. https://doi.org/10.1016/j.renene.2014.05.065. PE

[8] Yao Mingyao, and Bin Zhao. 2017. "Window Opening Behavior of Occupants in Residential Buildings in Beijing". *Building and Environment* 124 (november): 441-49. https://doi.org/10.1016/j.buildenv.2017.08.035.

[9] Rautlin de la Roy, Enguerrand de, Thomas Recht, Akka Zemmari, Pierre Bourreau, and Laurent Mora. 2023. "Deep Learning Models for Building Window-Openings Detection in Heating Season". *Building and Environment* 231 (March): 110019. https://doi.org/10.1016/j.buildenv.2023.110019.

[10] Luong, David, Russell Richman, and Marianne Touchie. 2022. "Towards Window State Detection Using Image Processing in Residential and Office Building Facades". *Building and Environment* 207 (January): 108486. https://doi.org/10.1016/j.buildenv.2021.108486.

[11] Sun, Cheng, Xumiao Guo, Tianyu Zhao, and Yunsong Han. 2022. "Real-Time Detection Method of Window Opening Behavior Using Deep Learning-Based Image Recognition in Severe Cold Regions". *Energy and Buildings* 268 (August): 112196. https://doi.org/10.1016/j.enbuild.2022.112196.

[12] Pandya, Sharnil, and Hemant Ghayvat. 2021. "Ambient Acoustic Event Assistive Framework for Identification, Detection, and Recognition of Unknown Acoustic Events of a Residence". *Advanced Engineering Informatics* 47 (January): 101238. https://doi.org/10.1016/j.aei.2020.101238.

[13] J Fergus Nicol. 2001. "characterising occupant behaviour in buildings: toward a stochastic model of occupant use of windows, lights, blinds, heaters and fan". *Seventh international IBPSA conference* (August): http://www.ibpsa.org/proceedings/BS2001/BS01_1073_1078.pdf.

[14] D'Oca, Simona, and Tianzhen Hong. "A Data-Mining Approach to Discover Patterns of Window Opening and Closing Behavior in Offices". Building and Environment 82 (1 December 2014): 726-39. https://doi.org/10.1016/j.buildenv.2014.10.021.

[15] Peuportier Bruno, and Isabelle Blanc Sommerreux. "Simulation Tool with Its Expert Interface for the Thermal Design of Multizone Buildings". *International Journal of Solar Energy* 8, n° 2 (1 january 1990): 109-20. https://doi.org/10.1080/01425919008909714.

# ANNEXES

## Data analysis

1. Outliers

Data points whose distance to the mean of their distribution is considered outliers and thus deleted:

$|T_t - \bar{T}| > 3\sigma$. (4)

with:
- $T_t$: Probe temperature at time step $t$.
- $\bar{T}$: Temporal mean of probe temperatures.
- $\sigma$ : Standard deviation of probe temperatures.

2. Data leaps

As the data are often uploaded, it is possible that some data points are missing or not representative of the environment. For instance, the probe may be poorly located or malfunctioning. This can be visualised easily by plotting the temperature time series.

To correct these "spikes" (Figure a.1), they are first detected using the formula below, then the data point affected is deleted from the time series.

$\min(|T_{t-dt} - T_t|, |T_{t+dt} - T_t|) > \varepsilon_1$ (5)

with:
- $\varepsilon_1$: temperature difference threshold, in K. Here, $\varepsilon_1 = 2$ K.

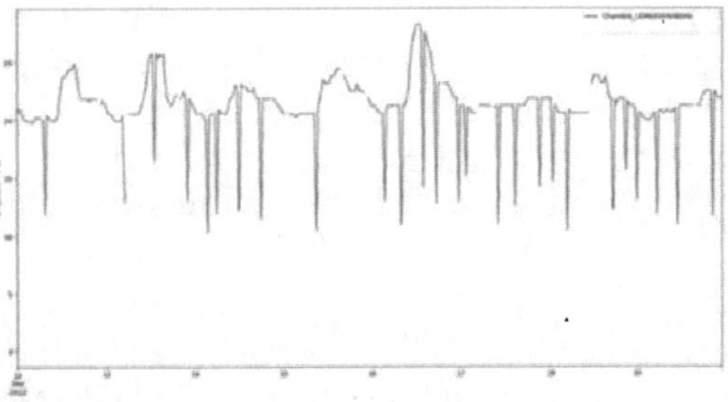

Figure a.1: Temperature time series with data leap over 1 data point

Another kind of spike we can observe in the data spans multiple data points (Figure a.2). In this case, however, it is not possible to identify which part of the signal is physical and which is erroneous. So, if the problem is detected, the probe is considered faulty and therefore entirely removed from the dataset.

$\frac{1}{n}\sum_{t=0}^{t=n}(T_t - T_{t-dt})^2 > \varepsilon_2$ (6)

with:
- $n$: number of elements in the time series.
- $\varepsilon_2$: temperature difference threshold, in K. Here, $\varepsilon_2 = 5\,K$.

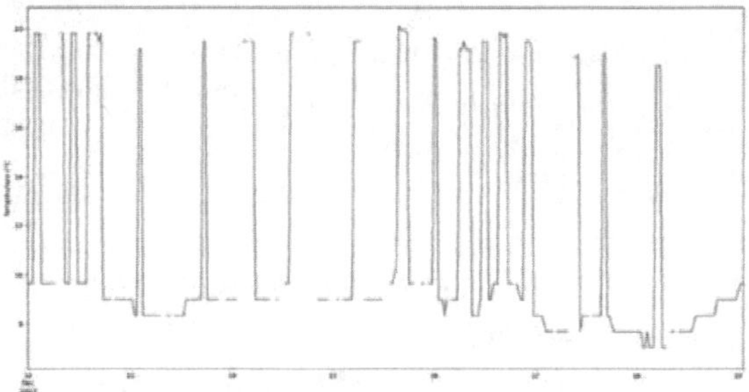

Figure a.2: Temperature time series with data leap over multiple data points

Constant probe

Some probes can stop working over a period without it being notified (figure a.3), leading to a constant signal.

In order to prevent this phenomenon, the formula below checks if the time series is constant over an interval, in which case the interval is deleted.

$\sum_t^{t+n} | T_t - T_{t-dt}| = 0$ (7)

$n$ : length (in number of time steps) of the interval.

In practice, for numerical reasons, a low threshold, rather than zero, will be used.

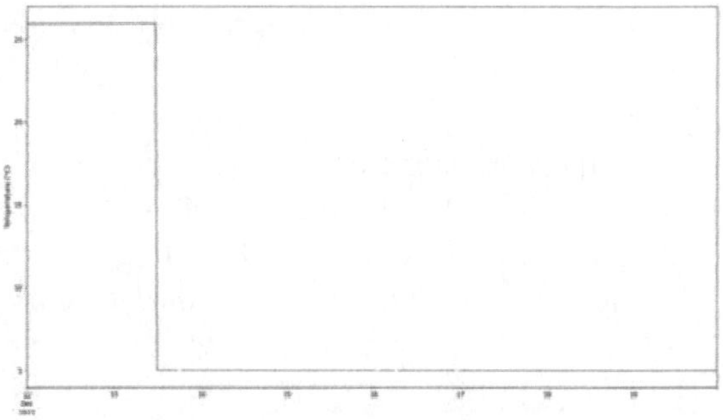

Figure a.3: Temperature time series with a constant probe

# Power Consumption Estimation of Love Wave Sensors using LTspice

Marcelo V. da Silva[1], Ewaldo E. C. Santana[12], Raimundo C. S. Freire[3], Marlo Andrade[345], Ollivier Tamarin[56], Corinne Dejous[5]

[1]*Federal University of Maranhão, UFMA, Av. dos Portugueses, No. 1966, 65080-805, São Luís, Brazil, marcelo.vs@discente.ufma.br*
[2]*State University of Maranhão, UEMA, 65055-310, São Luís, Brazil*
[3]*Federal University of Campina Grande, UFCG, 58429-900, Campina Grande, Brazil*
[4]*Feredal Institute of Pernambuco, IFPE, 50740-540, Recife, Brazil*
[5]*Univ. Bordeaux, CNRS, Bordeaux INP, IMS, UMR 5218, 33400, Talence, France*
[6]*Univ. Guyane, UMR 228 Espace-Dev, Cayenne, F-9730*

**ABSTRACT**: In this paper, the power consumption and efficiency estimation of a Love wave sensor was investigated using an electrical model in LTspice. Simulation results show how the sensor model electrical parameters, such as voltage, current, and frequency, influence the energy consumption of the system. The average estimated efficiency of 0.57% was obtained at the center frequency. The results of this study could be useful to design systems with Love wave sensors with low energy consumption.

**Keywords**: Surface acoustic wave sensor, Love wave devices, efficiency, power consumption, SPICE.

**Received** January 1, 20213; **In final form** January 31, 20213; **Published** June 20213



**Funding:** Research Support Foundation of Maranhão (FAPEMA), Research Support Foundation (FAPESQ), and Support Program for Center of Excellence (PRONEX).

**Corresponding author:** Marcelo V. da Silva, e-mail: marcelo-mvs@hotmail.com; Ewaldo E. C. Santana, e-mail: ewaldoeder@gmail.com; Raimundo C. S. Freire, e-mail: rcsfreire@dee.ufcg.edu.br; Marlo Andrade, e-mail: marlo.santos@ee.ufcg.edu.br; Ollivier Tamarin, e-mail: ollivier.tamarin@univ-guyane.fr; Corinne Dejous, e-mail: corinne.dejous@ims-bordeaux.fr

## 1. INTRODUCTION

In recent years, sensors have become increasingly integrated into the daily lives of individuals and industries, monitoring human health, the environment, or production quality. This growth is attributed to the high performance of the sensors, as well as their capability to be read passively and wirelessly [1]. Among the various types of sensors, surface acoustic wave sensors have been widely used for the detection of biochemical species in a liquid-gaseous medium [2], [3].

When applied to an aqueous environment, the Love Wave (LW) sensors are a type of Surface Acoustic Wave (SAW) sensor that has demonstrated high sensitivity and selectivity when using an appropriate selective coating dedicated to the biomolecule to be detected. These devices operate from the propagation of acoustic waves on the surface of piezoelectric materials. The electroacoustic conversion is performed by the Interdigital Transducer (IDT), which is a metallic structure placed on the piezoelectric substrate. The acoustic wave propagating on the surface can be modified by external disturbances such as temperature, liquids, and gases [4],[5].

These can be used as passive wireless sensors by connecting them to an interrogation unit using an antenna [6],[7]. For passive operation, the sensor has no local power and uses interrogation signal energy to make a measurement. The interrogation signal loses energy with distance, ambient and acoustic losses at the sensor. This affects the viability of the system, compromising wireless reading. The sensor power consumption estimate must be evaluated to be considered in an autonomous remote sensing link. One of the ways to carry out this study is through simulations of the sensor model. Simulations of SAW and LW sensors using different software were performed to validate models [8]-[11]. A particular simulation of SAW sensors for energy consumption investigation was done by Liu et al. [12]. In this study, the results were used for sensor design based on physical parameters (such as the central distance between two IDTs, piezoelectric substrate thickness, and IDT finger space) for optimization in the device manufacturing process. In this work, we investigate the energy consumption efficiency of the sensor based on electrical parameters like voltage, current, power, and frequency.

The objective of this work is to estimate the energy consumption and efficiency of a LW sensor based on the simulation of a SPICE equivalent circuit model. This paper is organized into the following sections: in Section 2 the LW sensors are introduced, the methodology for sensor simulation and estimation of parameters are described and the characteristics of the simulation model are presented. In Section 3 the simulated results are presented and discussed from variations of source signal parameters such as frequency and amplitude. Section 4 presents the final considerations.

## 2. MATERIALS AND METHODS

### 2.1. Love Wave Sensor Principle

The LW sensor detection mechanism is based on the mass effect and the variations of its mechanical and electrical properties. A diagram of a LW sensor is pictured in Figure 1. An input IDT fed by a sinusoidal signal generates an acoustic wave which propagates through the waveguide layer and is converted back to electrical signal by the output IDT. The alteration of acoustic wave propagation parameters like density, viscosity, thickness, and electrical conductivity by an aqueous medium modifies the amplitude and velocity of the LW. The delay line is composed of two IDTs on a quartz substrate, with an additional waveguide layer of $SiO_2$, and has an operating frequency of around 116 MHz [13].

### 2.2. Methodology

The methodology used in this work is described in Figure 2. From the SPICE simulation model, parameters like frequency, voltage, and attenuation on the propagation path were modified to obtain the voltage, current, and phase angle in the sensor. Finally, the input and output power were estimated and the efficiency was calculated using Matlab. The effective power consumption is the power estimated at the input port of the sensor.

The LW sensor model used in this work is described as a sequence of finger pair capacitances $C_s$ and resistances $R_s$ in parallel. These values can be obtained based on the total capacitance and resistance of one of the IDT measured between positive and negative inputs after the fabrication process [11], [15]. From these parameters, an equivalent model based on transmission lines was used to simulate the LW sensor [11]. The model also describes the Time of Flight (TOF) of the wave between the two IDTs and allows the addition of an extra delay and attenuation to represent external perturbations on the sensor. The parameters used in the Python code to generate the LTspice model are described in Table 1.

The LW sensor model setup used for power consumption estimation using LTspice is shown in Figure 3a. The schematic is presented in Figure 3b.

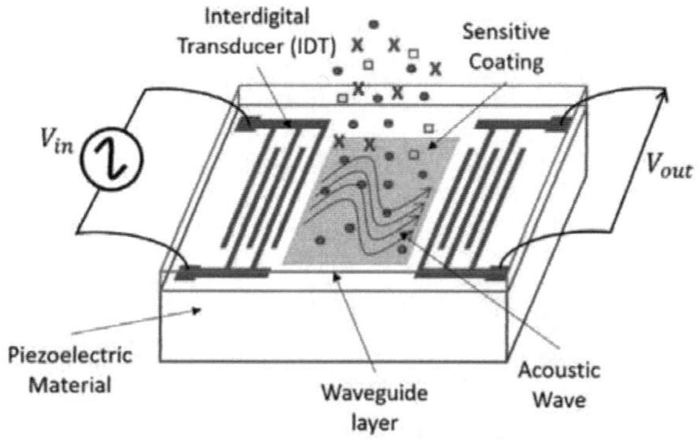


Figure 1. LW sensor with selective coating for biological detection.

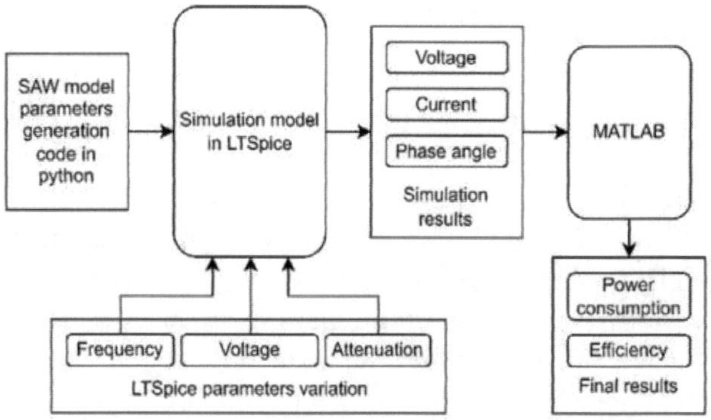


Figure 2. Methodological flowchart applied in the estimation of efficiency by simulation of the LW sensor model: with the description of the sensor model in Python and LTspice, it is possible to obtain the energy consumed.

**Table 1. Main characteristics of the LW sensor.**

| Parameter | Value |
|---|---|
| Center frequency | $f_0 = 116.5$ MHz |
| TOF between IDTs | $t_L = 2\ \mu s$ |
| IDT resistance | $R_T = 10.1\ \Omega$ |
| IDT capacitance | $C_T = 8.51$ pF |
| Number of finger pairs | $N_P = 44$ |
| Electromechanical coupling coefficient | $k^2 = 1.4\ \%$ |

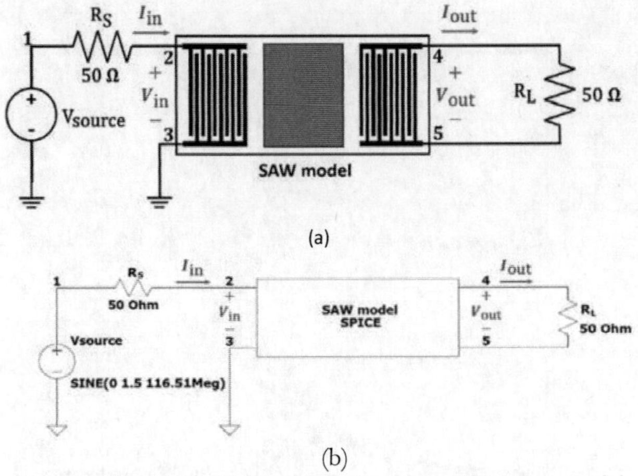


Figure 3. Electrical circuit schematic with a) LW sensor model and b) with LTspice configuration.

A sinusoidal voltage source of 1.5 V at 116.5 MHz feeds the input IDT through a series resistance equal to 50 Ω and the output IDT is connected to a load resistance of 50 Ω. The input ($V_{in}$) and output ($V_{out}$) voltages of the sensor are taken from the input (nodes 2 and 3 in Figure 3) and output (nodes 4 and 5 in Figure 3) IDTs respectively. The time interval of the simulations ranges from 0 to 6 $\mu$s to compensate for the TOF $t_L$ of the wave on the propagation path and consider the steady-state response. Two different analyzes were performed:

1) Frequency sweep between 106.5 MHz and 126.5 MHz with steps of 10 kHz with source voltage amplitude fixed at 1.5 V and without attenuation;
2) Varying the source voltage amplitude from 1 V to 4.5 V with steps of 0.1 V with a fixed frequency of 116.5 MHz and without attenuation;

### 2.3. Initial Characterization

A LW sensor unit was inserted into a test cell. The experimental setup is shown in Figure 4. A Vector Network Analyzer (VNA) was used to measure the scattering parameters. A computer (1) is connected via USB cable (2) to the nanoVNA v3.4 (3). Two 30 cm RG 174 ROHS coaxial cables (4) were connected to the test cell containing the LW sensor (5). A full two-port SOLT (Short-Open-Load-Through) calibration was performed in the range from 100 MHz to 130 MHz, with a resolution of 5.9 kHz. Details about the device and test cell are described in [5], [13], [14]. For the simulation, a Python code was used to evaluate the sensor model parameters based on the characteristics of the real sensor and generate a SPICE netlist describing the sensor equivalent circuit [11]. The magnitudes of the reflection and transmission coefficients measured and simulated of the sensor are shown in Figure 5. Those coefficients represent the power transmitted and reflected by the device when compared with the incident power. This information enables the evaluation of input impedance and insertion loss. It was possible to observe a good correspondence when comparing the simulated results with the measured ones (with maximum amplitude and phase differences of 5 dB and 1 MHz, respectively), as well as with previous works that carried out the measurement and simulation in terms of frequency response with these sensors [7], [11].

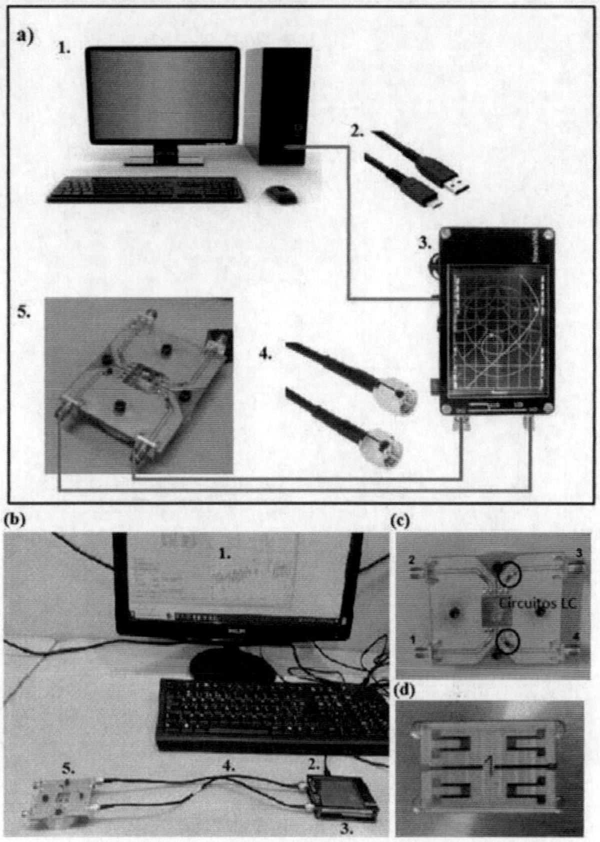


Figure 4. Experimental setup: a) Experiment diagram, b) Setup, c) Test cell containing the LW sensor, and d) LW sensor.

## 3. RESULTS AND DISCUSSION

### 3.1. Frequency Variation Analysis

The input and output voltage and electric current for the frequency variation is shown in Figure 6. The input voltage in Figure 6a remains constant at 1.05 V in all the considered range, except for the central

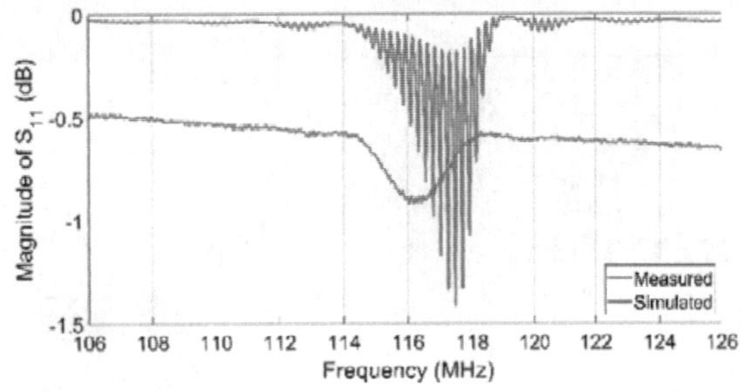


(a)

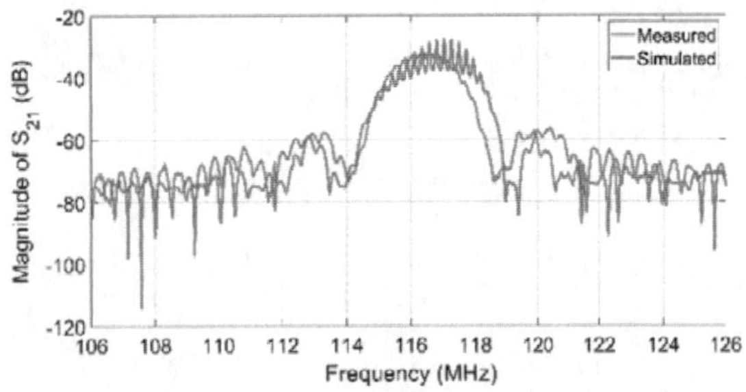


(b)

Figure 5. Frequency response measured and simulated of the sensor: Magnitude of a) reflection coefficient ($\boldsymbol{S_{11}}$) and b) Transmission coefficient ($\boldsymbol{S_{21}}$).

region around the resonance frequency from 114 MHz to 120 MHz where the voltage has a minimum peak of 0.92 V. For the output voltage, the characteristic is reversed with respect to the input voltage and the maximum output voltage is 20 mV. The input and output currents have a constant response outside the range around the resonance frequency of 1.6 mA and close to 0 mA, as shown in Figure 6b. In the region close to the center frequency, the input and output currents exhibit a peak of 3 mA and 0.45 mA, respectively. The input current presents a reduction between 118 MHz and 120 MHz with a minimum value of 0.5 mA. The reduction of the input voltage around the center frequency is expected since the magnitude of the reflection coefficient is smaller for this range, as shown in Figure 5a. Dually, the output voltage and current increase in this range in which the magnitude of the transmission coefficient is greater in the central region, as shown in Figure 5b.

The input and output power estimation and efficiency of the voltage are presented in Figure 7. The peak power consumption is equal to 0 dBm. The output power presents maximum values in the center region, with a peak at around −20 dBm, and is heavily attenuated as the source frequency moves away from the resonance frequency, reaching values

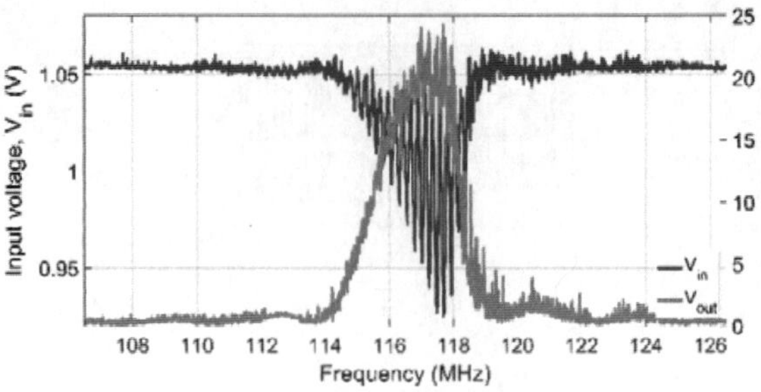


(a)

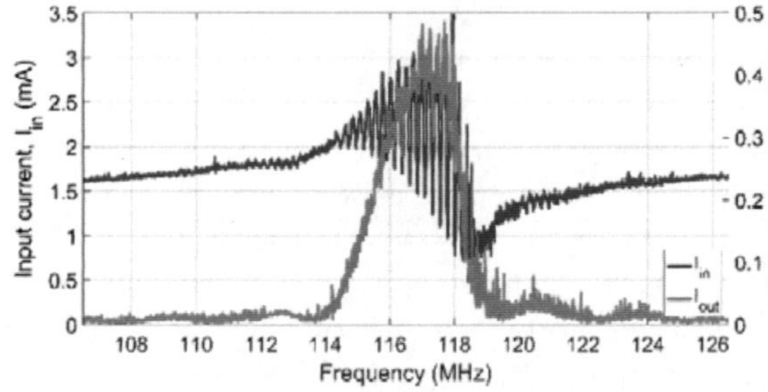


(b)

Figure 6. Simulations for LW sensor with respect to source frequency: a) input/output RMS voltage and b) input/output RMS current.

lower than −60 dBm. The efficiency has a peak value of 2.7 % at 116.68 MHz and an average value of 0.57 % in the range of 115.3 − 118.2 MHz, this value is consistent with the one obtained at the

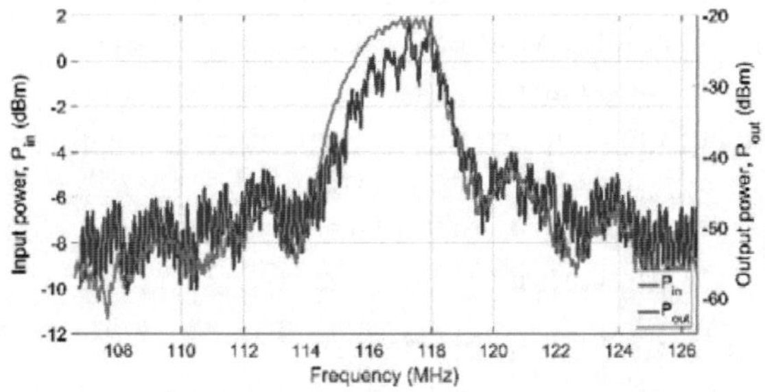


(a)

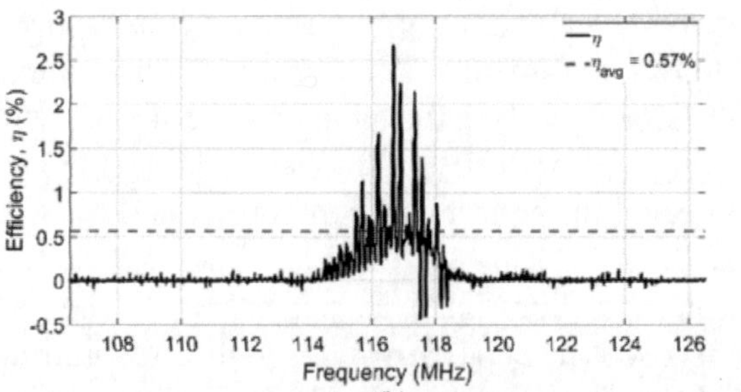


(b)

Figure 7. Estimations for LW sensor with respect to source frequency: a) input/output power consumption and b) efficiency with an average value of $\mathbf{0.57}$ % between $\mathbf{115.3}$ MHz and $\mathbf{118.2}$ MHz.

center frequency of 116.5 MHz. In Figure 7a we observe increasing input power consumption due to the growth of input voltage and current in the sensor operating range. At the center frequency, the increase in the input current is larger than the decrease in voltage in terms of percentage values, resulting in larger power consumption at that interval. As could be expected, the power consumption exhibits an overall shape similar to that of the $S_{21}$ parameter. The greatest efficiency is around the center frequency of the sensor, as the ratio between the output and input power has maximum value in this range. The average efficiency of 0.57 % is due to the small electromechanical coupling factor of the quartz substrate, but this material is the most suitable for LW sensing because it presents less damping when is liquid-loaded, among other reasons [16].

### 3.2. Source Voltage Amplitude Variation Analysis

The results of the simulation for voltage and current at the input/output of the sensor at the resonance frequency are pictured in Figure 8. The results for voltages and currents show that those parameters increase linearly with the source voltage as expected since the model is linear.

The results for power consumption and efficiency are depicted in Figure 9. The input power consumption has a logarithmic behavior starting from −3.3 dBm up to 10 dBm. The same occurs to the output power consumption, ranging from −25 dBm to −12.7 dBm as shown in Figure 9a. From Figure 9b, we can see that the efficiency tends to be constant with an average value of 0.57 %. The input and output power consumption are expected to be linear with the source voltage so are the voltages and currents. As the input and output power consumption grow at the same rate, the efficiency is constant. The average value shows consistency with the results obtained in the previous subsection 3.1.

## 4. CONCLUSIONS

In this work, an equivalent model for the LW sensor was simulated and the input and output power consumption and efficiency were estimated. The input and output power consumption are affected by source frequency and voltage amplitude. The efficiency depends on the source signal frequency but not on the voltage amplitude due to the mechanical filter behavior of the SAW delay line with a resonance frequency. The maximum output power consumption of −12.7 dBm associated with an input voltage of 4.5 V and a 50 Ω test setup is consistent with the preceding results obtained by Liu and Cui. [12] (around −13 dBm). The average

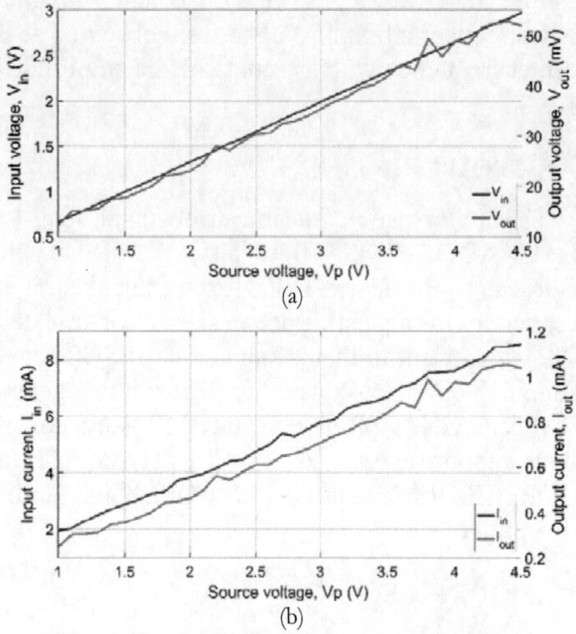


Figure 8. Simulations for LW sensor at the resonance frequency with respect to source voltage amplitude: a) input/output RMS voltage and b) input/output RMS current.

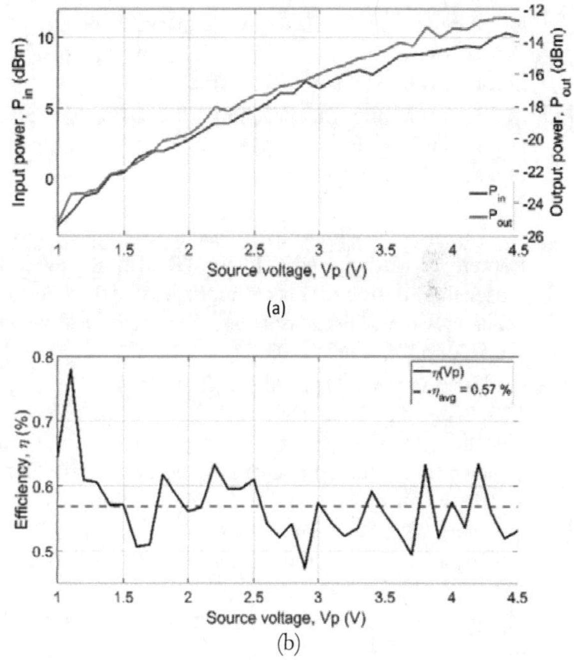


Figure 9. Estimations for LW sensor at the resonance frequency with respect to source voltage amplitude: a) input/output power consumption and b) efficiency with average an value of **0.57** %.

estimated efficiency of 0.57 % and maximum power consumption of 0 dBm were observed at the center frequency with an input voltage amplitude of 1.5 V.

## ACKNOWLEDGMENT

The authors would like to warmly thank Jean-Luc LACHAUD (IMS Bordeaux, CNRS, Univ. Bordeaux, Bordeaux INP) for technical support, especially in the test device design and fabrication. They also want to thank Raphael C. JESUS for the support on the code, the Brazilian agencies FAPESQ/CNPq/PRONEX and IMS-Bordeaux for their support as well as FAPEMA, UEMA, IFPE, COPELE/UFCG, and CAPES/COPEX for funding this project.

## REFERENCES

[1] H. Hallil, C. Dejous, S. Hage-Ali, O. Elmazria, J. Rossignol, D. Stuerga, A. Talbi, A. Mazzamurro, P.-Y. Joubert, and E. Lefeuvre, "Passive resonant sensors: trends and future prospects," IEEE Sensors Journal, vol. 21, no. 11, pp. 12 618–12 632, 2021.

[2] D. Mandal and S. Banerjee, "Surface acoustic wave (SAW) sensors: Physics, materials, and applications," Sensors, vol. 22, no. 3, p. 820, 2022.

[3] M. Agostini and M. Cecchini, "Ultra-high-frequency (UHF) surface acoustic-wave (SAW) microfluidics and biosensors," Nanotechnology, vol. 32, no. 31, p. 312001, 2021.

[4] O. Tamarin, S. Comeau, C. Dejous, D. Moynet, D. Rebiere, J. Bezian, and J. Pistre, "Real time device for biosensing: design of a bacteriophage model using Love acoustic waves," Biosensors and Bioelectronics, vol. 18, no. 5-6, pp. 755–763, 2003.

[5] C. Zimmermann, D. Rebiere, C. Dejous, J. Pistre, E. Chastaing, and R. Planade, "A Love-wave gas sensor coated with functionalized polysiloxane for sensing organophosphorus compounds," Sensors and Actuators B: Chemical, vol. 76, no. 1-3, pp. 86–94, 2001.

[6] T. Song, S. Y. Song, H. C. Yoon, and K. Lee, "Development of a wireless love wave biosensor platform for multi-functional detection," Japanese Journal of Applied Physics, vol. 50, no. 6S, p. 06GL09, 2011.

[7] M. A. Santos, R. C. S. Freire, H. Hallil, O. Tamarin, and C. Dejous, "Remote measurement of a VHF Love wave sensor for liquid detection," in 2022 Wireless Power Week (WPW). IEEE, 2022, pp. 536–540.

[8] A. Bhattacharyya, S. Tuli, and S. Majurndar, "SPICE simulation of surface acoustic wave interdigital transducers," IEEE Transactions on Ultrasonics, Ferroelectrics, and Frequency Control, vol. 42, no. 4, pp. 784–786, 1995.

[9] B. Achour, G. Attia, C. Zerrouki, N. Fourati, K. Raoof, and N. Yaakoubi, "Simulation/experiment confrontation, an efficient approach for sensitive SAW sensors design," Sensors, vol. 20, no. 17, 2020. [Online]. Available: https://www.mdpi.com/1424-8220/20/17/4994

[10] M. Rube, O. Tamarin, S. Hemour, M. Sebeloue, A. Choudhari, I. Sadli, L. Linguet, D. Rebiere, and C. Dejous, "A behavior-descriptive model of Love wave sensor in liquid medium for circuit-design and analysis with QucsStudio," in 2021 IEEE Sensors. IEEE, 2021, pp. 1–4.

[11] R. C. Jesus, E. A. Carvalho, O. Tamarin, R. C. Freire, and C. Dejous, "Equivalent circuit models for SAW delay line sensors," IEEE Sensors Journal, vol. 22, no. 12, pp. 11 810–11 818, 2022.

[12] Y. Liu and T. Cui, "Power consumption analysis of surface acoustic wave sensor systems using ANSYS and PSPICE," Microsyst. Technol., vol. 13, no. 1, p. 97–101, jan 2007.

[13] O. Tamarin, M. Rube, J. L. Lachaud, V. Raimbault, D. Rebière, and C. Dejous, "Mobile acoustic wave platform deployment in the Amazon river: Impact of the water sample on the Love wave sensor response," Sensors, vol. 20, no. 1, p. 72, 2020.

[14] M. Rube, O. Tamarin, M. Sebeloue, I. Sadli, H. Hallil, L. Linguet, D. Rebiere, and C. Dejous, "Unconventional protocol for SAW sensor: multi-physic response enrichment in liquid medium," IEEE Sensors Journal, 2021.

[15] W. Smith, H. Gerard, J. Collins, T. Reeder, and H. Shaw, "Analysis of interdigital surface wave transducers by use of an equivalent circuit model," IEEE Transactions on Microwave Theory and Techniques, vol. 17, no. 11, pp. 856–864, 1969.

[16] M.-I. Rocha-Gaso, Y. Jimenez, L.A. Francis, A. Arnau. "Love wave biosensors: A review," State of the Art in Biosensors - General Aspects. InTech, Mar. 13, 2013. doi: 10.5772/53077.

# Risk analysis assessment in working testing and calibration laboratories in accordance with ISO/IEC 17025:2017 standard]

Phd. Serap Köktaş Koca[1], Salih Ayvaz[2], Zeynep Naz Ayvaz[3], Funda Arslan[4]

[1]*National Accreditation Center, Quality Department, 1850 NW 84 th Ave Suite 114, Doral, FL 33126, Miami, USA, serap@nac-us.org*
[2]*National Accreditation Center, Quality Department, 1850 NW 84 th Ave Suite 114, Doral, FL 33126, Miami, USA*
[3]*National Accreditation Center, Quality Department, 1850 NW 84 th Ave Suite 114, Doral, FL 33126, Miami, USA*
[4]*National Accreditation Center, Quality Department, 1850 NW 84 th Ave Suite 114, Doral, FL 33126, Miami, USA*

**ABSTRACT**: With the publication of the EN ISO/IEC 17025:2017 "General requirements for the competence of testing and calibration laboratories" standard, a new process has started for laboratories that actively carry out accreditation activities and intend to be active in accreditation activities. In the ISO/IEC 17025:2017 standard, risk-based thinking, Impartiality, Personnel, Metrological Traceability, Hardware, Method have revealed the necessity of a detailed risk analysis. In this study, the necessity of risk analysis assessment was examined and sample risk analysis assessment studies were shared.

**Keywords**: Risk analysis, ISO/IEC 17025:2017, risk-based thinking

**Received** January 1, 2023; **In final form** March 31, 2023; **Published** June 2023



**Corresponding author:** PhD. Serap Köktaş Koca, e-mail: serap@nac-us.org

## 1. INTRODUCTION

As stated in the ISO 31000 standard, risk is the effect of uncertainty on goals [1]. The implementation of risk analysis in the testing and calibration laboratory started with the ISO/IEC 17025:2017 standard [2]. With this standard, laboratories must identify and evaluate potential risks that may affect the validity and reliability of calibration and test results, and then control them. For an effective risk analysis, the prepared risk analysis should be kept up to date.

## 2. METHODS

Risk analysis should begin by identifying current and potential risks associated with laboratory operations such as equipment and personnel qualifications, environment, methods, processes, and data management. There are basically two important components when determining risks. The first is the probability of the risk occurring while it is occurring, and the second is the effect of the risk after the risk occurs. Control measures should then be taken and implemented to reduce the impact of the risk. The methods used in risk analysis may be different. Among them, the most commonly used methods are:

Probability and impact analysis: It is one of the most basic methods used to determine the probability and impact of risks. In this method, risks are prioritized by evaluating the probability and impact of each risk separately.

System analysis: Potential risks are identified by analyzing an organization's activities and processes. This method requires a review of all the activities of an organization.

SWOT analysis: SWOT (Strengths, Weaknesses, Opportunities, Threats - Strengths, Weaknesses, Opportunities, Threats) analysis enables the identification of risks by analyzing the internal and external environment of an organization.

FMEA analysis: FMEA (Failure Mode and Effects Analysis) analysis is a method for minimizing risks by identifying possible failures of a process or product and their effects.

Bow-Tie analysis: Bow-Tie analysis identifies the link between the causes and consequences of a risk and the measures to be taken to break this link.

When choosing between these methods, factors such as the needs of the organization, the scope of the risk analysis process and the nature of the risks should be considered. At the same time, the method should be traceable and sustainable. [1]

Risks should be directed towards problems to be encountered in laboratory activities, to maintain impartiality, to guarantee the reliability of the results given, and to identify activities that will minimize deviation from quality targets. In the process of addressing and evaluating risks, the processes shown in Figure 1 are followed. [3]

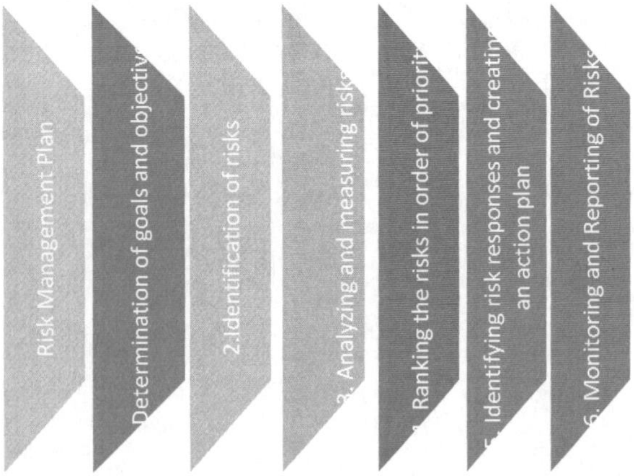


Figure 1. Risk Management Plan

Matrices such as 5x5, 3x3, 10x10 are used in risk assessment. The risk matrix is an evaluation tool used to analyse two variables, such as the probability of a risk and the impact it will have after it occurs. Each of the identified risks is given an impact value from 1 to 5 (left to right) and a probability value (top to bottom). A value of 1 is used for the lowest impact and probability level, and 5 for the highest. The risk score or risk score of each event is found by multiplying the probability values with the effect value, respectively. 5x5 matrix is given in Figure 2. In Table 1, Probability rating steps; in Table 2, Impact rating steps; in Table 3, Risk level determination matrix; in Table 4, Identification of risks and analysis are demonstrated.

| | SEVERITY (IMPACT) | | | | |
|---|---|---|---|---|---|
| PROBABILITY (LIKELIHOOD) | 1 VERY LOW | 2 LOW | 3 MODERATE | 4 HIGH | 5 VERY HIGH (SEVERE) |
| 1 VERY UNLIKELY | Insignificant 1 | Low 2 | Low 3 | Low 4 | Low 5 |
| 2 UNLIKELY | Low 2 | Low 4 | Low 6 | Medium 8 | Medium 10 |
| 3 POSSIBLE | Low 3 | Low 6 | Medium 9 | Medium 12 | High 15 |
| 4 LIKELY | Low 4 | Medium 8 | Medium 12 | High 16 | High 20 |
| 5 Almost Certain | Low 5 | Medium 10 | High 15 | High 20 | Extreme 25 |

Figure 2. 5X5 Matrix

| PROBABILITY RATING STEPS | |
|---|---|
| (1) | **Very unlikely**. Risk can occur in very exceptional circumstances. (In 10-50 years) |
| (2) | **Unlikely**. The risk is unlikely to occur. (In 5-10 years). The environment is not suitable for the risk to occur. The risk situation can only occur under very specific circumstances. |
| (3) | **Possible**. The likelihood that the risk will occur is moderate. (In 2-5 years). Risk can only occur in certain situations. |
| (4) | **Likely.** The risk is likely to occur. (In 1-2 years). The risk situation has happened many times. The environment is extremely suitable for the risk to occur. |
| (5) | **Very Likely**. The risk is almost certain to occur. (In 1 year). The risk situation has happened many times and is happening now. |

Table 1. Probability Rating Steps

| | IMPACT RATING STEPS |
|---|---|
| (1) | **Very Low**. Very low-level risks do not pose a threat to the body's strategic goals and objectives, main activities/ processes. |
| (2) | **Low**. Low-level risks do not pose a major threat to the body's strategic goals and objectives, main activities/ processes. |
| (3) | **Moderate**. Achievement of the body's strategic goals and objectives, main activities / processes may be hindered or delayed. It is sufficient for the management to follow up at a certain level. |
| (4) | **High**. There are situations that pose a significant threat to the achievement of the strategic goals and objectives, main activities/ processes of the body. The Top Management's attention and close monitoring are required. |
| (5) | **Very high (Severe)**. In case the action is not carried out, it may be the case that the body cannot achieve its strategic goals and objectives, basic activities / processes. Urgent Top Management attention and effort are required. |

Table 2. Impact Rating Steps

## Identification of risks and analysis

| No. | Category | Assessed Status | RISK | RESPONSE | RISK RATIO CALCULATION | | |
|---|---|---|---|---|---|---|---|
| | | | | | PROBABILITY | IMPACT | RR |
| R1 | Legal | Failure of metrological traceability of calibration equipment | -deterioration or loss in the shipping process<br>- deviant result | - the supply of new equipment creating a loss of time and cost<br>-disruption in operation | 2 | 5 | 10 |
| R2 | Operation | Lack of communication between the lab. supervisor and the customer representative | failure to complete the service on time | change in priority during lab. operation | 5 | 4 | 20 |
| R3 | Information | Customer Rep. keeping incomplete customer information | - invoice issuance delay<br>- tax office number is missing or incorrect receipt | change in accounting business planning | 3 | 3 | 9 |
| R4 | Technology | Programs used do not make backups | failure to find previous certificates | control of programs by IT | 3 | 5 | 15 |
| R5 | Operation | Label printing error | Label-certificate mismatch | re-printing labels | 5 | 3 | 15 |
| R6 | Operation | Misspelling in certificate | incorrect entry of measurement-related data | certificate revision | 5 | 1 | 5 |
| R7 | Technology | Review of computer programs used | -loss of customers<br>- disruption of functioning | - loss of earnings -disruption in operation | 1 | 5 | 5 |
| R8 | Finance | Giving the wrong offer to the customer | loss of customers | loss of earnings | 3 | 5 | 15 |
| R9 | Organization | Impartiality | - The customer puts The lab under pressure.<br>-personal interest of staff | -Incorrect declaration of measurement results<br>-Unnecessary discount | 3 | 5 | 15 |

| No. | Action to Control or Reduce Risk | RESPONSIBLE | RISK RATE CALCULATION AFTER CONTROL | | | CONCLUSION / DESCRIPTION |
|---|---|---|---|---|---|---|
| | | | PROBABILITY | IMPACT | RATIO | |
| R1 | purchase of replacement devices | Lab. Manager | 2 | 1 | 2 | Acceptable Risk |
| R2 | created new communication paths (notification settings changed) | Lab. Manager & IT | 2 | 4 | 8 | Medium Risk |
| R3 | the customer is contacted and the missing information is completed | Customer Representative & Accounting | 1 | 3 | 3 | Medium Risk |
| R4 | The frequency of backups to external disks is increased and this situation is checked by the lab manager | Lab. Manager & IT | 1 | 1 | 1 | Acceptable Risk |
| R5 | withdrawal of the old label and submission of the new label | Lab. Supervisor | 3 | 3 | 9 | Medium Risk |
| R6 | relevant staff alerted | Lab. Manager | 4 | 1 | 4 | Acceptable Risk |
| R7 | program review times have been reduced | Lab. Manager & IT | 1 | 3 | 3 | Acceptable Risk |
| R8 | Proposal form is revised and sent to customer | Customer Representative | 1 | 4 | 4 | Acceptable Risk |
| R9 | A confidentiality agreement is signed for the impartiality of each employee. | Laboratory management | 1 | 5 | 5 | Acceptable Risk |

| Size of the Risk | Degree of Risk | Evaluation | Colour |
|---|---|---|---|
| 15-25 | High Risk | Immediate Action Should Be Taken | Red |
| 8-12 | Medium Risk | Intervention As Quickly As Possible | Yellow |
| 1-6 | Acceptable Risk | May Not Require Urgent Action, Be Careful | Blue |

Table 3. Risk Level Determination Matrix

Table 4. Identification of risks and analysis

## 3. RESULTS

Identifying hazards and risks: Risk analysis identifies potential hazards and risks in laboratory activities and determines the measures to be taken to reduce these risks. This is very important for the safety of those working in the laboratory as well as others.

Increasing operational efficiency: Risk analysis can help increase efficiency and productivity in the laboratory operation. Risk analysis is especially important when there is concern about the quality, accuracy and consistency of work done in the laboratory.

Cost savings: Risk analysis helps prevent errors that may arise in laboratories and financial losses that may occur as a result. This can help businesses save money by reducing their costs.

Regulatory compliance: Risk analysis can help laboratories comply with regulations. In some industries, certain standards must be followed in laboratories. Risk analysis can help laboratories comply with these standards.

Good reputation: Performing risk analysis in laboratories is important for the credibility and reputation of the business. Businesses can gain the trust of their customers by demonstrating that they offer a reliable laboratory service.

Personnel health and safety: Risk analysis is important for the health and safety of personnel working in the laboratory. By identifying hazards, appropriate measures can be taken and risks to personnel can be minimized.

Opportunities for improvement: Risk analysis also offers opportunities for improvement in laboratory operations. Analysis results help the business identify weak points and areas for improvement.

Long-term planning: Risk analysis can help laboratories make long-term planning. Once hazards and risks have been identified, laboratories can try to minimize future risks by taking appropriate action.

Customer satisfaction: Performing risk analysis in laboratories can also help increase customer satisfaction. Businesses can increase their customers' satisfaction by demonstrating that they deliver reliable and accurate results.

## 4. DISCUSSIONS

Although risk analysis is explicitly mentioned in ISO/IEC 17025:2017 standard clauses, namely 4.1.4 Impartiality, 7.8.6 Declaration of Conformity (Decision rule), 7.10.1 Nonconforming business, 8.5 Addressing risks and opportunities, 8.6

Improvement, 8.7 Corrective Action, 8.9.2 Management Review, the entire standard should be addressed if necessary while conducting risk analysis. Only when entirely covered, the risk analysis has achieved its purpose and the risks of the laboratory are reduced to a minimum.

## 5. CONCLUSIONS

Risk analysis helps laboratories increase customer satisfaction. Providing quality measurements and documentation is critical to meeting customers' needs and exceeding their expectations. Risk analysis helps improve the quality of service that laboratories provide for their customers.

Risk analysis can help calibration and testing laboratories reduce their costs. Incorrect measurements or documents can waste time and money. Risk analysis saves time and money by reducing the possibility of laboratories making mistakes.

Risk analysis can help calibration and testing laboratories maintain their reputation. Customers look for reliable laboratories that provide quality measurements and documentation. Risk analysis protects the reputation of laboratories by improving their service quality.

Risk analysis ensures that calibration and testing laboratories comply with regulations. Laboratories must comply with certain quality management and regulatory standards. Risk analysis helps to ensure regulatory compliance by determining the compliance of laboratories with these standards.

For these reasons, conducting a risk analysis in terms of measurement and documentation in calibration and testing laboratories helps laboratories work more effectively and efficiently.

## ACKNOWLEDGEMENT

I would like to thank the entire National Accreditation Center team for their contribution.

## REFERENCES

[1] ISO 31000:2018 Risk management — Guidelines

[2] ISO/IEC 17025:2017 GENERAL REQUIREMENTS FOR THE COMPETENCE OF TESTING AND CALIBRATION LABORATORIES, December 2017, European Standard, CEN-CENELEC Management Centre, BRUSSELS

[3] M.P Alper, A.T İnce Metrics Symposium and Exhibition / 20-22 November 2019- Izmir-TÜRKİYE

[4]

# AUTHOR INDEX